CHRISTIAN ETHICS

CHRISTIAN ETHICS

A Case Method Approach

FOURTH EDITION

Laura A. Stivers
Christine E. Gudorf
James B. Martin-Schramm

ORBIS BOOKS

Maryknoll, New York 10545

Second Printing, October 2012

This is a substantially revised edition of *Christian Ethics: A Case Method Approach,* Third Edition, edited by Robert L. Stivers, Christine E. Gudorf, Alice Frazer Evans, and Robert A. Evans, Maryknoll: NY: Orbis Books, 1994.

Published by Orbis Books, Maryknoll, New York 10545-0302.
Manufactured in the United States of America.
Manuscript editing and typesetting by Joan Weber Laflamme.

Library of Congress Cataloging-in-Publication Data

Stivers, Laura A.
    Christian ethics : a case method approach. — 4th ed. / Laura A. Stivers, Christine E. Gudorf, James B. Martin-Schramm.
        p. cm.
    Rev. ed. of: Christian ethics / Robert L. Stivers et al.
    Includes bibliographical references.
    ISBN 978–1–57075–966–6 (pbk.)
  1. Christian ethics—Case studies. I. Gudorf, Christine E. II. Martin-Schramm, James B. III. Christian ethics. IV. Title.
    BJ1251.C49 2012
241—dc23
                                      2011036049

Contents

PART III
POVERTY

PART IV
THE ENVIRONMENT

PART V
BUSINESS

PART VIII
LIFE AND DEATH

Introduction

Christian Ethics
and the Case Method

The student pensively approached the case teacher after class and finally mustered some words: "That case really hit home. The characters were different, but they could just as well have been my family. Not long ago we went through exactly the same thing." Another student, waiting for the first to finish, finally edged up and joined in, "And the question that woman in the front row asked about euthanasia, that's the precise question I wanted to ask but couldn't find the right words."

These two statements, often encountered in one form or another by case teachers, reflect something enduring in human behavior: while every individual is unique, ethical problems and questions about what is right or good are persistent if not universal. These recurrences and the dilemmas they represent can be recorded and replayed to help others learn to make better ethical choices. Case studies are one way to capture past occurrences, and case teaching is a method to enable individuals and groups to make better choices.

This book is about making ethical choices and forming Christian character. It contains sixteen cases. Accompanying each case study is a commentary that is intended to aid understanding of the case from a Christian ethical perspective. The purpose of the book is to offer an approach to contemporary social issues and to underscore the importance of the Christian ethical dimension in the issues and in character formation. The authors are enthusiastic about the case approach as one way to prepare individuals and communities to make ethical decisions and form character. Since the method was first developed at the Harvard Law and Business Schools, it has moved far beyond these origins, receiving wide acceptance nationally in business and law schools. During the past three decades it has also been successfully applied to religious studies. This proven track record and personal experience with the case approach are the bases of the authors' enthusiasm for this teaching and learning approach.

MAKING ETHICAL DECISIONS

Ethical decisions are made on a number of levels. On one level decision-making seems to flow easily. Individuals follow their gut-level intuitions and muddle through situations reactively. This approach may be effective if the individual is caring and the situation is uncomplicated and more or less personal. It is less effective in complex social situations and can be disastrous when the individual is uncaring, ethically immature, or locked into a narrow social world.

On another level making ethical choices is both difficult and complex. Logical and abstract reasoning comes hard to some. In certain situations the decision-maker is bombarded by a bewildering array of conflicting and complex facts. Finding relevant ethical norms or guidelines from Christian traditions to apply to particular situations is difficult at best and can easily be short-circuited or sidetracked with simplistic appeals to authority.

Once relevant norms are discovered, their application is often tricky. The norms frequently offer conflicting counsel. Indeed, this is the primary reason that ethical decisions are problematic. There is seldom a straight path from a single norm to an easy decision. If there were, no problem would exist. The decision-maker is most often caught between equally attractive or unattractive alternatives. Worse, the path is usually made treacherous by intersecting problems and relationships that complicate situations and suggest exceptions to the rules. Last, and hardly necessary to point out, relationships themselves present complicating factors. The moral decision-maker possesses limited freedom and is quite capable of being arbitrary in its use.

The case method of instruction recounts real ethical dilemmas in order to assist individuals and groups through complexity to good or at least well-reasoned choices. Cases may help sort out the choices and give the person with the dilemma an opportunity to move down the path from the identification of norms through the maze of intersecting facts, relationships, and exceptions to the selection of the best alternatives.

There are many types of case studies. They range from imagined scenarios, to in-depth histories of organizations, to one-page "verbatims" that report a single incident. The cases in this volume are descriptions of actual situations as seen by a writer usually through the eyes of a participant involved in the problem. The situations normally entail a decision to be made that is left sufficiently open to allow students to enter the process of ethical reflection and decision-making.

Such a method is well-suited to the study of Christian ethics, for it drives the student to take the insights of tradition and theory, apply them to an actual situation, and then reconsider the adequacy of theory and tradition. Involved in this movement from theory to practice and back to theory are all the elements that go into an ethical decision.

THE ELEMENTS OF AN ETHICAL DECISION

Element I: The Relationship of Faith

A pervasive historical problem for most Christian traditions has been human sin. Sin results from deep-seated anxieties and separation from God, self, others, and nature. It issues forth in specific acts that break relationships. Sin is magnified in groups and hardens in institutions. From another angle, sin is the refusal to accept God's gracious power of love, a refusal that leads to a sense of alienation and judgment.

While sin runs deep and is universal, it does not necessarily paralyze the moral life. In his person and work Jesus Christ reveals resources for living with integrity in the midst of sin. Jesus identifies God, the source of these resources, as a power that creates inner wholeness and the possibility of right relationships.

Primary to most Christian traditions is the affirmation of God's power as love. Love redeems humans from sin and reunites them with others without violating human freedom. Love is a free gift, never a possession, and cannot be obtained by an effort of the will alone. The continuing presence of love in all situations is called the work of the Holy Spirit.

The starting point for Christian ethics is being in love. This is not something the self can do alone, however. It is something that God does in cooperation with the self, although the self is constantly tempted to think otherwise and take control, so furthering sin and alienation. Being in love is first a matter of receiving love and letting it work in the self to produce inner wholeness and transformation. Action follows being in love. This is more or less the central message of most Christian traditions, although there is considerable variation in particulars. Thus ethics or doing has its foundation in being or life in the Spirit. Faith is a matter of relationship, of being in love first with God and then responsively with self, others, and nature.

The word *spirituality* is often used to identify the core relationship to God. God's power is experienced in quite different ways, the common element being the integrated and transformed self that emerges. Most Christians readily recognize the customary religious ways of experiencing God: worship, prayer, singing, participation in the sacraments, and the preached word. God is not limited to these religious ways, but rather, according to most traditions, God is free to be present in a variety of ways consistent with love.

Spirituality, alternatively being in love or being in the Spirit, inspires acts of justice in society and nature and also leads the loving self intuitively to specific acts in particular situations. In coming to decisions, however, other things are needed, because inspiration and intuition by themselves are not always accurate guides for doing what is right or good. This is especially true in complex social situations. The doing of good acts requires thought as well as heart, knowledge as well as inspiration and intuition. The Christian doer, while inspired and empowered, is also sensitive to relationships in specific situations and deeply interested in the facts and theories that give order to situations as well as the traditions that provide ethical norms for human actions.

Sensitivity to relationships involves a strong element of good intentions. It also involves a sense of the Spirit already at work in a situation, of the character of the human actors, and of the needs of plants and animals. Sensitivity to relationships is constantly in tune with feelings and the subtle changes that make certain situations exceptional. It is aware of the self, its state of being, and its tendencies to sin, both in one's own self and in the selves of others.

Interest in the facts and norms that guide decisions are more a matter of knowledge than heart. They require the thoughtful analysis and assessment of a situation, the next two elements in making an ethical decision.

Element II: Analysis

Good ethical decisions and actions depend on good information, and getting good information depends on hard work and a certain amount of savvy. There are several components to consider in analyzing a situation or case study, not all of which apply in any given situation or case. First is to consider how *personal experience* shapes the way the self perceives a situation. One way to do this is for students to ask themselves what they personally have at stake, what personal history—for example, race, class, gender, habits, and attitudes—they bring to the situation.

The second component is *power dynamics*. Who are the key players, and how is power distributed among them? Whose voices are heard? Whose are ignored?

A third component is *factual information*. Are there historical roots to the problem? What are the key facts? Are there facts in dispute? Are the theories that give coherence to the facts in conflict?

Fourth is the larger *context* of the situation. Most cases are seen through the eyes of a single person and involve personal relationships. The decision-maker must go beyond the close confines of his or her own personal life to see how society and nature affect and in turn are affected by the actions of the people in the case. As the old adage goes: Don't lose the forest for the trees.

Fifth is attention to the *complicating factors* in a situation. Is this an exceptional case? Is crucial information missing? Are there things that are hard to grasp?

Sixth is a careful delineation of *relationships*. Sometimes relational factors produce a situation that is not normal and to which traditional ethical guidelines do not apply. Decision-makers must ask if there are relational or character issues that complicate choices.

Seventh is to identify the primary and secondary *ethical issues* in the situation. Case studies almost always involve multiple issues, and students must select among them in order to focus.

Finally, the eighth component is the identification of *alternative courses of action* to address the issues and the *consequences* of each. What seems to be appropriate action may on second glance reveal consequences that make it inappropriate or even harmful.

Element III: Assessment

The main task in assessment is locating norms or ethical guidelines in the traditions of the church that are relevant to a given situation. In ethics, norms refer to broad directives that provide guidance for moral life. Norms help to determine what usually should be done in a particular situation. They reflect the wisdom and experience of past decision-makers as they faced similar situations and generalized about what is good. Their insights are passed down in traditions and usually offer wise counsel as current decision-makers face the same kinds of situations or even new situations.

Norms

Norms come in many forms. A few illustrations will suffice to demonstrate this variety and to identify the most important norms. Three very important norms are love, justice, and peacemaking. The experience of God's love leads to an intention to love one's neighbor. In Christian ethics justice is a *general principle* and means fairness or equity with a special concern for the poor and those on the margins of society. In the ethic of ecological justice this norm is given further expression in the principles of sustainability, sufficiency, participation, and solidarity (see the case

"Sustaining Dover"). Peacemaking as a norm includes understandings of nonviolence and reconciliation and gives foundation to three normative *perspectives*: pacifism, the justifiable war, and the crusade (see the case "Vietnam's Children").

Virtues are norms insofar as they represent patterns of behavior worthy of emulation. The best, but not the only, example in Christian ethics is the person and work of Jesus. The popular but well-worn question "What would Jesus do?" points to how his example is a moral guide for many.

Theological interpretations also guide. Different interpretations of how God is at work in a given situation, for example, are important in cases of life and death. Theological understandings of sin, death, and the work of the Holy Spirit and the church are important to decisions in other cases.

Finally, the most familiar norms are stated as *rules*, *laws*, and *commands*. The Ten Commandments are the most obvious. In using laws as guides, care must be taken, however, to avoid legalism, the tendency to follow rules slavishly even if the consequences are unloving. In Christianity, all laws and rules are grounded in and tested by love, the most basic guideline of all.

Sources of Norms

Christians look to a number of sources for ethical guidance. The *Bible* has traditionally been the first and most important source. Gleaning ethical guidance from the Bible is not as easy as it might seem, however. The many books of the Bible were written in different periods and reflect quite a variety of contexts and situations. The biblical writers wrote from their own locations in diverse societies and culture. They saw and understood things differently from one another and certainly from persons of the modern age, who live in a thoroughly changed world. Biblical writers sometimes disagreed with one another, and what they thought was ethically acceptable in their own time—for example, slavery—has changed as culture has evolved. Compounding these differences, and complicating matters immensely, present-day decision-makers must interpret what biblical writers meant and then apply these meanings. The Bible does not interpret itself or make decisions. And while biblical scholars have developed a wide range of tools to do the task of interpretation and ethicists offer their best wisdom on interpretation, their disagreements are commonplace. Indeed, ethical conflicts are sometimes matters of interpretation and use of biblical texts.

In spite of these complications, themes do run through the Bible, and these themes can be identified with a degree of accuracy. The biblical writers experienced the same loving God as modern people and faced many of the same problems. The Bible remains a good source of guidance.

Theology is the second source of norms. Understandings of God's power and human sin have already been identified. The nature of God's power as love inspires and leads decision-makers to love their neighbors and to be sensitive to the work of the Spirit in situations. Different understandings of sin lead to conflicting views on matters of sexuality. Seeing sin as deep and universal leads decision-makers to realistic actions that factor in the human tendency to misuse freedom.

The third source of norms is the *historical traditions* of the church. Christians through the centuries have devoted considerable thought to issues of, for example, violence, sexuality, the poor, and nature. The traditions change and sometimes yield a multiplicity of guidelines, but they also show continuity and reflect a certain amount of practical wisdom. Traditions on justice are critical to this volume.

The fourth source of norms is the *church* in its many forms. The three previous sources all grew in church ground. The church ranges from the church catholic or universal, to specific church organizations such as the Roman Catholic Church and specific Protestant denominations, to associations of churches, to the local brick and mortar church, to what in the Bible is referred to as "where two or three are gathered together." Likewise, the ethical guidelines range from traditional historical perspectives, to comprehensive church studies and pronouncements, to rules of church organizations, and to the wisdom and guidance of a good friend.

The final source is the broad category of *secular ethical traditions and other religions*. Christian and secular philosophical traditions in the West have had a close and mutually edifying relationship for centuries. Native American traditions are rich in their sensitivity to nature. Taoism is likewise rich in its search for balance. Buddhism holds to the interrelation of all beings and talks about attachment or desire as the chief problem. Christians are free to appropriate the insights of these other traditions, to enter into dialogue with adherents of these traditions, and to join in common actions.

Using these five sources to establish norms that relate to a given case is complex and requires practice. The situation or case itself offers an obvious starting point. So, for example, if the situation involves violent conflict, norms dealing with violence and nonviolence apply.

Many aids are available to help in locating relevant norms. Concordances help to locate specific words in the Bible and texts containing these words. The critical commentaries that follow each case in this volume identify norms and help with interpretation. Dictionaries of Christian ethics are widely available and provide short summaries for those whose time is limited. Scholars have studied most ethical issues, and their publications usually develop norms. Most major denominations have well-established

positions on major ethical issues. If cases are discussed in a classroom setting, teachers may provide background in lectures. Also, decision-makers
may turn to the local church, where communities of believers frequently
work through ethical issues, often guided by competent leaders.

Conflicting Norms

Once decision-makers have identified the relevant norms and reflected
on their meaning for a specific situation, they must jump at least one more
hurdle. Ethical problems are frequently encountered because two or more
norms conflict. For example, in matters related to the use of violence, nonviolence is an obvious norm. So is justice. The conflict between the two in
certain cases has led some Christians to elect the normative perspective of
the justifiable war as their guide. So, if a large measure of justice can be
won for a small measure of violence, violence may be justifiable if certain
conditions are met. Another frequent conflict is between human economic
benefit and care for other species and ecosystems.

What should the decision-maker do when conflicting norms make for
a close call? There is no one right answer to this question. Prayer helps,
but finally choices must be made. Luther's famous dictum, "sin bravely,"
applies in some cases.

Method

Method is the process of pulling intuitions and norms together and applying them to analysis. No single method of relating norms, facts, theories,
contexts, and relationships to one another and to specific situations can be
called distinctively Christian. There are a number of methods, each with
advantages and disadvantages. The authors have not tried to impose a particular method in their approach either to the cases or to the commentaries
that follow them. They are convinced that method is important, however,
and that an adequate method seeks to touch base with the elements relevant
to making a particular ethical decision.

The case approach is conducive to the teaching of method. A specific
case can even be used to focus on method. Over the course of a semester or
study series the teacher can use and ask participants to use a single method
so that they will acquire skill in employing that particular methodology.
Alternatively, the teacher can employ several methods and request that
students experiment with and evaluate each. Or finally, consciousness of
method may be left to emerge from the process of doing ethical reflection.

The commentaries that follow each case are organized around the elements of making an ethical decision. The commentaries do not spell out

how these elements are to be put together to reach a decision. The authors would be remiss, however, if they did not indicate a few typical approaches.

The approach that starts with and stresses norms is called the *deontological* or *normative approach*. The word *deontological* comes from the Greek work *deon*, which means "binding," and refers to the study of duty and moral obligation.

The tendency in this approach is to let norms, rules, principles, standards, and ideals be decisive or binding in making choices. The degree of decisiveness that should be afforded to norms has been a matter of contention in Christian ethics. To call an approach normative means that norms have a fairly high degree of decisiveness. Most of those who take a normative approach, however, are willing to admit some exceptions to norms occasioned by contextual or relational factors and conflicting norms. Used in a flexible way, the normative approach is appropriate. Indeed, the authors are of a common mind that considerable attention should be given to norms in all situations.

The extreme of the normative approach, legalism, presents difficulties, however. Following rules to the exclusion of contextual and relational factors is a problem for Christians because of its rigidity, frequent heartlessness, and the obvious polemic against it in the sayings of Jesus and the epistles of Paul.

The second approach is called *teleological* from the Greek *telos*, which means "end" or "goal." Those who take a teleological approach are interested in achieving an end or maximizing a goal as much as possible. Another way to put this is to say they seek good consequences or results. Hence this approach is also called the *consequentialist approach*. People differ, however, about the goals they seek and the ends they pursue. Some may wish simply to amass wealth and power in life, while others may seek to maximize the welfare of others, including other species. Not all ends or goals are morally desirable, however. For Christians, norms derived from the five sources and especially fundamental norms like love and justice guide evaluation of these ends or goals. Teleologists weigh the costs and benefits of various alternatives as they figure out how to maximize the good they seek to achieve. For teleologists, the ends sometimes justify the means, even morally questionable means in some cases. A weakness here is that teleological thinking can run roughshod over others as it makes ethical concessions in order to maximize the good. So, ends do not justify all means. A strength of this approach is that it takes consequences seriously.

The third approach is called the *areteological approach* or sometimes *virtue ethics* or the *ethics of conscience*. The word comes from the Greek *arete* and refers to excellence of moral character. Those who take this approach think that good ethical decisions will be made by good people. The first task, therefore, is to cultivate excellence of character through education, training, and spiritual formation, that is to say, through the internalization of norms so that they become intuitive. One of the products of this moral formation is the conscience that exists within an individual or community. Those who employ this approach often appeal to their consciences as the basis of their perception of an ethical problem or as a justification for the particular solution they prefer. Ends and means are evaluated in terms of how consistent they are with one's moral character and conscience.

An advantage of this approach is that life is complicated and often requires ethical decisions that have to be made quickly. In situations where norms are not clear or there is insufficient time to calculate costs and benefits, recourse to one's conscience and moral intuition can be a very effective way to exercise ethical judgment. One of the problems, however, is that a sound conscience depends on a well-formed moral character. Many who perpetrate great evils sleep all too well at night. In addition, intuitive appeals to conscience can be very subjective. Ultimately, good ethics requires that reasons be given to justify decisions. Vague appeals to conscience can be a way to dodge this responsibility.

Few teachers have consciously used the case approach to form character. Case discussions are a good resource for character formation, however, and in the process of repeatedly making moral judgments, moral maturity may be expected to increase, or at least that has been the experience of case teachers. Character development may therefore be an unintended positive side effect of the case method. Many teachers may prefer leaving it that way, but there is no reason why character development cannot be made more explicit.

So which of these approaches is the best? All three are good and may be used effectively alone or in combination. The authors suggest a combination, although combinations will not be effective in all cases. Decision-makers should be self-conscious, however, about which approach they are using.

Ethical Assessment

The last step of assessment is actually to do it. Having done the analysis, identified relevant norms, and selected one or more of the methods, decision-makers should evaluate alternative courses of action, strategies, and tactics as well as their viability and consequences. No magic formula or foolproof way exists. The process is dialogical. Norms, methods, and the factors of analysis should be massaged together to find what is appropriate or fitting.

The decision follows. Sometimes difficult to make because alternative courses of action are equally satisfactory or equally unsatisfactory, the relationship of faith calls the decision-maker to decide. Cases do, of course, allow the luxury of "fence sitting," but the ethical dilemmas of life do not. Also, not to decide may be a wise course of action in some cases, but it is a decision nonetheless.

Once a decision has been made and a course of action chosen, these conclusions need to be justified to others. Ethics should normally be a community enterprise. Reasons supporting the decision should be consistent with analysis, appeal to relevant moral norms, use an appropriate method, and carry a sense of proportionality. A well-justified ethical decision will also explain why this is the best choice given the circumstances of the case. In addition, a well-crafted decision will also anticipate and respond to the most significant counterarguments others may raise.

Element IV: Action

Cases in this volume end with decisions to be made. They are open-ended. Discussions of cases usually end at the point of decision, but in life situations this will not be the case. In this final stage decision-makers are called not only to decide but also to act on their decisions.

Reflection should then follow action so that decision-makers will learn from successes and failures. Finally, there is even a tiny bit of reward. When decision and action are done well, decision-makers may bask in the glow and enjoy the inner peace that follows. And even when things do not turn out all right and mistakes are made, and wrong choices selected, with repentance there are resources of forgiveness. Guilt may be a mark of sin, but it is never the last word in Christian ethics. The Good News is the last word. You are forgiven.

FLEXIBILITY

Cases can be used to form character, to analyze problems, to teach method, to understand human relationships, and to employ a method. The case approach is flexible, and this flexibility makes the goals of the teacher in using the method of great importance. Cases lend themselves to one purpose or a multiplicity of purposes, and teachers need to be clear about what they are trying to accomplish. Purpose should govern the selection of cases, how they are taught, and the outcome. This cannot be emphasized enough. Purpose governs use.

What the authors have not done, and in fact cannot do, is set the purpose for participants and facilitators. We suggest a range of options, for example, introducing students to complex social issues, using cases as an entry into the tradition, the teaching of method, and the development of character, but application must remain with the user. This also means that cases can be misused for the purpose of indoctrination and manipulation. Teachers and students should be aware of this, although misuse of method is not peculiar to the use of cases.

Flexibility has still another dimension. The case method is appropriate to a variety of learning situations from the classroom, to church groups, and the informal discussions found in coffee shops, dorms, and living rooms. Those who use the method regularly find that it stimulates discussion, breaks up the one-way flow of lectures, and eliminates the silence that often permeates abstract discussions. The method is dialogical and thus meets the needs of instructors and learners who prefer more engaged pedagogy. But discussion is only the most frequent way cases are used, and discussion can be more or less structured by teachers depending on their goals.

The method also has internal flexibility. Role plays, small groups, voting, and mini-lectures, a fuller description of which can be found in the Appendix, are only a few of the ways cases can be engaged. Cases are not particularly good for presenting normative material and scientific theories. Experienced case teachers have found that lectures and outside reading are more appropriate for introducing this kind of material. Thus, where significant background information is required for intelligent choices, the authors recommend using cases for the purposes of opening discussions of complex problems, of applying theory and the insights of traditions, of bringing closure and decision, and of encouraging the development of a critical consciousness.

ISSUES AND COMMENTARIES

The issues that the cases raise were given careful thought. A characteristic of a good case, however, is that it raises more than one issue. Some cases raise numerous issues, and beyond these are what might be called connecting components. There is no case, for example, that is explicitly about women or men, yet several of the cases address problems associated with the changing relationships of contemporary women and men. Racism is a central issue in at least two cases and a related one in several others. Teachers may want to use these connecting components to structure their courses so themes are addressed consistently.

Each case is followed by a commentary that is provided because past experience shows that interpretive reflections help decision-makers by providing leads into avenues of analysis and assessment. These commentaries are not definitive interpretations. They are the observations of individuals trained in Christian theology, ethics, and the case method. They are not out of the same mold, although they do attempt to use the elements that go into an ethical decision as their starting point. There are stylistic differences and variations in emphasis resulting from their multiple authorship. They are intended as aids and not as substitutes for creative thinking, analysis, and decision-making.

As mentioned before, the content of the interpretive reflections is not arbitrary. It is organized around the elements that go into making an ethical decision; however, for the sake of variety and flexibility the authors decided that each commentary did not necessarily have to discuss all of the elements or to do so in the same order. The commentaries are designed to touch base with these elements, although for a given case each element may not be covered with the same thoroughness. Brevity has also governed design. In some of the cases, analysis of one or more of the components does not add significant insight. No doubt in these commentaries there are things omitted that teachers will want to add and points made that facilitators will disagree with and want to comment upon critically.

ADDITIONAL RESOURCES

Ahearn, David Oki, and Peter R. Gathje, eds. *Doing Right and Being Good: Catholic and Protestant Readings in Christian Ethics.* Collegeville, MN: Liturgical Press, 2005.

Crook, Roger H. *An Introduction to Christian Ethics.* 4th ed. Upper Saddle River, NJ: Prentice Hall, 2002.

Holland, Joe, and Peter Henriot. *Social Analysis: Linking Faith and Justice.* Maryknoll, NY: Orbis Books, 1990.

Lovin, Robin W. *Christian Ethics: An Essential Guide.* Nashville, TN: Abingdon Press, 2000.

Martin-Schramm, James A., and Robert L. Stivers. *Christian Environmental Ethics: A Case Method Approach.* Maryknoll, NY: Orbis Books, 2003.

Wogaman, J. Philip. *Moral Dilemmas: An Introduction to Christian Ethics.* Louisville, KY: Westminster John Knox Press, 2009.

PART I

FAMILY

Case

Rigor and Responsibility

David Trapp hung up the phone and paused to reflect. He had just spoken with his good friend Al Messer. Al had offered to build the cabin. For several months David and his wife, Nancy, had considered building on the two acres of Clark Lake property left to them the year before by David's uncle. The nagging question returned to David. Now that the means were there, was it right to build?

David lived with his wife and two children on a quiet residential street on the outskirts of Toledo, Ohio. David was a lawyer with a downtown law firm that encouraged him to spend up to 15 percent of his time with clients who could not afford to pay. David always used the full allotment, considering it one way he could respond in faith to a pressing human need. David was also active in community affairs. He was vice-president of a statewide citizens' action lobby for more progressive taxation. Locally, he was on the board of directors of an environmental organization whose goal was the cleanup, restoration, and preservation of Lake Erie, and he led adult education classes at his church. What troubled David the most was relating his sense of outrage at injustice to his enjoyment of good food, travel, and water sports.

Nancy Trapp was a buyer for an office-furniture supplier. Her work involved increasing responsibility, and she found it difficult to leave unfinished business in the office. Recently she had been elected to a two-year term as president of the P.T.A. at the children's school. She had not foreseen the constant interruptions such a position would bring. The telephone never seemed to stop ringing, especially on the weekends when people knew they could find her at home.

Decision-making was more or less a family affair with the Trapps. David and Nancy seldom disagreed on family matters and to David's recollection

---

This case and its commentary were prepared by Robert L. Stivers. The names of all persons and institutions have been disguised to protect the privacy of those involved.

never on a major one. The children, Darcy and Ben, ages ten and eight, were consulted on major decisions and their voices taken into account.

Nathan Ferguson was the pastor of the local congregation in which the Trapps were active participants. Nathan had recently sold a piece of property he had once intended for recreational purposes. The proceeds from the sale had been donated to a church-sponsored halfway house for drug addicts in downtown Toledo. Shortly after Nathan had sold the property, he had begun to preach and teach in a low-key way on the subjects of possessions, overconsumption, and the materialism of American society. His eventual aim was to have some of his parishioners understand and consider forming a community based on the one in Jerusalem described in the opening chapters of the Book of Acts. He envisioned this community as one that would be environmentally sensitive, hold possessions in common, limit consumption to basic necessities, and give liberally to programs among the poor that were based on a principle of self-reliance.

Clea Parks was David's colleague and an active participant in the church's adult education classes. What amazed David was how she could combine a concern for the poor with a way of living that allowed for occasional extravagances. Like David, Clea made full use of the firm's 15 percent allotment to work with poor clients. She was also on the board of the halfway house for drug addicts. In contrast, she and her husband regularly traveled to Bermuda for tennis and golf and to Sun Valley for skiing. Last year they had flown to the Amazon for an eco-tour. This fall they were headed to the Holy Land for three weeks.

Shortly after the settlement of his uncle's will, which in addition to the two acres included enough cash to construct a modest cabin, David and Nancy had discussed the matter of building. David expressed his ambivalence. He wondered about limits to self-indulgence. His desire for the cabin seemed to be locked in a struggle with his conscience. "How can we build a second place," he asked, "when so many people are living in shelters without roofs or simply do not have a home at all? Can we in good conscience consume as heavily as we do while others are crying out for the very things we take for granted and consume almost at will? And what about the animals? Our consumption contributes to the degradation of their habitat."

He also considered the matter of energy consumption. Again directing his reflections to Nancy, he said: "Think about the energy used in construction and the going to and fro that will follow. Is this good stewardship of resources? Does it reflect our responsibility as Americans to conserve fuel? What sort of legacy are we leaving to our grandchildren, not to mention the lessons we are teaching our own children?"

He then rehearsed once again a pet theme: the excessive materialism of American society. "The Bible is quite explicit about possessions," he insisted. "Possession can easily plug our ears to the hearing of God's word. A person cannot have two masters. The rich young ruler went away empty because he was unwilling to give up his possessions. The tax collector, Zacchaeus, is commended by Jesus for his willingness to give one-half of his possessions to the poor. And Jesus himself lived without possessions, commanding his disciples to do likewise."

He paused to think about this further. "Is it possible," he asked, "to avoid the spirit-numbing nature of possessions short of self-denial? And if I'm not going to opt for self-denial, then I at least have to ask in what way my consumption helps to perpetuate a system that is getting further and further away from the simplicity of Jesus." Again he paused, adding: "I guess it all boils down to the ethics of the Sermon on the Mount that Pastor Ferguson keeps talking about. Does the rigor of the sermon's ethic represent the only valid Christian option? Is it possible to live much in excess of basic needs if this ethic is taken seriously? And if we conclude that the sermon is not a new set of laws, what is its relevance anyway?"

Nancy's response was slow in coming both because she was sensitive to David's imaginative conscience and because she wanted a place to separate herself from work and to teach the children the water sports she and David both enjoyed. "I can understand your commitment," she told him. "It's not a matter of guilt for you. But I just don't feel quite as strongly about those things as you do. The pressure has been getting worse lately, and I feel the need to share with you and the children in a more relaxed setting. The kids are getting older fast, and in a few years they'll be beyond the age where they'll be around to learn water sports.

"The materialism you are so concerned about," she went on to say, "has also made for creative new possibilities. It's not possessions themselves, but how we use them that makes a difference. It's the willingness to give, and we give enough what with the 15 percent of your time and the giving of more than 10 percent of our incomes to church and charity. And think about what giving up our possessions will do. Without programs to transfer our abundance to the poor, giving things up will go for naught or perhaps contribute to the loss of someone's job. That is just the way things are. Think about Al Messer."

David was not quite sure what to make of Nancy's comments. The old nagging questions kept coming back. His conscience would not let him off easily.

Then Nathan Ferguson had begun his sermons and more recently had conducted a series of six sessions in the adult education class that David led. Nathan returned time and again to the teachings of Jesus: to the Sermon on the Mount, to the rich young ruler, to Zacchaeus, to the sharing in early Christian communities, to the call of the prophets to justice and care for the poor, and to Jesus' love for the birds of the air and fish of the sea. Nathan had not talked in a demanding or accusatory fashion, but neither had he let his parishioners off the hook. To David it seemed that Nathan's every thought had been directed straight at him.

At the office Clea hit him from the other side. At first she had merely commented on Nathan's sermons and classes. She thought Nathan was too much of a perfectionist. She appreciated his concern for the poor and the environment and how possessions can close one's ears to the word of God. She did not, however, see how individual sacrifices produced the social change they all wanted.

She also had a contrasting view of the Sermon on the Mount. "We cannot live the sermon," she explained. "It's impossible, and anyway, it wasn't intended for everyone. Ethical rigor is right for folks like Nathan, but what most of us are called to is responsibility: to the right use of possessions, to a willingness to give, and to advocacy of justice in word and deed. The choice is not between self-indulgence and self-denial. There is a third option: living responsibly with concern for all those issues Nathan talks about and still appreciating the finer things in life."

When David told her about the lake property and Nancy's needs, Clea had begun to push him a bit harder. "Come on, David," she said, half joking, "it's all right with Jesus if you build. Jesus enjoyed life and participated in it fully. The church tradition is quite ambiguous on possessions, wealth, and nature." Another time she put it bluntly, "What right have you to force your values and views on Nancy and the children?" Lately she had been twitting him. Just the other day with a big grin on her face she called him "the monk."

Al Messer's call had jolted David and increased his sense that something had to give. Al had told David that he could build the cabin out of used lumber and had found a place where he could get insulation and double-pane window glass at reduced prices. Al had also indicated he needed the work because business had been a bit slow lately.

Nancy entered the room and guessed what was troubling David. "I know what's bothering you," she said. "If we build, those old questions about the poor, materialism, and limits to consumption will nag at you. You might not even stick to a decision to build. If we don't build, you'll feel you have let the kids and me down and miss your favorite water sports. How should we decide this?"

Commentary

Taken at face value this case is about David and Nancy Trapp struggling to decide whether to build a vacation cabin. But at a deeper and more comprehensive level the case is addressed to all non-poor Christians; the issue is how to live as a Christian in a materialistic world where ostentatious luxury, grinding poverty, and environmental degradation exist side by side.

This question of how to live can be given greater specificity by considering the title of the case. Should an affluent family give up what it has and follow the rigorous "holy poverty" of Jesus, or is there an alternative called "responsible consumption" that stresses right use and good stewardship of material resources? Realizing that a continuum of options is possible between the "either" of rigor and the "or" of responsibility, these two options may be contrasted for the purpose of analyzing the decisions the Trapps must make.

Before addressing these two contrasting perspectives, however, there are several related issues that should at least be mentioned. The two most important are poverty and environmental degradation. David and Nancy's decision is not hidden in a vacuum. It stands out in a context where over a billion people are malnourished and live in miserable poverty. It stands out in a global economy in which the gap between rich and poor remains wide. It stands out in an economic system that needs high levels of consumption to stimulate growth and jobs. It stands out in a planetary system where unprecedented numbers of species are going extinct largely due to human actions and where there is serious concern about the sustainability of natural resources and the capacity of ecosystems to absorb pollution. These issues raised by the context of the case are the very issues raised to prominence by this volume.

There are six other issues important for this case but peripheral to the main concerns. The first is family decision-making. How is this family to decide? The second stems from the Trapps' need to "get away." Would the addition of a cabin really solve the more pressing problems of overwork and over-involvement in the community? The third is the matter of educating children. What messages do David and Nancy send Darcy and Ben by overwork and by building a second home? What sort of character are they trying to instill?

The fourth issue is raised by the inheritance. Are David and Nancy really free to give their inheritance to the poor? Although the case does not say, they probably live within the context of a larger family grouping, some of whose members might be a little upset with such unilateral action. The fifth issue is guilt. Should Christians and Americans feel a sense of guilt for their high levels of consumption? And what is the function of guilt in the Christian life? Sixth is the issue of individual action in a world of over six billion people that is dominated by large social organizations. How do people like David and Nancy influence others to do justice and exercise Christianity's call for solidarity? Will individual acts of self-sacrifice make a difference?

Beyond these six issues, there are a number of issues raised by Christian traditions. How should the Bible and theology, for example, guide the Trapps' choice? What in fact do the traditions say about the issues in the case?

THE MAIN QUESTION

So how are Christians to live in a world of continuing poverty and environmental degradation? Most students react to David's dilemma with at least mild astonishment. They seem to assume that consuming goods and services in quantity is the natural thing to do and have difficulty comprehending why building is a dilemma at all. This is not surprising given the daily barrage of commercial advertising whose main purpose is to sell a way of life that encourages heavy consumption. Indeed, heavy consumption has become a way of life to many Americans.

The norm of justice makes the gap between rich and poor and the grinding poverty of so many people that goes side by side with this consumption difficult to justify. The emphasis on material things underlying this consumption is difficult to reconcile with biblical norms on wealth and consumption. The environmental degradation that this level of consumption causes is a serious problem for sustainability of earth's ecological systems. On these grounds David and many Americans have good reason to be troubled by their consciences.

Consider first the norm of *justice*. Justice is rooted in the very being of God. It is an essential part of God's community of love and calls followers of Jesus Christ to make fairness the core of their social response to other persons and the rest of creation. Included in this biblical concern for justice is solidarity with the poor and also with nature.

The biblical basis of justice and solidarity with the poor starts with God's liberation of the oppressed Hebrew slaves in Egypt and the establishment of a covenant with them (Exodus). This theme continues in the prophetic reinterpretation of the covenant. Micah summarized the law:

> to do justice, and to love kindness,
> and to walk humbly with your God. (Mi 6:8)

Amos was adamant that God's wrath would befall Israel for its injustice and failure to care for the poor (Am 5:21–24). Isaiah and Jeremiah were equally adamant (Is 1:12–17; 3:13–15; 58:6–9; Jer 22:13–17).

In the Christian scriptures the emphasis on justice is somewhat muted in comparison to the prophets, but the concern for the poor may be even stronger. Jesus himself was a poor man from a poor part of Israel. His mission was among the poor, and his message was directed to them. He blessed the poor and spoke God's judgment on the rich. On the cross he made himself one of the dispossessed. In the early Jerusalem community, as recorded in Acts 1–5, the basic economic needs of all members were taken care of as the wealthier shared their possessions so none would be deprived.

Second are biblical and theological understandings of wealth and consumption. Two traditions have dominated, offering two not very compatible understandings of what it means to live sufficiently. One stresses a rigorous response to Jesus teachings, including self-denial, the giving of what one has to the poor, and a radical freedom from possessions. The other accents the right use of possessions and emphasizes responsibility and willingness to share. The first tradition may be called *rigorous discipleship* and the second *responsible consumption*. These are not meant to be polemical titles. Responsible consumption has its element of rigor, and rigorous discipleship is certainly responsible. While the differences between them are significant, it is possible to accept both as valid Christian ways of living.

Parenthetically, these two traditions also give a foundation for solidarity with the poor. Historically, many Christians have identified completely with the poor, even to the point of considerable self-sacrifice. Widely known modern examples, such as Mother Teresa and Dorothy Day, have continued this tradition. At the same time and not so spectacularly, Christians work responsibly in everyday vocations serving Christ with varying degrees of intensity and frugality.

The choice between these traditions is David's dilemma and is worthy of further exploration. The dilemma is the age-old one of the ideal and the real. On the one hand Jesus offers glimpses of the ideal in his teachings on the community of God and in his person. The community of God, he says, is already present with power, and Jesus asks his disciples to live in this power and to drop what they are doing and follow him. On the other hand, paradoxically, the community of God is still to come in its fullness.

Reality is a mixture of powers: human power rightly and wrongly used and God's power of love. God's community of love stands alongside and often in contradiction to human power, and Christians must live in a world where perfect choices are seldom presented.

These two normative traditions both have biblical bases. The Hebrew scriptures take the responsible consumption side. They praise the rich people and place a high value on riches gained through honest work (Gn 13:2; 26:13; 30:43; 41:40). Alongside this praise is the obligation to care for weaker members of society (Am 8:48; Is 5:8–10; 10:1–3). Nowhere do the Hebrew scriptures praise self-imposed poverty or beggars.

The two sides are found in the teachings of Jesus. His announcement of the coming community of God carries with it a call for unparalleled freedom from possessions and complete trust in God. The service of God and service of riches are incompatible (Mt 6:24; Mk 8:36; 9:43–48; 10:17–25; Lk 12:15; 8:14, 18–23; 19:1–10). Jesus tells the rich young ruler who has kept all the laws to go sell what he has and give it to the poor (Lk 18:18–24). Jesus himself had no possessions (Mt 8:20; Mk 1:16; 6:8–9; Lk 9:3; 10:4) and prodded his disciples to go out on their missionary journeys taking nothing with them (Lk 9:3; 10:4).

Nevertheless, Jesus took for granted the owning of property (Lk 6:30; 10:30–37; Mt 25:31–40). He was apparently supported by women of means (Lk 8:2) and urged that possessions be used to help those in need (Lk 6:30). Jesus did not ask Zacchaeus to give up all his possessions (Lk 19). He dined with hated tax collectors and was fond of celebrations, especially meals of fellowship. The examples echo the Hebrew scriptures' stress on the right use of wealth and possessions.

This mixed mind continued in the early church. On the one side was the Jerusalem community where goods were shared in common (Acts 1–5). This seems to follow Jesus' teachings about radical freedom from possessions. The letter of James offers little solace to the wealthy (Jas 1:11; 2:1–7; 5:1–6). On the other side is Paul, who did not address the problem of wealth, although he himself seems to have had few possessions and was self-supporting as a tentmaker (Phil 4:11–13). He did, however, stress right use, made clear his center in Christ, and called on the congregations he served to support the poor in Jerusalem. The letter to Timothy, while hard on the wealthy, leaves the door open to right use of possessions (1 Tm 6:6–10, 17–19).

From these two traditions a dual ethic emerged. For monks and nuns who surrendered their possessions and elected a life of chastity, holy poverty, and nonviolence, the rigor of Jesus was binding. For the great majority the rigor of Jesus became "counsels of perfection." It was deemed impossible of fulfillment and therefore binding only on those who would be perfect.

These two ways of living existed side by side with the authority of the church sanctioning both and holding them together. Implicit in this resolution of the dilemma was a troublesome hierarchy of perfection and the unbiblical notion of special merits that practicing rigor was claimed to confer. Thus, while the church held things together, it did so at the price of grading perfection and discouraging the rigor of ordinary Christians.

Protestants, following Martin Luther's dictum of the priesthood of all believers, eliminated special merit, but at the price of restoring the dilemma. Monasteries and convents were closed, and all believers were, according to Luther, to serve God in whatever vocation they found themselves. Where there had been two ways of life in one church, now there was one way of life with two tendencies in many churches. Still, rigorous discipleship has continued to the present in the monastic movement within the Roman Catholic Church and in many sects that have flourished in Protestantism.

One statement by Martin Luther during a "table talk" in the winter of 1542–43 catches the mind that is suspicious of wealth:

> Riches are the most insignificant things on earth, the smallest gift that God can give a person. What are they in comparison with the word of God? In fact, what are they in comparison even with physical endowments and beauty? What are they in comparison to the gifts of the mind? And yet we act as if this were not so! The matter, form, effect, and goal of riches are worthless. This is why our Lord God generally gives riches to crude asses to whom nothing else is given.

The biblical witness on consumption follows much the same twofold pattern. The basic issue is frugality versus contentment with a moderate level of consumption.

Theologically the two traditions take their cues from the paradoxical "here, but yet to come" teaching of the early church. This paradox appears in the earliest pages of the Bible. Human beings are created in the image of God (Gn 1) but with Adam and Eve fall away from God into sin (Gn 3). It reappears again and again in the history of Israel as the Israelites wrestle with the responsibilities of the covenant and their own unrighteousness.

Jesus advises his disciples to be sheep among the wolves and to have the wisdom of the serpent and the innocence of the dove (Mt 10:16). For Christians, this paradox is preeminent in the cross and resurrection. The cross is reality at its worst and points to the depth of human sin. Sin is not some minor defect to be overcome by new techniques. Ordering force and occasionally even coercion are needed to keep it in check.

Yet the cross is not the last word in Christianity. It is followed closely by the ever-new word of the resurrection. The resurrection points to God at work overcoming sin and death. It points as well to the possibility of the "new creation" in the lives of individuals and groups and to the creative potential of love and justice. It teaches Christians that while they still live in the age of sin and death, God's love has broken in, there is hope, and their efforts in response to God's love are not in vain. Christians are invited, as a result, to deal with a partly open future in which even small responses can make a difference.

Finally, the paradox is highlighted by Paul's sense that Christians live between the ages. They live in the old age of sin, death, injustice, and limits. Yet they are called to live according to the new age inaugurated by Jesus Christ and made present by the Holy Spirit. Insofar as they live in the old age, Christians give limited support to such things as prison systems, to less than perfect but still functioning economic and political systems, and even to wars of liberation and defense. Living in the old age involves compromises, many of which appear to be "cop-outs" to those who take the rigorous path.

Nevertheless, Christians are not to be serpents or to live according to the old age. They are to live in the resurrection according to the love and justice of the new age. This means pushing beyond what merely is and seeking just and sustainable societies. Living in the new age means witnessing to the ideal and may seem utopian to those who enjoy luxury and even some who follow the path of responsible consumption.

In summary, the rigorous tradition builds on Jesus' call to radical discipleship, his living without possessions frugally and simply, and his freedom from materialism. This tradition calls the disciple to a life of simplicity and sharing. It is a life of commitment to the community of God. And even if all the details are not lived perfectly, at least the disciple should aim in that direction and pray that the grace of God will provide the resources to reconcile aim and action.

As for living between the ages, the path of rigorous discipleship emphasizes the new age almost to the exclusion of the old. This exclusion comes not from failure to see the sin of the old age, but rather from the assumption that Christians are free from the old age through the power of God. Hence radical changes in ways of living come naturally, and followers make these changes with enthusiasm.

The path of rigorous discipleship is attractive. It does not bog down in the inevitable relativities and compromises of the old age. It is simple, direct, and often accompanied by communities that seem full of the Spirit. It is a valid Christian option.

Unlike the path of rigorous discipleship, the path of responsible consumption does not take its main cues from the teachings of Jesus. This does not mean it is less biblical, but that it rests more heavily on the main themes of the Bible, in particular on the theological tension between the old and the new ages. Like those on the path of rigorous discipleship, Christians on this path are concerned for the poor and aware of being tied to possessions. They do not, however, take the frugality and simplicity of Jesus literally or urge the surrender of all possessions.

Reduced to basics, those who follow this tradition wrestle with what it means to live between the ages, taking both ages seriously. In contrast to the heavy stress on the new age, they point to the realities of the old age or to the ambiguity of life between the ages. The problem for them is not rigorous discipleship but how to act responsibly and to begin a process of change that will lead to greater justice and more sustainable communities. Their mood is sober, their programs moderate and reformist in nature. They also have a greater appreciation of material consumption.

This path is attractive to less ascetic Christians and to those who are deeply involved in existing structures. It is a valid Christian tradition and avoids the excesses that sometimes accompany the rigorous tradition. Most important, it accounts for the complexities of living in the world as it is.

While Christianity has been of two minds, it has been clear on one guiding norm, *sufficiency*. Sufficiency for humans is the timely supply of basic material necessities, defined as the minimum amount of food, clothing, shelter, transportation, health care, and education needed to live at some margin above mere subsistence. Sufficiency is, of course, more than a given batch of goods and services. Philosopher Martha Nussbaum has established something she calls the "flourishing life" as the goal of her development scheme. She has advanced two lists of what constitute "the human form of life" and "good human functioning."[1] She insists it is the responsibility of political and economic institutions to ensure that everyone is capable of

---

[1] Martha Nussbaum and Jonathan Glover, *Women, Culture, and Development: A Study of Human Capabilities* (Oxford: Clarendon Press, 1995), 76–85. Nussbaum and Glover argue that the "human form of life" consists of (1) mortality; (2) the human body including the needs for food, drink, and shelter, and sexual desire; (3) the capacity for pleasure and pain; (4) cognitive capability including perceiving, imagining, and thinking; (5) early infant development; (6) practical reason; (7) affiliation with other human beings; (8) relatedness to other species and nature; (9) humor and play; (10) separateness; and (11) space to move around in.

"Basic human functional capabilities" include (1) being able to live to the end of a human life of normal length; (2) being able to have good health; (3) being able to avoid unnecessary and non-beneficial pain; (4) being able to use the senses; (5) being able to have attachments to things and persons outside ourselves; (6) being able to form a conception of the good and to engage in critical reflection about the planning of one's life; (7) being able to live for others; (8) being able to live with concern for and in relations to animals, plants, and the world of nature; (9) being able to laugh, play, and enjoy recreational activities; and (10) being able to live one's own life in one's own surroundings and context.

functioning at a human level. While her lists are exhaustive and beyond the capacity of most governments, they are a good starting place for understanding what sufficiency means.

Sufficiency for other species revolves first around the preservation and restoration of habitat for wild species. Humans do not have the capacity to oversee the survival of many species, but they can cease degrading critical habitats. Habitat loss is a major cause of species extinction. As for domestic animals, more is required. Sufficiency for them means the provision of basic material needs and proper care. This opens up a wide range of options including alternative farming techniques and even vegetarian diets.

Sufficiency must also include future generations. Sufficiency must be sustainable over long periods of time. Another norm influencing the Trapps' decision is therefore *sustainability*. The issue that sustainability raises for the Trapps is whether the forms of consumption they are contemplating degrade the environment. One small cabin on an already developed lake front will hardly do much damage, but if their behavior were to be generalized, it certainly would. The Earth can ill afford six billion people who consume as if they were affluent North Americans.

What then are David and Nancy to do? How are they to live? If they will to live responsively to the power of God and to be guided by Christian norms, they will avoid heavy consumption, materialism, and selfish individualism. They will live sufficiently free to pursue rigorous discipleship or responsible consumption as they feel called. They will put trust where trust belongs, that is to say, in God's community, not in material possessions. What this means in practice is something that finally is a matter of conscience. Blueprints and prescriptions are not available.

GUILT

Is David driven by guilt over his own privileged place in the world—white, American, male, intelligent, and wealthy—or is guilt an inappropriate word to describe his struggle with rigor and responsibility? The case does not reveal the answer. Giving David the benefit of doubt, however, it is better to see his struggle as a conscientious effort to deal with an ambiguous tradition and a changing environmental context. Christians like David may be genuinely perplexed as they try to figure out the right course, because valid norms sometimes suggest quite different courses of action.

Even if David did not feel guilty, it is important to recognize that guilt is an all too common human experience and should be taken seriously. Guilt may be a warning sign of serious inner alienation. It may be telling David that he really is living a sinful way of life and needs to change (repent).

More important for those who would categorize David as "guilt ridden" is the possibility that they are projecting their own guilt in order to be free for a life of affluence. To dismiss David's dilemma as guilt is to miss the main point of the case.

Finally, guilt is not something that needs to paralyze action. Guilt may be genuinely experienced and may legitimately point to sin, but it is not the place to rest. Just as the resurrection follows the cross, so do forgiveness and the possibility of new life follow sin and guilt.

INDIVIDUAL ACTION

Does it really make a difference what David and Nancy decide? Does David's struggle over options available to only a select few trivialize the more important problems of world poverty and environmental degradation?

Discussions of individual action are permeated with optimistic and pessimistic extremes. The optimists insist that successful social movements are usually started and led by individuals who are deeply concerned and motivated. They urge their listeners to take the challenge and change the world. The pessimists, in turn, dismiss individual action as not having a chance in a world of large organizations. They urge their listeners to join movements or counsel withdrawal.

Christians are neither optimists nor pessimists. They are hopeful and realistic; hopeful because God is at work in even the darkest times, realistic because of sin. Christians act first in response to the love of God they experience spiritually and only second to achieve results. If good results follow from faithful discipleship, they should be embraced. If they do not, action is still forthcoming because of its spiritual foundation.

This simple truth does away with the debate between optimists and pessimists over individual action. The debate is misplaced. It misses the essential inspiration of Christian ethical action and substitutes reliance on human action alone.

Is David's dilemma trivial? By no means! His struggle with his conscience over appropriate levels of consumption is essential in a poverty-stricken, environmentally degraded world. It is essential for everyone, especially for those who consume heavily or could potentially consume more. Whether it is a cabin, a television set, a new computer, or a trip to the Amazon, personal consumption makes an ethical statement. It says a lot about character. So while David's specific decision will not be recorded in history books, what this generation does to relieve poverty and preserve the environment will.

ADDITIONAL RESOURCES

Brueggemann, Walter. *The Prophetic Imagination*. 2d ed. Minneapolis: Fortress Press, 2001.

Cobb, John B., Jr. *Sustainability: Economics, Ecology, and Justice*. New York: Wipf and Stock Publishers, 2007.

Dauvergne, Peter. *The Shadows of Consumption: Consequences for the Global Environment*. Cambridge, MA: MIT Press, 2010.

Foster, Richard J. *Freedom of Simplicity: Finding Harmony in a Complex World*. New York: HarperOne, 2005.

Hengel, Martin. *Property and Riches in the Early Church*. Translated by John Bowden. Philadelphia: Fortress Press, 1974.

Horsley, Richard A. *Covenant Economics: A Biblical Vision of Justice for All*. Louisville, KY: Westminster John Knox Press, 2009.

Johnson, Jan. *Abundant Simplicity: Discovering the Unhurried Rhythms of Grace*. Westmont, IL: InterVarsity Press, 2011.

Kavanaugh, John K. *Following Christ in a Consumer Society: The Spirituality of Cultural Resistance*. Maryknoll, NY: Orbis Books, 2006.

McDaniel, Jay B. *Living from the Center: Spirituality in an Age of Consumerism*. St. Louis: Chalice Press, 2000.

Nash, James A. "Toward the Revival and Reform of the Subversive Virtue: Frugality." In *Consumption, Population, and Sustainability: Perspectives from Science and Religion*, edited by Audrey R. Chapman, Rodney L. Petersen, and Barbara Smith-Moran. Washington, D.C.: Island Press, 2002.

Rohr, Richard. *Simplicity: The Freedom of Letting Go*. Updated edition. New York: The Crossroad Publishing Company, 2005.

Shi, David. *The Simple Life: Plain Living and High Thinking in American Culture*. Athens: University of Georgia Press, 2007.

Sider, Ronald. *Rich Christians in an Age of Hunger: Moving from Affluence to Generosity*. Nashville, TN: Thomas Nelson Publishers, 2005.

Stevenson, Tyler Wigg. *Brand Jesus: Christianity in a Consumerist Age*. New York: Seabury Books, 2007.

Stivers, Robert L. *Hunger, Technology, and Limits to Growth*. Minneapolis: Augsburg Press, 1984. See Chapter 9.

Case

What God Has Joined

Linda glanced through the large glass window of the restaurant and saw Beth and Jennifer already seated in a corner booth. She hesitated a moment at the door, then moved toward them, hugging and greeting each in turn. They had been good friends in college, but after graduation they had drifted apart. When the fourth member of their college quartet, Joanne, had died of breast cancer eight years after graduation, the remaining three had come together again to support her in her last months and to share the pain of her passing. Over the next two years they had remained close. The lunch today was a kind of a celebration for Jennifer, who had concentrated on her career as an accountant after college rather than marrying and having children like the other three. Now, as the three survivors of the quartet approached thirty-five, Jennifer was engaged to be married to another partner in her accounting firm. Next Saturday there was to be a big party, but this lunch was just for the three of them.

Twenty minutes later, having admired Jen's ring and listened to the couple's wedding plans, Linda was shifting uncomfortably in her seat. She realized both Beth and Jennifer were staring, waiting for her to volunteer information. Finally Jennifer, not the most patient or tactful of the trio, blurted out, "Tell us what's the matter, Lin. We both know that things haven't been great for a while at home, but you seem desperately unhappy. We love you. What's going on?"

It was more than Linda could do to control the gulping sobs that rolled out of her. "I don't know what to do. It's all come back, and I can't go on. David's drinking, and he's hit me. I can't take it anymore."

When Linda had calmed down, Beth pulled the story from her a piece at a time. Beth and Jen knew that Linda's husband, David, had rarely used

---

This case and commentary were prepared by Christine E. Gudorf. The names of all persons and institutions have been disguised to protect the privacy of those involved.

alcohol before he lost his job as manager of a bank branch, but both had seen him inebriated at least twice in the last six months. They knew David had not found another job. But both were shocked to hear that he had hit Linda. They immediately asked for details, for neither would have thought David capable of violence. Both remembered the extraordinary gentleness he had displayed in the hospital nursery holding and feeding Megan, the couple's tiny premature firstborn.

Linda began by defending David, citing the pressures of unemployment on him, the stress of seeing their unemployment insurance run out, and the prospect of their savings running out as well. With only the part-time secretarial work that Linda had found with the school board, they would not be able to keep up house payments. "He's drinking, but he's not really drinking that much. He has hit me two or three times but always stops after the one slap. The real problem is me. It's all coming back. I love him, but I can't stand for him to get near me. And he thinks I'm rejecting him, that I don't love him anymore because he doesn't have a job."

Both Beth and Jennifer understood that Linda was referring to her memories of years of sexual abuse by her grandfather. From the time she was eight until his death when Linda was fourteen, her grandfather had used his position as her after-school baby sitter to sexually molest her. Her family had more or less dismissed both attempts she made to tell about the abuse. She later suspected that her mother had been abused before her. When she arrived at college, Linda never dated. When the topic of child incest came up in a sociology class, Linda spoke to the professor, who referred her to individual therapy and to a support group for child victims of incest. After six months of therapy Linda had met David, declared herself cured, and quit the therapy. But both Beth and Jennifer remembered Linda's screaming nightmares and her fear and distrust of men. And they knew that though she kept in touch with her family, she never went back home after college and never left her children with any of her family.

"Are you and David talking, Linda?" Jennifer asked.

"What can I say? He doesn't believe me when I say that he's not the reason I don't want sex. He keeps telling me I was over the abuse years ago, that I have loved sex for all these years, that the only thing that could be turning me off is him. Maybe he's right, and the memories are just an excuse. Maybe I have invented them. That's what mother and Aunt Lucy told me when I was little. That I made them up. I don't really know how I feel, or whether I love him, or what I want to do. But I can't go on. Sometimes I just go and hide in a closet for hours at a time. I can't face anyone. I don't know how I got here—I haven't been outside the house in weeks."

Linda was calmer by the end of the lunch. Both Jennifer and Beth were disturbed by Linda's depression and her expressions of self-doubt and self-blame. They urged her to seek therapeutic help. Beth volunteered to make appointments for both David and Linda separately to see her neighbors, the Spencers, a husband-and-wife therapy team. Beth assured Linda that they worked on a sliding-scale fee schedule.

LONG-TERM RECOVERY ISSUES

Six weeks later, when the friends met after Jen's wedding, Linda reported that some things were better and some things were worse. David had liked Dr. Dan Spencer from the start. By the second session he had stopped drinking, and though there were no more incidents of either verbal or physical violence, David continued to work with Dan Spencer on issues around alcohol and violence. Linda reported that Alice Spencer was pushing her to face the violent episodes, to look at the effect they had had on her and on the marital relationship, and to think about how she might react to violence or the threat of violence from David in the future. David was continuing to look for work in surrounding communities. But he still had trouble accepting that Linda was not rejecting him when she declined sex.

Sitting in Beth's kitchen while Linda's and Beth's children played outside the backyard window, Linda confided, "Sometimes I really do want him to hold me, to give me affection. But the minute it turns sexual, I want to scream. For him, if I don't want sex, I don't love him. He tries sometimes to just be affectionate, but it really hurts him when I panic and push him away from me. Sometimes I can't even stand him being close; other times I want to be held but then push him away later. He complains that he never knows what I want. And I don't know what I want. I don't know why it all came back. There was no clue for all those years. We were really happy until he lost his job. But it's been almost a year since we made love, and three months since I was last willing to try."

"What does Alice Spencer think of your situation?" asked Jennifer.

"She says that I need to concentrate not on David or the relationship but on my own feelings. She thinks that's why it all came back—I didn't stay in therapy long enough to heal from the abuse. I'm not good at explaining it, but what the years of abuse did was to teach me to respond to other people's needs and desires and to lose sight of my own. She says now I need to respond to my own feelings, but first I have to learn what they are. And in some areas of my life I don't have a clue as to which feelings are mine and which are David's, or my grandfather's, or even other people's—like yours. So many 'shoulds' in my life have come from outside me, without any conscious consideration or adoption on my part. She insists I can heal, that I can find my authentic self. But I don't know. In some things, yes, but I can't imagine ever having sex again and enjoying it without remembering the pain and hatred and ultimate emptiness inside. What does that mean for our marriage? Do I love David? Can I make him wait for what may never happen? Shouldn't I be working on accepting sex so I can stop hurting him? My rejection is hurting him much worse than his slaps ever hurt me. Can there be a marriage without sex? A real one with love and warmth, the kind we vowed to have?"

Jennifer responded, "That's a tough one. I remember that Christian churches used to forbid totally impotent men to marry, because sex was important to marriage, but I think so long as they had sex once, it didn't matter if they never did again. I don't know. I'm the newly married one here. Can there be a real marriage without sex? Won't that depend on what David wants and needs, too? Do you want to be married? Why don't you talk to somebody with some expertise? You like Pastor Link, and we've all known him for years. Why don't you and David talk to him?"

At that very moment David sat in Dan Spencer's office. "All right, all right. I am coming to see that she really is going back through all that past abuse. I don't understand why. I thought she was through it before we got married. She was never tense or nervous about sex, never afraid of being forced or hurt. She knew I would never hurt her. I just don't understand why it came back now, if not in response to me. But I can't do this much longer. I know that when I feel really threatened by her withdrawal that I want to drink too much, and I know that if I drink, the hurt and threat will come out in anger. I don't know how I'd live with myself if I ever forced her to have sex. But not drinking is only a little part of the answer."

David continued thoughtfully, "I know I haven't slept the whole night through in over six months. Some nights I have to get up and get away from her, so I won't start making love to her while she's asleep. I have to go lie down on the couch. I love Linda. When I hold her or hug her or just sit in the car with her driving the kids to Sunday school, I want to make love to her. And I want her to love me. It's not just selfish or lust. I want to give her pleasure, to make her feel better, to show her that she can trust me with her body and her heart. Sometimes I think it would be easier to just stay away from her. But to avoid her, to get separate beds, or even separate rooms when we could afford them, would be like divorce. When will this be over? How long does it take? Will she ever get better? Is divorce the only option?"

When Linda picked up David at Dr. Spencer's, she asked if he were interested in seeing Pastor Link. David agreed and offered to make the appointment. When David called the church, he was told that Pastor Link was out of town for three weeks but that the associate pastor, Reverend Deerick, was available. David made an appointment with Reverend Deerick, explained the general situation to him, and mentioned that he and

Linda were in therapy with the Spencers. Reverend Deerick asked for their authorization to speak with the Spencers. When David and Linda appeared the following week for their appointment, Reverend Deerick had briefly discussed the case with the Spencers. Linda and David began by describing their feelings about each other and their marriage, and ended with a flurry of questions about the nature of marriage. Was their marriage over? Could the wounded child in Linda ever really heal after all these years? If not, would remaining together be merely a hypothetical front, or would it be a heroic fidelity to the vows they had taken? Could there be a real Christian marriage without sharing either genital pleasure or touch and affection? What did the church teach?

When they had finished, Reverend Deerick was still for a few moments and then said: "I'm not sure that anyone can answer all your questions. I have never been married myself. And you probably know that our church, like most Christian churches, is in the midst of rethinking various aspects of our teachings regarding sexuality and marriage. I could tell you what Augustine or Luther would say to you, but I don't think that would do much good. From what you have told me, you didn't marry either to have children or to prevent fornication. You married because you loved each other in a deeply interpersonal way and because you found that the whole of the other person—body and soul—helped put you in touch with ultimate reality, with God. This contemporary understanding of the purpose and goal of marriage is radically different from Augustine's, or Luther's, or any of the other classical Christian thinkers. So their likely advice in this situation—that you purify and consecrate your marriage by giving up sexual intimacy, living as brother and sister as you rear your children—would probably strike you as effectively ending the marriage.

"Our theological tradition simply doesn't give us a lot of useful contemporary guidance about sexuality in marriage. But I do have some suggestions. The first one is personal prayer. I don't mean that you should pray that all this will mysteriously disappear. Prayer is communication with God. Sometimes it is spoken; more often it is silent. Sometimes we write our prayers. Think of prayer as a way of making a friend of God.

"David, I am very moved by your pain and your love for Linda. But you express a great deal of need for her, and that need clearly puts emotional pressure on her. Most men in our society are socialized to fulfill virtually all their intimacy needs in one sexual relationship. Developing an intimate relationship with God could not only take away some of your pain and need, but it could also let you focus on Linda's needs more clearly. Linda, prayer for you could be a source of hope and strength for healing. Some victims of sexual abuse by males have a difficult time with prayer and with God because of the traditional images of God as masculine. You may need to focus on the femininity of God, on God as Mother, to be able to pray. But regardless of what gender you attribute to God, the object is that you let yourself feel God's love for you and God's support for your healing. Feeling God's support for healing could help you feel more legitimate investing so much time and energy in the healing process. A prayerful relationship with God could help you reclaim feelings of trust, self-worth, and responsibility for your own life.

"You both have many questions about marriage and your future that I think only prayer can answer. Prayer can be a process of uncovering, one piece at a time, all our questions about who we are and what we should do. If you like, I would be glad to meet with you periodically to discuss developments in your individual prayer life. Or I have some books or articles you could read, if you prefer."

As David and Linda drove home from the meeting, they wondered how valuable Reverend Deerick's advice had been. In some ways it evoked simplistic notions of passive religion in which prayer is the answer to everything. But Reverend Deerick had supported their therapeutic process with the Spencers as helpful and seemed to want to coordinate this spiritual direction with that process. Perhaps prayer could help David find more patience with Linda's withdrawal and could help Linda feel stronger and more worthwhile. Halfway home Linda asked, "David, do you want to consider divorce as an option? I would understand if you did. I don't think it's right for me to ask you to continue with our marriage if that's not what you want, but for myself I prefer to work on our marriage. I'm just not sure how we work on rebuilding it, or what we can legitimately ask of each other. What do you want to do, David?"

Commentary

Some of the social and moral issues requiring analysis in this case include alcoholism, domestic violence, and child sexual abuse (child incest). But as David's and Linda's questions indicate, the central question for them is whether they should remain together. This question raises the theological issues undergirding the nature of marriage. Let us begin with the more specific problems.

ALCOHOLISM

Linda and David both seem to treat David's drinking as a minor problem; Beth and Jennifer also seem to accept that judgment. However, Dan Spencer continues to ask about and treat alcohol as a possible ongoing problem, for he is not sure that alcohol is only temporarily a problem due to David's loss of work or Linda's withdrawal. While the use of alcohol has not been regarded as a moral problem within most of Christianity—certainly not within scripture—the abuse of alcohol has been consistently condemned from scriptural times to the present. It is not clear from the case that David's alcohol abuse is part of a larger pattern of alcoholism, but David's misuse of alcohol under the pressure of unemployment and his wife's withdrawal might well signal a pattern of relying on alcohol to cope with pressure.

Research has not determined whether persons who have had trouble with alcohol dependency in response to stress are permanently at risk. Alcoholics Anonymous says yes and insists on lifelong abstinence. There are some people who seem to be able to return to moderate, even abstemious, use of alcohol after an episode of alcohol abuse and to maintain that lower level of use for years. But there are not reliable methods for separating those with such potential from those unable to use alcohol responsibly. If David does not decide to give up alcohol altogether, he needs careful monitoring and oversight of his consumption and response for some time.

DOMESTIC BATTERY

Linda's friends are perceptive to question her facile dismissal of David's violence against her. The Spencers need to elicit from both Linda and David their accounts of violence in the relationship. All too often domestic violence follows a pattern: psychological violence leads to verbal violence, which leads to physical violence (including sexual violence), which may even lead to homicide. It is important to discover whether there has been a pattern of escalation in the violence within the relationship.

Between one in seven and one in four homes in the United States are scenes of domestic violence. According to the national Coalition Against Domestic Violence, one in every four US women will be involved at some time during her life in a relationship of domestic violence. Christianity also bears some responsibility for high rates of domestic violence. Violence against women has been tolerated and sometimes actively supported in the churches. In Christianity before mandatory clerical celibacy was imposed at the end of the first millennium, and among Protestants after the Reformation, for example, clergy were encouraged to be especially severe in beating their wives, since their wives were to be examples of wifely submission for other women. Scriptural verses that embody the household code of the Roman Empire, such as Ephesians 5 and Colossians 3, enjoin wives to obey their husbands and husbands to love their wives. These texts were interpreted to require beating as a form of loving discipline, ignoring the fact that the Colossians text reads: "Husbands, love your wives and never treat them harshly" (Col 3:19).

The staggering level of domestic violence in modern society is supported by an attitude of social silence. Neighbors close the windows when they hear slaps, crashes, and shouting next door rather than intervene or call the police. Family members ignore bruises and black eyes in silence or whisper to one another that John and Mary "aren't getting along." Police sometimes treat domestic abuse as if it were another barroom brawl in which both parties are equally at fault and merely need a short separation to "cool down." Too often the churches are totally silent about domestic violence and sexual abuse, assuming that such things do not occur in the homes of church members but only among the unchurched. Such an attitude discourages victims from turning to the church as a resource and fails to call abusers to accountability.

Domestic violence is not accidental and is not typically about blowing off steam. Nor is the victim accidentally chosen. Domestic violence maintains control over the spouse. The batterer feels that he is losing control over the spouse and so "accidentally" loses control of himself in violence. Afterward, abusers frequently argue that they should be forgiven because they were not themselves; they were under the influence of alcohol, or temper, or fear, and did not mean the abuse. In fact, batterers' recourse to alcohol is itself usually deliberate, as is the attempt to find issues over which to explode (the quality of dinner, the size of a bill, the behavior of the children, the length of a phone call, and so on). These are pretexts for recourse to violent acts that then terrorize the spouse into capitulating to the control of the abuser. When the violence is done and his control restored, the typical abuser apologizes for the damage, pledges his love, and woos the victim into both remaining in the relationship and forgiving him. Even during this expression of repentance, however, abusers typically refuse to accept responsibility. They insist that the victim was responsible for triggering violence brought on by alcohol, stress, or other factors not under his control.

Given this common pattern in domestic abuse, the Spencers need to ask both Linda and David questions about control in the marriage. Is there any evidence that David's use of violence in response to Linda's sexual withdrawal is part of a pattern of David's controlling Linda through violence or threat of violence? It is important to probe the issue of violent abuse because of Linda's past victimization. Her earlier sexual abuse has obscured her own feelings and interests so that she seems better able to focus on David's suffering and pain than on her own. Does Linda's tendency to brush off the violent episodes mask a low self-esteem that makes her see herself as an appropriate object for violence? Or is her easy dismissal of violence the result of over ten years of knowing David as a gentle, non-controlling partner demonstrating abiding love for her and the children?

Questions need to be asked about violence in either Linda's or David's interaction with their children as well, and about how the children have been affected by David's violence and alcohol abuse and by Linda's emotional condition. We have no indications that either parent has directed violence at the children, and we do not know the ages of these children. The children should be told as much about what is going on with their parents as is appropriate for their ages. Linda and David should explain in simple terms why they are upset, that they are working on their problems, that the children have no responsibility for their parents' problems, and that no matter how they work out their particular problems, the parents will both continue to love the children. Having some idea of what is occurring may help the children feel secure enough to ask for additional reassurance when they need it.

CHILD SEXUAL ABUSE

The real prevalence of child sexual abuse is not known because so many victims do not disclose or report their abuse. According to a 2006 report by the US Centers for Disease Control and Prevention, however, adult retrospective studies show that one in four women (25 percent) and one in six men (16.7 percent) were sexually abused before the age of eighteen. One of every twenty young girls is the victim of stepfather-daughter incest or father-daughter incest, which is generally considered the most traumatic type of incest, though specific incidents of other types of incest can cause as much or more trauma. In this case we have no mention of Linda's father; her grandfather may or may not have functioned as a father substitute.

The extent of the trauma in child sexual abuse depends upon four factors: the intrusiveness of the abuse; the length of time the abuse continued; the degree of prior trust the victim had invested in the abuser; and the degree of pain, coercion, or threat used to obtain compliance from the victim. We have no information here about the intrusiveness of the abuse or the degree of coercion, pain, or threats in Linda's incestuous abuse as a child. But the abuse continued for several years, and it involved betrayal of trust. In Linda's case the abuser was not only a family member acting in a caretaker role, but the abuse was supported by her primary caretaker's refusal to believe her. Linda's experience is not unusual. Nor is she unusual in experiencing trauma from the incest many years after she thought she had put it behind her. It is often not clear what triggers such memories, but greater social awareness of incestuous abuse of children has supported many unhealed adult victims in getting help rather than remaining trapped in nightmarish fear, distrust, and self-loathing.

The United States is generally considered to have among the highest child sexual abuse rates in the world. But data is not readily available for most parts of the world, and even US data is incomplete. In general, researchers are coming to believe that large numbers of the world's children are at risk for sexual abuse. Both religious and secular cultures here and elsewhere include strong supports for child sexual abuse, including socialization of children to universal respect and unquestioning obedience to parents and other adults; failing to recognize children's rights over their own bodies; and a silence about sex that prevents both information flow and ease of communication around sex, even between intimates. Both church and society, which hold up the family as a protector of children, have been largely blind to familial abuse of children.

Healing from sexual victimization is almost always a long and painful process. When victimization is endured as a child and is unaddressed for decades, the internalization of the abuse, which usually does the most damage, is often unobstructed, even reinforced. In Linda's case, however, it is extremely positive that she did not suppress all memories of the abuse and that she seems to have a history of both sexual satisfaction and intimacy with David. Whatever deficiencies existed within that intimacy (and there are always greater depths of intimacy to achieve), the fact that both partners experienced the relationship as intimate for over a decade testifies to the advantage Linda has over incest victims in general. Many victims find themselves unable to trust others enough for intimacy and unable to feel that they have an authentic self worthy of being disclosed to another. While Linda may always carry some degree of damage from her childhood experience, she may well develop moral strengths from her battle that help her resist and heal from her family's sinful abuse.

It is important for Christians to insist that Linda can heal, both because there is objective evidence of the healing of other victims and because Christians believe in the resurrection, the ground of Christian hope. What Christians mean when they speak of Jesus Christ's resurrection as victory over sin is not that sin ceases to exist. Victims of child sexual abuse are victims of sin. Rather, Christians mean that sin is not final and decisive; because of Jesus Christ's resurrection, others can overcome and recover from the effects of sin. It is through healing from sin that we participate in the resurrection of Jesus. In this case there is a very real possibility that dealing with the present problems in the relationship—the memories that plague Linda, and David's recourse to alcohol and violence—may allow them to reestablish and strengthen their earlier intimacy.

In order for that to happen, David needs to move beyond his present step of acknowledging that Linda is not yet healed from the earlier abuse. He needs to become truly supportive of that healing. Perhaps, as Reverend Deerick suggested, prayerful intimacy with God could alleviate some of David's intimacy needs so that he could become more supportive of Linda's healing. Only support from David himself can remove the sense of demand Linda now feels about David's desire for sexual intimacy. Her feelings of guilt about not being able to give him what he wants echo lessons learned in the abuse and interfere with her ability to concentrate on her own healing process. If David could learn to rely less on sexual intimacy as symbolic of the overall intimacy of the relationship and be more open to emotional intimacy and non-genital physical intimacy with Linda, he could assist Linda's healing and satisfy physically some of his own need to be reassured of Linda's love for him.

At the same time, it would be wrong to demand that David immediately accept a marriage without genital relations or even physical touch. Human beings are integrated persons, and their relationships and growth and development should be integrated. While David seems to be extremely focused on physical and even genital activity for expressing his feelings for Linda and meeting his own intimacy needs, other avenues of interpersonal interactions should be developed in addition to, and not in place of, sexual activity. Genital activity in marriage is an important foundation for other forms of intimacy because of its symbolic power. Both nakedness and the letting go of consciousness and control in orgasm are powerful images of trust and self-giving, of vulnerability. Shared pleasure in sex both rewards lovers for their willingness to offer themselves to the other and bonds lovers together.

Linda should be encouraged to assume that she can heal and that the healing process will include her ability to reclaim her sexual feelings and activity. Healing will mean ending the power of the abuse to dictate her feelings, her actions, and her life. To assume from the beginning that she will never be able to resume a full marital relationship is "victimism," accepting that the effects of victimization are permanent.

SPIRITUAL COUNSELING

Reverend Deerick's offer of support for guiding Linda's and David's prayer life seems to include spiritual counseling around the specifics of their situations. Spiritual counseling when coordinated with psychological counseling frequently complements it and is often the most effective therapy for dealing with lingering feelings of guilt and sinfulness in victims of sexual abuse. Spiritual counseling for Linda might also include encouragement to approach her family as a mature adult who needs to have her suffering and the family's responsibility acknowledged in ways that allow her to get on with her life. We do not know whether she faced her mother (or her aunt) with the fact of her abuse after it ended, whether they feel estranged from her, or, if so, if they know the reason for the estrangement. Even though her grandfather is dead and Linda is not close to her family, she may need, for her own sake, to confront them with her abuse. Spiritual counseling could also help protect Linda from family pressure for premature forgiveness and reconciliation.

MARRIAGE AND DIVORCE

There is little doubt that both David and Linda are experiencing great pain and suffering and asking serious questions about the permanency of marriage (for more information about marriage and divorce, see the "What Makes a Marriage?" commentary). Even though some denominations recognize divorce, Christian understandings of marriage have always taught that marriage should be undertaken as a permanent commitment. Some variety of the "for richer or poorer, in sickness and health, until death do us part" vow has been a part of the Christian wedding service for centuries. The degree of suffering involved is not, in itself, an indication of the appropriateness of divorce. A physician would not help a patient with appendicitis to die merely because the immediate pain is severe. Far more important is the prognosis for restoring health and alleviating the suffering.

For many readers the question of whether David and Linda should remain married is moot, because they are both clear that they love each other. Until the twentieth century there would have been no theological support for the understanding that marriage endures only when love endures, even though it was increasingly common after the sixteenth century to understand that love was a motive for marriage. Because women were not economically franchised, and because of the association of marriage with the bearing and rearing of children, it was assumed that women and children required the presence of the husband/father for their well-being.

Today Christian churches are divided in their understanding of marriage and divorce. The Roman Catholic Church does not recognize divorce and therefore forbids remarriage. However, if Linda were a Catholic, she might be able to obtain an annulment—a declaration that no true marriage ever existed with David—on the grounds that she was not fully free to consent to marriage because of the unresolved trauma of child sexual abuse. Most other Christian churches do not exclude the divorced and remarried, though their preference for permanency is clear. Across denominational lines the criteria that divide marriages in crisis into viable and nonviable categories are disputed among pastors and pastoral counselors. The most common question is whether contractual obligations in marriage endure after feelings of love have been lost. A related question is whether fidelity to the contractual obligations can, over time, rekindle lost feelings of love. Is love more than a feeling? There are no clear answers to these questions, which is one probable reason for Reverend Deerick's focus on personal prayer in response to David's and Linda's questions about the future of their marriage.

A second reason for Reverend Deerick's shift of focus from church teaching on marriage to prayer is that the positive and useful insights on marriage in scripture are embedded within and often distorted by patriarchal depictions of women as men's property. Women achieve virtue through fruitful wombs, sexual fidelity, and homemaking skills. The Mosaic Law and scriptural authors allow little scope for the personhood of women; while a few women are singled out, only an exceptional handful of women are recognized for their own initiatives rather than for their submission or for the fruit of their wombs. For this reason it is difficult to apply any of the scriptural stories or teachings to the crisis in David's and Linda's marriage. From the perspective of many of the communities from which scripture emerged, Linda would have no right to deny David the sexual use of her body, and David would be expected to exercise his rights regardless of her wishes. Linda might not even feel sexual aversion from her childhood memories, for she would have been raised to understand women's bodies as the property of men and might well regard her abuse by her grandfather as a universal hazard of being female. At the same time, the expectations of David and Linda of their marriage would have been significantly different had they lived in scriptural communities. They would have understood the marital bond as characterized much less by interpersonal intimacy and more by contract, especially contract between clans or families.

Theological treatment of marriage as a covenant modeled on the covenant between Yahweh and Israel is a contemporary reversal of the biblical attempt to personalize the covenant relationship. Ancient Israelites came to see their relationship with Yahweh as more personal and intimate than the feudal covenant between lords and vassals that gave the covenant its form and name. The Israelites came to image the covenant as a marriage, the most personal and intimate relationship they knew. In a society in which women were chattel that husbands bought from fathers, the inequalities of power, status, and worth in the divine/human relationship were not barriers to the effectiveness of the analogy. Saint Paul later extended the marital analogy to Christ and the church. But when the contemporary church uses the relationships of Christ/church and Yahweh/Israel relationships to understand and explain marriage, it imports into the marital relationship assumptions about inequalities of power, worth, and initiative between the partners that are alienating, making the analogies less than effective.

Until the modern age, theological treatment of marriage focused almost exclusively on procreation as the purpose and chief blessing of marriage, rather than on the quality of the relationship, which has become the central theological concern over the last few centuries. Few helpful historical resources on the role of sexuality in Christian marriage exist. Between the early medieval era and the Reformation, Christianity taught total impotence as an absolute bar to marriage and sexual consummation of marital vows as necessary to finalize marriage. Before the Reformation, and in Roman Catholicism even afterward, couples were often encouraged to consider Josephite (celibate) marriages, and clergy regularly cautioned couples to abstain from sex on Sundays, holy days, and during Lent, as sex was understood as an obstacle to prayer and contemplation. Procreation was regarded as a sufficient good to justify sexual activity and consequent pleasure. But sexual pleasure was morally suspect and forbidden as a motive for marital sex. The difficulty of resisting sexual pleasure in marriage caused pre-Reformation Christianity and post-Reformation Roman Catholicism to understand celibate religious life as a holier vocation than marriage.

The Reformers raised the status of marriage compared with vowed celibacy and gradually abandoned some of the more negative traditional attitudes toward sex. For the most part, however, the churches of the Reformation continued to understand procreation as the primary purpose of marriage and sex. For limited numbers of Protestant Christians, sexual activity came to be seen as an important way to cherish the spouse and as a source for generating warmth and intimacy that could influence children and the wider community. Among the Puritans and Quakers, for example, new understandings of marriage as primarily a personal bond, within which children were an additional but not the central blessing, gave rise to an appreciation of sex in marriage.

Within American Christianity a positive understanding of sex in marriage has been in tension with a more traditional and more widespread understanding of sex as morally dangerous and sexual desire as something to be resisted by the virtuous. Contemporary Christian theologians are attempting to recover and develop the few examples of positive treatment of body, sexuality, and sex found in Christian theological traditions. Since Christian faith is grounded in the incarnation—the doctrine that the Second Person in the Godhead became fully and humanely embodied in flesh—there should be no room for hatred or suspicion of the human body, its appetite or actions per se.

Some Catholics point out that though the traditions of Catholic moral theology were decidedly anti-sexual, the sacramental tradition regarding marriage incorporated a number of positive elements, including the understanding that sexual intercourse (especially orgasm itself) operates as a primary sacramental sign. Marital sex does not merely represent the spousal love that it signifies but actually contributes to the creation and development of that love. It has even been suggested by a Catholic clergy/lay team commissioned and funded by the US Conference of Catholic Bishops, in its 1986 document *Embodied in Love*, that mutually pleasurable marital sex is perhaps the most accessible human experience of the love that characterizes the Persons of the Trinity.

CONCLUSION

What should David and Linda do about their marriage? Under what circumstances should they divorce? Despite all their problems and pain, they both state their concern for each other and act as if they care very much about the other. For that reason they may not want to abandon the marriage now but may prefer to continue work with the Spencers and perhaps to begin seeing Reverend Deerick to work on personal prayer as a means of clarifying what they should do. The teachings of Christian churches on the issues of permanency in marriage and sex in marriage have begun to shift away from fear and suspicion of sex in marriage and from insistence on marital permanence regardless of the costs to those involved. Christian churches have come to see that marital sex can be an integral part of both interpersonal intimacy and communion with the Divine, and that the costs of preserving marriage in some circumstances can include physical and emotional violence and the erosion of self-hood. Ultimately, only Linda and David can decide what level of cost is acceptable to them and to their children in the attempt to rebuild their marriage.

ADDITIONAL RESOURCES

Anjelica, Jade. *A Moral Emergency: Breaking the Cycle of Child Abuse.* Kansas City: Sheed and Ward, 1993.

Bass, Ellen, and Laura Davis. *The Courage to Heal: A Guide for Women Survivors of Child Sexual Abuse.* 4th ed. New York: Harper Paperbacks, 2008.

Bromley, Nicole Braddock. *Breathe: Finding Freedom to Thrive in Relationships after Childhood Sexual Abuse.* Chicago: Moody Publishers, 2009.

Brown, Joanne C., and Carole R. Bohn. *Christianity, Patriarchy, and Abuse.* New York: Pilgrim Press, 1989.

Ellison, Marvin. *Erotic Justice: A Liberating Ethic of Sexuality.* Louisville, KY: Westminster/John Knox Press, 1996.

Ellison, Marvin, and Kelly Brown Douglas. *Sexuality and the Sacred: Sources for Theological Reflection.* Louisville, KY: Westminster John Knox Press, 2010.

Farley, Margaret. *Just Love: A Framework for Christian Sexual Ethics.* New York: Continuum, 2006.

Gallagher, Charles A., George A. Maloney, Mary F. Rousseau, and Paul F. Wilczak. *Embodied in Love: Sacramental Spirituality and Sexual Intimacy.* New York: The Crossroad Publishing Company, 1985.

Gudorf, Christine E. *Body, Sex, and Pleasure: Reconstructing Christian Sexual Ethics.* Cleveland: Pilgrim Press, 1994.

Hammond, Adam. *Alcohol in the Home: An Analytical Guide to Understanding and Ministering to Families Affected by Alcohol Abuse.* Bloomington, IN: CrossBooks Publishing, 2011.

Jung, Patricia, Mary E. Hunt, and Radhika Balakrishnan, eds. *Good Sex: Feminist Perspectives from the World's Religions.* New Brunswick, NJ: Rutgers University Press, 2001.

Ruether, Rosemary Radford. *Christianity and the Making of the Modern Family.* Boston: Beacon Press, 2000.

Related Websites

National Coalition against Domestic Violence, http://www.ncadv.org/.
National Sexual Violence Resource Center, http://www.nsvrc.org/publica-
    tions/child-sexual-abuse-prevention-overview.

PART II

VIOLENCE/ NONVIOLENCE

Case

A Life for a Life?

There were only two days left in the 2011 Florida legislative session. Manny sighed in relief just thinking about it. He was tired of Tallahassee, tired of commuting home to Sarasota on weekends for the last two months. Florida, unlike many other states, was limited by its constitution to a two-month annual legislative session. The big work—getting agreement on the budget—had just been finished. No one was satisfied with the bill, but that was the nature of compromise, especially at what Manny hoped was the tail end of a recession, when state revenues were low.

As Manny picked up his briefcase and headed out the door of this office he spotted Alice Browner speaking with one of the House members from the Florida Keys. Manny ducked back within his office, shutting the door softly. He liked Alice, but he knew what she wanted and that she might latch onto him if she saw him now. Alice was an unpaid lobbyist for religious groups trying to get the death-penalty statute off the books in Florida. That was not likely to happen any time in the near future; Florida voters tended to be conservative. Polls showed that over 60 percent of them supported the death penalty. Alice's group was full of enthusiasm for full elimination of the death penalty, after having won their struggle to restrict the death penalty to adults, those over eighteen years of age, when the Supreme Court declared capital punishment for minors unconstitutional (March 2, 2005).

The issue of the death penalty for minors had arisen in Florida following a few recent trials that had become media affairs. Three Miami area boys, between twelve and fourteen years of age, had been arrested for murder in the last few years: one for shooting a teacher, another for beating to death a six-year-old girl, and one for slicing the throat of a classmate in the boys' restroom at a public school. The first two had been tried as adults, and in the first case the prosecutors had asked for the death penalty. But in the

This case and its commentary were prepared by Christine E. Gudorf. The names of all persons and institutions have been disguised to protect the privacy of those involved.

51

end both boys had gotten sentences of life in prison without parole. The case of the one who had killed the six year old while wrestling with her in his home had been a real mess, Manny recalled. The boy's mother had refused to let him take the plea to a lesser charge offered by the prosecutor because she was sure her son would be acquitted. But when he was found guilty of first degree murder, the mandatory sentencing statute kicked in, and he was saddled with life in prison without parole. He had just been released, however, after serving three years, because a court determined that the state should have done competency testing on him before going to trial since there was strong evidence that he was mentally impaired. Now the third of these child-killers was about to be tried, and it looked like he also would be tried as an adult and could face the death penalty. Due to the publicity over the possibility of these very young minors getting death penalties, many Floridians, including Manny, had come to agree with the Supreme Court that the death penalty was inappropriate for minors. His response to the Supreme Court decision in 2005 had been relief that now he would not have to explain to his strong law-and-order constituents why he was going to support the bill Alice had introduced to exempt minors from the death penalty in Florida.

But now Alice's group and a number of other civic and religious groups were lobbying to end the death penalty in Florida altogether; they had introduced a bill to that effect. With the state budget out of the way, they hoped the legislature would use some of its remaining days to deal with this bill.

Manny had talked to two other House members about the bill just days ago: John Benvenuti from Winter Garden, and Saul Weiss from Jacksonville. Saul had initiated the discussion over dinner one night as they finished revision of an amendment to an insurance bill they wanted passed.

"Do you know how you'll vote if Alice Browner and her group get the death-penalty bill on the agenda?" Saul had asked.

John had responded, "I don't see how I could live with myself if I didn't vote for it, but I don't see how I can get the voters to support such a vote. My district is strong on law-and-order issues, and when it sees death penalty, it thinks 'urban crime,' 'blacks and Hispanics.' My constituents don't see convicted criminals as belonging to the same species as their families and friends."

"Do you really see this as an issue of conscience, John? I didn't know you opposed the death penalty," asked Manny, surprised.

"My church did a program on the death penalty last year, and it really had an impact on me," said John. "You know, since the death penalty was reintroduced in 1973, over 138 people have been released from death row with evidence of their innocence. From 1973 to 1999 there was an average of 3.1 exonerations a year. From 2000 to 2010 there has been an average of five exonerations a year. Of the death-penalty convictions vacated in the United States, twenty-three have been in Florida—we have had the largest number in the country. Illinois is next with nineteen, then it drops down to twelve in Texas. The program at church brought in the sister of a guy named Smith who had been on death row for fifteen years when another man confessed, and DNA testing—not available when he was tried—proved he had not done the rape/murder for which he was convicted. But it came too late for him; he died of cancer in prison weeks before he would have been released. That's the piece of it that gets me—that some of them really are innocent. That's why in 2000 the governor of Illinois, George Ryan, put a moratorium on executions and commuted so many sentences, and why the current governor, Pat Quinn, signed a bill abolishing the death penalty in Illinois in March 2011. It became hard to have faith in the system's ability to deliver justice. I don't see how I could ever vote for the death penalty. It may cost me my seat. I'm glad we are only part-timers here." He added wryly, "Conscience would be a lot tougher to follow if this were my entire bread and butter." John referred to the fact that he, like almost all House members, had a normal career; they were lawyers, insurance agents, corporate officers, and a variety of other professions, but they earned $30,000 in addition to a per diem of over $133 for expenses in state compensation for a little more than sixty days of service every year.

"I hear you," said Saul, "but that's not where I am. I'm not pandering to my constituents here. I agree with them. There are monsters out there, and they deserve the death penalty. I'm all for improving the justice system— I admit all these people being released from death row doesn't inspire confidence in the system—but I think the answer is to fix the system, not junk it. And don't think for a minute that all these people released from death row are innocent—a lot of the reversals were for police or prosecutor misconduct in the first trials, but by the time those verdicts were reversed evidence had been lost, witnesses had died, so prosecutors simply didn't file for retrials. That doesn't mean those people were innocent. Our job is to write the rules that protect the innocent, and I think the death penalty helps do that."

Manny shook his head. "I just don't know. My district, like John's, thinks killers only come out of urban pits like Miami, that the death penalty is necessary for black and Hispanic criminals and a handful of white 'trailer-trash.' I'm not sure many of them would even care if they knew some of these vacated convictions were clear results of southern racism in the fifties and sixties."

John put in, "The role of race in death penalty sentences is scary, all right. Much higher percentages of blacks than whites get death sentences, but the real surprise is that regardless of the race of the killer those who kill whites are three times more likely to get sentenced to death than those who kill blacks, and four times more likely than those who kill Hispanics. That just shouldn't be."

"I agree that's wrong," responded Saul. "But just because there have been racists voting for the death penalty doesn't mean all death-penalty verdicts are racist. I think those prosecutors who decided to try twelve year olds and fourteen year olds as adults were wrong and that they were racially motivated. But they aroused what I think is an overreaction against the death penalty in the Supreme Court and among citizens. I don't have any problem with executing monsters of sixteen or seventeen, maybe even some fifteen year olds. We keep hearing that what we need to do to reform the system is to give judges more discretion in sentencing, instead of tying their hands with mandatory sentences. I say let the judges decide, but give them the option to grant the death penalty if that's what the state asks for and it's appropriate to the circumstances."

"Saul, do you really think that the criminal justice system is ever color blind?" asked John.

"Are you calling me racist?" asked Saul indignantly.

"No, I'm talking about the racism in our constituents, who so clearly intend the death penalty for minority groups. Or even the system itself—remember that series the *Miami Herald* ran a few years ago that showed the huge differences in how the juvenile justice system treats whites and blacks? When convicted of the same crime and with the same juvenile record, most white youth got probation or community service, and most black youth were sent to reformatories. People who work in the adult system say the same thing happens—whites have more money to hire private lawyers, and so they either get off altogether, or, when they are convicted, get lesser sentences."

"Wait a minute, John," protested Saul. "I do remember that series, and it explained that the reason for the different sentences involved the kids' support networks—family and community. Black kids less often had intact homes with effective parents who could monitor their behavior and also had fewer contacts with community organizations willing to supervise community service. Those sentences were based on the individual situation of the kids, not racism in the system."

"Kind of a vicious circle, isn't it?" asked John. "Because one kid has a father in prison, or who skipped town, and a mother who works three jobs to support her kids, the kid gets into trouble. And the very reasons he got into trouble in the first place are the same reasons he goes to reformatory, while a white kid in the same trouble goes free."

"I can't fix every broken home," responded Saul. "That's not my job. All I'm saying is that not everything that differentiates the races is due to racism. Some differences just occur, and individuals bear some responsibility for what happens to them. Not all kids with absent fathers and overworked mothers get into trouble. These kids had a choice."

Manny asked, "You know that Alice's latest argument is that we should eliminate the death penalty as a budget reduction measure? Some think tank figured out that Florida could save $51 million a year by commuting all its death penalty cases to life without possibility of parole. And some poll in California found that 63 percent of voters thought commuting all the death sentences to life without parole was a great idea, because it would save $1 billion over five years. What do you think, Saul? Would you and your voters go for that?"

"Maybe," Saul replied, "as a temporary budgeting solution. But I think that only death fits some of these crimes, and I know some of my constituents agree."

As the three of them left the restaurant to return to the session, John and Saul shifted the topic to procedural moves on the insurance bill, but Manny remained quiet. This was a really tough issue for him.

Manny had grown up thinking that unjust executions only happened in other countries, like Cuba, where one of his mother's brothers had been executed as a young man for opposing Castro. He had always seen the justice system in the United States as a model for the world. But his years in the legislature had taken some of the shine off that model. He saw how large a role politics, personalities, the press of time, and sometimes even corruption had in the creation of laws and state budgets, and it made him wonder if the implementation of laws was necessarily any more careful than the creation of those laws. The best evidence of that, he thought, was the March rape/murder of a nine-year-old girl abducted from her home not too far from Manny's district. It had taken many days to discover the body and catch the killer, an ex-con sexual predator who later confessed, because the state database that was supposed to track the registered locations of sexual predators was so out of date that it did not know that the rapist had moved into the girl's neighborhood months before. He tended to agree with his wife, Pina, that these sexual predators seemed to be impossible to reform and that the death penalty was the only way to safeguard society, especially the children.

Now Manny was torn. While he thought he could support capital punishment for sex predators, he knew that there could be cases in which people were wrongly convicted as sexual predators, too. He agreed with Saul that the level of death-row acquittals proved the system was not well run and should be improved, but he wasn't sure it could be fixed well enough to justify capital punishment.

Manny also knew that Pina would be appalled if he voted for Alice's bill to eliminate the death penalty. The little girl recently killed had been a student at the school where Pina taught kindergarten, and that had made Pina and most other parents see the perpetrator as a threat to all the children there, including Pina's and Manny's two little girls. But it was also true that Manny was a second-term legislator from a pretty safe district, and he and Pina had counted on the income from one more term to finance the master's degree in education she planned to finally begin in the fall. Their oldest son would graduate from a state university in December, and it was supposed to be Pina's turn now, while the younger kids were still in elementary and junior high school. Pina was a kindergarten teacher who had to earn a master's degree soon or lose her job, which she loved. If he lost the November election over this issue, his regular salary would only go up about $6,000 before taxes, because he already took one month of the legislative session as paid vacation from his job and only one month as unpaid leave. From $30,000 to $6,000 in salary for that month was a big drop. Could Pina understand if he not only defended the right to life of sexual predators who preyed on children, but if also, because of his taking that position, they weren't able to fund her return to the university? More than that, how would they manage to send the other kids to college if Pina lost her job?

Manny lifted his head and ended his reverie. Certainly he had waited long enough for Alice to leave. He walked down the hall, hearing nothing. But just as he turned the corner to the elevator, Manny saw Alice. She saw him, waved, and made a beeline toward him. It was crunch time.

Commentary

Christian tradition has not been historically unanimous on the issue of killing. While the first three centuries of Christianity saw a strong pressure for pacifism at all levels, in the fourth century earlier refusals to grant Christian burials to those who had taken life—whether in self-defense, military service, or wantonly—were relaxed, and Christian theologians such as Augustine began to argue that Christians could serve in the army, since the army protected the Roman Empire and, thus, Christianity. From that time on, the dominant Christian position has been that Christians are allowed to kill on behalf of the state in certain situations, and even in some very limited personal situations, notably self-defense.

This teaching has not been by any means unanimous. There have been, especially since the Protestant Reformation, a number of pacifist denominations who oppose killing in all forms. These denominations include the Mennonites, the Amish, the Quakers, the Brethren, and a number of other smaller denominations. Jehovah's Witnesses are often counted with this group, as they oppose all obedience to the state and deny the right of the state to demand military service or any other type of service, including oaths. Many theologians have agreed with the American courts that the Witnesses are not pacifist in the same sense as these other groups, however, since in their theology they insist they will take up arms in the last days to fight in the army of the Lord, punishing sinners.

Christian ethical analysis of this case must examine at least two questions: (1) the justice of capital punishment in general, and (2) whether for Christians there are other values (for example, forgiveness, mercy) that can or should trump justice in capital cases.

CAPITAL PUNISHMENT AND JUST WAR

The dominant Christian position regarding violence has been called the just-war position. Capital punishment has been subsumed under the just-war position, as it, too, argues that at some times the state must take human life in order to defend the common good against serious attacks—war from outside and capital crimes inside. The basic limitation was that the life taken must be guilty. While it could be permitted to kill, it was never permissible to kill innocent life.

The development of the just-war position occurred over many centuries; many theologians and churchmen contributed to it, including Augustine, Bonaventure, and Aquinas. In their arguments defending the possibility of a just war, they often used examples of capital punishment, which was generally accepted. At the same time that Christians generally accepted the need for the state to execute criminals (not always for what we might consider serious crimes), the question of whether Christians should be allowed to be executioners was raised again and again. Many jurisdictions ruled that executioners must be hooded, so that they might avoid some of the moral disapproval that generally accompanied the job.

While there has been a great deal of debate about just war—conditions for just war in particular—within the dominant tradition, there has been little debate about capital punishment until fairly recently. Historically, the self-understanding of the church as an institution parallel to, and similar to, the state, caused the church to assume that the legal system of the state was generally just and efficient. That assumption has been radically called into question in the last century in a new way.

In the past there were occasionally periods in which it was apparent to the church and to the wider society that the law and the legal system itself were being manipulated by the powerful, often by the monarch himself, to produce injustice: innocents wrongfully accused and executed, their property coveted and appropriated. Such things even occurred sometimes within the church itself. But when law and order were restored the interval that had just ended was considered an exception to the normal prevalence of justice.

This world view is still prevalent in many American Christians. The National Assembly of Evangelicals, the Christian Coalition, Christian Reconstructionists, the Southern Baptist churches, the Latter-Day Saints (Mormons), the Missouri Synod Lutherans, and many Pentecostal churches support the death penalty for serious crimes. Important for many of these churches is the biblical evidence that the Hebrew scriptures support capital punishment, even "requiring" the death penalty for over a dozen crimes in addition to murder. Most of these Old Testament "crimes" the churches would no longer see as deserving capital punishment (working on the Sabbath, being disrespectful toward parents, teaching another religion, being an unbeliever and entering the Temple). Furthermore, supporters of the death penalty quote Matthew 5:17–19 to the effect that Jesus intended the Mosaic Law to remain unchanged ("Do not think that I have come to abolish the law or the prophets; I have come not to abolish but to fulfill. For truly I tell you, until heaven and earth pass away, not one letter, not one stroke of a letter will pass from the law until all is accomplished").

But by the twentieth century there were many people who questioned not only the specific workings of one legal system or another, but the very assumption that human systems of legal justice could be more or less just. There were a number of reasons underlying such suspicions. One was the gradual acceptance by the majority of the idea, spread initially by Marxism, that modern societies are class societies in which power tends to be wielded by the wealthy in their own interests. In this conception the legal system functions to support social control by the wealthy elite.

Even many who do not accept that modern capitalist societies inevitably have legal systems in which the interests of those with less power and wealth carry less weight recognize that this is often the case. In the United States, for example, analysis of convictions and sentencing throughout the twentieth century has shown that the best predictor of the severity of punishments for murder, rape, and assault is the race of the victim. If the victim is white, conviction rates are higher and sentences are stiffer than if the victim is black or Hispanic. The second-best predictor is the race of the accused: blacks accused of crimes were convicted more often, and when sentenced for the same crime as whites, got higher sentences than whites when the victims were white, but not necessarily when the victims were black. As in the research reported in the *Miami Herald,* race-based economics undoubtedly plays a part in discrepancies in convictions and sentencing in general, in that higher percentages of blacks are poor and thus forced to utilize overworked and underpaid public defenders, who are not as successful in defending their clients as are the private attorneys more often hired by whites.

The statistics on death-row exonerations, updated May 4, 2011, come from the Death Penalty Information Center, whose website includes state-by-state data on executions and exonerations throughout the twentieth century in the United States. Since Florida first reintroduced the death penalty in 1976, and incidentally became the only state in which a jury vote for death need not be unanimous, there have been twenty-three exonerations on death row and six instances of clemency. The language used for the reversals of capital convictions is telling. Supporters of capital punishment point out that the vacation of these sentences does not mean that the person is innocent of the crime; sometimes it merely means that there is insufficient evidence to convict, or the process in the trial was faulty. Inevitably, some guilty persons are released, too.

Details on the twenty-three Florida cases in which death-row prisoners were set free illustrate that sometimes the reversals do indicate lack of proof or police or judicial misconduct rather than full innocence. Twenty-one of the cases fall into these categories:

- Two were pardoned by the governor after another man confessed;
- Three were set free after another suspect was charged (two) or convicted (one);
- Seven were set free after key witnesses retracted their statements;
- Four were released after new DNA evidence ruled the convict out as the perpetrator;
- One was freed by the appeals court because it said there was no evidence that the death of his wife was a murder;
- One charge was dropped when the prosecutor offered to be a witness for the convict if a new trial were granted; and
- Three were set free when the courts found that the police and the prosecutor had willfully misused evidence; in one case charges were dropped, in two cases the accused were acquitted in a subsequent trial.

The suspicion of unequal justice, supported by many different analytic reports of how the legal system actually works, has influenced American churches, even those with long histories of acceptance of capital punishment. Since 1974 the US Catholic Conference has opposed the death penalty, which was reinstated after a long legal hiatus in 1976, despite over a millennium and a half of ecclesial support for capital punishment. On November 19, 1980, the Catholic bishops of the United States issued a statement in which they declared: "Allowing for the fact that Catholic teaching has accepted the principle that the state has the right to take the life of a person guilty of an extremely serious crime, and that the state may take appropriate measures to protect itself and its citizens from grave harm, the question for judgment today is whether capital punishment is justifiable under present circumstances." Since that time the Vatican itself has become a strong supporter of abolishing the death penalty, frequently appealing in behalf of individual convicts awaiting execution, and the US bishops regularly repeat their opposition to capital punishment.

The Catholic bishops argued that there were significant problems impeding justice within the system of capital punishment, including the possibilities of mistakes, long delays, unfairness in sentencing due to poverty and racism, as well as the extinction of all possibility for reform and rehabilitation in the convict. The bishops pointed to racial and economic inequalities in the system of justice—that the poor and persons of color were disproportionately more likely to receive the death penalty than middle-class or white persons convicted of the same crimes.

Regardless of the continued criticism of the death penalty by the Catholic bishops of the United States, a majority of the Catholic population in the United States supports the death penalty. This is also true for many of the denominations that as institutions oppose the death penalty, a group that includes the Eastern Orthodox Christian Churches, the Methodist Church, the Evangelical Lutheran Church of America, the Episcopal Church, the Presbyterian Churches, the United Church of Christ, the Reformed Church in America, the Unitarian Universalists, and the National Council of the Churches of Christ. Black Christian churches have been especially prominent in their opposition to the death penalty, influenced by the history of lynchings in the United States, in which there was often collusion between officials of the justice system and the lynch mobs, and also by clear evidence of racial bias in the application of the judicial death penalty.

It is also important to understand the premises upon which a majority of Catholics or other American Christians approve the death penalty. When the question is asked in a vacuum (Do you support the death penalty or not?), many respond yes because they understand the alternative to be less than life sentences, which release on parole dangerous people, such as sexual predators who prey on children. When the question asked is whether one favors the death penalty or sentences of life without possibility of parole, there is a significant shift in the numbers, and a slight majority favors eliminating the death penalty. Elimination of the death penalty in the present situation of overcrowded prisons, which exerts pressure on prosecutors, judges, and parole boards to make prison space available by shortening sentences and granting parole, simply has not been acceptable to many. Since the crisis in state budgets began in 2010, a number of legislatures are debating whether their state should join the sixteen states that have abolished the death penalty, but the grounds for debate are not moral so much as economic. Death-penalty trials cost much more than trials over life sentences, and the execution process, with all its appeals, cost many millions of dollars more.

DNA TESTING DEEPENS OPPOSITION
BY EXPOSING ERRORS IN CONVICTIONS

DNA evidence was introduced into trials in 1989, and by the early 1990s it was responsible for freeing hundreds of persons charged with or even convicted of felonies across the nation. Opposition to the death penalty grew beyond the peace churches, black churches, Catholic bishops, and liberals in all the denominations in the mid-1990s, when a number of lawyers and law students began to petition the courts to use the new DNA testing in the cases of death-row convicts. Most of these cases had been tried before DNA testing was available, but the evidence had been preserved through the appeals process and was often still available. The most common DNA evidence involved semen, hair, or skin cells from the perpetrator. The University of Michigan Law School found that by June 2000 eighty-seven people had been released from death row because of DNA evidence, recanted testimony, or other new evidence—one reprieve for every seven executions in the same time period.

Nor were these problems only in the state criminal-justice systems. In the federal system there have been thirteen exonerations since 1988, twelve by DNA. Only two of these were death-penalty cases, though six were serving life sentences, one a fifty-year sentence, and one a 130-year sentence. The federal system enacted a death penalty in 1988 for drug kingpins. Of the sixty-one executions that have taken place under the act, 80 percent were of minorities, most of them local dealers.

As the number of vacated sentences increased, the Nebraska legislature voted a state moratorium on the death penalty in 1999, which the governor vetoed. The following year the governor of Illinois declared a moratorium on the death penalty in his state, citing statistics that showed that thirteen death-row prisoners had had their convictions overturned since 1977, one more than had been executed during the same period. The numbers continued to rise as police malfeasance in using torture to extract confessions was revealed. Just before the end of his term the governor also commuted a number of death sentences. In March 2011 the new Illinois governor, Pat Quinn, signed a bill abolishing the death penalty in Illinois, bringing to sixteen the number of states without the death penalty.

The average time spent on death row by the newly exonerated citizens was ten years, but some had spent over twenty. This spate of exonerations led many new groups to question the efficacy of the legal system, for these reversals were not based on difficult-to-understand statistical analysis. They were based on the real-life histories of people who had been unjustly deprived of decades of their lives, and almost of life itself. In the face of these exonerations it was impossible not to conjecture about how many of those who had been executed by the states had in fact been innocent.

To return to the central ethical questions in the case, we must ask to what extent the "errors" in the administration of capital punishment in this nation since 1977 are an inevitable part of a death-penalty system and whether they can be eliminated by reform. About this, people differ. Some point out that the justice system not only includes the original trial and sentencing, but also the very appeal process through which these men were exonerated ("men" because only 3 percent of death-penalty sentences are given to females). They insist that the high number of sentences vacated is proof that the appeals process works.

On the other hand, those who oppose the death sentence point to the fact that two-thirds of the vacated sentences came about through some kind of initiative from outside the justice system itself, usually from volunteer legal organizations such as the law-school class in Illinois that began the process of appealing for DNA testing in old death-penalty cases there. In the vast majority of capital cases, however, the convict does not have such advocates.

In 2009 a coalition pulled together by the Constitution Project published a report called "Smart on Crime," with recommendations for the Administration and Congress. That report listed the chief needs in the criminal-justice system as, among others, adequately trained counsel in all capital cases; protections for the mentally ill or disabled from execution; safeguards in habeas corpus (which anti-terrorism legislation since 1996 had undermined); and safeguards against racially biased capital prosecution.

JUSTICE: HIGHEST VALUE FOR CHRISTIANS

Beyond these questions of justice is yet another, often invoked by leaders of Christian churches, about the primary values of the gospel. They ask, When we stand before the throne of God, how do we want to be treated? With justice, or with mercy? What makes God worthy of worship is not power (in the sense of the ability to impose one's will on another), but the power of goodness, of compassion and mercy, even for sinners. This is the center of the incarnation and redemption: God's compassion and mercy for us as sinners. What God asks of us, say many authorities in the Christian tradition, is that we treat others as we are treated by God.

So strong is this argument from within Christian theology that it completely rules out arguments by Christians for retribution in the criminal justice system. Christians may make arguments for sentencing based on the need to protect the innocent in society from future victimization or on the need for action to reform and rehabilitate criminals (in order that they not be a danger to others), but Christians cannot make arguments that invoke the gospel for the necessity of making criminals suffer for their sins. That is not only exclusively God's prerogative, but it is one that God has been shown to forgo in the interests of mercy. Thus the question becomes one of whether or not we live in a situation in which the only way to protect the innocent requires us to give up any hope of rehabilitation in the criminal and end his or her life. Clearly in the past, many societies felt that there was no alternative to capital punishment if society was to be truly protected. But today, the United States is one of only a handful of developed nations that have not abolished the death penalty.

Some have argued that it is opponents of the death penalty who have imposed the heaviest burdens on those sentenced to death, in that they are responsible for the long delays before execution. These delays are not simply years—ten on average, but sometimes twenty or more—spent in prison.

Death-row prisoners are kept in isolation. They spend about twenty-three hours a day in their single-person cells, separated from the rest of the prison population, allowed out of the cell only for a shower every other day and a daily half-hour alone in the exercise yard. Two hundred years of prison studies have shown that because human nature is relational, solitary confinement is inhumane treatment that can and often does undermine sanity. Some feel that death-row conditions are so inhumane that it would be better to risk taking the lives of a few innocents by shortening the time between sentencing and execution in order to spare prisoners decades on death row. Opponents of the death penalty, however, insist that the proposals to limit appeals and speed up executions do not simply raise the risk of executing a "few" innocent people. The *average* death-row exoneration occurs slightly more than eight years after receiving the death sentence; cutting appeal time to under eight years means the majority of those now released would be executed. To cut the time until execution to one or two years, as proposed by some, would condemn almost all those who presently are exonerated.

Manny's decision in this case seems to hinge a great deal on his concern for his family. He is worried that his wife may not understand if he votes to end capital punishment, especially if it means that he then loses his seat and she is unable to return to the university. But if Manny's conscience speaks, it should be obeyed, regardless of the political or the personal consequences.

At another level, however, it is possible that his concern that Pina might not accept whatever stance he takes is rooted in a longstanding process of developing shared moral feelings, which is appropriate to marriage. One purpose of marriage is the "perfection of the spouse," as some vows used to say. Spouses often help each other recognize their moral blind spots and address them, and they learn to lean on each other for this. If Manny has been accustomed to take many of his moral signals from Pina, he may be uneasy at taking a differing position on this issue. But conscience is personal. Part of the process of moral development is being able to stand alone, even against our own community and our own family, when God speaks to us in conscience. Manny needs to listen to the voice of conscience and not let his anxieties about whether he will lose his seat, or whether Pina will understand, or how much clout Alice and her organization have, obscure that voice. Perhaps his problem is that conscience is not speaking at all, in which case he needs to continue to gather evidence, listen to both sides, pray, and listen for that voice. If conscience does not speak in a clear voice, then he will need to do the best job he can of weighing the risks and benefits of both options, and choose what seems the better option.

ADDITIONAL RESOURCES

Costanzo, Mark. *Just Revenge: Costs and Consequences of the Death Penalty*. New York: St. Martin's Books, 1997.

Gross, Samuel R., et al. "Exonerations in the United States: 1989 through 2003." University of Michigan Law School. April 19, 2004. Available online.

Kay, Judith W. *Murdering Myths: The Story Behind the Death Penalty.* Lanham, MD: Rowman and Littlefield Publishers, 2005.

Prejean, Helen. *Dead Man Walking: An Eyewitness Account of the Death Penalty in the US.* New York: Random House, 1993.

"Religious Groups' Policies about the Death Penalty." Ontario Consultants on Religious Tolerance website. July 3, 2001.

Steffen, Lloyd. *Executing Justice: The Moral Meaning of the Death Penalty*. Cleveland, OH: Pilgrim Press, 1998.

United States Catholic Conference. "Statement Opposing Capital Punishment," *Focus* 6, no. 10 (December 2, 1980): 1–5.

Westervelt, Saundra D., and John A. Humphrey. *Wrongly Convicted: Perspectives on Failed Justice.* New Brunswick, NJ: Rutgers University Press, 2001.

Wooten, Cindy. "Vatican Paper Condemns Death Penalty as Affront to Human Dignity." Catholic News Service, February 7, 2007.

Related Websites

Death Penalty Information Center. http://www.deathpenaltyinfo.org/reports.

Pro-Death Penalty.com. http://www.prodeathpenalty.com/.

Smart on Crime Coalition. "Smart on Crime: Recommendations for the Administration and Congress." www.besmartoncrime.org/pdf/Complete.pdf.

Case

Vietnam's Legacies

"What should I say to my grandchildren and to members of my study group at church about peacemaking and war?" Martin Paxton asked himself. "Should I remain silent, press my ideas on them, tell them what it is like to kill, or merely point out the options and remind everyone of our patriotic duty to serve?

"What Christian perspective makes sense in a world where terrorism and preemptive military strikes in the name of nation-building and peace have increasingly replaced more traditional methods of resolving conflicts? If Congress reinstates the draft because the current all-volunteer army is thought to be inadequate or discriminatory, how should my grandchildren respond if they are against being conscripted? Are there other ways of serving?

"More, what can I tell them? My grandchildren know nothing about Vietnam, although they seemed vaguely interested in the video I once showed featuring me as the leader of a gunfire mission. In my youth it was the same. Napoleon in Russia and Caesar in Gaul (in Latin, no less) were distant abstractions. Also, should I expose my own feelings about killing Vietnamese and my failure to be prepared for what would follow for my sense of self and my conscience? Human brutality sometimes overwhelms me. The false equation of military service with patriotism and Christian servanthood is troublesome. The pitiful excuses leaders fabricate after the fact to justify and distort the use of violence is appalling. And the dead, where do I pile them?"

THE MISSION

Then Martin's memory, or perhaps it was his conscience, began to work. The images of his own Vietnam experience came flooding back like an

---

Robert L. Stivers prepared this case and commentary. Names been changed to protect the privacy of those involved.

ever-flowing stream. He is the "gun boss" on a US Navy destroyer with six five-inch guns. Routine mission: to shell Vietcong positions from two miles off the coast of Vietnam. "General quarters, general quarters, all hands man your battle stations" booms the speaker outside in the passageway. "On station and ready," he reports to the spotter. The radio crackles the coordinates of the target. Calculation, then one round on its way. The spotter over the target in a light plane responds with a "left two hundred, down one hundred yards." Another round, another spot. Then in an electric voice the spotter yells: "You've got 'em on the run. Shoot! Shoot!" A quick correction to fire control, then the command: "thirty rounds, fire for effect!" The noise is deafening. The shock shakes loose twenty years of dust from the overhead. The spotter's voice returns, now even more excited: "You got 'em, you got 'em!" The combat center erupts with cheers. The captain races in from the bridge to congratulate everyone. Back slaps, high fives, spiking the ball, and hugs follow. God, it feels good!

Until the wee hours of the morning, that is. Then the small voices began to work: "Why did the gunners want to paint coolie hats on the sides of the gun mounts? Why did you hesitate granting their request? Why did you finally say: 'No, I don't think coolie hats would be appropriate'? What are you doing here in Vietnam? Why did you enjoy killing Vietnamese so much? Who are you anyway, a killer, a Christian, or both? Why didn't anyone prepare you for Vietnam and killing? Why didn't you think these things through before you got here?"

The questions never were answered. Discharge, graduate school, and years running a business; life has a way of intervening to block introspection just as the decisions of one's children and grandchildren have a way of releasing it. His son Chris had never had to face a situation in which he would be called into the military, although Martin had talked with Chris about his own Vietnam experience.

His grandson, Brad, now almost eighteen and required by law to sign up for the draft, did not seem to have a clue about military service or, for that matter, if there were any alternatives to serving in the military. He knew one option was to volunteer, but that's about all. Martin's two granddaughters were simply not interested, with Beth saying, "That's for boys." Amanda at least made several political observations. "None of our leaders wants a draft," she asserted. "It incites resistance and discord. The Vietnam experience and the 1960s were too much. And speaking as a woman, I don't think any woman should be drafted. The volunteer army we now have is just fine."

When Brad had asked his father about the draft and service in the army, Chris had told him what he knew and suggested that he talk to his grandfather. Brad had called and seemed worried by what he was seeing and hearing on the news. Martin felt some of Brad's anxiety, especially since a prolonged US military presence in countries like Iraq and Afghanistan, each at great expense and most with peril to our troops, seemed inevitable in this endless war on terror and tyrants. Both President Bush and President Obama had also made preemptive strikes part of their policies. Several members of Congress were talking seriously about legislation to put existing draft laws into effect to meet the military's personnel needs and to end the discriminatory elements of the current all-volunteer army. Some had added provisions for alternative service.

PACIFISM AND THE WAY OF THE CROSS

Martin was not without ethical resources for the questions and the new context in which Brad might have to make a decision. Members of the adult education class at his church had recently studied Christian views on violence and nonviolence. The classes had helped him sort out a few things. The early church, he learned, had been pacifist, and a continuing tradition had carried the option of nonviolence to the present in what Ronald Smith, the class instructor and professor of religion at the local college, had called the way of the cross.

A Mennonite from the local area, Jacob Kaufmann, visited the class on the first Sunday and explained his own pacifism. He spoke about his tradition and his own faith perspective within it. He mentioned the work of prominent pacifists and emphasized how important the church community is to maintaining the nonviolence of the way of the cross. "The church," he said, "takes its cue from the nonviolent but socially active model of Jesus Christ found in the New Testament." He went on to explain that the early church community followed Jesus and his non-violent ways not so much because Jesus commanded it, but because faith motivates it. "When Christ is truly in you and you in Christ," he said, "nonviolence is your automatic response. Love engenders love. That is the message of Jesus. I can never be a soldier. I must conscientiously object to military service."

Martin asked the first question in the period that followed. "Many of my friends tell me it's all right to serve in the peace-keeping and nation-building efforts of the United Nations. Would such service, even in the military, be appropriate for a pacifist?" Since he hesitated, Jacob had apparently not thought much about this. "There is a lot out there in academic circles making a case for 'active peacemaking,'" he said. "As long as the UN efforts are nonviolent, there is no problem. Nonviolent actions for justice, including nonviolent resistance, are the heart of my perspective. But the bottom line is still no use of violent means."

Martin's friend Jim Everett then pressed Jacob with another question. "How can I follow the way of the cross in a fallen world?" he asked. "What would you do if your wife and children were attacked?" Obviously Jacob had heard these questions before, because without hesitation he replied: "We are called to follow Jesus, not to make the world turn out right. Ultimately, we are called to suffer, not to inflict suffering. And, in almost all cases there are nonviolent alternatives."

Jacob's assurance had a certain appeal to Martin. The way of the cross was easy to understand, straightforward, and seemed to fit Jesus' radical call to discipleship and an exclusive reliance on God. He had to remind himself that it was a way of life, not a tactic or a strategy. He also recalled how Martin Luther King, Jr., had used nonviolent tactics to protest unjust segregation laws and the love ethic of Jesus to encourage integration. He remembered Gandhi had also made an appeal to Jesus.

Still, Martin was not convinced. "Justice is as important in the way of the cross as nonviolence," he thought. "On rare occasion a large measure of justice can be gained for a small measure of violence. Why prefer the ethical guideline of nonviolence to that of justice in these situations? Who does the dirty work of keeping order in a violent world? Doesn't the love of neighbor include defense in cases of premeditated violence?"

CHRISTIAN REALISM AND THE JUSTIFIABLE WAR

The next Sunday Ronald Smith presented a position he called Christian realism, out of which comes the doctrine of the justifiable war. Historically, Ronald explained, this position emerged after the Emperor Constantine converted to Christianity in the early fourth century and the church achieved a favored position in the Roman Empire. Christians took political office and became responsible for the general welfare, including the defense of the empire and the exercise of police functions. The ethical and political task for Christians changed in this situation, Ronald continued. They could not pursue the perfection of Jesus or follow Jesus literally. The best they could do was to use political power to push and pull sinful reality toward the ideal.

"Not best, but better," he insisted, "because best is impossible in a fallen world. The way of the cross may be lived personally, but it is not immediately relevant to politics. We human beings in our freedom can and frequently do ignore the power of God in our midst and alienate our neighbors. God doesn't set things right or organize them for us. We have been given dominion and are responsible for the stewardship of power. To serve one's neighbor, to steward resources well, and to achieve higher levels of justice in a sinful world mean a Christian must sometimes compromise and occasionally use means that are not consistent with the way of the cross. This is how anarchy is avoided and tyranny prevented. This does not mean the way of the cross is irrelevant, or that God does not work in the world. God's love and justice act like magnets pulling us out of sin and moving us to higher ethical levels, and we have a limited capacity to respond. God's power and this capacity are the basis of hope and make 'the better' a constant possibility. Simply put, those of this view are *realists* because of sin and *Christians* because there are resources for making this a better world."

Ronald went on to outline the justifiable-war tradition that is based on Christian realism. "Nonviolence is the norm," he insisted, "but on occasion violence is permissible if its use clearly meets certain criteria." He then set forth the criteria and indicated that they could lead someone who was using them either to enter the military and fight when they were met or selectively to object if they were not. In an aside he observed that our draft laws make only a few provisions for selective conscientious objection or alternative service in the community. Most young men don't qualify for these exceptions. He concluded by saying that if every nation took the criteria seriously, all war would cease. He paused and added: "But that is a big *if*."

Martin remembered leaving the class attracted to this position as well, but he was also troubled. How can Christian realism be reconciled with the picture of Jesus in the New Testament? Religiously, do the realists take the power of sin too seriously and the power of the Holy Spirit not seriously enough? Doesn't the justifiable-war doctrine open the floodgates to abuse? It is seldom taken seriously. Even Saddam Hussein claimed his cause was just, not to mention what Martin himself had been told about Vietnam. Each nation is left to judge its own case for the use of violence, and most fabricate ethical justifications after the fact that accord with their own interests.

And how about the preemptive strike by the United States on Iraq? Could that be justified, especially in hindsight, when no chemical, biological, or nuclear weapons were found and no definitive links to Al Qaeda established? Were the removal of Saddam Hussein, the so-called liberation of the Iraqi people, and the nation-building that followed sufficient justification for the attack, especially when the United States acted without UN approval and against the objections of several close allies?

Now we are also in Afghanistan and Libya under a different president, fighting still other wars on terrorism and trying to oust still other tyrants. Wars will continue to break out in different parts of the world. Why is the United States responsible for putting out all the fires, removing all the tyrants, and rebuilding failed states in our own image? When will terrorism and tyranny stop being used as justifications for endless violence and the extension of US power?

The next Sunday Ronald Smith split the class time between consideration of justifiable revolutions and the third of the primary Christian traditions, the crusade. To present the problems that revolutions create for the justifiable-war tradition, Ronald brought along a colleague, a Spanish teacher at the college, Maria Gomez. Maria came to the United States in the 1980s from El Salvador where her life had been threatened because she was thought to have associations with known revolutionaries.

Maria led off the discussion by telling her story about the violence and injustice in her own country. She painted a vivid picture of the atrocities perpetrated by government officials and so-called death squads. Maria ended by noting that some liberationists like herself are pacifists. Others justify violent revolutions in certain circumstances. Still others see the overthrow of oppressive regimes as a crusade against evil.

Ronald Smith followed by asking whether it is justifiable for citizens experiencing severe repression to rise up and violently overthrow those in power. He pointed out that the justifiable-war doctrine requires wars to be initiated by competent authority, which usually means those in charge of the government. Revolutionaries are not competent authorities in most interpretations of the doctrine. "So, how do the citizens of a country protect themselves against an autocrat like Muammar Gaddafi?" he asked. "Perhaps we need to modify the doctrine to allow for special cases when, to paraphrase the Declaration of Independence, a long train of abuses tend in the same direction." He then cited the violence in Sudan, Libya, Syria, Yemen, Iran, and Myanmar (Burma). He added the difficulties of separating out sectarian from justifiable wars.

THE CRUSADES

With that Ronald turned to the crusade tradition. He had not been able to find anyone to represent the tradition. "This does not mean the crusade is dead," he suggested, "only that few are willing to state it in its classic form. It is still alive, however, in the enthusiasm that surrounds going to war and in the tendency to demonize opponents and to see ourselves as highly virtuous."

"In the Christian tradition," he went on, "crusaders base their violent actions on the holy war texts in Deuteronomy, Joshua, and Judges. They see as God's clear command the call to stamp out evil and the designation of themselves as God's agents. Serving in the army of the righteous is a Christian responsibility. It is one of the meanings of servanthood."

Ronald dismissed this position by claiming it improperly literalized the biblical texts and then misapplied them. "Faith in God is the real significance of the texts." Then he added: "The portrayal of God in these texts as a general who commands and leads the holy army of the righteous in violent combat is incompatible with the picture of Jesus in the New Testament and the biblical witness taken as a whole. Even the picture of the holy army is inadequate. While holy warriors can usually identify the sin of their enemies, they seldom see their own sin." He concluded by observing that crusades are usually the bloodiest kinds of war and especially dangerous today given the destructiveness of modern warfare.

Martin agreed but reflected on the depth of the good/evil dualism in each of us. "Wouldn't we all like to stamp out evil if we could and be serving God at the same time?" he mused. "And how like us it is to represent our own cause by our best ideals and our opponents by their worst deeds." Martin also reflected on the comments of one of his employees who had been deeply troubled by the events of 9/11. She had passionately linked Osama bin Laden to evil and even used the word *crusade* to support the need to eliminate him. She didn't seem to see that Osama too was a crusader, a Muslim crusader, and those who have followed him have claimed they are under obligation to fight a holy war. Now that he is dead, his legacy goes on. Crusaders fighting crusaders, imagine that!

THE LAST CLASS

"So how are we as Christians to think about war in general and the wars we are now fighting?" Ronald concluded, asking each person there to carry this question home and reflect. "Which of the Christian perspectives is the most appropriate and how are we to advise young people who face the prospect of service in the military or some alternative, draft or no draft? How are we to understand Christian servanthood and service to our nation?" Martin was not quite sure where he stood and how his own experience in Vietnam applied.

The need to talk to his grandson took on greater importance. "I might be able to quiet my own conscience about Vietnam, but what do I say to Brad? Should I advocate the way of the cross and conscientious objection to serving? Should I suggest the realist's option that allows for justifiable wars in oppressive situations and counsels selective conscientious objection in others? Or should I tell him to still his doubts, to do his duty, and to serve his country if called? After all, that's what I did."

Commentary

Two generations of the Paxton family have matured since the Vietnam war. They know little about My Lai, the Tet offensive, Khe Sanh, or the final capitulation. The troubled waters stirred up by injustice, massive demonstrations, rhetorical flourishes, and challenges to traditional authority have stilled. But beneath the surface, currents of conscience and unresolved identity created by the Vietnam war still run deep in the memories of veterans. Few of their children and grandchildren know the face of war or think to ask. Even close friends who went through it seem to have forgotten. Now on the occasions of a phone call from his grandson, Brad, and a study group in his church, Vietnam veteran Martin Paxton has a chance to pass on some of his memories and possibly some of his wisdom about the face of war, the morality of the preemptive strike in Iraq, the ongoing war in Afghanistan, the bombing of Libya, and the Selective Service System.

Participation in killing presented a real challenge to Martin's conscience. Brad now faces a challenge to his conscience as he wrestles with the prospect of fighting alongside other US troops in far-off places, and the possibility that Congress will reinstate the draft. His challenge is both old and new. It is old because conscientious struggling with the use of violence is as old as violence itself. It is new because Brad is young and has never addressed violence as a matter of conscience. It is new also because there is no draft, globalized terrorism has changed the face of war, and the United States is more powerful militarily than any of its potential enemies.

To see that Vietnam and Brad's decision about military service or conscientious objection are related is important. They are related on the personal level through the exchange of thoughts and feelings. They are also related through the four Christian perspectives on violence presented in Martin's adult class. Finally, they are related through the education Brad has received in the Paxton family. Martin's conscientious ambivalence, which includes his lament about not being prepared for killing, has no doubt been communicated to Brad.

CONSCIENTIOUS OBJECTION

Brad's worries about what he is seeing and hearing on the news and his inquiry about the draft and service in the army do not reveal what he already knows. This may just be a lack of information in the case. More likely, Brad himself does not know what his views on violence might be, whether he might be a pacifist and conscientious objector to war or should take one of the other positions presented in the case and be ready to join up. One important difference he will face ethically is between conscientious objection and selective conscientious objection, and how US law treats each.

From 1948 through 1972 the US government used a combination of draft and voluntary recruitment to fill the ranks of its armed forces. In 1971 Congress put the draft on standby status, largely because it had become a platform for protesting the Vietnam war. Voluntary recruitment became the sole source of new soldiers. Draft registration continued until 1975, when it was suspended. In 1980 registration was reinstated, but the draft remained on standby status.

That is the status of the law today. All males ages eighteen to twenty-six are required to register by filling out a form available at the post office or online. In order to submit a Free Application for Federal Student Aid (FAFSA) male students must register with the Selective Service System. Failure to register can result in a fine, imprisonment, or both. After registration, the name of the registrant is entered into a computer for possible future use.

To make use of these names to induct draftees into the armed forces would require an act of Congress with the signature of the president. In an emergency a law to classify and induct could be passed on very short notice and be accompanied by all the emotions of nationalism that often cloud clear thinking.

Were such legislation enacted, local draft boards would quickly form, classify all those who are registered, and begin calling individuals for induction, first from the twenty-year-old age group according to a rank order of birthdays determined by lottery. If Brad was classified 1A and his name came up, he would receive an induction notice and have ten days to report. It is within this ten-day period that he would have to set in motion the machinery for deferment or exemption on grounds of conscientious objection. While the law makes room for conscientious objection to all wars, there is no provision for *selective* conscientious objection, that is, objection to particular wars. This is understandable, because such a provision would open up a host of problems for the military and the government.

Once Brad made an application for conscientious objection, the draft board would postpone induction and set a date for a hearing where he could present his case. His application would be judged on the basis of three criteria: (1) that he is opposed to participation in war in any form; (2) that his opposition is by reason of religious training and belief; and (3) that he demonstrates sincerity.

If approved, Brad would be reclassified in one of two conscientious objector categories. If not, the local board would have to declare in writing the reasons for its rejection, which Brad could then appeal.

The majority of conscientious objectors register for the draft, but a number of alternatives exist, including refusal to register and the indication of conscientious objector status in the process of registration. The latter is possible when completing the printed registration form at a US post office but not when registering online. The task for Brad is to think through the ethical implications, decide if he is a conscientious objector and, if so, what type, and make his decision about registration. If he elects to be a conscientious objector, he should seek the advice of a draft counselor and begin preparing his supporting material.

With the continuing violence in the Near East and troop commitments there and in other parts of the world, the army is hard pressed to meet its needs. As a result, there are rumblings in Congress about reinstating the draft. Pressures to reinstate the draft are not only a matter of the army's needs. They are also fueled by the inequities of the all-volunteer army, which attracts a disproportionate number of lower-income men and women and members of minority racial-ethnic groups. Very few sons and daughters of the wealthy, well born, and well educated are serving in the US armed forces.

The Selective Service System is also reactivating and restaffing long-dormant draft boards, the local committees that decide who is to be drafted. Spokespersons for the system say they will be prepared to call up soldiers about six months after the draft is reinstated.

THE VIETNAM WAR

The Vietnam war is not over. The hand-to-hand combat has long since ceased, but the meaning of the experience has not been settled. The Vietnam upheaval has never been adequately worked through and, as time passes, it looks more and more as if it never will be. Americans either cannot or will not come to terms with it, and now with all the new violence in areas of national self-interest, it looks less likely they ever will.

Martin appears bothered by two things. The first is the destruction of a social myth about the United States, the second the destruction of a personal myth about himself. For Martin and many other Vietnam veterans the destruction of their social and personal myths and the lack of adequate replacements have resulted in lost identity and the inability to comprehend what they went through.

The 1950s saw the United States with newfound power. Victorious in World War II and economically unrivaled, Americans had reason to be content with themselves in spite of serious unresolved social problems. They also had a vision with roots. America's social mythology depicted a new city set on a hill free from the cynical entanglements and imperial ambitions of old and decaying Europe. Stories of the American frontier told of rough but moral and hardworking pioneers pushing back the frontier and bringing civilization in their wake. Those who resisted were pictured either as uncivilized and in need of American technology and virtue, or evil and in need of a crusade.

The frontier closed in the nineteenth century, but its mythology remained open-ended in spite of changing conditions and rude shocks such as the Great Depression. The mythology was skillfully manipulated by politicians such as John F. Kennedy, who in his 1960 inaugural address described the foreign and domestic challenges facing the nation as a "new frontier." It was exploited by those who saw the spread of communism in Asia as the latest evil in need of a crusade and the Vietnamese as candidates for American technology and virtue.

In the end, this pervasive social mythology was not able to carry the day for an entire nation. The harsh realities of racial violence and the injustice and inconclusiveness of the Vietnam war combined to explode the myth, at least for a vocal minority. For men and women such as Martin Paxton, the bell is now cracked and no new bells have yet been cast.

Martin could not have avoided participation in this mythology. He would have been brought up on westerns, war movies, and patriotic instruction. The path of least resistance would have led him to the conclusion that for the first time in history, here was a moral nation. Because he was brought up in a middle-class America that almost without question saw itself as morally right, he probably saw himself and his nation as inheritors and purveyors of that morality. Abundance would have shielded him from the violence of poverty and class conflict. Entering the Navy was probably as natural as a trip to Disneyland.

That beneath the mythology of the American dream and his own peace in it lay a different reality would have only been dimly perceived. It apparently was not the injustice of Vietnam or the oppression of racism that revealed this reality to him, at least not initially. Rather, it seems to have been his participation in and apparent enjoyment of killing and the uncomfortable dreams stimulated by a vigorous conscience. The combat center erupted with the "happy" news of death, killed Martin's false consciousness, and left him with a good dose of guilt.

In a like manner, Vietnam blew the top off the dormant volcano of the American dream. Martin's crisis was the nation's crisis. The problem for both Martin and other Americans is how to build new mythic mountains to give order and justice to their landscapes. Martin may be building one in his Christian journey, but the nation still seems mired in the myth of its own righteousness as witnessed by efforts to justify the nation's most recent wars in Iraq and Afghanistan.

In Christian terms the problem is repentance and new life. Repentance must be the foundation of Martin's building. The first step must be to realize that he is one of those individuals who is capable of killing and enjoying it. Such an admission is hard for most individuals. It forces the sacrifice of the proud self and produces vulnerability. For modern nations it is much harder because pride is so strong and so central to national identity. With its glowing self-image and righteousness, it may be too much to expect the US as a nation to admit that the Vietnam war was unjust.

The guilt Martin feels is a sign of God's judgment and his first step toward repentance. But the recognition of judgment is not the end of the story. God forgives, and this forgiveness opens the door to new life. As soon as Martin goes through the door of repentance, the process of coming to terms with his role in Vietnam will begin. There are indications this process has already started.

The prospects for America in its continuing mental struggle are not as good. Nations have far fewer resources for coming to terms with their own injustices. A continuing infatuation with military supremacy does not improve the prospects. The church will have an important role to play in whatever rethinking takes place, because it has resources for announcing judgment, for coming to terms with guilt, and for moving beyond it.

Any rethinking that goes on must address Martin's question and lament: "Why didn't anyone prepare me for Vietnam or killing?" That question points up a shortcoming in the education of children in the United States. Experiences differ, of course, but a child of Martin's generation would normally have been exposed only superficially to peace education. History texts of his generation emphasized kings and great victories. The pacifist side of the Christian tradition was a well-kept secret, even in Sunday school. The media glorified violence and past wars as much as they do today.

It is no wonder Martin found himself on the firing line before he even had thought things through. His option, stated at the end of the case, was to "do his duty, and to serve his country." Is it not a problem that the state sees its internal cohesion as so important that it tries to make certain that this is the only option that can receive a hearing? Has the Christian church failed to present the full range of normative perspectives out of its own traditions? Or is the failure to question, to explore, and to reflect Martin's fault?

The answer to all three is yes, and from an ethical perspective the point is that those who are forced to make life-and-death decisions ought to be exposed to moral perspectives on violence. The state's need for compliance with its will and certainly the church's role in supporting the state do not warrant the exclusion of such perspectives. Young men and women should have the right to access different options.

CONTINUING WARS

The fall of communism in 1989 and the dissolution of the Soviet Union left the United States without major military rivals. During the 1990s leaders struggled with how to use this power effectively. The Gulf war in the early 1990s and involvement in Somalia and the Balkans seemed to push these leaders in the direction of selective military intervention using a few troops for a short period of time. They sought the support of international bodies such as the United Nations for these interventions. They seemed to have a sense of the limits of military power.

With the election of George W. Bush in the fall of 2000 and the events of September 11, 2001, a new direction was taken that has yet to play itself out. President Bush called it the war on terrorism. It was militant in attitude, unilateral in direction, and justified such things as preemptive strikes and regime change when the United States perceives itself to be threatened.

Not long after 9/11 a small group centered in the Pentagon began to lobby for the removal by force of Iraqi leader Saddam Hussein. They claimed he possessed weapons of mass destruction (WMDs), including chemical and biological weapons, and the capability to use them on his neighbors in the Middle East and even the United States. They were aided in making their case by Saddam Hussein's record of using chemical weapons in his war with Iran in the 1980s and on his own people. They further claimed he was actively pursuing the development of nuclear weapons, indeed, that he would soon accomplish this aim. They also linked him to Al Qaeda, the terrorist organization led by Osama bin Laden responsible for the events of September 11, 2001. In making these claims they apparently relied on intelligence gathered from dissident Iraqis bent on deposing Saddam Hussein.

They portrayed Saddam Hussein as a tyrant, the incarnation of evil, pointing to his invasion of Kuwait and the treatment of Shiites in his own country following the Gulf war. George W. Bush placed Iraq with Iran and North Korea on an "axis of evil." US military leaders and some elected officials pictured themselves as liberators bringing democracy and economic well-being to the entire Middle East. They steadfastly denied that Iraq's large reserves of oil had anything to do with their plans. In October 2002

Congress approved a declaration that gave President Bush wide latitude to initiate a preemptive strike.

The decision-makers also seemed to have made some critical assumptions. They thought the invasion would be over swiftly, and, indeed, President Bush declared it over in May 2003. They assumed the war could be won with relatively few troops and casualties and that the Iraqis would welcome them with open arms. Finally, they assumed that any occupation would be brief and quickly followed by a democratic regime friendly to the United States and a region where democracy and capitalism would flourish with Iraq as a model. In these assumptions they seemed to be more idealists than realists. This is ironic because they spoke as if they were the hardheaded, no nonsense, balance-of-power Republicans of the past.

In March 2003 the invasion of Iraq began. It was led by the United States but joined by Great Britain, Spain, Italy, and a few other countries. The United Nations Security Council refused to give its approval. Some in the Bush administration dismissed the United Nations as irrelevant. France and Germany, much to the disdain of the Bush administration, refused to support the US effort

Things have not turned out as well as expected, despite official statements to the contrary. It now appears as if fifty thousand US troops will continue to occupy Iraq for an indefinite period with the possibility of a civil war among Muslim groups after US combat troops depart. US troops have found no WMDs. The claim for nuclear potential was based on manufactured intelligence. Links to Al Qaeda have not been adequately established, although Islamic militants have flooded into Iraq in the aftermath of the invasion. That leaves the tyranny of Saddam Hussein as the main justification for a preemptive strike, a justification that has apparently satisfied many Americans who support the war.

The invasion was swift. Saddam Hussein fell from power in three weeks and was later captured. Some Iraqis welcomed US troops, although most were initially noncommittal. Immediately, however, looting became commonplace. Then the Bush administration dismissed the Iraqi army and most police, leaving US troops the job of maintaining order as new Iraqi forces were trained. Increasingly insurgent groups formed and targeted US troops, Iraqi collaborators, and the country's infrastructure. US casualties mounted, and Iraqi deaths, while uncounted, were estimated in the tens of thousands. The situation deteriorated further in April 2004 as insurgents mounted offensives in several Iraqi cities. To quell the insurgents, the US Army allowed them to keep their weapons and stay in place as long as they remained invisible. That left Sunnis, Shiites, and Kurds with well-armed militias ready to renew old hostilities. Iraqi acceptance of the occupation declined with the deteriorating situation.

The Bush administration admitted few mistakes, much less a failed policy, and remained officially optimistic. It saw these developments as a low point to be followed by an improving situation when the Iraqis took control of the reins of government. In part they were correct, as the violence diminished. The infrastructure of Iraq, however, is still in shambles. The insurgencies continue. The financial cost of the war and occupation have skyrocketed, while Congress and the Bush administration enacted tax cuts that primarily benefited the wealthy. Over eight years the Bush administration added over $6 trillion to the US federal debt. The result is a huge budget deficit that will be paid by future generations of Americans.

Was the deposing of Saddam Hussein worth all this? Are bleak prospects only the pessimistic projections of determined critics? Was this war justifiable? These are the questions that each American, not just Martin and Brad, needs to ask.

Then attention shifted to Afghanistan, where a war against the Taliban continues unabated using new tactics to involve local people. Whether these tactics will work in a context of power politics remains to be seen.

One thing is certain. These tactics reveal the new face of war introduced in Vietnam. War is local, not global, although the potential for the latter has not diminished. It involves local groups fighting for a cause and using guerilla tactics to resist. The US military has been slow to respond, although it has been trying. It is very expensive for major powers to fight local insurgents and their "terrorist" tactics. Few seem to understand that such tactics are the only option for groups that could never win if they had to face and fight massive armies head on.

Now the theater of war has shifted to the so-called Arab Spring, with Libya as a poster child. Since December 2010 there has been a wave of revolutions occurring in the Arab world against corrupt and undemocratic regimes that have concentrated wealth in the hands of a few and been unresponsive to the needs of the general population. What this new face will amount to is beyond our present view but has already involved violence. The complexities of all this must mystify eighteen year olds like Brad, not to mention folks of Martin's vintage and the president of the United States.

CHRISTIAN OPTIONS

Available to Christian thinking on conscientious objection and war is a normative tradition of great variety and richness. Three distinct options are presented within the case itself. The Mennonite Jacob Kaufmann offers the pacifist option, and Professor Roger Smith discusses the crusades and Christian realism, which includes the justifiable-war tradition. Maria

Gomez, who raises the question of justifiable violence in a revolutionary situation, assists him in discussing the justifiable-war tradition.

Pacifism

Pacifism appears first in the case. Christian pacifism is linked with what is called the way of the cross. Jacob Kaufmann presents a modern version of this very traditional perspective, a version often associated with theologian John Howard Yoder.

The way of the cross starts with and stresses what it takes to follow the New Testament view of Jesus Christ. According to this perspective, Jesus unambiguously models and calls Brad and Martin to only one option that is normative for life in society. No other options are valid; no other path but discipleship is authentically Christian.

This one option takes its cue from Luke 1:46ff. and Luke 4:5–8. In these texts Jesus is announced as an agent of radical social change who scatters the proud, puts down the mighty, exalts those of low degree, and sends the rich away empty. These texts portray Jesus in a new light. Jesus introduces a nonviolent but politically active way of life for Brad and Martin to live in the midst of the world. This way is best seen in the cross where Jesus stands up to Pilate but does not resort to mob violence or coercive political power to achieve his ends.

The way of the cross is not a new law. It cannot be forced on Brad or Martin, for its essence is freedom. It must be chosen by the disciple with recognition of its true costs, the ultimate being readiness to suffer. While all are called, few will follow because of the high costs. The few who follow will gravitate to small, sharing communities that understand that the church is the essence of the way.

The way of the cross almost always runs counter to prevailing cultures because the world of compromise cannot bear its single-mindedness. No compromises with secular values are brokered. A distinct lifestyle emerges. As disciples, Brad and Martin are called to live simply, bear hostility, serve others, to be oriented by God's self-giving love.

The way is emphatically nonviolent. Violence is antithetical to God's love even when some other good seems to justify it. Jesus makes clear that an authentic witness to the world is possible without resort to violence.

Nonviolence is not passive nonresistance. Jesus did not condone sin. He resisted it at every turn. Nor did he give in to the power of Rome. Likewise, Christians are called to resist evil and injustice up to the point of using violence. At that point resistance takes the form of suffering. Gandhi, King, and the tactics of nonviolent resistance offer a model for those who choose this option.

Finally, the way involves a radical break with calculations of consequences, power balances, and prudence. As followers of the way, Brad and Martin would not be responsible for getting results, making things come out right, or moving society to some higher level of moral endeavor. If good results come, fine. If not, then persevere. They are called first, last, and always to the way.

Pacifism was historically the first of the three Christian traditions on violence and nonviolence. The early church was pacifist and continued in this way until the early fourth century. Pacifism continues to be the perspective of the so-called peace churches and monastic orders. It involves a spectrum of options from nonresistance to nuclear pacifism. Pacifists are opposed to the wars in Iraq and Afghanistan because they are opposed to all wars. For Brad, the way of the cross points unambiguously to conscientious objection. To Martin, it calls for repentance and in the future active resistance to all forms of violence.

Christian Realism

Roger Smith presents the second option, Christian realism, which is presumably his own. In our time the best-known exponent of this position was the American theologian Reinhold Niebuhr.

Christian realism has its roots both in Luther's doctrine of two realms (the secular or earthly and the religious or divine) and Calvin's call to transform society. The nomenclature reveals the essence of the perspective: the holding together of idealism and realism.

Idealism is a disposition to be loyal to norms or to some understanding of goodness or right. Christian idealists usually look to the Bible and the tradition for their normative understanding and stress adherence to the rules and principles that they find in these sources.

Realism is the disposition to take full account of sin and other elements that frustrate the realization of the ideal. It starts with the way things are and stresses the brokenness of history, limitation, and the pride of individuals and groups. Instead of pushing single-mindedly toward the ideal, the realist asks: "Where do we go from here?"

In Christian realism Brad and Martin must keep the ideal or normative pole of the tradition together with the realistic pole of the way things are. Realism without idealism degenerates into cynicism; idealism without a sense of sin abstracts into illusion.

Brad and Martin are called in this view to live in freedom on the knife-edge between idealism and realism and to act politically to move the present situation toward the ideal without the illusion that they can or must achieve the ideal. The political task for them is not the rigorous following of the ideal, however important the ideal may be, but the use of political and sometimes even military power to establish the most tolerable form of peace and justice under the circumstances.

The idealism in this perspective comes from an understanding of God's work in Jesus Christ. Jesus Christ reveals the wisdom and power of God to be self-giving love untainted by self- or group-interest. This ideal is not achievable by Brad or Martin because of sin. Nevertheless, approximations of the ideal are possible for them because God's power of love is constantly at work in human affairs and their lives.

God's love judges and convicts Brad and Martin. It breaks their pride and prevents illusion. It brings humility and repentance. As a result, Brad and Martin can undertake political tasks motivated by God's love but with a healthy sense of their own sin as well as the sin of others.

The cross and the resurrection free Brad and Martin to work in the midst of suffering and contradiction and to serve without the need for reward. God's love is also a power at work in the world. It creates the possibility of justice and peace and sustains Brad and Martin against the power of sin.

The realism in this perspective comes from an analysis of human sin. Sin is the inevitable alienation that results from self- or group-centered attempts to gain security against the anxieties of the human condition, for example, using guns or waging war in response to political frustrations. This tendency to seek security in and through the self or the collective is strong in individuals and stronger still in groups. While the individual has a limited capacity for repentance, for shifting self to God, and for relationships with other persons, this potential is greatly reduced in groups. It is impossible, for example, for groups to love one another.

Such realism does not lead to pessimism and withdrawal. Rather, it leads to a new awareness about groups. Different norms apply. If groups cannot love, then the appropriate norm is justice under law. Groups can achieve some semblance of mutual regard and justice by balancing power against power. This view of groups as having a different set of norms than individuals is called the two-realms doctrine. In it the earthly realm is governed by justice, law, rules, and the sword; the divine realm is governed by love, the gospel, and sensitivity. Brad and Martin, provided they find their center in the divine realm, are freed by the cross and resurrection of Jesus Christ to live and work in the earthly realm and to get their hands dirty as soldiers.

From the Christian realist's perspective, the task for Brad and Martin is to serve in the earthly realm within reason, doing what is needed to make it a better place to live. They are called to exercise power and, insofar as they are able, to move the inevitable power balances that are prematurely called justice to higher levels of freedom and equality.

The call to exercise power as ethically as possible leads to the principles of the justifiable war. In the best of times Brad and Martin should work for justice and peace using nonviolent means. In the worst of times, when neither justice nor peace is possible, violence is sometimes the lesser among evils.

In such situations Christian realism considers violence, if not good in itself, at least acceptable as long as certain conditions are met. There are seven conditions or criteria for a justifiable war:

1. Last resort: All other means to achieve a just and peaceful solution must have been exhausted.
2. Just cause: The reason for fighting must be the preservation or restoration of a morally preferable cause against a clearly unjust adversary.
3. Right intention: The intention of violence must be the establishment or restoration of peace with justice.
4. Declared by a legitimate authority: Only a legitimate authority may declare war; private, self-appointed defenders of justice are disallowed.
5. Reasonable hope of success: While success does not have to be guaranteed, the useless sacrifice of soldiers, no matter how just the cause, is ruled out.
6. Noncombatant immunity: Civilians without direct connection with the opponent's war effort must not be intentionally attacked.
7. Proportionality: The force used should be proportional to the objective sought. The good sought should exceed the horrible evil of the violence.

The problem with these criteria is that each group that uses them is judge of its own case, the result being that unjustified and inflated claims are often made to satisfy the criteria. Critics wonder if this tradition is not honored more in the breach to sanction unjustifiable wars than to prevent them. Even Hitler persuaded enough Germans that his cause was just. He used justice as window dressing for the naked exercise of power.

The fourth criterion is also a problem because it seems to rule out justifiable resistance to oppressive regimes. Some would amend it to permit the use of violence in situations of oppression.

Finally, another criterion has emerged in recent years but has yet to find its way on to many lists. Increasingly, broad international support is required before a nation engages in a justifiable war. The United States sought such support at the start of the war in Iraq but the Security Council refused to give it.

This perspective puts pressure on Brad and offers several alternatives on Vietnam for Martin. Christian realists do not reject military service out of hand, but they are prepared to resist fighting in an unjust cause. Unfortunately, the current draft law does not allow for selective conscientious objection, which is the logical outgrowth of the perspective. Christian realists must therefore serve or suffer the legal consequences in the event that they conscientiously choose resistance.

Martin, should he accept this perspective, must decide on the justifiability of his own involvement in Vietnam and what to advise Brad. If he sees his involvement as unjustified, which seems to be the case, he should seek forgiveness and new life in Jesus Christ. He should also relate to Brad the lessons he has learned over the years as his conscience has reacted to his experience in Vietnam. For the future he should also be prepared to support just and resist unjust wars.

Finally, this tradition calls all Christians to judge whether the wars in Vietnam and Iraq were justifiable. US leaders claimed that both wars were justifiable. In both cases they met with bitter dissent. Brad and Martin, and all Christians, are left with the task of making this judgment.

CRUSADE

The final option presented in Martin's class is the crusade, which historically has been an option but does not appear to be so in this case. One reason the crusade has been popular is its simplicity. It divides reality into good and evil. The crusader is always on the side of the good; the enemy is always the incarnation of evil. God wills the eradication of evil; hence, the crusader is justified, even commanded, to kill. Another source of its popularity is its compatibility with tribalism, that seemingly natural human inclination to favor one's own group and accept without question its rituals, perspectives, and aggressions.

The crusade has had its moments in Christian history. It was at work in the conquest of the Promised Land by the Hebrews. Pope Urban II used it successfully in the Middle Ages to rescue the Holy Land temporarily from the forces of Islam. During the Vietnam war it was used in some Christian circles to call for opposition to "atheistic communism." In the Iraq war Saddam Hussein was placed on the "axis of evil" and put near the top of everyone's all-tyrant list. The United States, in turn, was pictured as the agent of redemption.

In this case the crusade is seen as foreign to the teachings of Jesus. Its dualism of good and evil is simplistic in the extreme, especially in its naivete about the sin of the crusader. Its embrace of violence is so alien to the central Christian experience of faith as to make a mockery of it. For these and other reasons Ronald Smith, the teacher, was correct in dismissing it as an option. It is out of the normative bounds of Christianity and offers no guidance to Brad or Martin. Its ethical importance today is that of a historical artifact and an example of what to avoid.

Still, the crusade is alive and well, not only in the claims of US leaders, but also in the emotional response to the war in Iraq and in the outpouring of war patriotism in support of US wars in general. The perennial tendency of groups to demand allegiance in time of crisis and to pull out the stops on moral rhetoric makes the crusade an ever-popular option.

SERVING AS A CHRISTIAN

Serving others in love is bedrock Christian ethics. More needs to be said, however, because both the guideline and its application to service in the military are ambiguous, and service to God is often confused with serving in the military, as in super-patriotism.

For the pacifist, service in the military is not what it means to be a follower of Christ. Violence of any kind is not the way of the cross. Conscientious objection and a refusal to serve are the only options, even if they mean suffering for some violation of the law.

Christian realists support service in the military as long as the use of violence is justifiable. Most realists oppose participation in unjust wars, but the decision to serve is left to the individual who may feel caught between conscientious objection and obeying the law. Support for conscientious objection in unjust wars applies even if the individual is not religious and conscription laws are rightly enacted and administered. Other realists think service is obligatory. Citing Romans 13:1–7 they claim we are to obey the governing authorities and should serve when called. Generally, realists cite the guideline of love of neighbor as their justification. For example, when a friend is threatened with violence or the nation is attempting to stem the advances of an aggressive country, participation in violence and serving in the military are justifiable.

The crusader has no concern for these distinctions. Wars fought by the crusader are holy because the opponent is evil. Violence and service in the military are automatically justifiable under these conditions. Conscientious objection is irrelevant.

One problem for all Christians is to avoid confusing service to God with nationalism and extreme forms of patriotism. No country's cause, much less its self-interest, is God's cause. This is idolatry. Christians serve in the military reluctantly and with a heavy heart, careful to use violence only when necessary and with a sense of proportion. Celebration of war and the more violent military virtues is out of bounds.

This confusion is ancient and understandable, even supportable. Love of country or group is good. Celebration of its capacity for peace and justice is good. It is extreme forms of this confusion that should be resisted. Examples abound. The flag is sometimes used to discredit opponents and bludgeon conscientious objectors. Death in combat is equated with Christ on the cross. Service to country becomes service to God. Leaders use religion to rally the troops and raise their emotions.

Only God is truly good. The governments of all countries are sinful to one degree or another. No nation represents God or is doing God's will, even those led by crusaders. Patriotic service in the military is a human choice that may be ethical in some cases, but the use of violence is always ethically suspect.

ADDITIONAL RESOURCES

Allman, Mark J. *Who Would Jesus Kill? War, Peace, and the Christian Tradition*. Winona, MN: Anselm Academic, 2005.

Bainton, Roland H. *Christian Attitudes toward War and Peace*. Eugene, OR: Wipf and Stock Publishers, 2008.

Bell, Linda A. *Rethinking Ethics in the Midst of Violence: A Feminist Approach to Freedom*. Lanham, MD: Rowman and Littlefield Publishers, 1993.

Cahill, Lisa Sowle. *Love Your Enemies: Discipleship, Pacifism, and Just War Theory*. Minneapolis, MN: Fortress Publishers, 1994.

Gray, J. Glenn. *The Warriors*. Revised edition. New York: Harper and Row, 1967. (Orig. pub. 1959.)

Gutiérrez, Gustavo. *A Theology of Liberation*. Fifteenth anniversary edition. Maryknoll, NY: Orbis Books, 1988.

Holmes, Arthur. *War and Christian Ethics: Classic and Contemporary Readings on War*. Grand Rapids, MI: Baker Academic, 2005.

Kolko, Gabriel. *Anatomy of a War*. New York: Pantheon Books, 1985.

Míguez Bonino, José. *Doing Theology in a Revolutionary Situation*. Philadelphia: Fortress Press, 1975.

Niebuhr, Reinhold. *The Children of Light and the Children of Darkness*. New York: Charles Scribner's Sons, 1944.

Stassen, Glenn H. *Just Peacemaking: The New Paradigm for the Ethics of Peace and War*. Cleveland, OH: Pilgrim Press, 2008.

Stone, Ronald H. *Reinhold Niebuhr: Prophet to Politician*. Nashville, TN: Abingdon Press, 1972.

Wink, Walter. *Jesus and Nonviolence: A Third Way*. Minneapolis, MN: Fortress Press, 2003.

Yoder, John Howard. *The Politics of Jesus*. Grand Rapids, MI: Eerdmans, 1994.

———. *When War Is Unjust: Being Honest in Just-War Thinking*. Eugene, OR: Wipf and Stock Publishers, 2001.

Related Websites

Catholic Peace Fellowship, http://www.catholicpeacefellowship.org/index. asp.

Fellowship of Reconciliation, http://forusa.org/.

Lutheran Peace Fellowship, http://www.lutheranpeace.org/.

Selective Service System, http://www.sss.gov/default.htm.

PART III

POVERTY

Case

Homelessness:
The How and Why of Caring

Walking to where she works as a counselor and case manager, Tracy drops a dollar bill into the paper cup in Gerald's extended hand. Gerald is fifty-five, nearly toothless, and debilitated due to a car accident years ago. As she walks on, Tracy wonders what Gerald will do if the new panhandling legislation is passed by the City Council next week.

While there is currently a law on the books against aggressive panhandling, citations are only issued when someone files a formal complaint. In such cases 80 percent of those arrested are convicted. The new legislation gives police the added power to offer citations for any intimidating conduct toward another person if the conduct is accompanied by an act of solicitation. If a "reasonable person" feels "fearful or compelled to give money" due to behavior such as intentional blocking or interference, use of threatening physical gestures or profane language, repeated solicitation, provision of unrequested services without consent, or solicitation by ATMs or parking pay stations, the conduct is considered intimidating. Under the new law Gerald could be fined fifty dollars and receive a civil infraction if a police officer thinks he has crossed the line and intimidated someone. Failure to pay the fine or show up in court could mean criminal prosecution and jail.

Gerald recently managed to secure a subsidized downtown studio apartment after being homeless off and on for a number of years, but he must panhandle to supplement the meager $338 a month he gets from the state disability program. Tracy has worked with Gerald and many other people

---

This case and commentary were prepared by Laura A. Stivers. The names of all persons and institutions have been disguised to protect the privacy of those involved. Some of the material from the commentary was previously published in Laura A. Stivers, *Disrupting Homelessness: Alternative Christian Approaches* (Minneapolis: Fortress Press, 2011).

who have ended up homeless, especially women with children, helping them negotiate the complex array of services available and the paperwork needed to secure them. Gerald had been lucky (after waiting for several years) to be placed in a "Housing First" subsidized apartment provided for individuals who have been chronically homeless. Gerald needs to pay only 30 percent of his income toward rent, but that leaves little to cover food, clothing, and other essentials.

Originally part of a fivefold program designed by the City Council to address homelessness, so far the anti-panhandling legislation has been the only piece of the program that council members have tried to put in place. Also part of the program is increased police presence and services for the homeless. The former includes more police foot patrols in downtown areas and hiring new police officers to enable the neighborhood policing plan. The latter includes street outreach offering support services to the homeless and increased housing capacity combined with support services for homeless individuals struggling with mental health and/or chemical dependency challenges.

Like most other urban areas nationwide, the county commissioned a ten-year plan to end homelessness several years back. Yet, due to the recession, city and county budgets are in crisis, and in this year alone human-services funding was reduced by half, youth shelters eliminated, and food-bank funding slashed. At the state level, funding for general assistance, the State Housing Trust Fund, drug treatment, and basic health care were also drastically cut or ended. Legislation against panhandling seems to Tracy to be a relatively cheap way for the City Council to appear to be addressing homelessness. She notes, however, that many panhandlers like Gerald are not even homeless.

While Tracy opposes the impending panhandling legislation, her employer, Fairmont Christian Housing Alliance, and several other service providers are publicly supporting the new law. In fact, she was hurrying this morning to the meeting the executive director had called to discuss the issue.

"As you all know, I've called this meeting to explain our organization's perspective on the pending panhandling legislation up for vote in the City Council next week and to answer any questions you might have," declared Bob Knowles, executive director of Fairmont Christian Housing Alliance. "Our mission is to help low-income and/or homeless individuals and families who are seeking to improve their lives and secure housing. As we all know, there are some homeless people on the streets of our city who have addiction disorders and who do not seek to better their lives but instead harass people to fund their drug or alcohol consumption."

While Tracy agreed with Bob's statement, she wasn't sure making criminals of these people was going to solve their addiction problems or stop their panhandling. Bob went on to state, "We believe that a combination of new laws, more officers on foot patrol, and increased services and housing will both address homelessness and improve the safety and quality of life for everyone in the downtown area."

One of the drug and alcohol counselors, Kurt Trimmer, spoke to Tracy's unease. "You seem to be saying that the people we serve are 'deserving' because they want help, but the people with addictions who are living on the street are no less deserving. They will never get off the streets if we simply recycle them through jails instead of helping them address the underlying roots of their addictions."

Fairmont Alliance chaplain David Smith added, "Until they surrender their lives to Jesus Christ, there isn't anything that is going to save them. We can offer all the support services in the world but unless people come to the realization that they cannot kick an addiction by themselves, they will continue to mess up their lives and end up in jail. All of God's children are deserving, but to help them we need to embody God's tough love and not be enablers. With God's grace homeless addicts can learn discipline and recover, but they have to want to do so. Sometimes it takes hitting bottom before such a conversion happens."

Bob replied, "The panhandling legislation is only a part of the fivefold plan the City Council intends to pursue. Our organization also supports more low-income addiction-recovery programs and housing." Housing coordinator Lynn Fields spoke up from the back, "Unfortunately, the City Council is only focusing on the anti-panhandling part of the plan. Coming out publicly in support of it pits us against many of the other organizations in the city that work with the homeless. The editors of the *Street Beat* homeless newspaper, the Interfaith Alliance Against Homelessness, the Star County Coalition on Homelessness, and even the American Civil Liberties Union all oppose the legislation. The ACLU claims that panhandling is a civil right and that this law targets the poor, especially people of color. That's racial profiling."

Jasmine Gould, a long-term volunteer peer mentor who was homeless at one point in her life, chimed in, "The city's Human Rights Commission is unanimously opposed to this law. In its fifteen-page report it shows that the majority of people cited under a similar anti-panhandling law in San Francisco were people of color. The report points out that 80 percent of the cases were dismissed, resulting in large administrative and court costs."

Another staff member noted, "The city that this upcoming legislation is patterned after never actually had to enforce the ordinance, but proponents said it acted as a deterrent nevertheless." Jasmine replied, "But our city already has a law against aggressive panhandlers that works fine when there is a complaint, so why do we have to give undue power to police officers to cite anyone they deem aggressive? I know from experience that many police officers despite excellent training are not immune from stereotypes about who is deviant."

Wanting to get on with the day's work, Bob cut short further comments and said, "I realize not all of you support our institutional stance on this legislation, but in the big picture we will be able to do our work more effectively if we publicly support this bill. While our stance might cause some difficulty with organizations we collaborate with on the issue of homelessness, we have to keep in mind our financial viability to further our mission." The room emptied quickly, Tracy noticed, except for Lynn and Jasmine. She thought that Bob had not adequately responded to the points they made and wondered what he had meant about keeping in mind the organization's financial viability.

Tracy overhead Jasmine say to Lynn, "I simply cannot in conscience support this legislation, even though I really like my position as peer mentor here at Fairmont. My community-organizer friends at *Street Beat* have invited me to a protest at City Hall tomorrow. Would you like to come with me? We're meeting at 11:00 on the front steps."

Lynn looked uncomfortable as she replied, "I agree with your position, but as a single mom of two children I can't risk losing my job over conscience. I also understand why Bob is supporting this legislation. He is on the board of the Downtown Association, a group of highly influential business leaders whose mission is to promote a healthy downtown core. This legislation is one of its three policy priorities this year. Fairmont Christian Housing Alliance relies heavily on city contracts and the beneficence of city business leaders, so it would not be prudent for Bob to oppose this legislation. There are at least five other service organizations in the same boat. Issues of funding sometimes limit organizational autonomy."

"I get the funding issue," Jasmine noted, "but what a waste of our time and energy to support a law that doesn't even address homelessness. The Downtown Association released a list of the thirty most prominent panhandlers to support its position, yet only three of them were labeled aggressive. I bet those three are not even homeless. This law will not address the public's discomfort and fear of the homeless. It will simply target the poor and people of color." Lynn agreed, "Yeah, the Downtown Association keeps trying to connect homelessness with deteriorating public safety, but as you and I both know, the homeless have more to fear from crime than anyone else. I think the association members are mostly interested in hiding poverty and homelessness so that their businesses can rake in the tourist dollars."

"I hope you will go to the protest and relay my tacit support to colleagues in service organizations opposing the legislation," said Lynn. "I know Jack Fields from the Interfaith Alliance will be there. He'll understand that while some of us are not there in body, we are there in spirit. I'm just sorry that his energy is being diverted to oppose this bill. His organization is doing such good outreach ministry to the homeless, and advocacy from the churches in his alliance got the new mayor to offer a permanent site for the homeless residents of the tent city."

Tracy joined the conversation, "The churches that have set up shelters and/or food pantries cannot keep up with the need. The recession and foreclosure crises are negatively affecting more and more people." Jasmine retorted, "Instead of addressing the structural issues of low wages, inadequate number of jobs, and insufficient affordable housing in our city, the council is focusing on individual deviance by intensifying surveillance and policing. In effect, it is blaming the poor for societal failure. In the neighborhood I grew up in, jobs were few and far between, drug sales were rampant, and housing was decrepit and dangerous." Exasperated, Jasmine passionately proclaimed, "I'm going to City Hall tomorrow with a sign that says 'Target poverty, not the poor!'"

At dinner that evening with John, her husband of twenty years, Tracy mentioned the City Hall protest the next day. "Despite my employer's stance for the anti-panhandling legislation and Reverend David's point about individual responsibility, I would like to join Jasmine in protesting a policy that seems to blame the poor." She continued, "I really respect the work the *Street Beat* organizers are doing to publicize structural causes of homelessness, most notably the lack of affordable housing and living wages, but also non-housing issues that affect family flourishing, such as safe neighborhoods and good schools, affordable quality child care, health care, and meaningful ways of citizen participation in setting public policies."

John replied, "The stories you've shared with me of the individuals and families you work with point to some of the structural issues that cause chronic poverty, yet you relate some pretty dysfunctional behavior and complain that many of your clients need to make better choices."

"I agree that people sometimes cause their own problems," Tracy replied, "but our own extended middle-class family and plenty of our friends have enough dysfunction to go around. The difference is that most of us have a safety net to fall back on in times of crisis."

She continued, "Perhaps there is a role for multiple approaches to homelessness. The structural causes of poverty must be addressed, but as Jack of the Interfaith Alliance said at the Forum on Homelessness the other day, many people cannot even access the resources that are already out there. He pictured the resources to help people who are homeless as a large apple tree with many branches, but argued that thousands of people cannot reach the fruit. For example, a single mother with two small children might want to take advantage of scholarships for education and job training, but if she doesn't have a place to live or cannot find affordable quality child care, how is she going to attend school?" John replied, "But that example only confirms that addressing the problem of homelessness requires structural changes to make basic needs accessible in many areas, not just housing."

"Jasmine clearly wants to move to the structural level first," Tracy noted. "Jack, in his outreach ministry, emphasizes how to help homeless people even get to the table. My work has a similar focus, but I think we need to come at it from both ends." Tracy thought about all the times she had heard Jack speak and shared some of his insights: "Jack says that most congregants come to the issue of homelessness as problem-solvers rather than listeners. Furthermore, when they come in contact with people who are homeless, they treat the relationship as a transaction, providing what they think people need. He argues that a relationship of trust needs to be built first. Presence and treating people with dignity, he says, is the most powerful response because of the isolation, separation, and shame that homeless people experience."

John thought about their recent adult Sunday School class on hospitality and the ministry of Jesus. "While we are called to open up God's banquet table to all (that is, address the structural issues so that all have access to the 'apples on the tree'), we are also called to see the divine in each person we meet and treat them accordingly. Through his presence Jesus continually brought healing and acceptance to marginalized people." Tracy nodded, "I try to remember that every time I pass a homeless person on the street and whenever I get frustrated with the behavior of my clients."

Tracy reflected: "I sometimes have trouble with the notion of hospitality, however. I think a lot of people in our Sunday School class have a patronizing form of hospitality. They talk about hospitality as a responsibility for those who have been blessed by God with abundance. It never occurs to them that hospitality is not practiced only by those with power and privilege. After all, God's blessings are not only about material abundance. They also seem to confine hospitality to charitable exchange rather than reciprocal relationship."

"One thing I have always admired about you is your ability to develop relationships with the people you serve," John replied. "You sure received hospitality the other day when four-year-old Evan gave you a drawing of the playground at the transitional housing unit he is living at, and his mom brought you hand-picked flowers. That relationship has taken time to form, but it has become one of mutual care, concern, and trust. Are we still going to have them over for dinner next week?"

Tracy was too deep in thought to respond to the dinner question. "I just worry that my power as counselor and case manager could lead to a form of patronizing compassion if I'm not organizing *with* the homeless for broader structural change to prevent poverty and homelessness. I often wonder what the best way to offer care and hospitality to those in need is. Can I be in solidarity with people on the margins when I control distribution of goods and services they are seeking? Is joining Jasmine tomorrow to protest the proposed anti-panhandling legislation the best use of my energy? Can I look Gerald and other homeless people in the eyes each day if I do not act on my conscience?" John smiled, "You've got a lot to think about, honey, but I know that whatever you decide, your heart is in the right place."

Commentary

Tracy is struggling with how best to put compassion and hospitality into practice in relation to the problem of homelessness. She takes seriously the Christian call to love our neighbor no matter who that is, as illustrated by her chosen profession and the deep relationships she has developed with people she serves. She is aware, however, that sometimes our most well-meaning efforts to help people are not what is most liberating for them and that we often settle for responses of charity without seeking to remedy the injustices that caused the need for charity in the first place.

Practical realities sink in, however. She has a secure job, and she does make a difference in the lives of people who become homeless. Can she be in solidarity with the people she works with, however, if she simply focuses on charity? How should she be involved in ending homelessness from a structural perspective? While protesting the anti-panhandling law would be a way to stand in solidarity with the homeless, what constructive change needs to happen to keep people from becoming homeless? Are compassion and hospitality on an individual level without attention to structural realities adequate? It appears Tracy tries to walk in the footsteps of Jesus and treat everyone as a child of God, but she seems to be questioning whether Christian discipleship requires more of her.

Tracy is also troubled by the fact that funding considerations have muted the prophetic voices that her workplace and other organizations could have. Does the potential loss of funding sources to help the homeless justify not standing up against policy that might result in unjust criminalization of some homeless people? And what about her organization's working relationships with other groups that are in solidarity with and advocating for the homeless? Working in coalitions is the only way that larger social change to end homelessness will occur. There is power in numbers. This power can be thwarted, however, by funding sources that use their donations to divide and conquer groups who are advocating for substantial policy changes to promote social and economic justice. How does Tracy follow Jesus as a role model when it comes to politics and social policy?

DEMOGRAPHICS AND CAUSES OF HOMELESSNESS IN THE UNITED STATES

The common denominator among people who are homeless is extreme poverty. Some people are transitionally homeless due to unemployment, divorce, or eviction. Others are episodically homeless; that is, they cycle in and out of homelessness for differing amounts of time. While the majority of people who are homeless are in these two groups, traditionally we associate the face of the homeless with chronic homelessness—people like Gerald who have lived on the streets or in shelters for prolonged periods of time. However, the fastest-growing segment of the homeless population today is children, like four-year-old Evan.

Estimates on the number of people who are homeless depend on how homelessness is being defined. For example, the Department of Housing and Urban Development (HUD) counts only those who are literally homeless (on the street or in homeless shelters), while the Department of Education includes people who are sharing the housing of others due to loss of housing or economic hardship as well as people who are living in such places as hotels, camp grounds, or parking lots. Gerald would be counted in HUD's homeless count, but Evan and his mom, as well as all the residents of the tent city supported by the Interfaith Alliance, would not be. Homeless organizations have estimated—using the broader definition of homelessness—that approximately 3.5 million people (1% of US population) experience homelessness in a given year, with 1.35 million of them children.

From the US Conference of Mayors' *Hunger and Homelessness Survey* it is estimated that of the single homeless population, 67.5 percent are male, but of the homeless families with children, 65 percent are households headed by a female. The national racial makeup of the homeless population is 47 percent African American, 47 percent European American, 4 percent Native American, and 2 percent Asian American. By ethnicity, 24 percent of the homeless are Hispanic Americans. Clearly, homelessness and racism are linked. A larger percentage of people of color experience poverty, and while overt segregation was ruled illegal with civil rights legislation, neighborhoods and schools continue to be segregated by both race and class, perpetuating inequality and unequal opportunity. Further, studies on racial discrimination have consistently shown unequal treatment in areas such as job hiring, housing, and banking.

The National Coalition for the Homeless says that up to one-fourth of the urban homeless are employed. Veterans make up 20 percent of people who are homeless, and about half of the people experiencing homelessness suffer from mental health issues. In addition, studies indicate that at least one-third and perhaps as many as two-thirds of all homeless persons suffer from addiction disorders.

While race, marital status, and health matters play important roles in homelessness, poverty and a severe lack of affordable housing are the central causes. Poverty has increased in the last thirty years due to eroding wages and benefits for work as well as declining public assistance, while affordable housing, especially rental housing, has decreased. After World War II there was plenty of affordable rental housing and inexpensive single room occupancy (SRO) housing, but rents increased in the 1970s and 1980s and SROs were demolished in urban-renewal efforts. According to the National Low-Income Housing Coalition there are now 5.8 million more extremely low-income households than there are affordable housing units. Today, many families are paying considerably more than the 30 percent of their income that is typically considered affordable for housing.

While poverty and lack of affordable housing are the predominant causes of homelessness, the personal factors determine *who* is homeless. Addiction, disability, mental illness, and experiences with foster care, jail/prison, and domestic violence can be contributing causes of homelessness, and oppression based on race, gender, class, sexual preference, or disability plays a factor in who is the most vulnerable in a competitive economy. The presence of a sufficient safety net in society determines whether structural or individual factors will cause homelessness.

A race and gender analysis of both declining wages and weakening public assistance helps explain some of the disparities of homelessness. For example, single mothers with children under the age of six cannot afford child care on low-wage jobs, yet according to the National Alliance to End Homelessness, only one of ten children who is eligible for child-care assistance under federal law gets any help. Studies from the Economic Policy Institute indicate that around 60 percent of minimum-wage workers are female and 40 percent are people of color.

Since the 1980s the *number* of people who are homeless has steadily increased, although the *percentage* of people in the overall population who are homeless has decreased. Although funding for homelessness has been one of the few areas of social-safety-net spending that has increased in recent years (mainly to address chronic homelessness through shelters and housing with services, like the Housing First apartment Gerald got), there has been little funding for low-income rental assistance. According to the Center for Budget and Policy Priorities, spending on public housing is minimal and rental assistance to offset the cost of market rate housing is available for only one in four households that qualify for it. The foreclosure and economic crises also increased the ranks of the homeless. RealityTrac's

2009 Year-End US Foreclosure Market Report showed that 2.8 million US properties received foreclosure notices. Twenty percent of the foreclosed properties were rentals. Job security is absent for many during times of recession. Low-income families and minority communities have been hit the hardest by both the foreclosure crisis and the economic recession. On the bright side, the foreclosure crisis has caused rents to go down in many urban areas because families are living with friends or relatives and renting their houses out to avoid foreclosure and banks with stocks of unsalable houses are offering low rents to keep the houses occupied in an effort to avoid vandalism and to pay for insurance and taxes until the market improves.

APPROACHES TO HOMELESSNESS

If poverty and lack of affordable housing are the predominant causes of homelessness, it would make sense for public policy and institutions to focus on addressing the causes of poverty and providing more low-income rental housing. However, approaches to homelessness have generally been punitive for those who are considered the "undeserving homeless" and charity-based for those who are seen as the "deserving homeless." Like many cities nationwide, the City Council in this case has focused its efforts on anti-panhandling laws that give police more authority to "clean up" the city—especially the downtown—by removing "undesirables." While many people like Jasmine and Tracy, who work in Christian organizations, might see the need for approaches focused more on justice than charity, long-term organizing to address poverty takes time and energy and often has no quick tangible gains to show for the work. Further, constructing low-income housing takes substantial capital. The efforts of low-income housing construction by nonprofits are laudable but remain small in scale in relation to the substantial need.

Punitive approaches are based on prevailing social myths including the claim that all homeless people are unreliable, incompetent, and/or mentally unstable and the belief that they are homeless primarily because of a personal fault or characteristic (laziness, addiction, lack of education, disability). Many even believe that people are homeless because they choose to be. These views lead some to think that the only way to stop people from being lazy and overly dependent on charity is to punish such behavior. Many cities have adopted anti-panhandling laws. Other cities have enacted "quality-of-life" ordinances under which police can arrest people for sleeping or sitting on sidewalks. Some argue that such criminalization of the homeless has led to an increasing number of attacks on the homeless, primarily by young men. Many believe, as drug and alcohol counselor Kurt

Trimmer points out, that recycling people through jails will not remedy the issue of homelessness but rather exacerbate it because it does not address the root cause of addiction.

Charitable approaches might or might not blame the homeless for their plight. Some people who offer direct charity realize that structural conditions in our economy are a major cause of homelessness. Others offer charity along with self-help assistance based on the assumption that homeless people need to be reformed in some way. That is, they believe the homeless need to gain a work ethic, a more virtuous character, middle-class values, or more job and life skills. Often the homeless who agree to the procedures of reform and assimilation are deemed "deserving" and offered charitable aid (housing assistance, welfare, shelter), but they remain subject to a whole array of social workers, rules, and regulations in their lives.

Some Christian programs of reform claim that the primary problem the homeless face is spiritual, not economic. Thus, their solution is for the homeless to accept Jesus into their lives. Chaplain David Smith voices this perspective when he claims the homeless cannot "kick an addiction by themselves" but can only do so through God's grace and through better discipline. His assumption is that most homeless people have addictions and that the solution to homelessness lies in changing the individual (the spiritual self), not in economic policies and structures.

Since the 1930s there has been an emphasis in the United States on promoting home ownership. Home owners are envisioned as everything the homeless are not—secure, autonomous, industrious, and virtuous (that is, they have middle-class values). Through tax deductions and credits (such as home mortgage deduction, deduction for property taxes, capital gains exclusion for home sales, and exclusion of net imputed rental income), state and federal tax systems have financially supported home ownership over rental assistance. While not technically budget expenditures and thus not considered part of the housing budget allotted to HUD, the amount of money not collected from home and rental property owners far exceeds any amount of money spent on low-income housing assistance. Half of the home mortgage-interest deduction actually goes to just 12 percent of taxpayers with incomes of $100,000 or more who often use the deduction to reduce the cost of owning two homes.

Ending poverty and homelessness is a goal shared by Christians from different theological backgrounds and denominations. Some congregations have worked to find ways to make their communities open and welcoming to people of all stations in life. Others have organized to respond to the needs of people who are marginalized in their local communities and cities through creation of programs and through advocacy for particular city and county policies. Still others are actively advocating for anti-poverty policies at state and national levels.

COMPASSION, HOSPITALITY, AND JUSTICE

While there is no perfect response to poverty and homelessness, any adequate response should include both compassion and justice. While structural changes are necessary to address the root causes of homelessness, advocacy efforts ought to be grounded in a deep level of compassion for *all* our neighbors. Church communities can and should offer a strong moral voice and commitment to the movement for a just and compassionate world; just as important, individual Christians and Christian communities must *practice* hospitality, compassion, and justice.

We often stop short of fulfilling these values out of fear. For example, we cite liability concerns to avoid letting homeless people sleep on church grounds or issues of safety and security to ban low-income housing in our neighborhoods. In the Fairmont Alliance case fear of losing funding becomes the obstacle. Often the real obstacle, however, is a stereotype that turns our neighbors into "others" who are dangerous. Many Christians volunteer at soup kitchens and shelters, or help build homes, or assist people they know who are struggling financially, but often we continue to hold stereotypes of the homeless unless we get to know them.

Tracy appears to do a good job of relating to the homeless without stereotyping them. Working shoulder to shoulder with people who are homeless might have aided her in doing so. Many parishioners in churches have contact with people who are homeless only at a distance or for short periods, and often their main experience is of street people who are chronically homeless. They might have known people who are episodically homeless without even realizing it. A handful of churches have challenged the turning of our neighbors into "others" by becoming radically inclusive. These churches have oriented their mission toward supporting the homeless and have developed outreach and worship that appeal to people in all walks of life. They hold that compassion requires solidarity, that is, a "walking with" others, not simply "doing for" others.

Getting to know the homeless and making their lives central to ethical analysis of social policy gives insight into what obstacles prevent flourishing lives. How would Christian approaches change if we quit seeing the homeless as having the problems? How would such approaches look if we saw the gospel as less about individual relationship with Jesus Christ and more about the physical, spiritual, and mental health of people within God's community? Assuming that the spiritual crisis is within specific individuals alone without addressing the ways our society is spiritually impoverished blames the victims of such a society.

Christian communities must ask what it means to take seriously a call to be disciples of Jesus Christ in the world. Compassionate responses of hospitality and charity, resistance to injustice and exploitation, and advocacy for systems and institutions that support justice and well-being are equally important. The way of Jesus suggests a bottom-up approach that moves from caring for each person in our life to making a flourishing home for all in God's community.

Thus, hospitality must be connected to justice. Hospitality as justice was a foundation of all morality in biblical times. Having been freed by God from slavery, the people of Israel understood that a covenant with God included caring for all within their midst by sharing their bread with the hungry and bringing the homeless poor into their houses (Is 58:7). Jesus also modeled hospitality as justice. At the Last Supper, and throughout his ministry, Jesus opened the banquet for all to be seated at the table in relationship with God and one another. Jesus envisioned abundant life for all, a life in which humans are not only physically housed but are truly at home within caring, inclusive, and sustainable communities. Paul sought to make such a vision of *koinonia* community a reality in the early church. Translations for *koinonia* include "fellowship," "contribution," "sharing," and "participation." The early church aimed to embody these values by caring for all its members, distributing goods according to need, and worshiping and praying together (Acts 2:42–47). Each member of the community participated fully in the fellowship and worship of the community because hospitality as justice was practiced with God's gifts shared sustainably by all.

The problem of homelessness is not about people who find themselves without a place to sleep; it is a reflection of our collective identity as a people and a society. Do we want to be a society that puts people in jail because they do not have a home, or do we want to be a society that claims homelessness simply is not an option? Our high value in the United States on individualism and each person being responsible for himself or herself can hinder our ability to envision alternatives to what seems inevitable. Many Americans have been socialized to accept a dominant cultural world view that promotes individual initiative, enterprise, and achieving the "American Dream," but a society founded on such a competitive world view privileges the winners and marginalizes the losers. The early church did not assume there must be losers, nor did it believe homelessness to be inevitable.

Jesus challenged those who tried to limit the seats at the banquet table and who were only willing to share crumbs rather than abundant loaves.

Hospitality as charity does not afford recipients full human dignity in ways that enable them to participate fully in community and fellowship. The bountiful goods at the banquet table are not earned but are gifts from God, meant to be sustainably shared by all (Lv 25:18–19, 23–24). God's creation is interdependent, with each one an intricate part contributing to the whole. Love of neighbor entails both being a neighbor to others and allowing others to be neighbors to us. As the story of the starving widow who serves Elijah (1 Kgs 17—18) attests, those who are poor and outcast can be just as hospitable as those who are rich and powerful.

While there is no single blueprint, there are basic levels of human and environmental flourishing for which we should aim. For one, all people in a society ought to have decent housing, access to adequate health care and a good education, and, if they are able, work that allows them to live healthy lives and contribute to a healthy society. For people who are not able to contribute through work, we ought to find other ways that they can contribute to society and have services and safety nets so they can live well. Basic goods are not all that is necessary for people to flourish, however. Meaningful avenues for participation for all individuals in communities and the broader society are also important. If we are all to participate in society and relate to one another as neighbors, then there also needs to be a rearrangement of wealth and power. While protesting anti-panhandling legislation is important, more deep-seated change is necessary. Substantial inequality as we have in our society today blocks solidarity among people and thwarts just and compassionate communities. Charitable paternalism that sustains the status quo supplants solidarity and justice.

Practicing hospitality as justice entails building a social movement to end homelessness and poverty. Such an agenda is not simply a liberal en- terprise; conservative and evangelical Christians are also concerned about ending homelessness and poverty. Top priority in such a movement would be advocacy for more affordable rental housing (not simply home owner- ship) and jobs with livable wages and benefits. Relying on nonprofits and churches to build and maintain affordable housing will not be enough. Being in solidarity with the homeless and working poor means advocating both local and federal government to ensure the number of decent low- income rental housing units meets the need. Government intervention is needed to promote zoning for rental housing, require developers to include a certain percentage of low-income rental housing in their developments, and hold landlords accountable to fair rental practices and safety standards. The ways to eradicate homelessness are well documented, but the political will waxes and wanes (usually the latter) without a sustained movement to promote change.

Both Tracy and Jasmine are beginning to see that Christian disciple-ship requires more than charitable hospitality. They are clear that being disciples of Jesus Christ includes care and compassion for those who are marginalized in society, but they are still figuring out how to practice and organize for hospitality as justice so that all may have a home not only in God's community but in our all-too-human communities as well. While organizing against poverty and for more affordable rental housing is clearly an important long-term goal, Tracy must decide how to respond in the short term to legislation that serves to punish rather than empower the homeless. She has to keep in mind, however, her institutional role and how she can continue to work directly with people who experience homelessness. Such work requires funding. Thus, pragmatic as well as prophetic concerns are on Tracy's mind.

ADDITIONAL RESOURCES

Bouma-Prediger, Steven, and Brian J. Walsh. *Beyond Homelessness: Christian Faith in a Culture of Displacement.* Grand Rapids, MI: Eerdmans, 2008.

Kusmer, Kenneth L. *Down and Out, On the Road: The Homeless in Ameri-can History.* New York: Oxford University Press, 2002.

Rennebohm, Craig, with David Paul. *Souls in the Hands of a Tender God: Stories of the Search for Home and Healing on the Streets.* Boston: Beacon Press, 2008.

Russell, Letty M., Shannon J. Clarkson, and Kate M. Ott. *Just Hospitality: God's Welcome in a World of Difference.* Louisville, KY: West-minster John Knox, 2009.

Stivers, Laura. *Disrupting Homelessness: Alternative Christian Approaches.* Minneapolis: Fortress Press, 2011.

Related Websites

Housing Policy Debate, http://www.mi.vt.edu/publications/housing _policy_debate/hpd-index.html.

National Alliance to End Homelessness, http://www.endhomelessness.org.

National Coalition for the Homeless, http://www.nationalhomeless.org.

Shelter Force: The Journal of Affordable Housing and Community Building, http://www.shelterforce.org/.

Case

Who Cares about Haiti Anyway?

I

"It seems to me," Pierre mused, "that the outside world does not care a bit about Haiti. No one takes anything that happens to Haiti seriously. Haiti is treated like some bizarre part of the world; strange things are supposed to happen in Haiti or to Haiti. Nothing good is supposed to come out of Haiti. Compare how America treats Haiti to how it treats Cuba! These two neighbors have similar histories and cultures. When Cubans cross the seas and land in Miami they are welcomed. Yet Haitians are either turned away on the high seas or arrested and deported when they manage to make it to Miami safely. Who cares about Haiti anyway?" Pierre's face was puckered with concern as he pulled up a chair to sit down.

It was a bright Wednesday morning in late August 2010. Life on the campus of this state university in Florida had just begun. Professor Mensah was in his office cleaning up the final version of the course syllabus for his graduate seminar on Caribbean religions when Pierre Jean Mapou, a master's-degree student in the African Diaspora Studies program, burst in. Pierre had enrolled in the seminar late; he had added the course only because a Haitian Creole class had been canceled due to low enrollment. Pierre had come to Professor Mensah's office to pick up a copy of the syllabus before classes began on Monday.

Pierre was in the middle of a story about how his parents had migrated to Florida from Haiti in the mid-1970s in order to escape the Duvalier dictatorship when he suddenly started talking about Haiti's predicament after the

---

This case and commentary were prepared by Albert Wuaku. The names of all persons and institutions have been disguised to protect the privacy of those involved.

earthquake of 2010. His troubled musings reflected the broader sentiment of the Haitian community in Miami that the Western world had once again abandoned Haiti when it needed help the most. Quite typical of his generation (the children of Diaspora Haitians born in the United States), Pierre was passionate about Haiti. He wanted to know more about his heritage, and that was why he had enrolled in the M.A. program in African Diaspora studies. Driven by this passion, Pierre had spent the summer working as a volunteer interpreter for a nongovernmental organization (NGO) in Port-au-Prince that was involved in the rebuilding effort after the earthquake. In an earlier conversation he had told Dr. Mensah that this volunteer work was just a small way he could give back to his people. Unfortunately, Pierre had returned to Miami later in the summer appalled at the slow pace at which things were moving in Haiti. He seemed defeated and disappointed that the Western media was not focusing as much attention on the post-earthquake recovery efforts in Haiti as they had done in the days immediately following the earthquake. He felt the media response was lackadaisical. The Western media, he lamented, had shifted the eyes of the world away from Haiti. He attributed the slow pace of recovery in Haiti to the failed promises of Western donor nations, especially the United States.

After Pierre left his office, Professor Mensah mused that Pierre's passionate frustration was not unjustified. The earthquake that struck Haiti in January 2010 killed over 300,000 people and rendered about two million more homeless. Eight months later many Haitians still lived in miserable conditions. A report issued by the United Nations Office of Coordination of Humanitarian Affairs (OCHA) shortly after the earthquake stated that 60 percent of government, administrative, and economic infrastructure had been destroyed, including the Presidential Palace, Parliament, and the cathedral. The report also said 25 percent of the standing houses in Port-au-Prince had been damaged so badly they would have to be torn down. In addition, 80 percent of schools and more than half of the hospitals in the affected area had been either destroyed or damaged.

Eight months after the quake over 1.5 million Haitians were still huddled in over a thousand make-shift camps that occupied all sorts of spaces from the plaza across from the almost completely destroyed National Palace to the medians between roads and golf courses in the vicinity of Port-au-Prince. Professor Mensah brushed his hand over a report titled "We Have Been Forgotten," which had been compiled by the Institute for Justice and Democracy in Haiti. It stated that 75 percent of families in these camps had sometimes gone an entire day without food, 44 percent were forced to drink untreated water, and 27 percent had no access to sanitation and therefore had no choice but to defecate on the open ground. Moreover, according to the International Organization for Migration, twelve thousand refugees had been evicted from their camps and another eighty-seven thousand were on the verge of eviction. Meanwhile, the international medical NGO Médecins Sans Frontières/Doctors without Borders reported that 10 percent of Haiti's medical professionals either had been killed in the earthquake or had left Haiti thereafter. Professor Mensah felt depressed. He sat in his office chair and looked out his window—south, toward Haiti.

II

A few months later, in January 2011, Professor Mensah found himself driving to work and listening to a report on National Public Radio (NPR) that focused on the welfare of Haiti one year after the earthquake. The NPR correspondents reminded their listeners that after the earthquake Haiti had been flooded with promises from NGOs and heads of governments from around the world that they would provide material and financial support to rebuild Haiti. His own university had collected aid and sent a contingent of emergency workers to deliver it, some of whom worked with him in the African Disapora Studies program. Two months after the quake in January 2010 the wealthiest nations of the world had met at a conference in New York City, set up the Interim Haiti Recovery Commission (IHRC), and pledged $10 billion in aid for reconstruction, with $5.3 billion specified for 2010 and 2011. Now, a year after the quake, the Office of the United Nations Special Envoy was reporting that although most of the humanitarian aid pledged for the first year had been received, six months after the quake only 2 percent of the aid pledged for reconstruction in 2010 had arrived, and one year later over 60 percent of pledged reconstruction funds had yet to be delivered. Even the United States, the wealthiest of the nations and the one closest to Haiti, had only sent the first installment of its reconstruction aid seven months after the quake and was still holding back about half of its pledge.

To add insult to injury, the NPR anchors noted that the NGOs who had raised money by capitalizing on the overwhelming sympathy of the world's people had similarly fallen short in promises to aid quake victims and help reconstruct the country. Professor Mensah found himself shaking his head as he heard a spokesperson for the Haiti Response Coalition tell the NPR anchor that "the large charities have a lot of money in their bank accounts that's not getting spent in Haiti. For example, the Red Cross is reported to have spent in Haiti only a third of the $480 million it raised after the quake. Not surprisingly, Haitians are annoyed with the NGOs." The NPR anchor turned next to an anthropologist who was involved in the reconstruction effort in Haiti. The anthropologist said: "Most people are angry at the NGOs because, like it or not, they are the ones that have taken over from the state the job of providing vital services. Lots of Haitians think the NGOs are getting rich off of their misery and don't really want things to change, because if the problems were solved, the NGOs wouldn't exist."

The NPR program then shifted to focus on the vulnerability of Haiti to the threats of diseases and hurricanes. One of the NPR anchors noted that, as if on cue, both phenomena hit Haiti in November 2010. There was a cholera outbreak in Haiti's Artibonite region and Central Plateau. The outbreak resulted from dilapidated or nonexistent sanitation systems across the country. Carried by human waste, the cholera bacteria wound up in the Artibonite River, an important source of water for drinking, bathing, and irrigation. The World Health Organization reported that the outbreak had sickened 9,100 people and killed 583 within two-and-a-half weeks. It spread into the slums of Port-au-Prince as well as the camps. The NPR anchor interviewed a reporter for the Associated Press in Port-au-Prince who said that some Haitians blamed the United Nations for the cholera outbreak because they linked it with the presence of Nepalese soldiers who had been stationed at a UN base near the Artibonite River earlier in 2010. Word had spread that Nepal was also plagued with the particular strain of cholera that had infected Haitians. An investigation of the base found open and cracked sewer pipes. A pipe from a septic tank was leaking foul-smelling black fluid into the Artibonite River. As a result, an overpowering smell of human waste pervaded the UN base. Angered by this news, hundreds of Haitians marched from Mirebalais to the base demanding the expulsion of the Nepalese soldiers.

The NPR anchors emphasized that Hurricane Tomas, which struck on November 5, 2010, almost turned the cholera outbreak into a full-blown epidemic. Luckily, the hurricane had weakened considerably before it hit, but it still killed twenty-one people and left 6,610 more Haitians homeless. Professor Mensah listened as a female public-health worker employed by Partners in Health told the NPR audience that Tomas's winds ripped apart tents and tarps; its rain turned Port-au-Prince's refugee camps into muddy swamps; and its floodwaters spread cholera. She went on to say that "living conditions at the camps have deteriorated as a result of the storm. Standing water, lack of garbage collection, and limited sanitation availability make the camps a potential flashpoint for another cholera outbreak." She concluded by saying she was surprised the United States had hardly lifted a finger to aid Haiti during the hurricane. It deployed just one aircraft carrier, the *Iwo Jima,* to conduct aerial surveys of the damage done to the country.

III

Professor Mensah pulled into the campus parking lot just as the NPR program was ending. He found himself deep in thought as he walked slowly to his office. He agreed that the United Nations, individual nations, and many NGOs had proven themselves incapable of solving the crisis in Haiti. He knew that some Haitians view the West as the principal source of most of Haiti's problems and feel these powers must be compelled not only to make good on their promises of aid for rebuilding the country after the quake, but also to pay reparations for the decades of damage they have done to Haiti. They argued that only when the Haitian masses receive such funds and are able to rebuild their own society will Haitians be able to pull themselves out of the endless crises. Professor Mensah knew there were other Haitians, like Pierre, who thought reparations were a pipe dream. They thought the only way Haiti would get back on its feet was by Haitians pooling their meager resources together to help other Haitians.

Professor Mensah knew that Pierre had been debating during the fall semester what his own responsibilities were toward Haiti. He wondered whether he should change his major from art—he had loved painting since he was a child—to something more "practical" that would be of immediate use in alleviating suffering in Haiti. "Perhaps art is something that should wait until people stop dying early," he had thrown out one day in Professor Mensah's class as the class pondered the situation in Haiti. "I pray to Le Bon Dieu to guide me in the right direction." Others in the class had argued that art, too, had its role in the rebuilding of Haiti, that public art could inspire people. But Pierre was not sure.

Just after the semester ended Pierre left a note on Professor Mensah's door. He was on his way to Port-au-Prince the next day. He would spend the Christmas break at a camp in Port-au-Prince helping homeless persons who are deaf and dumb relocate to a safe haven that an NGO had constructed for them. Pierre had written at the end of the note: "Only Haitians can save Haiti. We cannot rely on anybody else. They will always promise us, but fail to deliver."

Professor Mensah sighed as he reread Pierre's note. What to do about Haiti was not just Pierre's question. He wondered about his own and his university's responsibility. Was sending food and water and a delegation that distributed it and surveyed the damage for two weeks after the earthquake all that was required of the university? Tom, one of his friends in the African Diaspora Studies program, had been in the delegation. When Tom had returned, he told Professor Mensah that once their supplies for distribution had run out, he had felt helpless, even like a voyeur, peeping at the suffering and misery of the Haitian people.

The sermon Professor Mensah's pastor had delivered the previous week had been on the parable of the Good Samaritan. The professor had been thinking of Pierre and Haiti ever since. Haiti was clearly a near neighbor of the United States, especially, to Miami, with its large Haitian community. The questions turned over and over in Dr. Mensah's mind: Is it enough for me to encourage Haitian students, and write an occasional check to the Red Cross? How good a neighbor am I? What can I do? How much do I care about Haiti?

Commentary

There are two related contexts in which many Haitians locate their understandings of the developments presented in this case. While the United States is not the only nation guilty of reneging on its promises to Haiti, many Haitians have directed their anger toward it because they feel it has betrayed them. The United States, they argue, should be leading the rest of the world in Haiti's post-earthquake reconstruction effort. After all, it is the most powerful nation in the world and is Haiti's closest neighbor and ally among the nations that promised funds. But many Haitians say they are not surprised the United States is one of the countries that has not fulfilled its promise to Haiti because it has not always lived up to the expectations for a good neighbor. *Bel dan pa di zanmi*—"A beautiful smile doesn't mean he's your friend"—goes a Creole proverb, a staple of Haitian popular culture. Haitians tend to agree that America's invasion, occupation, or intervention in Haiti's political and economic life, often with help from homegrown Haitian despots, has often been motivated by America's own greed and selfishness, although it has used the provision of aid to Haiti in one form or the other as the guise.

Two stories stand out as illustrations of how aid from America has helped turn Haiti, a nation of low-tech subsistence farmers, into a dumping ground for American agribusiness. The first has to do with rice, which was once a staple crop in Haiti. Food aid from America has turned Haiti, a nation of rice growers, into a market for the subsidized rice crop grown in the United States. In 1986, after the Haitian dictator Jean Claude "Baby Doc" Duvalier was forcibly removed from office, the International Monetary Fund (IMF) loaned Haiti $24.6 million in desperately needed funds because Baby Doc had looted the treasury before he fled into exile. But as a precondition for securing the IMF loan, Haiti was required to reduce tariff protections for its rice and other agricultural products as well as some industries, and to open up the country's markets to competition from outside countries. As the largest and most powerful voice in the IMF, the United States pressed for these stipulations. This is how rice from the United States invaded Haiti. By 1987, there was so much cheap rice coming into Haiti that many local rice farmers stopped working the land. Having lost their businesses, rice farmers from the countryside started moving to the cities.

After a few years of cheap rice from the United States, Haiti, local production went way down. By 2008, Haiti was the world's third-largest importer of US rice, receiving some 240,000 tons that year alone. Meanwhile, US rice growers were heavily subsidized by the government. For example, between 1995 and 2006, US rice growers received $11 billion from the federal government. The American rice industry is also protected by tariffs—the same kinds of tariffs the IMF demanded Haiti remove. With the average family income standing at about $400 a year, most Haitians could not afford to pay international prices for a product they once grew for themselves, so they had to turn to America for food aid. The United States provided the aid, but half the money did not go to buy the food; it went not only to US farmers, but also to food processors and to shipping companies, because the food had to be transported in US ships. A good part of the so-called handout to Haiti actually went to US agribusiness, which needed markets for its overflowing bins of farm products.

Another infamous "aid" story involves the destruction of native pig farming in Haiti following an outbreak of Asian Swine Flu in the late 1970s. As described by Paul Farmer, the physician and anthropologist famous for his work among Haiti's poor, pigs were once a centerpiece of Haiti's peasant economy, providing a reliable source of income and an insurance policy against hard times. But American agriculture experts, fearing that Haiti's pigs could spread the disease to the United States and destroy its massive pork industry, bankrolled a $23 million extermination and restocking program. By 1984, all of Haiti's 1.3 million pigs had been killed. The US Agency for International Development and the Organization of American States thereupon announced a plan to replace the Creole pigs with brand new Iowa pigs—if the peasants committed to building pigsties to US standards and demonstrated they had enough money to buy feed. Even the peasants who could afford these "free" pigs found that they didn't flourish under Haitian conditions. The fragile *kochon blan* ("foreign" or "white" pigs) frequently became ill and they had few litters compared to the native pigs that had been exterminated. Soon, the project was abandoned—leaving Iowa hog farmers enriched and hundreds of thousands of Haitian families without a key means of survival.

Forced out of small-scale farming by the elimination of two basic staples, Haitian peasants moved to the cities to work in sweatshops producing panties, bras, and dresses for mega stores in America such as Sears, Walmart, and JC Penney. Even before the earthquake these initiatives, driven by American interest, offered little promise of restoring and reinvigorating indigenous farming or providing any sort of real, homegrown economic base for Haiti. Many Haitians interpret American reneging on the promise of reconstruction aid in the context of this legacy. America does not really care about Haiti, they insist.

ROOTS OF HAITIAN CYNICISM

Many Haitians do not feel they need to search hard to explain how America and the rest of the West treat them. A consensus among Haitians is that Haiti is not one of those countries the rest of the world, especially the West, takes seriously. This is exactly the point of Pierre's musings about nobody expecting anything good to come from Haiti. The roots of this attitude toward them, many Haitians agree, lie in their history. Ever since African slaves in Haiti freed themselves from the bondage of their colonial masters through a violent revolution, they and their indigenous religion, Vodou, have been subjected to ridicule, feared, and demonized. Moreau de St-Mery, author of one of the earliest portraits of Vodou in Haiti at the time of the revolution, painted a picture of a religious culture in which fear, lust, and violence were core ingredients. Vodou spirit possession experiences were characterized as out of control and potentially contagious for any outsider that happened to stumble upon such rituals. These themes shaped the scholarly and popular discourse. The blunt portrait that emerged gave the impression that a person from the so called civilized world could be consumed if he or she ventured too close to Haiti, its religion, and its out of control sexuality and violence.

Contagion is a theme that runs through the larger world's imagination about Haiti. Haiti contaminates. In the sixteenth century the source of syphilis in Europe was attributed to Haiti. Haitians were supposed to have introduced tuberculosis to the United States in the nineteenth century. When acquired immune deficiency syndrome (AIDS) first broke out in the 1980s, and it was not yet clear where it came from, it was referred to as the 4-H disease—homosexuals, heroin addicts, hemophiliacs, and Haitians were identified as the primary sources. Haiti was an epicenter of AIDS. Even well-trained scientists in the United States promoted the rather absurd narrative that the human immunodeficiency virus (HIV) made its entry into the human population through routine sexual intercourse with animals during Vodou rituals. Today the origin of HIV is known to be a mutation of Simian immunodeficiency disease, found among apes, especially chimpanzees, in West Central Africa; at some time in the last decades the mutation allowed the disease to pass from apes to humans. Yet the early stigma of a Haitian origin lingers in the public mind. Haiti is seldom treated with the seriousness Haitians feel they deserve.

The slow response of the richer nations to help Haiti after the earthquake seems to make its citizens conclude that such negative perceptions are so deeply ingrained in other peoples' thinking about them that not even a humanitarian crisis as grave as a devastating earthquake can erase them. By way of example, Pat Robertson, the conservative televangelist, and Rush Limbaugh, the conservative radio talkshow host, attributed the earthquake in Haiti to a "pact with the devil" purportedly entered into by the Haitian people in the late eighteenth century in a bid to defeat French colonizers. These sickening remarks confirm what Haitians think has been typical of and wrong with how the world thinks of them. Some Haitians believe the powerlessness of poor nations like Haiti allows people to get away with such reckless views. *Lè ou malere, tout bagay samble ou*—"When you are poor, everything can be blamed on you"—says a Haitian proverb.

THE ETHICS OF PROMISING

Human beings make promises. Our very existence as social, self-conscious, creative, and productive human beings depends in large part on promises made in myriad forms. Our day-to-day lives are filled with promises, though not all of them are consistently or easily discharged. There is a rationale behind promising. As human beings, our needs and wants greatly supersede our natural capabilities. This leads us, as William Vitek says in his book *Promising,* to "invent artifices to supplant our defects." One of these "defects" is our inability to conceive the future with any clarity or detail. The practice of promising represents an attempt to remedy this problem by allowing otherwise disinterested parties to cooperate with one another in the future.

Ethics concerns the norms and principles groups accept and set forth as proper guides and directives for moral action. Actions considered ethical have peculiar characteristics: objectivity, a generalized or universalized validity, rational intelligibility. All of these become the basis for a shared morality. A very good example of such a universal requirement is the idea that when one makes a promise he or she must endeavor to fulfill it. In fact, making a promise alters the moral or ethical status of the future action. It is generally considered ethical to go through with what one promises and unethical not to, all things being equal.

There is a paradox inherent in promising, however, that makes it a more complex human process than we often imagine it to be and that we must consider before we rush to judge the actions of the nations that reneged on their promises to Haiti. When we promise, what we are doing is boldly asserting that the future will turn out as we say. The paradox here is that it is precisely because we are blind to the future that we are required to predict it boldly through promising and then to guide our lives and the lives of others toward fulfilling it. Hence, the promise demands assertiveness, a sense of commitment and certainty at precisely the point when the promise-maker is least able to give it. This makes promising something of a risky business. Perhaps one reason we make promises in public or to God—as in an oath, the marriage ceremony, or the signing of a contract—is that we do not trust our own abilities to follow through with them without external support. Such ceremonies and public expressions of intent serve to inspire, cajole, and threaten the promise-maker. To promise then, as the nations in this case did, is to commit to an uncertain future, even though one is exposed to unforeseeable vulnerabilities. To fail to deliver on these promises is considered immoral and can lead to loss of one's standing in the global community. Christians understand promises, such as the promises made in marriage ceremonies, to be weighty, and broken promises to be serious moral failures. To fail to keep a promise is in effect to make that promise a lie, to violate one of the Ten Commandments, and thus to invite distrust into all our relationships.

Despite assurances, promises are broken all the time. Broken promises are found everywhere in history and literature. Many times people have decided not to do as they promised due to unforeseen circumstances. In the absence of explanations and in the context of the understanding that countervailing circumstances can lead promise-makers to renege on their promises, we can only second guess why the nations that promised Haiti failed to deliver. Perhaps many of these nations had to rethink their commitment after a more realistic assessment of their own financial situations. With the current economic problems worldwide, few nations are prepared to expend their much-reduced financial resources on projects they don't believe would yield their own distressed citizens much dividend. Bill Clinton indicated this when he tried to offer an explanation for the delay of the nations in releasing the funds they had pledged to Haiti. Clinton said, "I think that they're all having economic trouble, and they want to hold their money as long as possible." Thus the timing may not have worked in Haiti's favor, coming in the midst of a global recession and financial crisis.

The apparent reluctance of the nations to honor their promises could also have stemmed from concerns about how much change the funds could effect in Haiti. They may have bought into the popular view that Haiti was already a mess before the earthquake, and nothing any nation could do would help Haiti get out of this mess. A 2010 article published in the *Washington Post* gave voice to this view: "Development efforts have failed there, decade after decade, leaving Haitians with a dysfunctional government, a high crime rate and incomes averaging a dollar a day." Developments in

Washington and in the governmental circles of the nations that pledged to help Haiti show that while crucial rescue efforts are still supposedly under way, policymakers are still debating "how a destitute, corrupt and now devastated country might be transformed into a self-sustaining nation" before they dole out any money. Whatever pragmatic concerns the nations may have had is not important, ethically. The key issues still remain. It is unethical to promise and fail to deliver. It is immoral not to follow through with the promised response when a disaster strikes a neighboring country and the lives of its people are at stake.

CHRISTIAN VIEWS ON GIVING TO THE NEEDY

Questions about caring for others and what it means to be a good neighbor turn over and over in Dr. Mensah's mind. The parable of the Good Samaritan can lead directly to some key Christian moral principles that can guide the right course of action with regard to the situations presented by the case. The good neighbor in the parable is the one traveler who shows compassion for the man beaten and robbed, even though as a despised Samaritan he was least expected to be neighborly. Those who are nearer neighbors, and more closely related, should have even more responsibilities toward the needy than did the Samaritan.

The general moral practice of fulfilling a promise made is found in all religions. In Judaism and Christianity it underlies covenant, the relationship between God and Israel, and between Christ and the church. Covenant is a reciprocal set of promises: Israel promised fidelity to Yahweh, and Yahweh promised to protect and be with the Chosen People; the church promises to follow Jesus the Christ, and Christ promises to be with the church and guide it. Most Christians make promises at baptism specifying their role in the covenant.

In addition to the moral practice of fulfilling promises in Christianity, there is a strong Christian tradition of help—giving, caring about others, and demonstrating faith through kind actions. These actions are considered to be important obligations of Christians. Some biblical references can serve as useful reminders here:

- "What good is it, my brothers, if someone says he has faith but does not have works? Can that faith save him? If a brother or sister is poorly clothed and lacking in daily food, and one of you says to them, 'Go in peace, be warmed and filled,' without giving them the things needed for the body, what good is that? So also faith by itself, if it does not have works, is dead" (Jas 2:14–17).

- "Bear one another's burdens, and so fulfill the law of Christ" (Gal 6:2).
- "Let each of you look not only to his own interests, but also to the interests of others" (Phil 2:4).
- "Do not neglect to do good and to share what you have, for such sacrifices are pleasing to God" (Heb 13:16).

Christian sources supporting compassionate care for the needy are not limited to scripture. The history of Christianity is full of Christian institutions created to care for the needy: hospitals, foundling hospitals, orphanages, and more recently, nursing homes. Christian monasteries and convents historically fed the poor, sheltered travelers, and cared for the sick and dying. In the modern age, Christian churches not only have food pantries and soup kitchens for the poor but have spun off organizations that build housing for low-income families both in their own neighborhoods and in other countries. Many NGOs working in poor nations around the world are Christian in origin.

Thus, even if countervailing situations create a cause for concern about the promise, should the weight of such Christian teachings and practices about helping one's neighbor not be heavy enough to move these nations forward? These reminders also prompt an important question for which each of us must seek an answer: Did we as Christians do as much as we could to help our next-door neighbor in need, or did we allow stereotypes to keep us from lending a hand?

CHRISTIANITY AND OTHER RELIGIONS

The treatment of Vodou by some Christian figures in the press in the wake of this disaster should be an embarrassment to all Christians. Christianity has a long history of exclusivism, of teaching that salvation is limited to those who profess Jesus Christ. Although theologians in the Catholic tradition as early as the fathers of the Church and continuing through to the modern period have identified baptism of blood and baptism of desire[1] as two ways that non-Christians can be saved, the general teaching has been that there was no salvation outside the church. While several Christian denominations, including the Anglican Church in its catechism, continue to teach exclusivism, during the twentieth century the Catholic Church (in

---

[1] Baptism of blood is the baptism attributed to unbaptized people who voluntarily give their life for the love of God; baptism of desire is baptism attributed to those who turn their heart to God and would have chosen baptism if given the opportunity.

the Second Vatican Council), as well as many Protestant theologians and churches have changed this teaching, recognizing that other religions are not devoid of revelation and that salvation is open to members of other religions. Often, however, this openness is only extended to members of the major world religions (Islam, Buddhism, Hinduism, and Judaism) and not to indigenous/tribal and local religions such as Vodou, which are understood as pagan superstition, not "real" religions. The prevalence in Haiti of Vodou, with its West African roots, alongside the religion of its colonial past, Catholicism, has been one source of prejudice against Haitians and often has been connected to general racial prejudice against those of African descent. Today, all Christian churches have the responsibility not only to denounce any form of racism, but also to instruct their members in respect for all religions that recognize and support both human dignity and the presence in human life of its source, the Divine.

THE HAITIAN ETHIC OF SELF-HELP

In closing, we consider Pierre's decision to go home to help in the rebuilding of Haiti during Christmas. There are antecedents within Haiti to make sense of this moral gesture. Beneath Pierre's decision to go Haiti to help is a fundamental Haitian cultural emphasis on self-reliance and communal responsibility, which runs counter to the widely accepted stereotypes about Haiti and its people as helpless victims of all that has gone wrong for them. The tendency to conclude that Haiti's problems are irresolvable, not only because Haitians do not engage their challenges with rational analysis—as Westerners supposedly do—but also because they lack political maturity, moral will, and economic wherewithal to overcome their existential predicaments, is a result of such stereotypical notions. Pierre reminds us that giving up on their own efforts to solve problems and relying solely on outside help would morally be disempowering. It would be an example of despair, the opposite of the virtue of hope.

Like Pierre, many Haitians calling up reserves of hope have rallied their own resources in the reconstruction effort. Recently, Gabriel Thimothe, general director of Haiti's health ministry, said: "It's not only a matter of money coming from outside sources. . . . We need to train more of our own people to provide good quality care." Thimothe went on to make a case for a new ten dollar tax on visitors to Haiti to fund a $149 million upgrade to the health-care system. "After the earthquake foreign nongovernmental organizations have overrun Haiti, but the country cannot remain reliant on international aid."

This thinking that Haitians can do something to help themselves is a dominant theme in the Haitian religious and moral world in which social responsibility or communal well-being is valued. The common notion that "we are all Bondye's [the high god in Vodou] children, and must always extend our hands in help to one another if we can" underlies the emphasis placed on service to the community as the highest good of Haitian life. In fact, it is through the act of passionately choosing to serve the community that the self finds its authentic expression in Haitian thinking. There is no act that is too much for an individual to undertake if the intended beneficiary is the collective "we" within which the individual finds his or her own being. This sense of obligation to one's community, which almost four centuries ago provided a moral justification for Haitian slaves to rally their resources in pursuit of freedom for all through revolt, is the very source of Pierre's motivation for foregoing Christmas to travel to Haiti to help in the reconstruction.

This case challenges us to consider not only the moral status of promise-keeping on the part of individuals and nations, but also the centrality of compassion for the needy in the gospel of Jesus Christ. In making and keeping promises based on compassion, it is always important that our actions and decisions not be influenced by racism, Christian exclusivism, or despair, but that we keep in mind Paul's wish for all: " And now faith, hope, and love abide, these three; and the greatest of these is love" (1 Cor 13:13)

ADDITIONAL RESOURCES

Astier, Henry. "Voodoo Religion's Role in Helping Haiti's Quake Victims." BBC News. February 21, 2010. Available on the news.bbc.co.uk website.

Cohen, Marc J., and Amélie Gauthier. "Aid to Haiti: Reconstruction amidst Political Uncertainty." Real Instituto Elcano. March 29, 2011. Available on the realinstitutoelcano.org website.

MacGillis, Alec. "From Haiti's Ruins, a Chance to Rebuild a Nation," *The Washington Post*, January 17, 2010. Available on the washingtonpost.com website.

McCarthy-Brown, Karen. "Vodou in the Tenth Department: New York's Haitian Community," in *Beyond Primitivism: Indigenous Religious Traditions and Modernity*, ed. Jacob Olupona, 164–71. New York: Routledge Press, 2004.

Miller, M. E. "Haiti's Wounds," *Miami New Times,* July 7, 2011.

Miller, Talea. "Haiti Reconstruction Aid Falls Short, New Figures Show," January 10, 2011. Available on the pbs.org website.

Nelson, Anne, and Ivan Sigal, with Dean Zambrano. "New Media and Humanitarian Relief: Lessons from Haiti." A Knight Foundation Report. January 11, 2011. Available on the knightfoundation.org website.

Office of the Special United Nations Envoy for Haiti. "UN Special Envoy's Office Releases Report on Aid to Haiti: Analysis Shows 37.8% Disbursement Rate for Haiti Recovery among Public Sector Donors," June 22, 2011. Available on the haitispecialenvoy. org website.

University of Haiti/Tulane University. *Haiti Humanitarian Aid Evaluation— Structured Analysis Summary Report.* January 2011. Available on the drlatulane.org website.

Vitek, William. *Promising.* Philadelphia: Temple University Press, 1993.

Related Videos

"Gallery: Religion & Ethics Newsweekly in Haiti." Episodes. Available on the pbs.org website.

"The Quake." 55 minutes. PBS, *Frontline.* 2010.

PART IV

THE ENVIRONMENT

Case

Oil and the Caribou People

Ron Blanchard had eagerly accepted the invitation from Bill Sanders. As head of social ministries at church headquarters, Bill had invited Ron to represent the church and society committee of their denomination at the clan gathering of the Gwich'in people during mid-June in northeastern Alaska. Ron had never been above the Arctic Circle in mid-summer. The prospect of visiting such a remote place and learning more about Native American culture seemed like high adventure and something good for his social-studies teaching at Western High School in Seattle.

Now that the trip was over, he had to produce a report on the gathering for the church and society committee. Bill Sanders had also asked for Ron's recommendation on proposed oil drilling in the Arctic National Wildlife Refuge (ANWR) on the north slope of Alaska's Brooks Range adjacent to the Gwich'in reservation. Bill indicated that sixteen other religious organizations and thirty-two Native American groups had already endorsed Gwich'in opposition to the drilling. The Gwich'in, it seemed were interested in gathering further support and so had invited Bill to send a representative.

The Gwich'in are Athabascan people with a population in the range of five to seven thousand. They live primarily in northeastern Alaska and northwestern Canada. Legend and archeological evidence support a long human presence on the lands now inhabited by the Gwich'in. Traditionally, the Gwich'in roamed the boreal forests of the region as hunter-gatherers in bands of six to eight families. They lived a harsh life in an unforgiving land with cool summers and long, frigid winters when starvation was an ever-present danger.

Over the last century this rigorous way of life has radically changed by a regrouping in larger social units in small villages. The arrival of the

---

This case and commentary were prepared by Robert L. Stivers. The names of all persons and institutions have been disguised to protect the privacy of those involved.

Episcopalian missionaries, the building of schools, and the acceptance of modern technology, in particular the rifle and snowmobile, hastened these changes. Ron learned that Gwich'in opposition to oil exploration stems from the threat they perceive to their main source of subsistence, the Porcupine Caribou Herd, and to the culture and spirituality they have developed in relation to the herd. The Porcupine Herd, with approximately 123,000 animals, is one of the largest herds of caribou in the world. It winters south of the Brooks Range on Gwich'in lands. In spring a great migration takes place. First the females and then the males trek through the passes of the range onto the north slope, where calving occurs almost immediately, reaching its peak in early June.

The herd migrates to the north slope to take advantage of the rich tundra vegetation in the brief but fertile Arctic summer; to avoid its natural predators, who seldom venture onto the slope; and to gain respite from the hordes of mosquitoes in the winds off the Arctic Ocean. Beginning in late summer the herd makes its way once again south of the range and disperses across Gwich'in lands to endure the winter.

For centuries the herd has been the primary source of food for the Gwich'in's subsistence economy. The Gwich'in have harvested animals from the herd in substantial numbers and developed a culture closely bound to the herd and its migration patterns. The herd continues to do well in this habitat. The Gwich'in, in turn, have survived as a people, though not without considerable hardship.

To prepare himself for the trip, Ron had read scientific reports on the potential effects of petroleum development in ANWR and an anthropological study that described the ancient ways of the Gwich'in. The scientific reports on the Porcupine Caribou Herd were inconclusive, Ron thought. Its numbers had declined in recent years due to natural causes, not oil production. Thirty years of oil drilling at Prudhoe Bay had apparently done no harm to the smaller Central Arctic Herd, whose range included the production facilities. In fact, the herd's numbers had increased in recent years for reasons that eluded scientists. Nevertheless, scientists were concerned. The parts of ANWR slated for drilling, the so-called 1002 lands, were among the best feeding grounds for the caribou. Would the caribou of the Porcupine Herd seek other, less nutritious feeding grounds more populated with predators? One thing the reports made clear was that reproductive success depends on summer weight increase and avoidance of predators. The scientists urged caution.

From the anthropological study Ron learned about the traditional nomadic way of life of the Gwich'in, their main food sources, and their relation to the caribou. He understood intellectually their concern for the loss of both their primary food source and their traditional culture. He was not prepared by his study, however, for the degree to which their traditional culture already seemed to be in jeopardy, something he learned after arrival at the clan gathering. He was not sure he understood enough about these people, the technology of oil, or the ecology of the north slope to make a recommendation on drilling in ANWR. To make any recommendation might well be an exercise in disinformation, harmful to meeting the nation's energy needs, or worse, harmful to these people who had so kindly hosted him for five days.

Throughout his stay during the clan days, Gwich'in tribal elders had been eager to recount the old days and their experiences. Barbara Frank, whose age was difficult to judge, but who looked to be in her seventies, told about the old days and of summer movements in small family groupings. The warm days added nuts, berries, and fruit to their steady diet of moose and small animals. In winter she remembered a harsh life in crude shelters and a diet of caribou and whatever other animals trapping produced. She expressed in deeply spiritual terms the close relationship of her people to the caribou. Although she spoke with nostalgia, she never once urged that the modern comforts of the village be abandoned for a return to the wilderness.

Another elder, John Christian, remembered the coming of the missionaries and the schools they established. He related how his parents and grandparents were attracted to the village that grew up around the church and school. They were fascinated by the new technologies that added a margin to subsistence in the Arctic and by the amusements that brought variety and diversity. His family was subsequently baptized. They abandoned their given names for Christian names and assumed the superiority of the new and the inferiority of the old.

Alongside these private conversations were daily public gatherings with starting times that baffled Ron. It was confusing to have no schedule, no appointed time to begin. Things just happened. The sessions began when the spirit moved and ended when there were no more speakers. Other more experienced visitors dismissed his confusion as "Gwich'in time." There was no set agenda. An elder kept order and transferred to each speaker the large decorative staff that conferred the right to address the assembly.

The general topic for the first public gathering was oil exploration in ANWR. Moses Peters, an important tribal elder, spoke in English and presented his assessment of the situation. He reviewed existing production procedures at Prudhoe Bay and the shipment of oil through the Alaska pipeline. He claimed that operations at Prudhoe Bay had adversely affected the smaller Central Arctic Caribou Herd that summered in the vicinity. He acknowledged the increase in the size of the herd but dismissed it as normal fluctuation. The herd, he asserted, was reluctant to cross the pipeline and did not graze in the vicinity of the wells.

Moses went on to say that the oil companies expect their next big find will be in ANWR. He feared that the one hundred miles of pipeline, four hundred miles of roads, the gravel pits, the production facilities, and the air strips would seriously disturb the migration routes of the Porcupine Herd at a crucial time in its annual cycle. "Caribou survival," he insisted, "depends on being born in the right place at the right time, and all of the caribou depend upon these summer months on the north slope to rest and restore food reserves. It is this period of predator-free resting and feeding that prepares the caribou to reproduce and to survive the winter. I know the oil companies have improved their drilling techniques, but I am still worried."

Moses handed the staff to his daughter, Mary, who added: "Oil waste and the burn-off of natural gas would contaminate the tundra. The caribou would not be able to eat." She concluded with alarm: "We will starve again, as it happened before, but this time it will be worse."

Mary returned the staff to her father, who concluded by saying that they needed to continue to press for the permanent protection of ANWR. "The refusal of the US Congress over the past few years to pass energy legislation that includes developing ANWR for oil is not enough. The oil companies are keeping the pressure up. They are arguing that terrorism and dependency on foreign sources of oil, especially in the unstable Persian Gulf, necessitate opening ANWR. Now that the price of oil has increased, as supply dwindles in coming years, gas-hungry Americans will make known their demands for new sources of supply. Environmentally conscious members of Congress may not be able to withstand all this pressure. We must get permanent protection now. The caribou is our main source of life, our very survival. We can't live without the caribou. All our traditional skills, our whole way of life, will be lost if there are no caribou."

Ron was impressed by the sincerity of these appeals and the efforts of the Gwich'in to secure reliable scientific evidence. He was troubled, however, by some of their conclusions. He also recalled his conversation with Glen Stone, a friend who worked as an engineer at Northern Oil. They had discussed the issues prior to Ron's departure for Alaska. Glen had talked about his own involvement on the north slope at Prudhoe Bay. He painted a rosy picture of the benefits of oil production to all Alaskans. "Oil money," he said, "builds schools, roads, and other public works projects. It keeps personal taxes low and enables the government to pay each resident a yearly dividend. The Native Americans benefit too, perhaps most of all."

Glen went on: "Production at Prudhoe will not continue forever. We need ANWR to maximize our investment in the pipeline and to keep those benefits rolling to Alaskans. Northern Oil geologists say they can technically recover sixteen billion barrels of oil. The US Geological Survey, basing its numbers on what is economically recoverable, has much lower, but still considerable, estimates. There is a lot of oil there, enough for nearly a year's worth of US consumption. Why lock up such a valuable resource? As for ecological concerns of the environmentalists and Gwich'in, I think they are wrong about the effects at Prudhoe. The Central Arctic Herd is in fine shape. Modern construction and containment techniques minimize negative environmental impacts. Believe me, we take great precautions. The Gwich'in have little to worry about."

Glen continued by pressing one of his favorite themes, the coming energy crisis. "Oil, gas, and eventually even coal will be so expensive in the future that we will have to switch to alternatives. Appropriate alternatives are not in place and will require considerable development. In the meantime, we will need all the fossil fuels we can get our hands on. Otherwise, production of goods and services will decline and unemployment increase. It won't take long under those circumstance to unlock ANWR. We can be patient; it's just a matter of time."

Glen ended the discussion by pointing out that other native groups in Alaska, in particular the Inupiat on the north slope, have far fewer problems with exploration than do the Gwich'in. He wondered aloud why the Gwich'in were so troubled but offered no opinion since he had not been in contact with them. Ron wondered too, especially about Glen's evaluation of the scientific evidence at Prudhoe and his claim that oil revenues had benefited groups such as the Gwich'in.

As the days of talk continued, Ron thought he detected something deeper at work. Oil exploration seemed to be symbolic of the invasion of modern technology and the threat it presented to traditional Gwich'in culture. It was an obvious enemy: alien, capitalist, consumer-oriented, and potentially destructive to the environment. What really seemed at issue was Gwich'in identity.

The little that was said about oil exploration after the first day seemed to support this conclusion. Instead, the question of identity dominated public sessions. Speaker after speaker decried the erosion of Gwich'in culture. Some in prophetic voice condemned the erosion outright. Others reflected their own personal struggle to preserve the best of the traditional culture while adopting chunks of modern life.

The speakers focused their concern on language. Mary Peters reported through a translator that in some villages only 20 percent of the children understand the Gwich'in language. She was troubled that the local schools taught English as the primary language and, worse, that some schools ignored native language altogether. For the most part she herself did not speak in English, believing that speech in her native tongue was a mark of integrity.

As he thought about it later, Ron certainly agreed that language was crucial. But the matter seemed to run still deeper. He reflected on the one school in the village that was hosting the clan gathering. It was by far the largest, best-equipped, and most modern structure in the village. Built by the state of Alaska with money from oil royalties, its facilities were state of the art. Villagers could not avoid making comparisons between it and their own humble dwellings.

Even Ron, a total stranger, made the comparison, although he had not taken the time during the meeting to explore the implications. As he thought about it later, it seemed odd that Gwich'in from other villages and non-Gwich'in like himself were not housed in the school but were put up in make-shift tents. He thought about his own backpacking tent and the mosquitoes that were so big villagers were said to build bird houses for them. How much easier it would have been to lay his pad on the floor of the school, away from the swarms of mosquitoes and in easy reach of flush toilets and showers. How much easier indeed! He too could understand the attractions of modern technology.

Ron's reflections returned to the village itself and the things he had observed while hanging out and wandering around. Snowmobiles, while out of use for the summer, were everywhere in storage. Satellite dishes for television reception were common. The table in the laundromat was covered with glamour magazines. The teenagers roamed the village in groups without apparent direction, much like teenagers roam malls throughout North America. Joy riding and kicking up dust on big-tired, four-wheeled vehicles was a favorite pastime.

Perhaps the most obvious symbol of all this was the five-thousand-foot gravel runway that ran like a lance through the center of the village. As the place where visitors, fuel, mail, and supplies entered, it was the symbolic center of town, he reflected.

Although wary of his untrained eye, Ron concluded that the matter of oil exploration on the north slope was also a matter of the invasion of an alien culture and ideology. Yes, saving the caribou herd was important. Yes, teaching the kids the language was also important. But the deeper questions in these deliberations seemed to be, How can caribou and language survive the onslaught of modern technology and thought? How can a traditional people maintain its identity when much that is attractive to them comes from a more powerful and alien culture and seems to make life easier and more interesting? The problem for the Gwich'in was not just the oil on the north slope. It was also the school, the runway, the motorized vehicles, the glamour magazines, and maybe even the churches.

The Gwich'in gave the last days of their gathering to stories of flight and return. A procession of witnesses including Mary Peters testified to the horrors of migration to the outside. Lost identity, alcoholism, drug addiction, a final bottoming out, and then a return to roots were common experiences. For each witness, Ron wondered, how many were lost in the bars of Fairbanks?

Ron had been impressed with the integrity of those who testified. They were no longer innocent about modern culture. They seemed to have returned much stronger for their trials and with a healthy respect for their traditions, the land, and the ambiguities of their situation. Perhaps these survivors and their children were the hope for a future that would be both easier and more satisfying. Maybe a new and stronger identity was being forged right before his eyes. He was moved to tears by Mary Peters's concluding remarks, this time in English: "It is very clear to me that it is an important and special thing to be Gwich'in. Being Gwich'in means being able to understand and live with this world in a very special way. It means living with the land, with the animals, with the birds and the fish as though they were your sisters and brothers. It means saying the land is an old friend and an old friend your father knew, your grandmother knew, indeed your people have always known. . . . We see our land as much, much more than the white man sees it. To our people, our land really is our life."

Ron's attention turned to the present and his report and recommendations to the church and society committee. Should he merely report what he had seen and write in pious, uncritical generalizations? Despite his ignorance as an outsider, should he try to state his misgivings about what is happening to this alien but very rich culture? Should he accept Glen's optimistic assurances about environmental impacts and the benefits or mention the Fairbanks taxi driver who condescendingly observed that the controversy over ANWR was so much Indian smoke and mirrors to exact higher royalties from the oil companies? Should he recommend that the church support further oil exploration on the north slope or take up the cause of the Gwich'in, feeling as he did that more was going on with these people than the dispute over exploration? And how should he factor in his own strongly held attitudes about social justice for traditional peoples and his conviction that Americans were consuming far too much energy in the first place?

Commentary

Under similar conditions fifty years ago North Americans would have ignored this case. Led by oil companies and backed by federal, state, and local governments, they would have moved in to tap the resource with little hesitation. They might even have done to the caribou herd and the Gwich'in what they did to the buffalo and the Plains Indians. The Gwich'in would have been silent, and observers such as Ron would have noted little out of the ordinary, much less questioned their powers of discernment.

Today corporations and government are often more sensitive, a new breed of environmentalist is crying for the preservation of species and ecosystems, the Gwich'in are speaking out, and observers are questioning their own assumptions. Oil demand remains high, however, and with the depletion of reserves this demand may have the last word.

AN ETHIC OF INTEGRITY

To understand this case, a new appreciation of an old virtue, integrity, is helpful. The word integrity comes from the Latin *tango,* meaning "to touch." The past participle of *tango* is *tactus.* Add the preposition *in,* and the English word *intact* emerges. Further consideration yields other relevant related words such as *integration* and *integer.*

The Christian tradition speaks of the immanence of God, of the God who is revealed in Jesus Christ and continues to relate to the world through the Spirit. In an ethic of integrity, God is the power of integrity that creates and sustains in three distinct but related dimensions of existence: (1) personal integrity, (2) social integrity, and (3) nature's integrity. Jesus Christ is the embodiment of God's power of integrity and points to the experience of inner wholeness or integration that is God's primary work with humans.

Personal integrity, the first dimension, involves an inner harmony that is the foundation and source of inspiration for an outer harmony that seeks a consistency between act and intention. God's integrating power of love creates internal harmony in the self when the self is receptive. This internal harmony also creates the spirit and will to respond with love and justice. The relationship of God and the self that produces internal harmony is called faith. It empowers and frees the self to act in accordance with intentions.

For Christians, intentionality is informed by norms derived from the Bible, the traditions of the church, and the personal experience of the Spirit. Sin is the power of disintegration that blocks integrity. Sin results from the refusal of the self, others, or the community to receive the power of integrity and is experienced as something done to a person or something the person does willfully. The continuing power of sin prevents the full realization of integrity. The presence of God in the midst of sin provides the resources for partial integrations and the assurance that the full realization of integrity is God's final aim. Integrity is dynamic, something that is partially realized, lost, to be hoped for, and received again.

Personal integrity is part of Mary Peters's reluctance to speak English in the public gatherings. She apparently sees speaking in her native tongue as an important element in the reinvigoration of Gwich'in culture and wants to match her words and deeds.

Ron Blanchard's personal integrity is also an issue in this case. Given his limitations as an observer, how is he to report his experience and make recommendations so that his intentions for the well-being of the Gwich'in, his own society, and the Porcupine Caribou Herd are realized?

Finally, personal integrity is a matter for everyone. In this case it involves knowledge of the issues, accurate understanding of the history of Native Americans, and sensitivity to finding one's way in a different culture.

Social integrity, the second dimension, is the harmony of act and intention in a community. Communities have integrity when peace and justice are foundational ethical concerns. While communities have fewer resources than individuals for receiving and acting on the power of God's integrity, peace and justice are deep wellsprings. To the Greeks, justice was the harmony of a well-ordered community where equals were treated equally, unequals unequally. For the Hebrews, *shalom* and righteousness resulted from keeping the covenantal relation with God and following the guidelines of the law. They included a special concern for the poor. For both Greeks and Hebrews, peace and justice fed on each other and together nourished social integrity.

Christians melded Greek and Hebrew traditions, emphasizing basic equality in Christ and seeing in the person of Jesus the model and the power for both peace and justice. These understandings of peace and justice have developed further in Western traditions with the norms of equality and freedom. Persons should be treated equally and left free unless some ethically justifiable consideration justifies a departure from equality or freedom. Such departures, when adequately justified, are called equity.

From the seventeenth and eighteenth centuries came the notion of rights as a further development of the norm of justice. Rights are a human way of giving greater specificity to equality and freedom. One of the best examples is the Bill of Rights found in the US Constitution. At first only a few enjoyed rights. As time went on, rights were extended to ever more groups, for example, minority groups and women. Today some would extend the concept of rights to animals and plants. So, for example, animals have a right to be treated with care and the right to have a clean habitat. In the thinking of those who maintain that animals have rights, the caribou in the case have a right to their feeding grounds in ANWR.

While peace and justice are the spiritual and ethical foundation of social integrity, they presuppose the provision of sufficient consumption. The equal sharing of poverty can be as disintegrating as war and injustice. The definition of basic sufficiency is notoriously difficult, of course. Clear in the extremes of absence and excess but vague at the margins, the concept of sufficiency is useful for setting floors to poverty and discriminating about levels of consumption. As the commentary on the case "Rigor and Responsibility" makes clear, the norm of sufficiency establishes a floor below which a just society does not let its members fall. On the upside, it calls into question nonsustainable consumption and efforts to justify environmentally destructive consumption. Sufficiency applies to plants and animals as well. They too need what is necessary to sustain their evolutionary trajectory.

Basic also to peace and justice are elements of a common culture. No society can long remain integrated without some minimum of shared understandings, symbols, values, and traditions. A culture can become so fragmented by invasion from without or conflict within as to lose its identity.

A consideration of social integrity is central to this case. From the side of the Gwich'in, the integrity of their culture appears to be in jeopardy. Their way of life depends on the land and their subsistence on the Porcupine Caribou Herd, which needs its special summer habitat in order to flourish. Their identity as a people depends on the maintenance of their language and respect for their traditions. Sensitivity to their situation calls for an understanding of the difficult changes they are facing, changes from the outside that may be too rapid for them to preserve that basic minimum of common culture.

From the side of the wider North American society, the Gwich'in and other native peoples deserve respect. In Christian perspective, this respect stems from the love of neighbor that stands at the center of the tradition and the norm of justice. There is also a need to address the dependency of industrial societies on the consumption of copious amounts of energy. Can such consumption be justified on grounds of economic sufficiency? Is it sustainable? Is it really integral to North American identity? These are questions North Americans should address before drilling begins in ANWR.

The third dimension is the integrity of nature. While human integrity and nature's integrity are separated in many people's minds, they are related because humans are a species in nature like any other species. All species must use nature as a resource to survive. The human species and other species are distinct because other species do not exercise intentionality, at least not in the same way or to the same degree. Therefore, it is incorrect to speak of a harmony of act and intention, justice, or sin in the rest of nature. These terms apply to humans. Still, the concept of integrity may be even more relevant to nature, considering the root meaning of the word.

The integrity of an ecosystem or species is its intactness, its capacity to evolve dynamically or sustain itself so that a variety of individuals and species may continue to interact or fit together. What comes first to mind is a pristine (untouched) wilderness. This is too static a concept, however, and today a rare exception as humans have made themselves at home in an ever greater number of earth's ecosystems. Rather than some abstract, pristine ideal, it is better to speak in terms of the norm of sustainability. This norm allows for human participation in and use of nature without endorsing activities that cause the disintegration of systems and species. Such activities should be named for what they are—sin.

Maintaining the integrity of ecosystems is not solely a prudential matter for humans. Nature in biblical understandings has more than use or utilitarian value. It also has intrinsic goodness, at least in the understandings of the writers of Genesis 1, where God sees nature as good independent of humans, and in Genesis 9, where God makes a covenant with all of creation. In Christian perspective, nature is much more than a resource, or backdrop, or something to be overcome. Nature is to be cared for ("till it and keep it" in Genesis 2:15) as Jesus himself cared for others and sought their fullest realization. Humans are called to be good stewards in the image of God as that image is revealed in Jesus Christ, a concept discussed more fully in the "Sustaining Dover" commentary. God will eventually redeem the whole creation (Rom 8). Nature's integrity is represented in this case by the Porcupine Caribou Herd. Oil drilling in its summer range has the potential to degrade habitat critical to the herd. The integrity of the herd is threatened and with it the social integrity of the Gwich'in.

ENERGY AND AMERICAN INTEGRITY

The era of cheap and abundant energy is almost over. The fossil fuels (oil, gas, and coal) that currently support industrial societies are being depleted rapidly and are not renewable. Oil and gas will be in short supply and very expensive sometime in the next century. Already production at Prudhoe Bay adjacent to ANWR is declining and will be a mere trickle of its former self by 2015. According to a recent report by the US Geological Survey, economically-recoverable coal reserves may only last another one hundred and twenty-five years due to increased consumption. Of great concern with fossil fuels, however, are their serious drawbacks, notably air and water pollution, degradation of the land, global climate change, and eventual depletion.

Global climate change is particularly troublesome. Fossil fuels are decomposed organic matter that grew millions of years ago. When burned, fossil fuels produce a variety of gases that pollute the air. They also produce nontoxic carbon dioxide (CO_2), the levels of which in the atmosphere have increased 20 percent in the past forty-five years. They continue to rise rapidly. The vast majority of scientists think that increasing levels of CO_2 and other so-called greenhouse gases will result in a temperature rise of four to ten degrees Fahrenheit by 2100. They say average global surface temperatures have already risen over one degree over the past century.

Evidence of warming is now available, including retreating mountain glaciers, a thinner arctic ice pack, animal and plant shifts, rising ocean levels, and heat-damaged coral reefs. Scientists are not altogether clear what will happen if this increase continues unabated, but some predict the inundation of low-lying areas, more extreme weather events, hotter summers with more drought, and more heat-related illnesses and deaths. A minority of scientists disputes the theory of global climate change and dismisses the evidence as natural variation.

In terms of supply, the prospects for nuclear energy are brighter, but the environmental impacts of present technology are as bad as or worse than those of coal. Energy from the fission of heavy atoms is more or less on hold because of economic costs, continuing concerns about safety, the threat of terrorist attack, and the vexing problem of waste storage. Energy from the fusion of hydrogen atoms holds great promise but may never be commercially available due to the difficulties and dangers of containing the great temperature and pressure necessary for a sustained reaction to take place. It is also likely to be very expensive.

Unless fusion is harnessed at a reasonable cost, nations will eventually need to meet their energy needs from sources that are sustainable over a long period of time, essentially renewable resources. Solar power is frequently mentioned is this regard. Conservation, the name given efforts to save energy either by cutting back or by producing with greater efficiency, will also be essential.

The realm in which renewable sources of energy and conservation reign will be markedly different from the present realm where economic growth, as measured by the Gross Domestic Product, governs. Sustainability and sufficiency will necessarily guide energy decisions, not growth, at least not growth of energy and resource-intensive production and consumption.

Between this realm and the one to come there will be a difficult period of transition that is already beginning and whose duration is difficult to predict because the rate of technological innovation cannot be known. The realm to come can be delayed if limits to growth are aggressively attacked with the so-called technological fix, that is, a commitment to find technological solutions to resource constraints.

Certainly new technology will have a role to play, but if the shape of human communities and the distribution of costs and benefits are disregarded in the rush for technological solutions, the new realm will hardly be worth inhabiting. Groups like the Gwich'in, if they can continue to exist in such a climate, will be peripheral. Social scale will be large and structure complex, with hierarchical, centralized, and bureaucratic administration. Materialism accompanied by great disproportions of wealth will continue as the reigning philosophy. In short, social integrity will be under severe pressure from the demand to find "fixes" and to pay those who can.

Alternatively, a society geared to renewables and conservation will bring pressure on everyone to live sustainably and to be satisfied with basics. It will be a society where appropriate scale, simplicity, a greater degree of decentralization, and greater equality will prevail.

Energy choices are social and value choices. If a critical mass of North Americans decides on lives that consume large amounts of energy and natural resources, or alternatively, to live sustainably, it will simultaneously choose the economic and political structures to organize and sustain such decisions.

The decision to explore for oil in ANWR is thus much larger than meets the eye when technological and economic calculations are the only factors. In its largest dimension the question is, What kind of society do present stewards of the earth want for themselves and their children? And beneath this lurks the basic question of social identity and character. Who are North Americans as a people? What should be the center of their common culture?

The question of basic identity goes even deeper. In the commentary on the case "Rigor and Responsibility," two normative Christian traditions governed the analysis—rigorous discipleship and responsible consumption. The amount and style of energy consumption currently enjoyed by North Americans are difficult, if not impossible, to justify in terms of either tradition. Energy sufficiency can certainly be endorsed and a case made for oil as necessary in any transition, but the unnecessary and wasteful consumption of the present not only violates the norm of sustainability but also the model of frugality and simplicity seen in the person of Jesus Christ.

In sum, Christians will have difficulty justifying exploration in ANWR even before they consider environmental effects. Yes, oil will be needed in the transition to a more sustainable society, but until North Americans reduce their high levels of consumption and consider their identity in a world of limited resources, all the oil in ANWR will make little difference. The worst possible outcome stares them in the face: further depletion of oil reserves, no long-range alleviation of supply problems, and the possible loss of the Porcupine Caribou Herd with its consequent impact on Gwich'in culture.

THE CURRENT ENERGY DEBATE

Today, two primary visions of energy futures vie with each other to dominate the direction of US energy policy. The traditional vision behind recent Republican Party initiatives calls for increasing the supply of energy and would assign large corporations the primary task of finding new sources and generating power. Advocates of this vision assume technological innovations and market mechanisms will overcome resource limits and pollution problems. Willing to entertain a few conservation measures and endure limited environmental regulation, these advocates hold out for a minimum of government intervention in markets. Their vision of the future is largely economic. In their vision economic growth will provide ample wealth for every person as long as the nation stays the course of market capitalism. Drilling for oil in ANWR follows easily because human economic good takes first priority.

In contrast, a new vision of a sustainable energy future with broad support in the environmental community has emerged. Its proponents see government and the corporate sector cooperating to provide sufficient energy supplies while protecting the environment. They recommend dispersed and less intrusive technologies and a more equitable distribution of income, wealth, and power. They are more ecocentric as opposed to anthropocentric and focus on environmental limits to continued economic expansion. They would not drill for oil in ANWR.

GWICH'IN INTEGRITY

The view of the Gwich'in in this case is through the eyes of a nonnative on a short stay who is unfamiliar with their culture and has no formal training as an observer. Any one of these limitations might skew his observations.

While caution is warranted, a few things are clear. First, the Gwich'in are deeply concerned about the Porcupine Caribou Herd for reasons of subsistence and social integrity. Their history is tied nutritionally and spiritually to the herd. Were the herd to lose its integrity, the Gwich'in would receive another rude shock to their identity.

Second, Gwich'in culture, like most native cultures in the Americas, is in jeopardy. Ron wonders whether there is enough common culture left to maintain social integrity. The Gwich'in worry about this too but also express words of hope and show signs of reinvigoration.

One way to approach the situation is to advocate closing ANWR to exploration and to pursue a policy of disengagement, leaving the Gwich'in to work out their own future. Such an approach has its attractions, given past injustices. The perceived need for oil, the many linkages between cultures in Alaska, and the intermingling of peoples on the land, however, make disengagement all but impossible.

Alternatively, policymakers could continue to pursue the two patronizing approaches that have governed US policy in the past. The first of these two approaches pictures Native Americans as backward savages in need of superior Western technology, social institutions, and culture. While still widely held, this picture must be dismissed outright and confession made for the expropriations, massacres, and deceptions it has promoted. The chapter on the domination and elimination of Native Americans by people of European origins is one of the ugliest in the annals of world history.

The other traditional approach is to idealize Native Americans as "noble savages." This idealization, while more sensitive than the first, leads to confusion about native care of the land, the moral superiority of native peoples, the ease and comfort of nomadic life in a harsh climate, and the place of native religions in modern technological society and in the environmental movement.

The Gwich'in have a different—not a superior or inferior—way of life. They are a shrewd and politically interested community of people who have learned how to negotiate from strength. They know of the potential monetary rewards of oil production in ANWR. They know that the Porcupine Caribou Herd is resilient and that the environmental consequences of oil production at Prudhoe Bay are not altogether clear. They know they have political support in the rest of North America, and they know how to use it. They know as sub-Arctic people that they have different political interests than the Inupiat on the north slope. They know that northeastern Alaska is no Eden.

How then should North Americans view the Gwich'in? Most appropriate is a perspective that begins with respect and exhibits a concern for their social integrity. Included should be a frank recognition that a conflict continues between two cultures, the one closely linked to a subsistence way of life on land, the other more powerful, linked to modern technology and capitalistic economic organization.

Traditionally, the Gwich'in were hunter-gatherers who long ago migrated from Asia and settled in the sub-Arctic south of the Brooks Range in Alaska and the Yukon and Northwest Territories in Canada. They subsisted directly off the land, primarily on the Porcupine Caribou Herd, which they harvested in sustainable numbers. Life was difficult, but the people were resourceful. They relied on sharing, the extended family, and respect for the wisdom of others, especially elders.

Necessarily, they had a special relation to the land and to its flora and fauna. To the Gwich'in, the land is sacred. It is inalienable. It cannot be bought or sold but is held in common as the basis of subsistence. Subsistence is much more than a way of securing food. It is a productive system that entails living directly off the land and demands the organized labor of practically everyone in the community. There are countless tasks in a subsistence economy, each requiring specialized skills. Subsistence is also a system of distribution and exchange that operates according to long-established rules. It links the generations and knits the community into a common culture. It is the material basis for Gwich'in values and underlies the relation of the Gwich'in to the land.

Modern industrial society is obviously different, perhaps most obviously in how it relates to the land. Those in modern society are not as close to the land. They do not see it as sacred. They buy and sell it and encumber it as private property. They view it through the eyes of the economist as a factor of production and obtain its produce by selling their labor and purchasing the means of subsistence in markets far removed from the land.

The traditional Gwich'in way of life persists in spite of deep inroads by modern industrial society. Cultures are never static, of course, but the rapidity of the changes, many of which have been imposed, not chosen, have the Gwich'in worried about their future. Imported goods and food; movement into villages under the influence of Christian missionaries; the introduction of schools, welfare payments, and wage labor; and the acceptance of labor-saving and recreational technologies have brought unprecedented and swift changes. With them have come values and methods of social organization quite foreign to native peoples and a sense of inferiority and powerlessness.

That identity and alcoholism are problems is not surprising. The imports from modern society form a barrier separating Native Americans from their traditional cultures. The words of Inupiat Polly Koutchak, quoted in

Thomas R. Berger's *Village Journey*, express this sense of being walled off that also seems to characterize the lives of many Gwich'in:

> I always feel deep within myself the urge to live a traditional way of life—the way of my ancestors. I feel I could speak my Native tongue, but I was raised speaking the adopted tongue of my people, English. I feel I could dance the songs of my people, but they were abolished when the white man came to our land. I feel I could heal a sick one the way it was done by my ancestors, but the White man not only came with their medicines—they came with diseases. What I'm trying to emphasize is that I am one in the modern day attempting to live a double life—and, from that my life is filled with confusion. I have a wanting deep within myself to live the life of my ancestors, but the modernized world I was raised in is restricting me from doing so.

The future of the Gwich'in's subsistence way of life is in jeopardy. Ron Blanchard's account, however, reveals considerable evidence of continuing social integrity. The Gwich'in have organized themselves to defend their interests. A spirit of resistance is expressed in the refusal by some to speak English and in opposition to oil production in ANWR. The Gwich'in recognize shortcomings in their school system and the importance of language to a cultural identity. Younger people are returning to the villages to raise their families. Many seem determined to overcome the ravages of alcoholism. Skeptics might view this evidence as staged by the Gwich'in to impress unsophisticated observers or as a failure to assimilate to a superior culture. In contrast, eyes of respect will interpret this evidence as a triumph of the human spirit.

Nor should the Gwich'in's subsistence way of life be dismissed. Granted the Gwich'in have purchased tools to make that way of life easier and as a result must resort to wage labor. Granted also, they have supplemented their diets with food from the outside, thereby improving nutrition. These actions are not decisive, however. Their subsistence way of life will continue as long as they choose to live in rural Alaska, for the simple reason that a market economy will never produce a sufficient economic base to support them in this setting. Except for the oil, which is not on Gwich'in lands, there are not enough commercially valuable resources in rural Alaska.

Respect for the Gwich'in in their subsistence way of life is important in this case. From the outside it is a matter of justice and recognizing the legitimacy of Gwich'in concern about identity, the land, and the caribou. From the inside it is a matter of economic sufficiency and the maintenance of a common culture.

The Porcupine Caribou Herd is central to Gwich'in integrity. The caribou are the means of continued subsistence. Cultural identity is bound up with the land and the herd. Oil exploration is viewed as a threat to the herd and as another one of those barriers that wall the Gwich'in off from their identity. Respect in this case means listening to what these people are saying.

NATURE'S INTEGRITY

When anthropocentrism dominated discussions such as this, a commentary would have ended with the preceding section or with a short statement of the value of the Porcupine Caribou Herd as a resource for Gwich'in subsistence. Utilitarian considerations dominated analysis. The intrinsic value of landscapes, species, and ecosystems was left out or separated off into the realms of philosophy or theology. This is no longer the case. Analysis needs to be fully integrated and nature's systems viewed as having value of their own.

The issue for the integrity of nature in this case is the sustainability of the Porcupine Caribou Herd, whose survival depends on the preservation of summer habitat on the north slope of the Brooks Range in ANWR. On the one hand, the need to preserve this habitat is symbolic of a more general problem: the worldwide degradation of land and ecosystems that causes the extinction of species and the reduction of biodiversity.

The causes of this wider degradation are complex, but certainly an increased human population that consumes more and uses more powerful technologies is principal among them. Oil exploration and development in ANWR on fragile Arctic tundra is simply another example of behavior that degrades the natural environment, Glen Stone and his safeguards notwithstanding. In some cases, and this may be one, any intrusion whatsoever can be destructive, and humans should probably stay out.

On the other hand, the issue is quite specific: the impact of oil exploration and development on the herd and other species that inhabit the Arctic ecosystem. Exploration itself may be innocent enough if all it means is looking around, overturning a few rocks, probing the ground here and there, and then leaving. Who could object? Producing oil is another matter.

The case itself offers important information about the Porcupine Caribou herd, not all of which bears repeating. According to the US Fish and Wildlife Service, the herd currently numbers about 123,000 animals, down from a high of 178,000 in 1989. Critical to the herd is its summer calving and feeding in areas believed to have the greatest potential for oil discovery. If the herd is displaced from its richest feeding grounds to others where the vegetation is less nutritious and predators are more numerous, the herd may suffer. Less nutrition means less weight gain. Weight gain is critical for the females and is directly related to calf survival and birth rates the following summer. Predators are found in greater numbers to the south in the foothills of the Brooks Range. Presumably the herd would move in that direction with displacement, since this is what occurs in years of heavy snowfall in the prime feeding areas. In good weather years, displacement might have little effect, but scientists are concerned about other years where displacement would add to already bad conditions and put the herd under stress.

The more than thirty years of experience with the Central Arctic Herd at Prudhoe Bay is the only evidence that scientists have to predict effects on the Porcupine Herd in ANWR. The Central Arctic Herd numbers about 32,000 animals. It grew rapidly in the late 1970s and early 1980s. After 1985 the ratio of calves per one hundred cows dropped, more so in areas in the herd's western range near oil production at Prudhoe Bay. More recently, the herd's numbers have been increasing. Scientists are cautious about these data, however. There is no long-range information on numbers or calf/cow ratios. The estimates of herd size are based on aerial surveys. Natural fluctuations in ratios and size are to be expected, and without base-line date, causes of short-range fluctuations are difficult to determine. The data suggest little impact but are not conclusive. Until more data are gathered, scientists are reluctant to make predictions on the basis of trends in the Central Arctic Herd.

Scientists have arrived at several significant conclusions, however. The Central Arctic Herd avoids humans, roads, and production facilities at Prudhoe Bay, the females more than the males. In other words, production facilities displace the herd. Also, the herd as measured by calf density is in worse shape the closer its animals are to production facilities. This is the evidence that worries scientists and the Gwich'in, for displacement in ANWR would drive females to less favorable calving and feeding grounds.

PERSONAL INTEGRITY

Mary Peters's reluctance to speak English in public gatherings is probably difficult for most North Americans to understand. English is, after all, the main language of international communication, not to mention the language of common culture in the United States. If Mary's first priority is to get the Gwich'in's message out to observers such as Ron, it would behoove her to communicate directly instead of through an interpreter.

Mary is, however, speaking to her own community as well, and it is probably more important for her to establish her own integrity within the community before she speaks to outsiders. Whatever else, her reluctance to speak English should not be viewed by outsiders as a snub or as culturally backward. To expect Mary to give up what is central to her culture and her own identity is the epitome of cultural imperialism. Mary's act is in keeping with her intention to reinvigorate Gwich'in culture.

As for Ron Blanchard, he must decide how to word his report and what to recommend concerning oil exploration and production in ANWR. Personal integrity depends on receiving God's power of integrity. Ron's first act should be a prayer for openness and discernment.

Ron might next reconsider his intentions. The case makes clear that he is troubled by the threats to Gwich'in social integrity. The disintegration of the Porcupine Caribou Herd would threaten their subsistence way of life and arrest efforts to reinvigorate old traditions. Ron is no doubt aware of the tortured history of Native Americans in post-Columbian North and South America. Under the norm of justice with its concern for the poor and oppressed, he might well give the Gwich'in the benefit of the doubt about their motivations, their reading of the scientific evidence, and the political nature of their appeal. He should be careful not to cloud his judgment with patronizing illusions about Gwich'in nobility, however.

The case also reveals that Ron has convictions about excess energy consumption. He listens carefully to Glen Stone, who is convinced that energy sufficiency for North Americans is at stake, but does not appear to be swayed.

The evidence on the threat of oil production to the integrity of the caribou herd should also be a consideration. If he is perceptive, Ron will pick up the caution of scientists who have studied the possible consequences. The lack of conclusive evidence should lead him to be cautious himself. No longer, he might conclude, can an ethic that considers only human integrity control outcomes. He should also remember that the Porcupine Caribou Herd has intrinsic value as part of God's good creation.

Finally, Ron will want to bring a special awareness to his decision, an awareness that applies to any visitor to a different culture. Ron is not alone in his lack of understanding of Gwich'in ways or training in methods of observation. In such situations humility about one's own capacities and respect for the integrity of others are paramount virtues. He should be careful to qualify his recommendation with an admission of his own limitation. He should also be prepared to do more studying and listening and to look at his own consumption of energy.

What Ron decides to do with his observations is finally his responsibility, as it is the responsibility of every visitor to other cultures. Ethical analysis can pave the way to good decisions, but good character and personal integrity are needed to translate analysis into good actions.

CONCLUSION

The case against exploration and production in ANWR is strong. It rests on three pillars: (1) respect for Gwich'in social integrity, (2) respect for nature's integrity, and (3) the failure of North Americans to curb their energy appetites. The case may not be as strong as it seems, however. ANWR is not on Gwich'in lands or even in the same ecosystem. The main link of the Gwich'in to ANWR is the Porcupine Caribou Herd. If it can be demonstrated beyond a reasonable doubt that oil production represents little or no threat to the herd, then Gwich'in integrity is not threatened and the first two pillars fall. Should North Americans curb their demand for energy and thereafter use the oil in ANWR to fuel the transition to sustainable energy consumption, then the third pillar crumbles.

For the moment, however, the three pillars stand. The effects on the herd are not clear, the herd is central to Gwich'in integrity, and North Americans have yet to make a determined effort to change their habits.

ADDITIONAL RESOURCES

Bass, Rick. *Caribou Rising*. San Francisco: Sierra Club Books, 2004.

Berger, Thomas R. *Village Journey.* New York: Hill and Wang, 1985.

Brown, Joesph Epes. *The Spiritual Legacy of the American Indian*. New York: Crossroad, 1993.

Duke, Winona. *All Our Relations: Native Struggles for Land and Life*. Cambridge, MA: South End Press, 1999.

Madsen, Ken. *Under the Arctic Sun: Gwich'in, Caribou, and the Arctic National Wildlife Refuge*. Englewood, CO: Earthtales Press, 2003.

Martin-Schramm, James. *Climate Justice: Ethics, Energy, and Public Policy*. Minneapolis: Fortress Press, 2010.

Martin-Schramm, James A., and Robert L. Stivers. *Christian Environmental Ethics: A Case Method Approach*. Maryknoll, NY: Orbis Books, 2003.

Matthiessen, Peter, and Subhankar Banerjee. *Arctic National Wildlife Refuge: Seasons of Life and Land*. Seattle: Mountaineers Press, 2003.

Nash, James A. *Loving Nature*. Nashville, TN: Abingdon Press, 1991.

Nash, Roderick. *Wilderness and the American Mind*. Fourth edition. New Haven, CT: Yale University Press, 2001.

O'Brien, Kevin J. *An Ethics of Biodiversity: Christianity, Ecology, and the Variety of Life*. Washington, D.C.: Georgetown University Press, 2010.

Robb, Carol S. *Wind, Sun, Soil, Spirit: Biblical Ethics and Climate Change.* Minneapolis: Fortress Press, 2010.

Rolston, Holmes, III. *Environmental Ethics: Duties to and Values in the Natural World.* Philadelphia: Temple Univ. Press, 1988.

———. *A New Environmental Ethics: The Next Millennium for Life on Earth.* New York: Routledge Press, 2011.

Smith, Shirleen. *People of the Lakes: Stories of Our Van Tat Gwich'in Elders.* Edmonton: University of Alberta Press, 2009.

US Energy Information Administration. "Analysis of Crude Oil Production in the Arctic National Wildlife Refuge." Washington, D.C.: Department of Energy, May 2008.

Related Videos

"Energy Crossroads: A Burning Need to Change Course." 55 minutes. Tiroir A Films. 2010.

"Oil on Ice." 90 minutes. Bullfrog Films. 2004.

Related Websites

American Council on Renewable Energy, http://www.acore.org/.

American Petroleum Institute, http://www.api.org.

Arctic Power—Arctic National Wildlife Refuge, http://www.anwr.org/.

Gwich'in Steering Committee, http://www.alaska.net/~gwichin.

Gwich'in Tribal Council, http://www.gwichin.nt.ca/.

National Resources Defense Council, The Arctic National Wildlife Refuge, http://www.nrdc.org.

US Fish and Wildlife Service, Arctic National Wildlife Refuge, http://arctic.fws.gov/.

Case

Whose Water?

"How are you going to vote, Mike?" Sheila Bloom asked her husband as he prepared to leave home for the County Commission meeting.

"I'm not even sure that we are going to vote on the issue tonight," Mike replied, knowing the issue she was interested in. "Julie called and said there are so many people who have signed up to talk to the commissioners on the water issue that the commissioners might have to postpone our own discussion and vote at the next meeting, an extra one in two weeks."

As Mike put on his jacket and headed for the front door, Sheila impatiently said, "You know what I was asking—how do you think you are going to vote on it?"

"I still don't know, Sheila. I have to listen to all the different points of view first. That's why I was elected." At that, Mile went out and closed the door behind him.

"Humpff!" snorted Sheila in dissatisfaction. She was concerned for her brother Eli's interests and for those of many of her neighbors. Eli had been hired as assistant manager of the new bottled water plant that was to open in Butler six months from now. He was already deeply involved in overseeing aspects of the construction of the new plant, at which a number of her neighbors, some unemployed since 2008 and no longer receiving unemployment, hoped to work. The plant would employ about one hundred people when it was complete.

But now all that was threatened by a mix of lawsuits that had been stirred up by a coalition of local and national environmental organizations.

Butler is a small city of five thousand in Pendleton County, a rural county of fifteen thousand. Butler, like the county seat, Maysville, and virtually all

---

This case and commentary were prepared by Christine E. Gudorf. The names of all persons, places, and institutions have been disguised to protect the privacy of those involved.

of the county, gets its water from Cimery Lake, a dammed stretch of the Licking River. The year before the state water-testing service had notified the county's water-treatment plant that its water quality had failed to meet state standards for the previous six months. As a result, the county was being officially cited. The County Commission, which oversees the treatment plant, would have six months to file a plan for bringing the water quality up to standards, after which it had eighteen months to demonstrate the effectiveness of that plan.

The reason for the notice of water-quality failure was obvious—the state itself had been cited by the federal Environmental Protection Agency (EPA) for insufficient state water-safety standards two years before, and when the state in response had set new higher standards, a number of municipalities and counties had failed to meet those new standards, including the Pendleton County plant. Most of those municipalities had neither the expensive equipment necessary to test for those pollutants that were either to be tested for the first time or were to be allowed at much lower levels than before, nor the ability to treat them. In fact, one of the problems the state pointed to in Pendleton County's water was excessive levels of chlorine—chlorine that the treatment plant had been putting in the water hoping to knock out some of the things they were now supposed to test for but couldn't. An additional problem was that every spring, following winter runoff, the water in Cimery Lake required a level of filtration to remove manganese that the old plant was not capable of. The new standards would require a completely new state-of-the-art-treatment facility at a cost of over ten million dollars, a figure that was well beyond the county's reach, especially with the county's lower property-tax yield since the real-estate bubble burst in 2008. County and city officials had been stymied about how to become compliant with state demands—until they received the offer from the bottling company.

The bottling company offered to lend the county the funds without interest so the county could build the treatment facility at the current county site and to operate it for the first three years at the current schedule of charges to users, and after that to keep increases under 4 percent per year. In return, the bottling company would build its own bottling plant on adjacent land bought from the county, and, after the county had paid back the loan in water for the bottling plant at current user rates, it would continue to buy water at the prevailing commercial rate. The only concession the bottling company asked was deferment of property taxes on the bottling plant for the first three years of the thirty-year contract. County and city officials had been more than relieved when this offer was made—they had been overjoyed. A free water-treatment plant without a raise in rates, a new industry to give jobs to locals, and, after five years, new property-tax revenues as well! What could be better?

So construction on the plant had begun. And then came the news about legal suits by environmentalists. Sheila was not alone in thinking that any environmental problems down the road should take second place to current problems, like families without income. Eli's situation was especially worrisome. He had been out of work for twenty months when the new job offer came in. He and Betty had used all their savings in addition to his eighteen months of unemployment and her salary as a school-bus driver to feed the kids, to pay the mortgage, and to pay the premiums for health insurance. They were just about to default on the mortgage on their house when an even bigger disaster loomed. Betty had felt a lump in her breast, which a biopsy revealed was cancerous. Only weeks before this diagnosis the eighteen months of COBRA health insurance from Eli's job at the Sara Lee plant had ended. It had been a horrible time. Sheila and Mike had offered their own savings to help, but they did not have enough to pay the mortgage more than a few months, and not enough to make even a dent in cancer surgery and chemotherapy costs.

It was then that Eli got the interview with the bottling company and the job offer. Since his insurance had been lapsed less than sixty days, Betty's treatment was covered under the new insurance, and his new job allowed them to pay up on the mortgage and keep the house. Betty had had her surgery and was well into chemo—things were looking much better for them, and better for many of their neighbors, some of whom had just been hired to construct the new treatment plant and some of whom were hiring onto construction on the bottling plant. And then the news about the court suits had hit the radio and papers.

Sheila helped the kids finish their homework and take their baths, then heard their prayers and put the youngest two to bed. An hour later she was finally getting the oldest, Curt, to head to bed when she heard the garage door and looked up to see Mike come in.

"How did it go?" she asked.

"Come in the kitchen and get us both a cup of coffee while I hang up my coat, and I'll tell you," he replied.

Settled at the kitchen table, Mike began. "I have no idea what will happen, Sheila. I'm not even sure the commission is going to have much say in how this gets settled. It is really a mess. The crux of the issue is that the contract Butler and Maysville signed with the bottling company did not put any limit on the amount of water that the company could take from Cimery Lake. Some of the environmentalists have data that show that in other places, both in the United States and abroad, similar contracts with bottling companies have led to the companies taking so much water from the local reservoir that the municipalities had to buy water from other districts to have enough for their own people. That would be crushingly expensive, considering we would have to construct a pipeline to bring the water in from miles away. Additionally, in our case, since the dam constantly releases water from the lake to keep the Licking River flowing below the dam, a major draw down of the level of water in the lake could dry up the flow of the Licking into the Ohio, depriving all those who depend on the Licking of the water they need—not just the rafting and canoeing businesses, or the sport fishermen, but also the barge businesses docked on the Licking that work on the Ohio River.

"On the other hand, the bottling company seems to have a strong legal case that since constitutionally corporations must be treated as persons, they cannot be limited in their water use any more than any other customer. We have no regulations limiting water use for residents or for other businesses. In fact, Harry Bertram, who has been on the commission for forty years, thinks we signed a contract with the Sara Lee plant back in the 1970s that gave them unlimited water access at the residential rate for fifty years, the life of the contract. Bob Marshall, the town attorney is checking on that. I think we are screwed either way it goes. We are going to be paying a fortune to lawyers to take it to court, and who knows how long it will take to settle."

"What is the interest of the environmentalists in this?" asked Sheila.

"Any significant draw down in the level of the lake would endanger the flow of the Licking below the dam, and that would have an impact on a number of species, a couple of which only exist here. I had never even heard of them, but one is a fish and two are some kind of local frogs," said Mike.

"What will this mean for Eli and Betty?" Sheila asked.

"Who knows?" Mike replied. "The company could stop construction, fire him, and wait out the results of a court fight. Or it can continue construction, open on time, and wait out the decision that way. I have no idea. Eli is not the only person concerned here—all the people with jobs in construction either at the treatment plant or the bottling plant are at risk.

Two weeks later, at a spaghetti supper at the high school held to help raise money to send the band to a competition in Washington, the table Mike and Sheila sat at was deep in debate about the plant and the contract. One of their neighbors, Mary Posey, had just declared that everything would have been fine if the state had not adopted the new water standards. Another neighbor, the Methodist Sunday School teacher Ted Nelton, disagreed. "I don't think so, Mary. Our son is an engineer for the Water and Sanitation Department in Charleston, West Virginia, and he has been telling us for years horror stories about the inadequacies of water treatment plants around the country, especially the little old rural ones like ours. Our treatment plant thought that adding chlorine alone made the water safe. But Tim explained that cities in the United States, even major cities, have had their water loaded with microorganisms that can cause serious disease in humans, such as giardia, because these old systems cannot detect them. There are regular outbreaks of water-caused disease around the country, and over nine hundred people a year, especially those with weak immune systems, die from these, and almost a million get sick. But under the new standards there has to be testing for giardia and other microorganisms. Who knows how many people here have gotten sick or even died because of stuff in the water?"

Mary retorted, "But why do we never hear such things on the news? I have never seen a story on unsafe city water."

Ted's wife Grace leaned forward: "I asked Tim the same thing, Mary, and he said that there are a number of reasons why we don't hear much about it. The really big cases, when thousands of people in a big city get sick from giardia in the water, for example, do make the news, but they are not that frequent. More often, smaller numbers of people get sick, many of them so mildly that they don't go to hospitals. The few who get most sick are often diagnosed without anyone knowing the source of the infection until long after the epidemic is over, and even then the cases are not always connected. Often, these water-borne infections are simply the last straw for persons who are already seriously ill or immune compromised. When they die, their deaths are attributed to their chronic illness. But beyond that, most of these outbreaks are not publicized for fear of public panic. When they do publicize it—and we have all seen this—the water company tells people to boil their drinking and cooking water for a few days because there has been a 'break in the system.'"

David Cook, the local sheriff, addressed Mike: "Mike, do you really think that we have to worry about the bottling plant taking so much water it drains the lake? That is a huge lake! I don't understand it—there has to be some way to prevent the plant from increasing its draw on the plant to that extent. Doesn't the state—and the local commission, too—have to approve the plans for the new treatment plant? Surely there is a limit to how much water the new plant can treat, and at that limit, the bottling plant couldn't take any more."

"Yeah, you would think so, but the way it was explained to us, if that point comes and the company is told it can't have more water, neither could any other user. Further, no new users could be added. That would mean no new homes could be built, no new businesses. It was made plain to the commission that this is a constitutional issue: The bottling company has the same right to water as you or I or any homeowner."

Sheila turned to Mike, "So tell them about some of the things the commission is looking into."

"We have just begun to look at a number of possibilities, but we don't know if any are realistic. The state is giving us some help, but it is over-extended because there are so many counties and municipalities in similar straits. They sent an engineering and accounting team here that did some research and determined that we are treating about 40 percent more water than people are using. When they reported that, we thought we were home free and had enough water after all. But what they were reporting was a *leakage rate* of 40 percent—the old plant sends out 40 percent more treated water than ever gets delivered to users. It turns out that we are only slightly higher than the average in our state, especially in the hilly eastern counties. The same shifts that cause mud-and rock slides put pressure on old pipes, which leak at joints and sometimes even crack along their length. If we could capture that 40 percent lost to leakage, it would give us a margin for supplying the bottling plant without drawing down the lake level or lower-ing the downstream flow," reported Mike. "But fixing the delivery system will be expensive, maybe more expensive than building the new plant. And some of that cost will be passed on to customers—we would all pay a surtax for pipe repair as well as be required to pay for fixing any leaks between the meters at our homes and the spot where we tap into the mains."

"I still don't understand why the environmentalists got into this issue," complained Sheila.

Grace looked surprised, "Well, they were the ones who knew of other ecological problems when bottling plants start draining high proportions of local water. They looked into it here when they read of the new contract with the bottling plant. If Cimery Lake disappears, so will the environment for many local species of animal and plant. But the biggest loss would be the downstream Licking, which actually has two or three species of fish and frogs that have not been found anywhere else. That is the primary envi-ronmental interest in the issue, but those environmentalists were smart and publicized their research on the possible disappearance of the downstream Licking so that the businesses on that stretch of river would know that they had a bone in this dogfight, too. Lot of people who don't take the rights of fish and frogs seriously do know somebody with a business or a job that depends on the downstream Licking."

Just then Sheila's brother Eli walked over and sat down at the table. As he approached, conversation hushed. Eli looked around, "Guess I know what you all were talking about here. I know it's a mess. But the bottling plant is not the villain here. And I don't say that just because I have a job there. The company wants a good relationship with the county, and that's why it was willing to build the new treatment plant on a no-interest loan, so that there would be a solid foundation of cooperation that would lead to renewing the contract again in thirty years. It has complied with the 1988 law that requires non-agricultural, non-thermoelectric users of more than 10,000 gallons a day to register with the state Department of Environmental Protection, even though the company's initial plans call for using considerably less than that. All the workers, and more than half of the management at the company will be local. Do really think we would recklessly overuse the lake and dry up the river?"

When no one else answered, Mike lifted his head. "I'm not sure that what any of us thinks really matters, Eli. Until the commission gets a formal answer from your company about how much water it will need for the next three to five years and what the maximum capacity of the new treatment plant will be, and we get some idea of how much we can draw from the lake in an average year without endangering local species, we won't know whether the county can go ahead with the present plans. If so, could we use zoning in the future to prevent an extension of the bottling plant that would overstrain the new treatment plant? Or would addressing the leakage problem be enough?" At that, the group at the table began to turn in their trays and put on coats, ready to go home. After all, it was a school night.

The following Sunday the local public high school, Pendleton Senior High, played the local Catholic high school, St. Xavier, in boys' basketball—an event that always generated lots of excitement and was guaranteed to draw a crowd. Mike and Sheila sat next to Father Polk, the pastor at the local Catholic parish. He had been Mike's coach when he played basketball at St. Xavier. During half time their conversation turned to the water issue when Father Polk asked Mike what was happening on the County Commission. Mike said that it looked as though the contract with the bottling plant might be continued, but the issue of whether the county could institute a new rate structure that would have higher commercial rates than residential rates, and higher commercial rates for larger users—which could potentially discourage huge expansions of the bottling plant—was still in the hands of wrangling lawyers. He concluded, "The one thing we are all sure of is that all of our rates are going to go up, and go up considerably."

The priest responded: "Mike, this is a county with a lot of very poor folks. Families have lost their jobs, then lost their homes—some of them are living two and three families in two-bedroom homes. The elderly who were already living very simply on Social Security are now trying to support their kids and grandkids on that same check. Water is the gift of God, intended to serve the needs of all. We all have an obligation to see that the poor continue to get water, no matter what the rates are. We have gone through this issue with the electric cooperative. It took us ten years to get its agreement that the poor who are on disability or the elderly who fall behind on their heating bills in the winter will not have their electric and heat cut off. We need to do something like that for water, too, and do it in the planning stages for the new plant."

Mike squirmed a little, then looked up at Father Polk and said: "I have been learning a lot about water and water systems and the role of water in the environment in the last few months. And I have to say that I think we need to be very careful in implementing the kind of program that you are talking about. I don't want the poor to have their heat *or* their water cut off. But a big reason that the price of water must go up is that we do not have a surplus of it, and clean drinking water is becoming more scarce all around the world, not just where new bottling plants are going up. If water is free, or extremely cheap, it is easy to waste it. When I was growing up, we thought nothing of forgetting to turn off the sprinkler at night. It watered the backyard all night long.

"After all the kids left home, my parents rented out the bottom floor of their home, but after the first two years of offering free heat to the renters, they put in a separate furnace and meter because the heating costs for the whole house more than doubled that first year with the renters—and stayed that high the second year. If it doesn't cost you, then you don't worry about turning down the heat when you go out or go to bed. If heat—or water—is free, people have much less incentive to conserve water."

"But how will the poor be able to pay high rates?" asked Father Polk.

"We need to look at various ways to go," Mike replied. "You know Ben Arabi, the recorder at the courthouse? He told the commission that in some Muslim countries, like Saudi Arabia and Iran, they have different rates for different kinds of use, based on the Qur'anic verses that speak of care of the poor. Residential customers get a certain amount of water, enough for drinking in the average household, at a fraction of its normal cost. Then they get enough for the typical household to wash themselves and their clothing at a somewhat higher but still subsidized level. Any water use after that is charged at the rate that is necessary to cover the cost of obtaining, treating, delivering, and reclaiming (recycling) the water in a closed-loop system. This full-cost rate—that is what we need to be moving toward if the county is not to deplete its water resources below the level needed by the next generation or two. We need a full-cost rate to establish a closed-loop system. You are pointing to the needs of the poor now—but I think we need to think about the needs of those in the next generations too. My kids, and hopefully my grandkids, if I am blessed, will need to have water at affordable rates, too."

Father Polk bowed his head as the teams came back out on the floor and said, "We need to pray that God will take care of the future."

As Sheila and Mike herded their kids to the car after the game, Mike related to Sheila his conversation with Father Polk. "It's all very well to pray that God will take care of the future," he groused," but those of us on the commission need to take care of the present *and* plan for the future. Lord knows we all pray about this, but we still have to make decisions that will affect thousands of people now and more in the future. Does he think we don't have obligations to future generations?"

Commentary

This case ends with Mike irritated that Father Polk suggested praying to God to take care of future generations, interpreting it as an abdication of human responsibility. It is perhaps natural for Mike to be annoyed, given the strain he and the other commissioners have been under. But, in fact, Father Polk had already shown his interest in addressing community problems rather than simply sitting back and waiting for God to take care of them. He had been involved in the campaign with the local utility to prevent the poor who were behind in their bills from having their heat and electricity cut off in winter. In addition, the concern he now voiced to Mike was the need to ensure that the new water rates would neither exclude the poor from access to water nor make it impossible for them to pay for other necessities. By suggesting praying for help in addressing the interests of future generations, he may not have meant to exclude planning for them now. He could be recognizing that such planning is difficult, due to not knowing the conditions that will exist in the future. Prayer can sometimes be an aid to deciding on action, not a replacement for action.

Both Mike and Father Polk voice important values. As Mike indicated, urban planners all over the world are clear that virtually everywhere it will be necessary to have closed-loop systems if potable water is to be available to meet human needs. A closed-loop system is one in which no water is lost; all treated water is recycled, retreated, used, and then recycled, retreated, and used again in a never-ending loop. Various cities and counties in the United States and around the world are already working on three of the most important aspects of progress toward closed-loop systems: solving systemic leakage problems, stopping the discharge of untreated sewage water into streams and oceans, and keeping down the volume of water that needs to be fully treated by separating sewage from storm water. Sewage and storm-water runoff are combined in many places during heavy rains, and the combined volume requires the highest level of treatment in order to become potable. In fact, in many cities the capacity of the treatment plants is overwhelmed during storms so that the excess of combined raw sewage and storm water is discharged into rivers and oceans. If the two waste streams can be separated, the storm-water runoff can be collected, minimally treated, then used for purposes that do not require the high standards of drinking water, such as irrigation in agriculture, cooling in power plants, and lawn watering. Many new suburban neighborhoods have done such separation and require that only "dirty" water be used for watering lawns and washing cars. A number of tests have shown that there are no health dangers in using this "dirty water" to water crops eaten by humans.

But Father Polk brings up another value often understood as opposed to the environmental planning values that Mike advocates. Father Polk's concern is for the poor and their right to water as a basic human need. It is because water is such a basic human need that many issues around water are so contentious. Privatization of water supplies, like privatization of garbage pickup, prisons, and jails, and even some highways, has become increasingly common all over the world. In many places in the developing world there have been riots and political controversies because private companies that replaced municipal services have raised rates beyond the capacity of the poor to pay or have refused to extend water-system services to neighborhoods from which they could not make back their investment in a timely manner. Officials in these corporations understand that their primary responsibility is to their stockholders, unlike municipal services, which must answer to voters. The primary reason for the spread of privatization is that so many municipal governments, like the Pendleton County government in this case, are unable to raise the capital required to invest in replacing or expanding services like water.

The county commissioners are not privatizing their plant, but their contract with the bottling company amounts to a partnership that could have many of these same tensions. In fact, the whole issue of how much water the bottling plant would use in the future may pit the interests of stockholders, who may want to expand the plant in order to increase profits, with the interests of the residents, many of whom are poor or who have businesses or employment that depend upon the downstream Licking River. Environmental interests in preserving biological life in the area here cohere with the interests of many humans.

WATER AS A BASIC HUMAN NEED

What status should the human need for water be accorded? Some respond that because humans require both food and water simply to survive, water is a human right, an aspect of the right to life. The limitation on assertions that water, or any commodity, is a human right is that rights must be enforced, they must be provided by the larger community. Some people, in the form of institutions, must be obligated to provide those rights. In Pendleton County, this is the task of the county commissioners; in most societies, protecting human rights is the task of government—local, regional, or national. But governments have limited resources. Many governments around the world do not have the resources to provide potable water to all of their citizens. As in Pendleton County, government resources are dependent upon tax revenue; poor communities often do not generate enough tax income to meet all their obligations. In fact, privatization of basic services has often been the governmental response to such revenue shortfalls.

Religious responses to water as a basic human need support understanding water as a human right but go beyond this. Christian treatment of the human need for water takes two forms; one is symbolic, and the other is an imperative. Water appears frequently as a symbol in the Christian and Hebrew scriptures and in ritual. Wells and pools figure prominently in bible stories as the center of villages and towns. These wells were public; all citizens used the water to meet their needs for sating human thirst and that of animals, and for washing. Because everyone needed the water in the local well, wells were frequently meeting places. In the gospel Jesus meets the Samaritan woman at the well, and she draws water for him (Jn 4:11–26). Rebecca becomes the wife of the patriarch Isaac when the emissaries from his parents encounter her at the well near her home (Gn 24:11–27). In larger cities, such as Jerusalem, there were not only wells but pools from which residents could draw water for washing as well as drinking and cooking. Jesus heals a man among the many infirm he encountered at the pool of Bethesda in Jerusalem (Jn 5:2–9).

Water in the Christian tradition is a prominent symbol both of washing and of life itself. John the Baptist baptized thousands, including Jesus, in the waters of the Jordan River (Mk 1:9–11). For centuries the Christian ritual of baptism used complete immersion in water to signify the washing away of sin and the emergence of a "new" person, who was often given a new name as a further symbol of his or her new status. Just as babies emerge from the waters of the amniotic sac in birth, so emergence from water has signified new life in the Spirit through baptism.

The symbolic uses of and references to water in scripture reinforce for Christians the intimate relation between humans and water, and inculcate in Christians a sensitivity to water as a universal human need. There are also imperatives—commandments—in the tradition that bind all Christians both collectively and individually to respect the basic needs of everyone. The first commandment of this kind comes in the creation story in Genesis, when God appoints Adam and Eve the stewards of the earth and entrusts them with all the earth's resources (Gn 1:26–31). Through Adam and Eve all humans inherit this stewardship of the resources of the earth. But while God has gifted humans with water and all the other resources of the earth, this gift comes with obligations. Stewardship is not ownership. As stewards of God's creation, humans must manage creation for the benefit of all.

This includes managing water to meet the needs of all. Thus stewardship encompasses both Mike's concern for future generations and Father Polk's concern for the poor of the present day. (For more on stewardship, see the commentary in "Sustaining Dover.")

The second commandment that is directly relevant to Christian understandings of water usage is Jesus' command that his followers love their neighbor (Mt 22:39). This is not simply one commandment among many but the overarching commandment that sums up all the commandments of the Jewish Law under which he lived. When Jesus was asked by those attempting to discredit him which was the greatest of the commandments, he did not cite any one specific part of the Law but instead replied, as had previous great rabbis, that the greatest commandment is the sum of all the others: we must love God with our whole body, mind, and spirit, and love our neighbors as ourselves (Mt 22:34–40). Thus, if we recognize our own need for water and love our neighbor as ourselves, we must acknowledge an equal need in our neighbor.

Nor can we arbitrarily decide who our neighbor is. In the parable of the Good Samaritan (Lk 10:25–37) Jesus taught that the good neighbor was the outsider, one of the despised Samaritans, a group thought to be heretical by other Jews. The Samaritan was the good neighbor because he responded to the needs of the Jew who had been robbed and beaten and left to die in a ditch. Jesus instructed his disciples that the obligation to love our neighbor cannot discriminate between intimates and strangers, even enemies, but requires loving all. One cannot love one's neighbors and allow them to go without water.

BALANCING RESPONSIBILITIES

There is a universal temptation to understand the command to love our neighbor as applying only to the persons in close proximity, those with whom we personally interact, and thus to avoid applying the command in complex social situations. In this case Sheila is tempted by such an approach in that she is impatient with Mike's determination to take all sides into consideration. She insists that priority should go to the needs of her brother and his family, and those of her near neighbors. She is not alone in such an approach, nor is this approach based necessarily in selfishness.

Many persons are intimidated by the complexity of economic and political decision-making and interpret Christian morality as involving only the personal avoidance of prohibited activity such as adultery, theft, or lying. They leave the complex decisions to experts and only become involved in wider political activity when their self-interest is threatened by policies of political and economic experts. But individual Christians in democracies, where citizens have responsibilities for making laws and policies, have an obligation to engage in the process of social decision-making based on their dual obligations to stewardship and love of neighbor.

Social policies involving water are extremely complex, and must differ from place to place depending on local circumstances. In this case the question of what Mike and the other commissioners should decide is not completely open. There are legal issues that constrain their decisions. It is possible that the EPA could become involved and prevent any decision that would endanger the local species in the downstream river. The constitutional construction of corporations as persons before the law, having the same rights as citizens, has served important purposes historically in promoting economic prosperity, but in this case and many others today includes some very real dangers due to the size and wealth of many corporations. Mike seems to think that perhaps the only legal way to prevent the bottling company from expanding its water use to the detriment of the rest of the county is to use zoning to control the size of the plant.

It might be that constitutional interpretations of the status of corporations should be reviewed. It does not seem just that understanding a corporation as having the same rights guaranteed to individual citizens should allow a rich and powerful corporation to usurp local resources that belong to all. Certainly such an outcome seems contrary to all Christian social justice traditions, in which the integrity of divine creation, especially the dignity of humans, must take precedence over all human creations such as corporations.

In the past, water resources in the United States have only been understood as a problem in some limited areas of the nation, mostly in the West, where policies were established to allocate water for irrigation and to balance the rights of upstream and downstream river communities. These policies attempted to implement just water allocations to various human groups but did not take into account the environmental impact on other species or on preservation of water resources for the future. In the next decades policies must be established to deal with these issues and with the increasingly complex new problems around water. These complex issues include many densely settled cities having depleted their underground water table, cities buying large amounts of water from other communities, and regions where underground water tables and surface waters have been polluted. In some coastal places the draw down on the water table from heavy settlement has resulted in saltwater seeping into the water table. While the Clean Water Act of 1972, amended in 1977 and 1987, has vastly improved the water quality of many US rivers and streams, comprehensive law regarding water systems and usage has yet to be developed—and is urgently needed.

Ironically, if Pendleton County did have a closed-loop water system, the issue of bottling plant usage would be moot, because except for the bottled water produced and sold by the bottling plant, all the water from the plant would be used over and over. In this case the county could legislate limits on, or higher rates for, all treated water that is not recycled. In the absence of such a system, Mike and the other commissioners must choose the most just option available, one that best protects everyone's interests.

SOURCES FOR FURTHER STUDY

Alvez, Alejo. "Water as Private Property." *Latinamerica Press* 20 (October 31, 2007), 4.

Arnone, R. D., and J. P. Walling. "Waterborne Pathogens in Urban Watersheds," *Journal of Water and Health* 5, no. 1 (2007): 149–62.

Babak, Alyona, and Vincent Byrne. "Tariff Reform in the Municipal Water Supply." Paris, 2002. Available on the oecd.org website.

Bronsro, Allen. "Pricing Urban Water as a Scarce Resource: Lessons from Cities around the World." In *Proceedings of the CWRA Annual Conference*, Victoria, B.C., Canada. Cambridge, Ontario: Canadian Water Resources Association, 1998.

Eckstein, Gabriel. "Precious, Worthless, or Immeasurable: The Value and Ethic of Water." *Texas Tech Law Review* 38 (2005–6): 963–70.

Florez-Estrada, Maria. "CAFTA Threatens to Turn Water into Merchandise," *Latinamerica Press* 20 (October 31, 2007), 6.

Gudorf, Christine E. "Water Privatization in Islam and Christianity," *Journal of the Society of Christian Ethics* 30, no. 2 (2010): 26–55.

Hall, David, and Emanuele Lobina. "Private and Public Interests in Water and Energy," *Natural Resources Forum* 28 (2004): 268–69.

Mallat, Chibli. "The Quest for Water Use Principles." In *Water in the Middle East*, ed. M. A. Allah and Chibli Mallat. New York: I. B. Taurus, 1995.

Marshall, Liz. "Water on the Table." Available on the wateronthetable.com website.

McKenzie, David, and Issha Ray. "Urban Water Supply in India: Status, Reform Options and Possible Lessons," *Water Policy* 11, no. 4 (2009): 442–60.

Schultz, Jim. "Another Water Revolt Begins in Bolivia," Pacific News Service, December 16, 2004. Available on the newsamericamedia.org website.

Shiva, Vandana. *Water Wars: Privatization, Pollution, and Profit.* Cambridge, MA: South End Press, 2002.

Stivers, Laura. "Water as Earth's Bloodstream or Commodity? Latina Eco-feminist Responses." In *Spirit and Nature: The Study of Christian Spirituality in a Time of Ecological Urgency,* ed. Timothy Hessel-Robinson and Ray Maria McNamara, 201–19. Eugene, OR: Wipf and Stock Publishers, 2011.

Related Videos

"Tap into Prevention: Drinking Water Information for Health Care Providers." Washington, DC: U.S. E.P.A., 2004.

"Water and Life: A Delicate Balance." Princeton, NJ: Films for the Humanities, 1986.

"Water for Tonnoumassé." By Gary Beitel. New York: Filmmakers' Library, 1990.

"When the Water Tap Runs Dry." By Ron Meyer. New York: Ambrose Video Publishing, 2009.

PART V

BUSINESS

Case

Sustaining Dover

I

John Yeoman was relieved to be sitting in the folding chairs instead of his customary seat as a City Council member. "I could get used to just being a regular citizen again," John thought. "It's been a long seven years." In fact, division had been growing among the eight thousand citizens of Dover for more than a decade. When he was first elected to the City Council, the city was still licking its wounds financially after a failed effort to block a large developer from building Sunrise Plaza, a new retail center on the south edge of town. Concerned that the shopping center would harm the downtown business core, the city had denied the landowner's request to rezone the property. After a judge ruled in favor of the landowner, and all appeals were denied, the city of Dover was left with over $85,000 in legal fees. So John's first duty as a City Council member had been to figure out where to cut thousands of dollars out of the city budget over the next few years in order to pay legal bills racked up by City Council members who had preceded him.

Now, at the end of John's second term on the City Council, emotions were running high over the news that Walmart intended to build an 184,000 square foot Supercenter on the eastern edge of Dover. Dwarfing all other stores in the community, including Walmart's 74,000 square foot store in Sunrise Plaza, the Supercenter would be built on thirty-one acres of land, one-third of which had up to now been designated as a flood plain.

James B. Martin-Schramm prepared this case and commentary. While the case is based on actual events, names and places have been changed to protect the privacy of those involved. This case is a condensed and updated version of "Sustaining Dover: Urban Sprawl, Habitat Fragmentation, and Sustainable Communities," in James B. Martin-Schramm and Robert L. Stivers. *Christian Environmental Ethics: A Case Method Approach*, 80–111.

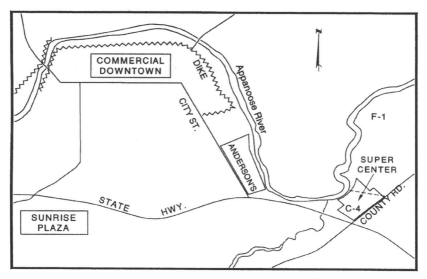

Map of Dover, Iowa

Sitting in chairs reserved for the general public, John had come to attend the last public hearing the Dover Planning and Zoning Commission would hold regarding Walmart's request to fill in the portion of their property in the flood plain and to reclassify the land from F-1 (Flood Plain) to C-4 (Shopping Center Commercial District). Tonight, the Zoning Commission had to make a recommendation to John and the six other members of the City Council who would make the final, binding decision.

Wincing at the thought of being back in the hot seat in a few weeks, John listened as the regional representative for Walmart, Max Walters, began his presentation. Dressed in casual business attire, Walters made three points in his presentation. The first was the news that the Iowa Department of Natural Resources (DNR) had just approved Walmart's plan to bring fill to the site in order to raise the land above the one-hundred-year flood plain level. "I am sure you are as gratified as we are to receive this vote of confidence from the DNR," said Walters, holding the letter aloft. "Once the fill process has been completed, the land will no longer be in the flood plain; our land will be at the level of other commercial establishments in the area.

"Like all of you, Walmart is concerned about the water quality of the Appanoose River, which forms the western boundary of our property. As a result, we have worked with the DNR to design an eight-acre detention basin and riparian buffer zone. These two design features will filter petro-chemical and other wastes from our parking lot so that they do not enter the river. This will probably be the 'greenest' parking lot in the county! To our knowledge, every other parking lot in Dover and the city's forty miles of streets discharge their waste directly into the nearest storm sewer and thus ultimately into the river. In addition, the detention basin and riparian buffer zone will create a small area of wetlands that will create habitat for wildlife. Our plans for the site include a prairie-grass demonstration project, bat houses, and houses for songbirds. Ecologically, we want to do our part to be a good steward.

"Finally, whereas some developers have strenuously negotiated various tax breaks before investing in the community, Walmart will pay for all improvements to our site. We will bring city water and sewer lines to our property and add a turning lane to the county road that feeds the entrance to our store at no expense to the taxpayers of Dover. In addition, we have secured federal funds to provide walking and biking trails to the store. As always, Walmart will continue to be a good neighbor in the city of Dover."

Clapping heartily, Buck Sorensen, chair of the Planning and Zoning Commission, thanked Walters for his presentation and turned the podium over to Clara Laursen, coordinator of the Appanoose River Alliance—a loose coalition of environmentalists, bird watchers, anglers, hunters, and canoeists. Twenty years younger than Walters and a foot shorter, she addressed the audience dressed in khakis and a t-shirt emblazoned with the logo of the Alliance.

"Members of the Zoning Commission and fellow citizens of Dover, the Appanoose River Alliance opposes Walmart's request to fill in and rezone this portion of the flood plain for several reasons. The first and perhaps most important reason is that filling in flood plains destroys wildlife habitat. Habitat destruction is the single most important variable in the loss of biodiversity on our planet. Here in Iowa, more than 50 percent of neotropical migrant bird species have been in decline for the last thirty years. The loss of wetlands and flood plain areas is directly related to the decline of songbirds in our backyards. We would much prefer the wetlands nature provides to one constructed artificially and laced with toxic chemicals.

"Second, flood plains serve as natural sponges that soak up excess water in the spring after snow melts and in the summer after major storms or extended rain events. Without these flood plains, floodwaters are confined to the main channel of the river until they spill over the banks and cause considerable damage to dwellings and agricultural property—especially to communities further downstream. Flood plains are nature's way of spreading out floodwaters so that they do the least damage and provide the most benefit through the dispersion of river nutrients and the provision of wildlife habitat.

"Third, the Alliance is not convinced that Walmart's detention basin and riparian buffer zone will protect the river from contamination by the road wastes collected on its eleven-acre parking lot while also controlling the volume of water from its four-acre roof. It is our understanding that the state DNR is only required by law to consider the effects of a 100–year flood upon the property in question. Left unstudied is the virtual certainty that the detention basin would fail in floodwaters that exceed the 100–year flood level. When we experience another flood of this or greater size, all of the concentrated petro-chemical wastes would suddenly be flushed into the river where they could seriously degrade the quality of the water for fish and other species. We can prevent this by retaining and enforcing Dover's more stringent flood plain standards.

"Finally, given the fact that the state of Iowa has designated the Appanoose as a 'protected water area,' the city of Dover has no right to spoil the natural and scenic quality of the river by allowing a big-box retailer like Walmart to construct a Supercenter right along its banks. Given these concerns, we strongly urge the Planning and Zoning Commission to reject Walmart's bid to fill in the flood plain and reclassify this portion of the land from F-1 to C-4. Any decision otherwise would constitute bad land stewardship."

As the room erupted in applause, Buck Sorensen thanked Clara somberly and then announced that there would be one more presentation before the floor would be opened for public comment. Coming to the microphone now was Tom Bittner, director of Dover Citizens for Sustainable Development (DCSD), a coalition of local merchants, advocates for historical preservation, and farmers in the area committed to community-supported agriculture. A recent college graduate in political science, Bittner cared passionately about sustainable development but had little experience in local politics. Nevertheless, here he was, looking a bit uncomfortable in a shirt and tie, addressing a packed crowd.

"Ladies and gentlemen, Dover Citizens for Sustainable Development is in favor of economic growth when that development is conducted in a responsible manner and contributes to the sustainability of this community. We are not anti-growth, but the construction of a Walmart Supercenter in this flood plain would be both ecologically irresponsible and economically ruinous. This community worked long and hard after the Sunrise Plaza fiasco to develop Dover's comprehensive development plan. As those of you on the Zoning Commission know, that plan designates the downtown business area as a vital commercial district in Dover. In addition, the plan states that protecting the flood plain of the Appanoose River and its tributaries from 'incompatible development' will be given 'high priority.' Walmart's request to build a Supercenter on the banks of the river violates both of these major features of Dover's comprehensive plan. Sprawling development in the flood plain on the eastern edge of town will destroy our downtown, and it will forever end responsible farming in the flood plain. It is your responsibility, and the duty of the City Council, to enforce the comprehensive plan so that these two things do not happen.

"As you know, just the rumor that Walmart was going to build a Supercenter was enough to cause one of the three grocery stores in our town to close. Take a walk down Main Street. Count the number of empty storefronts. Yes, the downtown area survived the initial battle when Walmart moved into Sunrise Plaza, but a Supercenter is too much. It will be the death knell for local merchants, and it will certainly clobber all of the other stores in Sunrise Plaza when Walmart moves to its new store. Just as important, it will be a devastating blow to the distinctive, historic character of our community. People come from far and wide to canoe in the Appanoose, to camp in our campgrounds, and to enjoy the blessings of small-town life that all of us take for granted. The construction of a Walmart Supercenter along the banks of our lovely river is not progress; it is yet one more denial of our heritage and an irrevocable step into the boring homogeneity of American culture. We don't have to be like everybody else. We can control the nature of economic growth in our community. We can harness the power of that economic activity to preserve this community for our children and grandchildren as well as the countryside around us. Members of the Zoning Commission, I implore you: Don't sell our community down the river. Do the right thing: Say no to Walmart!"

Bittner's populist rhetoric struck a chord with many who leapt to their feet and applauded as he left the podium. Watching Bittner return to his seat like a slugger rounding third base, John found himself wondering if anyone in the room supported Walmart's bid to open a Supercenter in Dover. He didn't have to wait long.

Paul Petersen was the first to speak. "Forgive me, Mr. Bittner, but you were probably in middle school when Walmart first came to Dover. We had a lot of 'doom and gloom' rhetoric back then, too, but take a look around. Did downtown Dover dry up and blow away? Is Walmart the only game in town? Hardly. Many merchants downtown are thriving. Things are going so well that the city just spent $3 million on historic preservation and street improvements downtown. Dover has become a major retail hub in this corner of Iowa. We didn't enjoy that status before Walmart came to town."

Dale Murphy, a contractor in Dover, spoke next. He noted that Dover was built in a valley carved out by the Appanoose and that the eastern edge of town was the only outlet for growth in the region. Murphy went on to point out that the city's comprehensive plan acknowledged this reality because it designated this area as a corridor for future growth. "Close that end off, and the town will die. If you're not growing, you're dying," said Murphy.

Speaking next, Charlie Tieskotter commended Walmart for working so closely with the DNR and warned everyone that, if the Zoning Commission or the City Council ignored the DNR permit and denied Walmart's legitimate request to fill in and rezone the land, the city could find itself back on the losing end of a court case.

Last, but not least, Gail Banks addressed the audience. Banks and her husband operate a modest dairy farm on the outskirts of Dover. Speaking forcefully, she said: "I'm tired of people turning their noses up at Walmart. Some of you only seem to be concerned about Dover's historical heritage. I've got news for you. I'm proud of our heritage, but I'm more interested in the present and the future. Maybe some of you can afford to spend extra money on groceries and cleaning supplies, but we can't. We don't buy our clothes over the Internet from Eddie Bauer. We need the low prices that Walmart gives us, and we're not alone. Take a look at its packed parking lot. The reason Walmart wants to build a Supercenter here is because we're all shopping a lot at its current store. It is giving us more of what we want!"

II

Two weeks later John left his Goodyear dealership early, ate dinner with his pastor, and then took a long walk along the river on the eastern edge of town before the City Council meeting that evening. He knew that the vote would be close; in fact, it might come down to him breaking a tie. With a name like Yeoman, he was always the last one to vote.

He rehashed the arguments in his mind. On the one hand, Tieskotter was probably right. If they ignored the judgment of the Iowa DNR and rejected the recommendation of the Planning and Zoning Commission to rezone the land after it is filled, Walmart would almost certainly take them to court and a judge could rule again that the City Council's decision had been "arbitrary and capricious." On the other hand, if they approved the landfill and rezoning request, the newspaper had reported yesterday that property owners upstream and adjacent to the Walmart site intended to sue the city for increasing the danger of flooding on their land. John sighed. No matter what decision they made, it looked like the City Council was going to get sued.

He still didn't understand how the DNR could approve the filling in of a flood plain. Buck Sorensen had been helpful on that score, however, when he reminded him that the DNR's responsibility is to protect the lives and property of the people of Iowa. In this situation they had concluded that filling in this small portion of the flood plain did not produce a significantly increased risk of flooding. But the DNR's decision did not mean that Dover's hands were tied, because the state left final control of flood-plain areas and planning-related issues to local officials. It was up to the City Council to interpret the comprehensive plan and decide whether the Supercenter amounted to "incompatible development" in the flood plain. The problem was that the comprehensive plan did not provide any definition of this key term. The reality was that much of Dover was built in the flood plain and had regularly flooded until the 1930s, when the Army Corps of Engineers built the dikes that now protected the town.

But John still didn't like the idea of passing even more floodwaters along to communities downstream from Dover. Just because a dike protected Dover didn't mean the city shouldn't do something about the floodwaters it could still control. Just as important, he worried about the impact that commercial development would have on wildlife that relied on the habitat offered by the flood plain. Even though John knew that the Walmart land had once been home to a drive-in theater, it had been planted in either soybeans or corn for as long as he could remember. There was no doubt that the land provided habitat to some wildlife, especially near the river. And it *was* beautiful—even with Anderson's big gravel pit and road construction equipment parked on the western bank. How should he juggle his responsibilities to others downstream with his duties to the citizens of Dover? And what about the birds? Who represented their interests? Was this good stewardship of the land?

Having reached the site, John surveyed the 586–acre watershed and knew why it was so appealing to developers. Dale Murphy was right when he pointed out that this was the only area within current city limits that provided the kind of space necessary for large-scale commercial development. There certainly was no other thirty-acre undeveloped parcel available to Walmart elsewhere in Dover. As a businessman he understood the benefits of economic growth, but he also had a personal stake in the matter. It was likely that he would lose a good share of his tire and auto service business to Walmart. And even though he felt up to that competition, he found himself thinking about the impact the Supercenter would have on other business owners.

John also found himself thinking about the impact the Supercenter would have on the community of Dover and the county as a whole. He loved living here. Every year he could count on reading letters to the editor that praised the beauty of the town and the kindness of its citizens. It was true that Walmart's entry into Sunrise Plaza had led some local business owners to close their stores, but several years later the economy seemed strong, and it appeared to John that Dover was a stable and growing community. He wasn't so sure about the other towns in the county, however. The Supercenter's sixty thousand square feet in groceries would exceed the total amount of space in grocery stores in the county outside of Dover. Given the chance to couple savings with the convenience of one-stop shopping, John feared people who now patronized these rural grocery stores would probably take their business to the new Supercenter in Dover.

Finally, was Dover on the brink of losing its distinctiveness? Certainly Dover had changed a great deal since John had arrived twenty-five years ago to enroll at the college in town, but the town still seemed healthy. Fast-food chains had moved in around the same time that Walmart arrived, but Sally's Kitchen was still a thriving downtown eatery for locals and college kids. Lawn-chair nights still pulled big crowds to listen to local entertainment on the steps of the County Courthouse in the summer. And the annual ethnic-heritage festival remained a huge draw for tourists. John found it ironic that one of the parties that had sold land to Walmart's land developer was Dover's museum. Recognized nationally for its unique collections honoring Dover's ethnic heritage, the museum board of directors had realized that the only way it could raise the funds to expand the museum was to sell land that had been given to the museum as a bequest. How do you preserve the identity of a people or a town? At what price?

Commentary

Ethical questions raised by this case are being debated all over the world as cities, suburbs, and towns grapple with the growth of big-box retailers in their communities. While the environmental aspects of the case are very important, there are also significant economic and social issues at stake. This case is not just about urban sprawl and its environmental consequences; it is also about jobs, the character of a major corporation, the heritage of a town, and the quality of life in Dover. Will Dover be a *sustainable* community if it allows Walmart to build a new Supercenter there?

In order to answer this question it is necessary to introduce the much-debated concept of *sustainable development,* a term used since the 1980s to describe development that, according to the United Nations, "meets the needs of the present without compromising the ability of future generations to meet their own needs." Since then people around the world have been examining various ecological, economic, and social goals that need to be integrated in order for life to flourish on earth.

Sustainable Development Goals and Sustainable Community

As an elected member of the Dover City Council, John Yeoman is wrestling with ethical questions related to each of the three key dimensions of sustainable development: environmental integrity, economic prosperity, and social justice. Environmentally, will the Supercenter development diminish habitat for migratory birds and other wildlife? Will filling in this portion of the flood plain increase the likelihood of flooding in the future? Will wastewater run-off pose a water-quality problem for the Appanoose River? The economic questions are also difficult. Will the Supercenter help or harm the merchants in Dover? Is it more important for the Dover economy to grow or for there to be a larger percentage of locally owned stores? On the social front, is it really the case that the character of the community is at stake? When do quaint towns lose their distinctiveness and tourist appeal?

As if these problems were not enough, Dover's comprehensive development plan requires John and the other members of the City Council to prioritize the three key dimensions of sustainable development. The comprehensive plan does a good job of identifying various social, economic, and ecological goals, but it is not clear how these goods should be reconciled when they conflict. The plan calls for protection of ecologically sensitive areas, but it also calls for economic growth that will benefit the citizens of Dover while preserving its downtown business core and the town's unique heritage. It is not evident how these goods should be ordered, and thus it is difficult for John to know what position he should take on Walmart's request to landfill and rezone a portion of the land for the site of the Supercenter.

THE IMPACT OF WALMART

Walmart is the largest retailer in the world. According to the company's website, in 2010 Walmart employed 2.1 million people in over eighty-eight hundred retail stores under fifty-five different store names in fifteen countries. Walmart's sales of $405 billion in 2010 enabled Walmart to claim the number-one spot on *Fortune* magazine's list of the top five hundred corporations in the United States.

Much of this case revolves around the economic impact a Walmart Supercenter would have on a relatively small city in Iowa. Researchers at Iowa State University have studied the impact of Supercenters on communities in Iowa and Mississippi and have reported three important findings. First, once a Supercenter opens, total local sales usually increase because the huge stores encourage residents to shop in their own community rather than travel to larger communities nearby. In addition, Supercenters attract residents from outlying areas and thus affect the retail establishments in those areas. In many rural parts of the United States the size of the population is at best stagnant and often declining. As a result, retail competition is often a zero-sum affair, which means that increased sales in one community often result in reduced sales in others.

Second, merchants in towns that host a Supercenter do better if they do not compete head to head with Walmart on products. Examples are furniture stores, restaurants, various service businesses, upscale stores, and so forth. These firms tend to benefit from the spillover effect caused by new shoppers drawn to the community by the Supercenter.

Third, the opposite is true for those who compete directly with Walmart. Merchants selling the same merchandise as a Supercenter are in jeopardy. Local grocery stores and drugstores are usually the hardest hit, with sales declines of some independent stores reaching 25 percent or more a year. Other businesses that are hit hard by Supercenters are those that sell clothes, jewelry, sporting goods, tire and auto services, eyewear, and photo services.

The bottom line is that a new Supercenter makes the host community more of a regional trade center. Often other chain stores follow suit, which magnifies the economic impact. At the same time, there is no question that some businesses in the host city or county and surrounding areas will fail.

Other issues related to Walmart's business practices are not discussed in the case but bear some mention here. One of these pertains to a class-action lawsuit that was filed against Walmart in 2001 by six female workers who said the company was guilty of sexual discrimination. At the time the suit was filed, the plaintiffs claimed that 72 percent of Walmart's hourly sales employees were women but only one-third of the company's managers were women. Drawing on corporate data furnished to government regulators, the plaintiffs contended that 56 percent of managers at Walmart's largest competitors were women. Walmart resisted the lawsuit, claiming the complaints filed by these six employees were not sufficient to justify a class-action lawsuit that could affect 1.6 million workers. Ten years after the lawsuit was filed, the US Supreme Court voted unanimously in June 2011 that the case could not proceed as a class action in its current form. Lawyers for the plaintiffs vowed to restructure the class-action lawsuit in order to seek justice for their clients.

On the labor front, unions are not very fond of Walmart. From its outset the company resisted efforts to unionize its workers. In 1970, Sam Walton hired a professional union buster to break up union organizing efforts in two small towns in Missouri. To this day unionizing efforts have borne little fruit. In 2000, eleven meat packers at the Walmart Supercenter in Jackson, Texas, voted to join the United Food and Commercial Workers Union. In response, Walmart declared that it would only provide pre-packaged meats in all of its stores, thus eliminating the need for meat packers. In 2004, union organizers in a town in Quebec managed to unionize the workers at a Walmart store, but Walmart then closed the store. It said the increased labor costs would make the store unprofitable. More recently, Walmart has negotiated with construction labor unions in Chicago and New York in order to get new stores built in these communities, but none of the workers in these stores are yet members of a union. Interestingly, Walmart's 2009 "Standards for Suppliers" manual stipulates that "suppliers must respect the right of workers to choose whether to lawfully and peacefully form or join trade unions of their choosing and to bargain collectively." Walmart insists it respects the right of its workers to unionize, and it is proud that few have thought it would be in their best interests to do so.

Another set of issues that has plagued Walmart, and frankly all other clothing merchandisers, is the frequently proven allegations that child labor has been used to manufacture garments. Bob Ortega, a journalist for the *Wall Street Journal*, chronicles this sad story in his book *In Sam We Trust*. Fueled with information supplied by union activists, television journalists confronted Kathie Lee Gifford, whose name is featured on a line of clothing at Walmart. After denying the accusations at first, Gifford became convinced by the evidence and insisted that Walmart monitor its vendors to ensure that child labor would not be used to manufacture her clothing line. With some reluctance the company acceded to her wishes and has made significant efforts, along with other clothing retailers, to eliminate the use of child labor in garment production.

Walmart has made many efforts over the last decade to counter its critics and to burnish its reputation as an ethically responsible corporation. The company's website trumpets a host of philanthropic initiatives by the company and its foundation, including disaster assistance for the victims of Hurricane Katrina and for those left homeless by earthquakes in Haiti and Chile. In May 2010, Walmart announced it would donate $2 billion to fight hunger in the United States over the next five years. In addition, the website provides a state-by-state summary of the benefits Walmart brings to communities in these states through wages, taxes, and charitable gifts.

Recent commitments Walmart has made in the area of sustainability have surprised many who have viewed the corporation's global reach, sprawling growth, and poor labor practices as the best example of unsustainable business practices. Edward Humes recounts Walmart's unprecedented and unexpected change of course in his book *Force of Nature*. In 2005, Walmart set various sustainability goals for the corporation and its suppliers, which included improving the energy efficiency of its transportation fleet, increasing the use of renewable energy in its stores, and reducing packaging waste. In October 2010, Walmart announced plans to double the percentage of locally grown produce it sells to 9 percent. In January 2011, at the urging of

Michelle Obama, Walmart announced a five-year plan to reduce the salts, fats, and sugars in the packaged foods it sells and also to lower prices on fruits and vegetables. Specifically, Walmart pledged to reduce sodium by 25 percent, to eliminate trans-fats, and to reduce added sugars by 10 percent. Some critics note, however, that Walmart is not proposing to reduce the sugar in soft drinks and other beverages, which studies show are directly related to childhood and adult obesity. Other critics claim Walmart's broader sustainability measures are little more than "green-washing."

In defense of Walmart, the company's unrivaled economic success could not have taken place without high rates of customer and employee satisfaction. As Gail Banks testifies, people around the world love to shop in Walmart stores. They certainly appear to be doing some things very right. Why shouldn't John Yeoman support construction of the Supercenter? At this point it is time to do some moral assessment of the ethical issues posed by this case.

STEWARDSHIP AND SUSTAINABLE DEVELOPMENT

Over the centuries Christians have drawn on the stewardship tradition when they have been faced with balancing the various ecological, economic, and social goals associated with sustainable development. Several people in the case appeal to the concept of stewardship. Max Walters points to the detention basin, riparian buffer zone, and the accommodations for wildlife as evidence that Walmart wants to be a good steward ecologically. Clara Laursen takes the opposite view in her presentation. For her, the destruction of wildlife habitat, the increased dangers of flooding and water pollution, and the construction of a massive store on the banks of the scenic Appanoose all add up to a clear case of bad land stewardship. John Yeoman seems to sympathize with Clara's concerns. He finds it hard to see how filling in flood plains can constitute good stewardship of the land, though he acknowledges that dikes protect Dover from floods that used to plague the town.

It is clear, however, that John is wrestling with more than just the environmental matters related to this case. As a member of the City Council he is also concerned about the economic impact the Supercenter would have on other businesses as well as the social repercussions this project could have on the distinctive quality of Dover. Though he does not refer explicitly to the concept of stewardship when he considers these matters, it is clear that he feels an obligation as an elected public servant to make decisions that are in the best interests of the citizens of Dover, both now and in the future. John wants to be a good steward of Dover's resources.

This broader conception of stewardship is revealed through comments by some other characters in the case. Tom Bittner casts stewardship primarily in terms of preservation. He urges the Planning and Zoning Commission to preserve and protect the flood plain, local businesses, and the distinctive quality of Dover. Dale Murphy takes the opposite approach. For him, good stewardship is equivalent to economic development and growth in the area. Finally, Charlie Tieskotter's comments remind John that fiscal prudence is another important dimension of good stewardship. The city can ill afford another failed lawsuit. It would also not fare well if Walmart built the Supercenter in a different town instead.

Virtually nothing is said in the case about John's faith background, only that he has an early dinner with his pastor before the City Council meeting. The case does not say what they discussed, but it is possible that stewardship was one of the topics. If so, the pastor might have helped John trace the biblical foundations for the concept of stewardship in the Hebrew and Christian scriptures. With this background John would better understand how the concept of stewardship applies not only ecologically to the stewardship of land, but also to wise decisions involving everything God has made.

In the Hebrew scriptures interpretations of the two creation accounts in Genesis can render different concepts of stewardship. In Genesis 1:26–28 God creates human beings in God's image and blesses them, saying, "Be fruitful and multiply, and fill the earth and subdue it; and have dominion over the birds of the air and over every living thing that moves upon the earth." In Hebrew, the word that is translated "subdue" *(kabash)* means literally to put something under one's control, like a conqueror placing his foot on the throat of the vanquished. The term finds colloquial expression in the phrase, "He put the kibosh on that," which means that someone stamped out the possibility of a certain option. In this text the implication is that human beings have divine permission to control nature as they fill the earth and exercise dominion over it. This authorization to "subdue" the earth is tempered a bit, however, by two other key elements in Genesis 1. God's blessing to "be fruitful and multiply and fill the earth" is actually pronounced *first* to the birds of the air and the fish of the sea (Gn 1:20–22). Thus, even though God wants human beings to fill the earth, it would appear that this should not come at the expense of birds and fish. They have a right to flourish too. Also, the Hebrew word translated "dominion" *(radah)* refers to the type of rule that kings or queens exercise over their subjects. While this rule could be harsh or benevolent, it is clear from the rest of the Hebrew scriptures that God prefers rulers who care for the poor and vulnerable, maintain justice, and avoid idolatry.

Thus, the concept of stewardship that emerges from this interpretation of the first creation account in Genesis is one that views human transformation of nature as perfectly legitimate so long as it contributes to the flourishing of human beings and is not achieved through unjust means or by unduly imperiling the welfare of other living animals. The problem, however, is that too often stewardship as responsible dominion has been replaced with the notion that ownership sanctions rapacious domination. As modern notions of private property and increasingly powerful technologies have been joined with a permission to subdue the earth, the result has been enormous ecological and social harm. This logic of domination has sanctioned slavery, destroyed civilizations, and caused enormous ecological damage. In no way, shape, or form can this sort of behavior be construed as good stewardship. God's command to have dominion over the earth is not a license to exploit it ruthlessly.

Another conception of stewardship can be located in Genesis 2:4b–24. In this second creation account God forms the first human being *(Adam)* from the dust of the ground *(adama)*. Then God plants a garden in Eden and puts Adam in the garden with instructions to "till it and keep it." Next, concerned that Adam have a partner and not be alone, God forms out of the ground every animal of the field and every bird of the air and allows Adam to name these animals. When none of these animals proves to be a sufficient partner for Adam, God uses one of Adam's ribs to form Eve.

The conception of stewardship that can be drawn from this text is significantly different from the view in the first creation account. Whereas Genesis 1 emphasizes that human beings are created in the image of God, Genesis 2 emphasizes humanity's humble origins; God molds the first human from humus. In addition, humans share kinship with all other living creatures, because they too were formed from the ground. Later, in Genesis 3, Adam is reminded that he was created from dust, and to the dust he shall return when he dies. If the first creation account emphasizes humanity's independence and reign over all that God has made, the second emphasizes humanity's fundamental interdependence with the earth and kinship with other forms of life. Here the vocation of human beings is not to "subdue the earth" but rather to "till and keep" God's garden. In Hebrew, the word translated "till" *(abad)* also means "bless," "serve," or "benefit another." The Hebrew word translated "keep" *(shamar)* means "to watch or preserve," "to guard and protect." These terms render a more static and less dynamic conception of stewardship. The emphasis is on serving and protecting what God has made. Humans are invited to care for the earth as God "blesses [*abad*] and keeps [*shamar*]" them (Nm 6:24). Human beings are not set above other living things with permission to exercise dominion over them. Instead, God sets human beings apart to address the needs of other forms of life through acts of service.

The reality, of course, is that both texts are part of the book of Genesis, and thus both texts should inform contemporary conceptions of stewardship. It would appear that the ancient Hebrews realized that human beings would always be torn between the desire to preserve all that God has made and the need to use parts of God's creation in order to flourish. Stewardship is a complicated vocation.

Other texts in the Bible further illuminate the concept of stewardship. Good stewards are those who know their place and do the work of their masters (1 Chr 28:1), while bad stewards receive severe condemnation (Is 22:15). In terms of duties stewards manage substantial economic assets and sometimes also wield political responsibility (Gn 43:16–19; Gn 44:1–4; Mt 20:1–16). For Jesus, the ideal steward is the one who stays on the job while the master is away and manages resources so well that all members of the household have "their allowance of food at the proper time" (Lk 12:35–48). Jesus even extols the example of a dishonest or shrewd steward in one of his parables (Lk 16:1–8). When a rich man confronted one of his stewards and charged him with squandering the master's money, the steward decided to cut deals with the master's debtors in order to ingratiate himself with them and also to recover at least some of the money that was owed to the master. When the steward presented these returns to the master, the master commended the steward for his shrewdness. At this point Jesus laments that the children of light are less shrewd than others in society. On another occasion Jesus encourages his followers to be "wise as serpents and innocent as doves" (Mt 10:16). From these texts it is clear that stewardship requires trustworthiness, skill, experience, and cunning. It is not just a matter of preserving what God has made but also a matter of taking some risks and using God's resources wisely.

THE ETHIC OF ECOLOGICAL JUSTICE

This summary of the stewardship tradition provides a helpful background, but it does not resolve John Yeoman's dilemma. Somehow John needs to figure out what good stewardship entails in this particular situation. He has to prioritize and integrate the three key dimensions of sustainable development that function as interlocking but also competing spheres of moral concern. One resource John might use to reflect further on this case is the ethic of ecological justice, which has grown out of conversations in the World Council of Churches and has been utilized by member churches to develop official policy statements. The ethic of ecological justice, which is sometimes called eco-justice, is an attempt to unite in one broad scope of moral concern the ethical obligations Christians have both to present and future generations, and to all human and natural communities. Four norms rooted in scripture and Christian theology are central to this ethic: sustainability, sufficiency, participation, and solidarity.

The eco-justice norm of sustainability expresses a concern for future generations and the planet as a whole and emphasizes that an adequate and acceptable quality of life for present generations must not jeopardize the prospects for future generations. Sustainability precludes short-sighted emphases on economic growth that fundamentally harm ecological systems, but it also excludes long-term conservation efforts that ignore basic human needs and costs. Sustainability emphasizes the importance of healthy and interdependent communities of life as the basis for the welfare of present and future generations.

It is obvious that much economic activity in countries like the United States is not sustainable ecologically in the long run. Global warming, topsoil erosion, habitat destruction, and water degradation are all harming the ecological foundation upon which economic activity takes place. It is difficult, however, for most local politicians to consider seriously their duties to future generations because the voters that elected them are the ones that call on the phone and demand that their interests be represented *now*. This is why policy documents like Dover's comprehensive development plan are so important; they can give politicians some cover to make difficult decisions. But ultimately politicians have to muster the courage to use the plan to protect the future and not sacrifice it to the present. Since the protection of flood plains is a priority in Dover's plan, it is hard to see how filling in a flood plain reflects this priority. Given the high costs that are incurred each year as a result of flooding in the United States, it is clear that development in flood-plain areas is wise neither economically nor ecologically. Raising land to bring it out of the flood plain simply passes the burden of floodwaters further downstream, thus violating the norm of solidarity that calls for the equitable sharing of burdens and benefits. It is also reasonable to expect that wildlife will be affected by this development, though it is not clear to what extent. The case does not mention any specific species that would be endangered or threatened, but it is likely that loss of habitat would further contribute to the decline of songbirds in the area.

The norm of sustainability, however, can also be applied to the economic and social dimensions of this case. One of John's primary duties as an elected member of the City Council is to make decisions that enable Dover to flourish as a sustainable community. Economically it appears clear that

Dover would be better off with a Walmart Supercenter than without one. If Walmart closed its store in Dover and built the Supercenter in a nearby town, Dover would lose a large number of jobs and a sizeable portion of its tax revenue due to decreased sales. At the same time, other long-range studies produced by Iowa State University indicate that total sales eventually decline in most towns whether they have a Walmart or not because larger cities in Iowa are gradually capturing an increasing share of total sales. This trend does not bode well for the future, but it is clear that having a Walmart store in the community helps to forestall this trend.

On the social side there are reasons to be concerned about the impact a Supercenter could have on Dover and the rest of the county. Some businesses undoubtedly would fail, especially grocery stores and others competing head-on with Walmart. Would the loss of these businesses erode the sense of community in Dover and diminish its vitality? It is true that Walmart's sales revenues are not recycled substantially in communities like Dover since they are transferred electronically to Arkansas, but it is reasonable to wonder how much money is currently recycled from the shaky local businesses that John fears will be tipped into bankruptcy by the arrival of the Supercenter. It is likely that the cash flow and financial assets of these businesses are already weak. At the same time John needs to consider what would happen to Dover if hundreds of Walmart jobs left the community. This would significantly harm the economy of Dover, and it would deal a blow to the town's self-image. While the preservationists would be delighted, others might well be discouraged about the long-term future of Dover.

There is no denying, however, that a Walmart Supercenter built on the banks of the scenic Appanoose River would be one of the first things people would see when they approached Dover from the east. The question is whether it will deal a decisive blow to the distinctive character of the community. Since dikes protect downtown Dover from floods, commercial enterprises will only encroach upon the aesthetic beauty of the Appanoose as development takes place beyond the dikes in the watershed on the eastern edge of town. In addition, since the Supercenter would be built on land on the fringes of the community, the homogeneity of its architecture would not detract from the historic character of Dover's downtown business district. At the same time it is likely that the Supercenter will result in another round of business failures for merchants on Main Street. Thus, tourists may arrive only to tour a downtown with quaint buildings but a growing number of empty stores. Optimists will see this as an opportunity for new ideas and investment, but pessimists will look at the decimated downtown areas in other Iowa towns and be discouraged. No matter how one looks at it, however, change is going to occur in Dover. The issue is what kind of change will take place and whether it will help Dover to be a sustainable community or not.

The other eco-justice norms address additional ethical considerations in the case and deserve brief mention. The norm of sufficiency emphasizes that all forms of life are entitled to those things that satisfy their basic needs, but it also repudiates wasteful and harmful consumption and encourages the virtues of moderation and frugality. It is clear from Gail Banks's remarks that she is looking forward to low prices on more items at the Walmart Supercenter. There is no doubt that these savings will be a significant boon to people with limited means in Dover and in the rural parts of the county. But will the Supercenter actually increase the selection of goods available in the community? The failure of competing local stores could reduce the range of goods available. Will low prices also encourage higher rates of consumption among wealthier people? Undoubtedly they will, but virtues are always tested by vices. Mass discounters will always appeal to greed and envy, but this is not a new phenomenon, and avarice is an ancient character flaw that is not unique to any particular economic class.

Another factor to consider under the norm of sufficiency is that construction of the Supercenter in the flood plain will destroy some habitat that currently helps to provide basic needs to various animals. While the development does not apparently pose a dire threat to any particular species, it will perpetuate a pattern of habitat degradation and fragmentation that is a key factor in the loss of biodiversity.

The participation norm emphasizes that the interests of all forms of life are important and must be heard and respected in decisions that affect their lives. The norm is concerned with empowerment and seeks to remove all obstacles to participation constructed by various social, economic, and political forces and institutions. The norm places importance on open debate and dialogue and seeks to hear the voices or perspectives of all concerned. The participation norm is relevant to certain dimensions of this case. For example, like small merchants, small towns find it nearly impossible to match the power of the world's largest retail corporation. This lack of power can be seen in the fact that, apart from denying the landfill and rezoning request, there appears to be little the City Council can do to prevent Walmart from building the Supercenter. The city's comprehensive development plan does not define "incompatible development" in the flood plain, and the Iowa DNR's permit to fill in the flood plain makes the issue largely moot because the land would no longer be in the flood plain. Thus, if the City Council wants to prevent the construction of the Supercenter because it constitutes "incompatible development" in a flood plain, it is likely that

Walmart will sue and present to a court the DNR permit that allowed it to fill in the land. The point is that the deck appears to be stacked in favor of economic growth and large corporations. While communities have the power to regulate where growth takes place, this power is limited; the more jaded might say that it is largely illusory. These power dynamics are not an insignificant aspect of this case, and for some they may constitute the primary moral problem.

Finally, John grapples with the solidarity norm when he considers the impact the Supercenter will have on various merchants, especially grocers. This norm highlights the communal nature of life in contrast to individualism and encourages individuals and groups to join in common cause with those who are victims of discrimination, abuse, and oppression. Underscoring the reciprocal relationship of individual welfare and the common good, solidarity calls for the powerful to share the plight of the powerless, for the rich to listen to the poor, and for humanity to recognize its fundamental interdependence with the rest of nature. There is no question in this case that consumers assume they will benefit from lower prices, increased selection, and one-stop shopping, but the costs will be borne by some merchants who will not be able to compete, by workers in other nations paid meager wages, and by various species that used to rely on the habitat provided by the land that has now been developed. Thus, one could argue that the burdens and benefits of the Supercenter will not be shared equitably.

This is not a new problem. It is inherent in the capitalist economic system. Competition leads to survival or failure in business, but the customer always benefits from increased competition so long as monopolies do not form. Given Walmart's market saturation strategy, this is a real concern, but not one that the Dover City Council can resolve by itself. In the end, fervent societal beliefs in the pursuit of self-interest and the value of competition make it very difficult for individuals or communities to act in solidarity with those who might be adversely affected by the construction of a Supercenter. John was elected to champion the interests of his constituents, not those of residents elsewhere. It is very difficult to take a step back to see the broader picture, and politicians who do so are normally not reelected.

Nevertheless, the case indicates that as many as three of the seven City Council members may be leaning against approving Walmart's request to landfill and rezone the land. Should John join them and thus form a majority? Could he justify his stance by appealing to the stewardship tradition and the eco-justice norms? Or will those same moral norms lead him to conclude that the land should be filled and rezoned so that the Supercenter can be built? How should John vote?

ADDITIONAL RESOURCES

Duany, Andres, Elizabeth Plater-Zyberk, and Jeff Speck. *Suburban Nation: The Rise of Sprawl and the Decline of the American Dream.* San Francisco: North Point Press, 2000.

Evangelical Lutheran Church in America. *Caring for Creation: Vision, Hope, and Justice.* ELCA Social Statement. Chicago: ELCA, Division for Church in Society, 1993.

———. *Sufficient, Sustainable Livelihood for All: A Social Statement on Economic Life.* Chicago: ELCA, Division for Church in Society, 1999.

Fishman, Charles. *The Walmart Effect: How the World's Most Powerful Company Really Works—and How It's Transforming the American Economy.* New York: Penguin Press, 2006.

Halebsky, Stephen. *Small Towns and Big Business: Challenging Walmart Superstores.* Lanham, MD: Lexington Books, 2009.

Hall, Douglas John. *Imaging God: Dominion as Stewardship.* Grand Rapids: Eerdmans, 1986.

———. *The Steward: A Biblical Symbol Come of Age.* Grand Rapids: Eerdmans, 1990.

Hiebert, Theodore. *The Yahwist's Landscape: Nature and Religion in Early Israel.* New York: Oxford University Press, 1996.

Humes, Edward. *Force of Nature: The Unlikely Story of Walmart's Green Revolution.* New York: HarperBusiness, 2011.

Martin-Schramm, James B., and Robert L. Stivers. *Christian Environmental Ethics: A Case Method Approach.* Maryknoll, NY: Orbis Books, 2003.

Moreton, Bethany. *To Serve God and Walmart: The Making of Christian Free Enterprise.* Cambridge: Harvard University Press, 2009.

Ortega, Bob. *In Sam We Trust: The Untold Story of Sam Walton and How Walmart Is Devouring America.* New York: Random House, 1998.

Rome, Adam Ward. *The Bulldozer in the Countryside: Suburban Sprawl and the Rise of American Environmentalism.* New York: Cambridge University Press, 2001.

Related Videos

"The New Age of Walmart" 56 minutes. CNBC Original. 2010.

"Rocktown: From the Small Farm to the Big Box." 90 minutes. CreateSpace. 2009.

"Store Wars: When Walmart Comes to Town." 56 minutes. Teddy Bear Films. 2002.

Walmart: The High Cost of Low Price. 95 minutes. Brave New Films. 2005.

Related Websites

United Food and Commercial Workers International Union, Making Change
    at Walmart, http://makingchangeatwalmart.org/.
Walmart Corporation, http://walmartstores.com/.
Walmart Watch, http://walmartwatch.org/.

Case

Executive Pay: Reward or Excess?

Sally Young leaned back in the black leather chair that graced the expansive, polished table of the Cotto Inc. board room. The task before Cotto's board compensation committee was review of the compensation package for Cotto's chief executive officer (CEO), Robert Mossman. Deliberations had convened at nine o'clock, and it was now approaching noon. Young, in her role as committee chair, had anticipated a short discussion of the CEO's compensation package leading to quick agreement by the three-member compensation committee to forward a recommendation to Cotto's board for final approval.

Cotto Inc. started manufacturing office furniture in 1953 in Bancroft, Illinois. The company quickly became a respected employer and earned a good reputation for its high-quality products. The growth of Cotto contributed to the growth of Bancroft. By the early 1960s Cotto was the largest local employer. The company expanded in the 1970s through acquisition of complementary product lines. Cotto's stock started trading on the New York Stock Exchange in 1975. The funds generated from selling the stock were used to purchase four other United States companies that manufactured mail-processing equipment and copiers and two regional office-supply retail companies. By 1999, Cotto had an international market, reported $40 billion in annual sales, and was the second-largest company in the business equipment industry. Throughout the incredible expansion and growth, Bancroft continued to be the corporate

This case was prepared by Ramona Nelson and the commentary by Laura A. Stivers. The names of all persons and institutions have been disguised to protect the privacy of those involved.

headquarters location, and the original Bancroft manufacturing plant was in full operation.

Since 2000, Cotto had endured multiple business challenges. Customers decreased their buying following the 9/11 terrorist attack. The recession in 2008 again decreased sales because business customers quit buying equipment as they reduced office space or encouraged their employees to work from home. Finally, Cotto experienced less customer demand for the traditional office supplies as businesses went paperless.

To Sally Young's surprise the compensation committee's discussion took a turn when director John Jones voiced concern that Mossman's cash bonus was slated to be 20 percent higher than the previous year. A year ago the board had established performance goals for Cotto's management team: to improve Cotto's operating income; to reduce the company spending on expenses not directly related to product costs; and to improve the reputation of the Cotto stock in the public investor community. The CEO's annual performance incentive compensation targets were structured to reward him if these goals were achieved.

Three years earlier the compensation committee had engaged a compensation consultant who designed a CEO compensation package that incorporated a base salary, short-term performance-based bonus pay, and restricted awards of Cotto stock. Both the base salary and short-term performance-based bonus are paid in cash. The restricted stock shares are awarded in the current year, but Mossman does not receive full ownership of the stock until four years after the shares are awarded. If he leaves Cotto before the end of the four years, all of the restricted stock is returned to the company. It is expected that Mossman will act in the best interest of all shareholders during the period of holding the restricted stock to improve the value of the company, which is measured by a higher market price for Cotto stock. If this happens, both Mossman and the Cotto shareholders reap the benefit.

The objectives of the Company's CEO compensation program are to align the financial interests of the CEO with those of its shareholders, in both the short and long term; to provide incentives for achieving and exceeding the Company's short-term and long-term goals; and to attract, motivate, and retain a highly competent executive by providing total compensation that is competitive with compensation paid at other well-managed companies in Cotto's industry.

Mossman was hired as CEO shortly after the new compensation program was adopted. At that time Cotto's profitability had declined as the overall economy slumped. The market price of Cotto's stock was at $19, a five-year low, when Mossman took the helm. The Cotto board had set high expectations for Mossman.

The board was impressed with Mossman's executive experience; he had led two other major corporations to improved profitability and increased share market price. Early in the board/CEO relationship it was evident that Mossman was motivated to make tough decisions and meet the board's expectations.

To achieve the targeted performance in three years, Mossman immediately instructed his executive team to increase the effectiveness and efficiency of the Cotto business model. Over the course of the next three years, twenty-five employees were laid off, another twenty thousand were moved to lower-paid positions, and the remaining employees had a two-year pay freeze. Six months before this compensation meeting, Cotto announced that the Bancroft manufacturing plant would be shut down the following year, with plans to move the production to Mexico. Fifty under-performing office-supply retail stores, located throughout the country, were also closed.

Mossman has announced plans to implement a new employee performance incentive pay plan next year. The base pay of existing employees will not change. All employees will participate in a profit-sharing bonus plan designed to pay a 4 percent bonus if the operating income increases by 5 percent. If the year four operating income increase is less than 5 percent, the non-executive employees will not receive a bonus. Mossman hopes the new employee performance incentive will motivate employees to improve their productivity.

The three-year executive performance incentives produced positive economic results for Cotto and its shareholders. The following table summarizes key information for the three years Robert Mossman has served as CEO:

($ amounts in billions)	Year 1	Year 2	Year 3
Revenues	$37	$38	$45
Operating income	$1	$2	$5
Operating expenses	$11	$9	$8
Number ofemployees	150,000	148,000	130,000
Stock market price	$19	$21	$32
(actual $ amounts)			
CEO base salary	$1,000,000	$1,200,000	$1,500,000
CEO performance bonus	$1,800,000	$2,500,000	$3,000,000
CEO restricted stock awards (shares)	500,000	650,000	1,500,000

Sally Young's stomach was starting to growl. Three hours after they had begun the meeting, the board's compensation committee appeared to be no closer to resolution.

Young, Jones, and Ralph Smith, the third member of the board's compensation committee, found themselves locked in debate over rewarding Mossman according to the terms of his pre-approved compensation package with clearly articulated performance incentives or reducing the bonus to make the CEO's pay consistent with the rank-and-file employees who were caught in the layoffs, pay reductions, or pay freeze. The three board members had reached a stalemate, each representing a different view on what action should be recommended to the Cotto board.

"The CEO's first obligation is to increase shareholder value," said Sally Young. "He's clearly achieved that, and he has exceeded the performance goals the board established a year ago. Prior to Robert's hire, Cotto was clinging to an outdated business model against competitors who were better at managing their costs. The board hired him knowing cost-cutting measures would require personnel reductions. Robert has demonstrated strong leadership. The stock market's reaction is positive, as evidenced by the exceptional increase in Cotto's share price. We need to be true to our previous compensation agreement with Robert. We offered incentives for performance, and he has performed."

John Jones squirmed in his chair before collecting his words to respond. "I've always thought a corporate board and management team should make increased shareholder value the first priority, but this situation is causing me to reflect on the fairness of paying a bonus to the CEO when the rank-and-file employees are forgoing pay increases, adjusting to reduced pay, or even worse, out of a job. Cotto has always had a good reputation in the communities where we operate. This year our employees are feeling the pressure of less pay and the community of Bancroft will suffer the loss of a major employer when the plant is closed. How can we claim Cotto is a responsible corporate citizen if so many people are negatively affected by this year's business decisions? If we reduce Robert's bonus, it will convey a message that everyone associated with Cotto is doing with less, with hope for long-term recovery. I trust that Robert will understand why we think his compensation should be decreased. If he doesn't, perhaps his personal values are in conflict with what Cotto needs from a CEO leader."

A third perspective was advanced by Ralph Smith. "It is too early to change our direction with Robert. A talented leader needs time to identify a strategy, implement it, and then measure the results. If we reduce Robert's bonus this year, we are conveying the message that we don't value his leadership. The tough decisions he has made have improved the company's performance. Can we risk him leaving the company before the business improvements and increased profits are sustainable? The pay freeze is a temporary action until the new employee performance incentive pay plan is implemented next year. A guy with his talent has many opportunities, and we need to commit to him for the long term. The reduction of the work force and facilities will prove in the long term either to be brilliant or a knee-jerk reaction with only temporary cost reductions. Let's be patient and see how he can continue to reinvent Cotto with the remaining employees and a more focused business plan. To react now and alter the incentive for the performance he demonstrated will tarnish the trust he has in the board. That will harm Cotto and all of the company's stakeholders in the long term."

The three board members sat in silence. John Jones slowly turned to Sally and started to speak. "Sally, I had hoped the three of us would find a reasonable method to adjust Robert's compensation and demonstrate to the employees that we are sensitive to the negative effects they have suffered. I'm sure you remember Larry Able and Marcy Holmes from your high school class. They contacted me recently with concern about the abrupt change in Cotto's loyalty to its employees. Cotto has been their only employer since they finished high school. They are great examples of what the company has meant to Bancroft. Both Larry and Marcy have advanced to production management jobs. They called me to express their disappointment in the layoff decisions and the pending plant closure. Even though they went to school with you, they did not want to pressure you to change Robert's compensation, but they felt they had to speak up. They hoped I could express their concern to you and Ralph. Finally, they asked us to consider the message the CEO's compensation package conveys to the employees and the community."

Shifting uncomfortably in her chair, Sally's memory flashed back to her high school class. Since graduating as valedictorian, thirty-two years ago, Sally had moved beyond her hometown roots, taking advantage of a full scholarship to Harvard. The prominent undergraduate degree presented Sally with many opportunities, and she joined the New York City office of Mercer Benham, a large international consulting firm. Through the years her talent was recognized and she advanced to her current position of senior vice president. Numerous invitations to join corporate boards had crossed her desk. Sally had been selective in accepting the invitations. When the Cotto board extended her the invitation to join six years ago, she accepted immediately. Even though Cotto was suffering decreased profits and was confronted by many business challenges, Sally accepted the position, viewing it as a chance to give back to her hometown. She remembered Larry and Marcy, both quality individuals who did not have the chance to earn a college degree. In fact, the three of them had grown up going to the same church. Larry's mom taught the fifth-grade Sunday School class. Sally had lost contact when her parents moved to Florida, twenty-five years ago.

When Sally agreed to join the Cotto board, she did not anticipate the internal conflict she was now facing. She started today's meeting thinking her expertise in executive compensation and her sense of commitment to the CEO's compensation agreement would guide her actions. Now she was confronted with her personal values. Thinking of Larry, Marcy, and the many other long-time employees tugged at Sally's sense of fairness and equity. No longer did Sally have a clear decision regarding the CEO's compensation.

Commentary

Sally came to her position as a board member of Cotto with a pro-business perspective, not realizing that her roots in the town of Bancroft and her Christian background might challenge some of her beliefs. While supportive of the need for corporations to cut employee pay and benefits and downsize jobs to become more economically efficient and competitive, Sally is confronted this time by the actual people affected by these actions. If not for her connections to former classmates, she probably would not have thought twice about her beliefs that the main obligation of a CEO is to increase shareholder value or that contractual agreements that reward strong leadership and performance should be honored.

Once ensconced in an elite circle of executive leadership, it is hard to step outside one's position and ask ethically sensitive questions about what constitutes fair pay in a free-market economy and how pay should be structured to offer incentive for good performance while also ensuring equitable relations within society. Even more important is to ask what role corporations have in promoting healthy communities. Having grown up in the small town of Bancroft, Sally is aware of the importance of a major employer like Cotto for community well-being. And from her church roots there she has likely experienced the bonds of compassion and care within a close-knit community. Yet her Harvard degree and her New York jobs as international consultant and senior vice president have taken her a distance from her small-town upbringing and world view.

FAIR PAY

While twenty-five thousand people have been laid off from Cotto and twenty thousand more have been reassigned to lower-paid positions, CEO Robert Mossman's pay, benefits, and perks have grown exponentially. Even though the US economy is still not out of recession and millions are trying to hang on to homes and jobs, CEOs of major corporations are making as much today as they were before the recession. According to a study produced for *The New York Times,* the median total compensation for top executives in two hundred major corporations was $10.8 million in 2010, up 23 percent from 2009. At the top of the list was Philippe P. Dauman, chief executive of Viacom, who made $84.5 million in 2010.

According to the Economic Policy Institute, in the 1960s CEOs were paid about thirty times the average wage of US workers, while today they receive around three hundred times the average pay. Many economists justify this wage differential by claiming it is simply what the market sets and is not about any sort of value judgment. In other words, if demand is high and supply of workers is low, pay will be higher and vice versa. In relation to CEO pay, the argument holds that there is high demand for the extraordinary leadership skills and talents that only particular top executives have exhibited, and therefore these executives are highly compensated. Executive pay consultants argue that just as there are few superstars like Michael Jordan in athletics, so too are there few gifted leaders in business. There are all sorts of other factors in addition to the market that determine pay, however.

The largest factor that determines CEO pay in relation to other jobs is how public policy is structured, especially tax policy. For example, in 1960 income over $400,000 (equal to about $3 million 2011 dollars) was taxed at 91 percent. In comparison, today's top tax rate is only 35 percent. And salary is only one piece of executive compensation. Mossman's compensation package includes a base salary, a performance bonus, and restricted stock awards. His executive compensation may also include health insurance, life insurance, a retirement plan, chauffeured limousine service, use of executive jets, club memberships, paid expenses, a housing allowance, and interest-free loans for the purchase of housing. In the 1990s, stock options rose from a quarter to a half of executive compensation. US corporations favored using stock options as compensation because stock-option accounting and tax rules allowed them to report stock-option expenses on their financial books at one value but use a different value when claiming an expense on their tax returns, resulting in substantial tax savings. When legislation was proposed that would have made firms report the costs of stock options like other compensation (thus limiting the growth of stock options), it was soundly defeated in the Senate.

In other countries corporations use stock options, but payouts are linked to performance. Mossman does not receive full ownership of his stock options until after four years. The board expects that a higher market price per share will be an incentive for him to improve the value of the company, but they do not link his ownership of stock options to actual performance. The fact that the average CEO in the US makes so much more than executives in comparable countries illustrates the effects of public policy. According to Jacob Hacker and Paul Pierson, authors of *Winner-Take-All Politics,* Switzerland has the second-highest CEO pay levels and yet executives are paid three-fifths of what American executives earn. In many European countries the role of CEO and board chair are separate, resulting in more independent boards. Studies have shown that CEO compensation is higher when board members have been appointed by the CEO. In the United Kingdom, shareholders vote on executive pay, and although their vote is only advisory, this policy can also serve to curb CEO compensation. The European Union is currently exploring whether to grant shareholders a final, not simply an advisory, vote on executive compensation.

Another justification for high CEO compensation, especially in the form of stock benefits, is that such incentives will ensure good corporate performance (and thus increase shareholder wealth) by putting the CEO's interests in line with the shareholders' interests. It is not clear who is serving whom, however. Often boards are more beholden to CEOs than the reverse because the CEO influences the nomination of board members (often personal friends) and their pay and perks for their service as board members. There is usually a separation between the ownership of a corporation and the management of it. Most boards do not have the time or expertise to manage companies, and therefore shareholder votes only rarely alter corporate decisions. Furthermore, most shareholders are not individual investors but groups of investors (mutual funds) and insurance companies. Stock options are often less about aligning CEOs' interests to those of board members and more about disguising the total amount of compensation CEOs receive. They are also a way to avoid the vagaries of the market by such maneuvers as "backdating" particular options or deferring compensation to avoid taxes and interest.

Mossman did increase Cotto's shareholders' wealth substantially, but there is ample evidence that executive compensation is not necessarily linked to the profitability of companies. A recent study of 483 companies found that in 179 of them the average value of their stocks fell between 2008 and 2010, yet their top executives still got raises. There are numerous stories of CEOs being rewarded for failure. According to *CNN Money*, John Mack received $118 million despite a 25 percent decline in Morgan Stanley's stock, and Chuck Prince took Citigroup close to insolvency but walked off with $113 million in four years.

So what is a fair wage or level of pay? There are various ways to define justice, each of which results in differing understandings of fair distribution of resources and opportunities. A classic Western definition of distributive justice, explicated by Aristotle, defines justice in terms of equality. This means similar cases should be treated similarly and dissimilar cases differently. But by what criteria do we consider cases similar? For example, are executive leaders and rank-and-file workers to be paid equally based on their common humanity, or are they to be compensated differently based on their roles, talents, responsibilities, or productivity? Most people believe incentives are important; that is, the CEO should be offered more pay as an incentive for increased responsibility, leadership, and expertise. Are current pay distributions based on the value of what people produce? Should they be based on performance? If so, then justice is being defined more on the basis of merit than equality. That is, justice requires people getting what they deserve. Mossman has achieved the high expectations set by the board, but do his results warrant the extravagant pay he was promised?

While a biblical view does not discount justice according to equality or merit, it has a communal orientation and therefore places greater emphasis on fair burden and need. More often than not, biblical authors conceive of justice in terms of equity rather than equality or merit. That is, burdens should be distributed on the basis of one's ability to bear the burden, and benefits should be distributed on the basis of need. If cutbacks, including layoffs, are necessary to improve the efficiency and financial health of a company, who should shoulder the burden? If the point of wage cuts is to save money to benefit the whole, then wouldn't it make sense to cut the largest salary? A handful of CEOs, in solidarity with workers, have refused raises, and some have even taken pay cuts, but such action has usually been voluntary, not mandated by their board. According to Christian norms of concern for the poor and a common good, there is something morally wrong with legal contracts that disproportionately reward a few but do not support equitable community relations.

Apart from legal responsibilities to honor the contract it made with Mossman, the Cotto board also has a moral obligation to keep its promise to compensate Mossman for a job well done. He not only achieved the performance goals the board established, but he exceeded them. It is only just that he be remunerated according to the stipulations of his contract for work done. Furthermore, the common good requires that contracts be honored. Companies will be unable to retain good leadership if they routinely renege on promised contracts, and societal stability and cohesion will disintegrate if there is no way to enforce contracts.

Modern contracts have roots in religious covenants that are central to Judaism and Christianity. While there is a reciprocal nature to much of biblical law that emphasizes divine blessing for human faithfulness, what is unique about God's covenant with humanity is that it ultimately is unconditional and not reciprocal. Despite human sin and humanity's persistent failure to keep up its end of the bargain, God remains faithful, loving, and merciful. The prophet Isaiah compares God's faithfulness to the care and compassion a mother has for her nursing child (Is 49:15–16). Human contracts are not the same as God's covenant because there is not always a personal relationship between the parties—and humans, unlike God, are fallible. Nevertheless, the covenant tradition can guide Christian thinking about keeping promises both out of duty and with respect to promoting the common good. As a covenant people, Christians have a duty to take seriously the importance of trustworthiness. At the same time, Christian morality requires pursuit of the common good. For example, *all* workers, not just CEOs, should be paid what they have been promised by their employer.

Often people view the morality of CEO pay on an individual rather than a societal level. Some decry the lack of virtue or sinfulness of CEOs who accept such excessive reward for work. The Bible has plenty to say about the idolatry of putting one's self and one's own desires in the place of God and of placing trust in material wealth over God (Ex 20:1–26; Ezek 16:48–50; Lk 15). We are not told much, however, about Robert Mossman's personality or desires, except that he is good at executing what he was tasked by the board to do. Many believe that those who work hard and rise to the top should be rewarded well. Mossman, like many CEOs, might believe that his compensation is the result of his own individual efforts, forgetting that he cannot run Cotto without the work performed by numerous other employees. His understanding of freedom might be a libertarian one—that wealth and income belong to the individual, not to the community. Paul taught, however, that God's love, sustenance, and salvation are a gift of grace, not merited by works (Eph 2:8–9). Before God, we are all equal, and furthermore, we are all part of the larger body of Christ (Rom 12:3–8).

From scripture comes the theological claim that all our wealth in this world is created and gifted by God to be used to establish justice, not for some to live in luxury while others struggle in poverty. The profits of a company like Cotto are a result of many factors, which include the efforts of the CEO, investors, managers, workers, and even the government through various corporate subsidies. In the biblical view that workers like Larry Able and Marcy Holmes hold, it is a violation of both freedom and equality that a few line their pockets while others suffer pay cuts. The Hebrew scriptures teach us that we are not autonomous beings but are called to be stewards of that with which God has entrusted us. All of creation is God's property, to be subordinate to the purposes of the Creator. The biblical prophets were continually calling the people of Israel to account for their covenantal responsibility of making justice (Is 3:14–15; Jer 5:28; Am 2:6–7). While God's grace is freely given, humans are nevertheless called by God to care for creation. In the Christian scriptures James warns the rich of future misery for their lack of stewardship: "You have laid up treasure for the last days. Behold the wages of the laborers who mowed your fields, which you kept back by fraud, cry out; and the cries of the harvesters have reached the ears of the Lord of hosts. You have fattened your hearts in a day of slaughter" (Jas 5:3–5).

Workers like Larry and Marcy might believe that Mossman was being idolatrous by accepting such extravagant compensation when he was laying off workers and decreasing the pay of those who were left. While they might see the need for both layoffs and pay cuts to keep Cotto competitive, a focus on proportional justice would hold that the sacrifice be shared more equitably.

A few CEOs are amazingly virtuous people, giving back to their communities a substantial percentage of their gains. An individualistic culture like ours deems it the prerogative of individuals to make as much as they can and to contribute to charitable causes if they see fit. On an individual level CEOs might be reminded of Jesus' injunction to the rich man to sell all that he owned and give the money to the poor (Lk 18:18–23), yet most people would find such a command to be an impractical and idealistic understanding of discipleship. The problem with focusing on an individual level is that it does not challenge cultural understandings about work and pay and the structures and policies that have institutionalized such widely differential compensation. We might ask whether Jesus' injunction is primarily about the rich man's salvation or about redistribution of wealth within society.

EQUITABLE SOCIETY

Interpreting Jesus' message to the rich man as a call for redistribution of wealth would put him in the long line of Hebrew prophets who argued for economic justice. God is a God of justice throughout the Hebrew scriptures. "For the Lord your God is God of gods and Lord of lords, the great, the mighty, and the terrible God, who is not partial and takes no bribe. He executes justice for the fatherless and the widow, and loves the sojourner, giving him food and clothing" (Dt 10:17–18). God repeatedly calls the people of Israel to act justly and reminds them that they were treated unjustly as slaves in Egypt: "You shall also love the stranger, for you were strangers in the land of Egypt" (Dt 10:19). The Mosaic economic laws were centered on limiting property rights so that all families had access to basic material goods. For example, farmers were instructed not to harvest all their crops so that people without adequate sustenance could glean the remaining grain (Lv 19:9–10). Furthermore, land could not be sold in perpetuity. If a family had to sell its land due to poverty, the land was to be returned in the year of Jubilee, a celebration that occurred every fifty years (Lv 25:8–17). While there is no evidence whether the redistribution of land ever occurred, Jubilee justice nevertheless functioned as an ideal for the people of Israel to strive toward.

While our individualistic and capitalist culture tends to glorify the ability of executives and others to become massively rich, accumulation of wealth for those at the top is linked to the poverty of those on the bottom. This truth was fairly obvious in the agrarian societies of biblical times when those who owned the most land had the lion's share of power. Mainstream economists claim, however, that capitalism is not a zero-sum game, one in which the economic pie is static and some lose out when others eat too much. Instead, they argue, capitalism increases the size of the pie, and while some might get bigger pieces, everyone gains. For example, industries like Cotto create jobs, and corporate profits are reinvested into other productive endeavors that spawn new jobs. Board member Ralph Smith acknowledges the sacrifices Cotto workers experience in the company's short-term transition to better performance, but he believes that the reduction of the work force and facilities will in the long run put Cotto in a more competitive position, ultimately benefiting workers.

Non-mainstream economists and others critical of capitalism argue that while it creates wealth, not all benefit. The labor of many is exploited through poverty-level wages inadequate to sustain a family. Others are simply marginalized through unemployment, but even their status serves to keep wages down, creating more profit for the investors and owners. Workers like Larry and Marcy who are left at Cotto end up accepting lower pay simply to keep their jobs, knowing that there is a reserve of unemployed people ready to step in. Critics argue that the welfare of workers is subordinated to the quest for capitalist profits. Shareholders pay executives handsomely to increase the profits they receive, even if it requires the exploitation of workers and the degradation of nature. The unemployed and the degraded are made invisible through this relentless drive for profits.

Biblical justice is not simply about compensation for work done; it is also about right relations. A God of justice and liberation wants communities based on mutuality and respect. Such community building is difficult when executives make three hundred times what average workers make. Further, according to the Economic Policy Institute, 10 percent of the US population owns 75 percent of the wealth, and 1 percent owns 36 percent. This is a degree of economic stratification that approaches biblical proportions. Such a large gap between the rich and poor inhibits mutuality and exemplifies injustice.

Jesus criticized relationships of unequal power and patronage. Religious purity laws provided the ideological basis for who had status and power in his time. The Pharisees and Sadducees, the Jewish religious elite, justified their power and wealth by claiming to be more pure than others. They made a show of keeping the same purity code as the priests, such as a kosher diet, circumcision, and observance of Temple ritual and the Sabbath. Jesus, however, was concerned with the heart of the Jewish Law over the letter of the Law, teaching that the Law was created to promote the common good, not to justify new forms of oppression. In Jesus' time women, Gentiles, and those who lacked bodily wholeness, such as lepers, blind people, or eunuchs, were deemed impure and considered outcasts. Yet Jesus continually challenged such status distinctions by creating inclusive community and purposely welcoming the "impure" (Mt 8:1–4; Mt 9:10–13). Crossing status boundaries as he did provoked hostility and resistance from those who used their positions of power to control and oppress people.

Paul was grappling with how the early church was to be organized. Would it adopt the cultural status distinctions of the Greco-Roman world, or would it embody the new form of community of mutuality and respect modeled by Jesus? He argued that both Gentiles and Jews should be included as participants in God's community and that membership should be by faith not works (Gal 3:23–29). That is, God's community, or in Paul's words, the *koinonia* community, includes all who believe in God, not simply those who appear religiously pure by human conventions. *Koinonos* in Greek refers to partner and companion. The *koinonia* community, in Paul's view, is one in which fellowship in God's grace abounds; it is a fellowship where sharing and generosity are prevalent and care and compassion for all are evident (Acts 4:32–37). True happiness and wealth are found in the relationships of love and hospitality, not in what members own.

While no community is perfect, and Larry and Marcy realize that Cotto needs to stay competitive to remain a viable business in a global economy, they are worried that the layoff decisions and pending plant closure will irreparably rupture their community. Furthermore, they expressed concern over the message conveyed when the executive leader of a company with long and deep ties to the community accepts exorbitant compensation in the face of such cuts. Such action is contrary to the fellowship, care, and sharing embodied in God's community. Implicit in the view Larry and Marcy hold is the value of solidarity—that if workers need to make sacrifices for the good of the whole, the budget cuts should be enacted in a fair way that respects all members. If we are all created in God's image and are part of Christ's body, then our institutions and institutional policies should respect the dignity of each and every member. This raises an important question: Should the norms of solidarity and inclusion be confined only to intentional *koinonia* communities or can they be applied to corporate board rooms and guide public policy?

What the people of Bancroft are experiencing is happening in multiple local communities. Many businesses are transferring production or services overseas in search of cheaper labor and production costs, leaving communities with a lack of employment opportunities. And for those businesses that remain, the threat of job loss is enough to lower wages and stifle workers' efforts to organize for better working conditions or pay. Those who retain their jobs are often overworked, and those who lose their jobs become demoralized. In both cases meaningful participation in community is lessened. On a national level the disparity between the rich and poor, and even between the rich and the middle class, threatens democratic participation, especially in a system where "money talks."

CORPORATE RESPONSIBILITY

Connected to the issues of just compensation and equitable communities is the question of corporate responsibility. Should corporations have responsibility only for their bottom line and return investments along with profits to shareholders, or should we expect more of them? Should Cotto be loyal to the workers and the community that have supported the company for years? Board member John Jones notes that Cotto has always had a good reputation in the communities where it operates and that he is concerned it will lose this reputation if it does not treat all employees fairly in its attempt to become more efficient.

The corporate charter, developed in the sixteenth century, was a grant from the governing king or queen that limited an investor's liability in the event of corporate loss to the amount of his or her investment. Such a privilege encouraged private investment in New World exploration and productive initiatives. In early America corporate charters were adopted to serve the public good but were only granted for a fixed number of years and were carefully monitored by citizens and government alike.

By the late 1800s, however, corporations had gained sufficient control over legislative bodies to influence the passage of laws that basically limited their liability and extended their charters in perpetuity. In 1886, the Supreme Court ruled that corporations had the rights of a natural person under the US Constitution, thereby entitling them to protections that individuals have under the Bill of Rights. These changes gave corporations even greater freedom and greatly decreased corporate accountability to the public. Today's corporations reach into every corner of the globe, and many are larger in size and power than most governments. International and domestic policy agendas are often more beholden to corporate interests than to labor or environmental interests.

A God of justice and liberation wants economic institutions and structures to promote the flourishing of God's amazing creation. Today's corporations are important for production of goods and services that support human welfare, and they are a crucial source of employment. But although corporations provide employment, not all jobs promote human flourishing, nor is all corporate activity environmentally sustainable. Not only must people have access to the basic necessities to survive, but the opportunity to work and to participate in community life is important to individual self-esteem. Humans were created to be God's co-creators, to be faithful stewards in caring for God's creation. Thus, economic institutions should be designed so that people can participate as co-creators. Workers should be paid a just wage that allows families to afford the basic goods necessary for a sustainable and healthy lifestyle. Work places should encourage creative contributions, both so that workers can be fulfilled and so that organizations and businesses, and ultimately the economy, can benefit from the full array of gifts and skills workers possess. Economic institutions should also value the flourishing of human communities and the ecosystems that support them. To change the focus of corporate governance from short-term profit to sustainable community and environmental flourishing, however, would entail a radical transformation in corporate accountability to communities around the world.

Organizers in the late 1800s were able to institute some forms of accountability, such as child-labor laws, an eight-hour workday, minimum-wage standards, and modest safety regulations. However, transnational corporations like Cotto are increasingly transferring production to countries that do not have these same regulations. Workers in all countries are negatively affected by lack of corporate accountability. Solidarity among workers worldwide becomes important if any transformation is to be successful. While capital flows across borders freely, families suffer from displacement and communities become harder to sustain when employment opportunities are transient. Larry and Marcy are right to be concerned about the fate of their community if the Bancroft plant shuts down and moves production to Mexico, leaving an insufficient number of jobs for residents. Economic institutions should support the flourishing and freedom of all members of society and tread lightly on the ecosystems that they depend on.

How will Sally's connections to the Bancroft community influence her perspective on Mossman's remuneration for the work he has performed? Should the Bible's views regarding economic justice influence her views about corporate responsibility? Will she side with John Jones's perspective that reducing Mossman's bonus will show that Cotto is a responsible corporate citizen? Or should Sally side with Ralph Smith's claim that continued support in the form of a bonus for Mossman is crucial for the long-term success of the company? Will consideration of Cotto's legal and moral responsibilities to uphold contracts be most important to her? Or will she listen to the requests from her former classmates Larry and Marcy for proportional justice in light of the sacrifices Cotto workers have made? Issues of fairness, equity, and corporate responsibility were not topics Sally thought she would have to grapple with when she accepted the invitation to be on the Cotto board. Now she and her fellow board members must decide what is best for Cotto, its stakeholders, and its employees.

ADDITIONAL RESOURCES

Brubaker, Pamela. *Globalization at What Price? Economic Change and Daily Life*. Cleveland: The Pilgrim Press, 2001.

Childs, James M. *Greed: Economics and Ethics in Conflict*. Minneapolis: Fortress Press, 2000.

Estey, Ken. *A New Protestant Labor Ethic at Work*. Cleveland: The Pilgrim Press, 2002.

Finn, Daniel, ed. *The True Wealth of Nations: Catholic Social Thought and Economic Life*. Oxford: Oxford University Press, 2010.

Hicks, Douglas A. *Inequality and Christian Ethics*. Cambridge: Cambridge University Press, 2000.

Horsley, Richard A. *Covenant Economics: A Biblical Vision of Justice for All*. Louisville, KY: Westminster John Knox Press, 2009.

Long, Stephen D., Nancy Ruth Fox, and Tripp York. *Calculated Futures: Theology, Ethics, and Economics*. Waco, TX: Baylor University Press, 2007.

National Conference of Catholic Bishops. *Economic Justice for All: Pastoral Letter on Catholic Social Teaching and the US Economy*. Washington, D.C.: USCCB, 1986.

Stackhouse, Max L., Dennis P. McCann, and Shirley J. Roels with Preston N. Williams. *On Moral Business: Classical and Contemporary Resources for Ethics in Economic Life*. Grand Rapids, MI: Eerdmans, 1995.

Wallis, Jim. *Rediscovering Values on Wall Street, Main Street, and Your Street: A Moral Compass for the New Economy*. Brentwood, TN: Howard Books, 2010.

Related Videos

ABC News. "Inside AFLAC: CEO Dan Amos." Princeton, NJ: Films for the Humanities and Sciences, 2008.

Smith Business School. "Setting CEO Pay: Executive Compensation." www.youtube.com/watch?v=veplldWz6ng.

"These People Are Idiots." U.S. Senate Executive Compensation Bill Discussions: Sen. Claire McCaskill." www.youtube.com/watch?v=yt90KUwCCoE.

PART VI

HEALTH

Case

How Many Children?

As the students filed into her classroom, Jennifer Blair smiled as she overheard isolated lines of their conversations. Many of them were already discussing the reading for today, an analysis of the Octomom case.[1] Her bioethics class had just begun the section on reproduction, a topic that was close to the hearts of many of her students in this community college classroom. A number of them were already parents, and most of the rest anticipated becoming parents soon. One woman in the class was already a grandmother, though not yet forty. The extensive publicity about the Octomom case had ensured a great deal of student interest.

As Dr. Blair brought the class to order, hands were already raised with comments and questions. "That chick is really nuts!" exclaimed Xavier Suarez, a twenty-year-old engineering student. "Who in her right mind wants fourteen children?"

Debbie Chandler, an older nursing student, agreed: "I can hardly manage my three, and I have a husband to help, which she doesn't. Even her mother finally gave up and moved out. No one can raise that many kids alone—and even her oldest kids are much too young to be any help with the babies."

"Maybe she didn't think that the last implantation would produce so many," offered Nick Wiell, a usually quiet Liberal Studies student. "After all, many times the implantations of embryos don't take."

"Yes, that's right. Most of the time they don't. But she already had six kids, all by in vitro, so she should have known the possibilities. She said she

---

This case was prepared by Christine E. Gudorf and the commentary by Laura A. Stivers.

[1] In 2008, Nadya Suleman, a thirty-three-year-old single Californian with six living children, conceived octuplets after being implanted with twelve embryos. The octuplets were born in January 2009, at which point the media dubbed her Octomom. All fourteen of her children were conceived by *in vitro* fertilization. Her fertility specialist, Dr. Michael Kamrava, was subsequently expelled from the Society for Assisted Fertility and his medical license was revoked by the California State Medical Board in 2011.

wanted to use all of her frozen embryos," added David Gutierrez, "though that turned out to be a lie."

Alison McCrea declared, "For anyone who believes that human life begins at conception, it would be murder to discard some of the embryos. Of course, they didn't have to be implanted in her. She could have given them to a childless couple."

"Tell me what you think of that," asked Dr. Blair. "Donating embryos— what about it, class?"

Xavier pointed out: "I was adopted, and I don't see any difference between giving up an embryo to a childless couple and giving up a baby. That would have been better than having eight more babies herself."

Most of the class nodded, but Debbie remarked: "Yes, maybe it would be better, but I can't imagine giving up one of my babies. To know that she was out there somewhere with another mother, that I would never know what or how she was doing—that would be real torture."

Alison asked: "So wash that baby down the drain so you don't have to wonder what she's doing? It may not be ideal to give her away, but it is certainly better than killing her."

Maria Migoia raised her hand and at Dr. Blair's nod softly stated: "My mom is one of thirteen children, and her father died in a coal mining accident when she was eight. Her mother raised all of them after my grandfather died. And they all turned out fine. I think there is a prejudice against big families now."

"For some very good reasons," David responded. "The world cannot afford families that big. We are at a crisis point right now at many different levels of the environment. No one should have more than the replacement rate—two children a couple. And given that we Americans consume so much more of the world's resources per capita than any other people, we ought to have fewer than two children per couple."

"Nobody has the right to tell me how many kids I can have," protested Debbie, the mother of three. "That would be like the Chinese with their one-child policy."

"Well, there were some abuses there, especially in places where overzealous officials forced late-term abortions, but most Chinese accepted the need for the one-child policy and did the world a tremendous favor," insisted David, an environmental studies major. "Without the one-child policy that began in China in 1979, the world would have close to another billion people right now. Can you imagine where global warming would be with another billion people in the world?"

"I don't believe in global warming. This last winter was the coldest on record across the United States and Europe. How can the world be warmer?" inserted Ben Palaver, an education major.

"I can answer that, but it would take a while. So for right now," David replied, "don't look at global warming. What about a billion more people needing energy—what do you think that would do to the price of oil, or to the number of oil spills like the BP Deepwater Horizon one in Louisiana or the Exxon Valdez?"

Liz Sanchez, a senior philosophy major, responded: "But environment is not the only reason, and for me not the principal reason, for limiting the number of children one has. How is she going to support fourteen children? How can she even pay the bills for their births? According to the article, she doesn't have a job, or insurance, and even before she got pregnant with the octuplets, she was getting almost $500 a month in food stamps! I bet the hospital bill was over a million just for the delivery and neonatal care. They had over a dozen professionals working on her and her babies when she delivered. California has a multi-billion dollar budget deficit, and she is going to be adding to it for years at the expense of taxpayers."

At that point, Phillip objected: "Wait a minute. I think even poor people have a right to have kids, including assisted reproduction if they need it. Having children is an important part of human life, and she should not be excluded because she isn't working. She is going to school to train for employment."

Liz replied: "I'm not saying that she shouldn't have had any kids or shouldn't have been able to use assisted reproduction. But she already had six living children! All by assisted reproduction!"

At that point Dr. Blair asked if anyone in the class approved of Ms. Suleman having so many embryos implanted in her. Not one hand was raised. "So then we need to decide why we disagree with her actions. Are all the reasons out for discussion?"

Debbie raised her hand: "I think she is psychologically immature, and that she did this in hopes of celebrity status, even wealth. There is a long history of families with large multiple births receiving lots of corporate gifts and of the media paying big fees for pictures and stories of the babies. I think that's why she did it, and that is not a good reason to have children."

Several heads nodded. Alison added: "I agree. She is a publicity hound. She says she just loves kids and wanted a large family. But in this day and age, nobody can think that one person can provide enough quality parental time for fourteen kids, and that is what a good mother would want for her kids."

Maria, who had earlier defended big families, also agreed. "I guess so. You know, my mom has talked about growing up on a small farm in West Virginia and how all the kids worked together on the farm to make a go of it after her dad was killed in the mine, but she has also said that when she married and moved to the city, it wasn't practical to have so many kids, so she and Dad only had three. Not many people live on farms today, where children are extra workers and easily fed."

Dr. Blair inserted: "You know the other intervening variable here is technology. Until relatively recently, multiple births were accidents of nature that could not be predicted. And until the contraceptive pill was introduced in the 1960s, there were not many options for effective birth control at all. If you look back at the help given families with the first quintuplets, for example, everyone understood that these multiple births just happened. They hadn't been expected, much less planned."

"You know, I think we are all coming to agree that she is a nut. Even her parents disapprove of what she did, and she didn't even tell them until after it was done," said David. "But what about her doctors? Didn't they know she already had six kids?"

Liz replied, "That's the really incredible part. She had one obstetrician, this Dr. Michael Kamrava, who performed all her in vitro fertilizations, implanted them, and delivered them all. So he knew exactly how many children she had and how old they were. And still he not only implanted those last embryos, four to six times the advisable number, but he lied about it initially."

Alison added, "Yeah, the story that Ms. Suleman and Dr. Kamrava told after the birth, that he had implanted her last six embryos, was clearly a lie, because when the babies were tested some months later, no two of them were identical. And to get eight babies from six embryos, you either have to have two sets of identical twins, or one set of triplets or greater multiples. But these babies all seem to be simply siblings, which means at least eight embryos were implanted, not six. But then the investigation by the State Medical Board of California found that he actually implanted twelve embryos!"

At that, Debbie burst out, "That doctor should lose his license to practice! The dangers to both mother and babies go up with each additional fetus. His professional society sets a guideline of no more than one or two, in special circumstances three, embryos to be implanted in a woman of her age (thirty-three). Big multiple births can involve disastrous, life-threatening complications, lifelong disabilities such as cerebral palsy, and crushing medical costs for the babies, and health risks for mother, too. In fact, Suleman receives disability payments for three of her first six children from the state of California. Wouldn't that in itself be reason not to implant her again? I don't understand that doctor—what reason could he have to agree to this?"

David suggested, "He had as much to gain as she did. She had had five pregnancies from five previous implantations. Her five pregnancies—resulting in six babies—were five of the twenty-four pregnancies resulting in live births that constitute his success rate. People choose fertility clinics based on their success rates, and she was certainly helping his. Suleman initially said that each of her previous implantation cycles consisted of six embryos being implanted, and each of those cycles produced only one to two babies. So they might have thought that implanting twelve embryos this last round would only produce two or three babies. I don't think Kamrava should have agreed to take her as a patient after the first two pregnancies, but I can see that maybe they didn't think so many embryos would take, and they wanted to be sure to get a pregnancy out of it."

Debbie persisted, "But the risks are so high if they all take!"

"Are there any important elements of the case that we haven't discussed?" asked Dr. Blair.

Ben suggested, "The article we read also raised some issues about regulation. It contrasted insurance coverage in the United States for assisted fertility treatments with the situation in Europe. In Europe, government-sponsored health insurance covers fertility treatments, but in the United States only fourteen states require that health insurance policies cover assisted fertility treatment, and the degree of coverage varies a lot. California law forbids health insurance to cover fertility treatments; it is an attempt to keep down the cost of insurance policies. So in this country, most patients who get assisted fertility treatment are paying for it themselves. Since each cycle costs $12,000 to $18,000, and has an average success rate of 20 percent, patients put a lot of pressure on doctors to implant multiple embryos in order to raise the chances of a pregnancy. Economic considerations are often behind patient appeals—if this is the last cycle that I have the money for, I might pressure the doctor to implant more, too, in hopes of being a parent."

Maria hesitantly volunteered, "I wasn't going to say anything, but my husband and I have been married seven years with no kids, so we are seeing a fertility doctor now. My parents have said they will help us if we need it, but we know that the most we can afford, even with their help, is two cycles. So would I want to be implanted with more than the guidelines suggest? Maybe, probably not much more. But if it were the second cycle, and I knew this was my last chance, then maybe."

Greg Lockyear, who had been silent until now, added: "My sister and her husband are both engineers who met in university. They were married for twelve years without kids. They just had twin girls with in vitro last year. Their company's insurance paid for the whole thing. That's the way it should be. It's what insurance is for. People who don't have cancer help pay for cancer care for those who do, and people who don't need fertility treatment help pay for fertility treatment for those who do need it. I don't see a problem with this. But what I do have a problem with is the scams in fertility clinics. The first clinic my sister went to lied about its rate—it listed the number of children they had produced instead of the number of pregnancies. Due to multiple births, a success rate of 9 percent was presented as a 25 percent rate. If she had not done her research, she would have been taken in. This ought to be regulated. There ought to be penalties for this kind of scam."

"You know, Greg, your sister's insurance plan sounds like one of those 'Cadillac' plans that is going to be taxed in coming years under the 2010 government health-care program that Congress passed," said David. "The unions are going to be dropping those plans like hotcakes in the next few years for that reason. If we want everyone to have health insurance, then we can't keep pushing up the cost by adding 'life enhancement' treatments like this. My grandpa is excited because he just learned that his insurance will pay for three $10 Viagra tablets a month. There are lots of things like that which can enhance the quality of our lives, but we have to consider the cost. These enhancements are not on the same level as treatment of disease. They are not necessary. If people want children and can't have their own, there is always adoption. Lots of kids in foster care need adoptive parents. Next we'll have proposals that insurance should cover the cost of joining eHarmony or Match.com so that people can find marriage partners."

"Not such a terrible idea, David," said Alison. "Some of us could use some help in that area!" Seeing David ready to respond, she added, "I'm kidding, I'm kidding!"

"Well," concluded Dr. Blair with a glance at the clock, "I think we finally have all the major issues on the table. We have questioned the motivation and judgment of the mother herself in being implanted for yet another pregnancy and the motivation and judgment of the doctor to implant her, as well as their decision to double the number of embryos implanted and to lie about it. We have also raised questions about possible moral grounds for limiting fertility, the social question of the appropriate status of fertility treatments within health-care insurance, and the legal question of what responsibility the state has to either pay for the consequences of such treatments or require/forbid insurance companies to cover them. For your assignment for this week, please write a four-page paper choosing one of these topics. Then research it further, take a position on it, and lay out the supporting evidence for your position. Be sure to anticipate the arguments that would come from someone taking the opposite position, and respond to them. As Dr. Blair glanced around the room, some students looked thoughtful upon hearing the assignment, while others groaned. "Some things never change," she thought to herself as she packed up her briefcase.

Commentary

Medical ethicists in the United States have historically placed great emphasis on individual autonomous decision-making, especially with decisions that affect one's own body and do no harm to others. Having control over one's own body is central to human dignity, as autonomy allows people to pursue what is meaningful in their lives. Decisions about reproduction are deeply related to our human identity, our well-being, and our relationships with others. In the United States the general population values reproductive freedom, that is, that women should have a choice about when or whether to take on the responsibility of pregnancy and childrearing, and if they so choose, how to do so. We also generally hold that women have a right to reproduce, or at least they should not be hindered from doing so. As Debbie says in her critique of China's one-child policy, "Nobody has the right to tell me how many kids I can have." In vitro fertilization (IVF) as one form of reproductive technology appears at first glance to be a straightforward issue of individual choice, but in fact it has multiple social implications.

In vitro fertilization is a process where the egg cells are fertilized by sperm outside of the body. The process involves removing the eggs from a woman's ovaries and fertilizing them with sperm in a fluid medium, then transferring the fertilized egg (or zygote) to the patient's uterus. The first successful use of IVF was in 1978, and it has been used since to assist many people have children. IVF can be used with a female's and male's own egg and sperm, or it can be used with donated egg and/or sperm. In cases of surrogacy the woman providing the egg(s) might not be the same person who carries the pregnancy to term. Many heterosexual couples use IVF due to medical infertility, while many gay and lesbian couples or single people use IVF because they are not in a heterosexual relationship. The success rates of IVF vary by clinic but the average national rate of live births hovers around 20 to 30 percent and account for about 1 percent of all infants born in the United States every year. Often IVF pregnancies result in more than one child being born because clinics usually implant more than one fertilized egg to increase the odds for a successful pregnancy. According to a 2008 study by the U.S. Centers for Disease Control and Prevention, "148,055 assisted Reproductive Technology cycles were performed at 436 reporting clinics in the United States during 2008, resulting in 46,326 live births (deliveries of one or more living infants) and 61,426 infants."

REPRODUCTIVE FREEDOM AND AUTONOMY

Reproductive freedom has not always been a reality for women in the United States, and a majority of women in the world do not have such freedom. Supporters of reproductive freedom argue that women will achieve real equality with men only if they are not thought to be biologically destined to be mothers, but rather have a choice over how to live their lives as well as control over those choices. Artificial reproduction can be one means for having choice and control. While many would view Ms. Suleman's decision to have eight children in one pregnancy as irrational and an exceptional case, most women who opt for artificial reproduction are simply availing themselves of technology to be able to bear a child.

Many Christians are sympathetic to the use of IVF by married heterosexual couples who are medically infertile, like Maria and her husband in the case. Conservative Christians are generally less supportive of IVF for single women, surrogate mothers, or lesbian couples. Advocates of reproductive freedom would argue based on the value of equality and the right to reproduce that IVF should be extended to all women, no matter their circumstances.

While most people in the United States agree with the value of autonomy, IVF and artificial reproductive technologies in general are not simply matters of autonomous choice. They take place in a wider context, as many of the students in the case point out with their comments about environmental implications, the regulation of fertility clinics, the moral status of embryos, and questions about insurance, access, and who pays for such technologies. Furthermore, while a Christian perspective values individual human dignity and freedom of choice, it insists that humans are not isolated decision-makers apart from the communities in which they are born, nourished, and hopefully flourish. Thus, a Christian perspective on IVF and other reproductive technologies should value more than simple autonomy and ought to have some grounding in a larger vision of human and environmental flourishing. Such a vision ought to respect the human dignity of each person created in God's image while also giving attention to issues of both social and environmental justice within broader human and ecological communities.

NATURAL PROCREATION, ARTIFICIAL MANIPULATION, AND SANCTITY OF LIFE

In support of infertile couples, many churches, especially most Protestant churches in the United States, are open to IVF as long as it is reserved for married heterosexual couples and no embryos are discarded. The Catholic Church, in contrast, prohibits almost all procedures associated with artificial reproduction. Based in natural-law thinking and in line with its stance on birth control, the church argues that separating intercourse from its inherent biological reproductive goal is not God's intention. Furthermore, it claims that marriage between a husband and wife is the appropriate venue for procreation, and that procreation is a natural act of love and should not be an artificial manipulation of egg and sperm in a petri dish by a technician. The 1987 papal encyclical *Donum vitae* says, "Homologous artificial fertilization, in seeking a procreation which is not the fruit of a specific act of conjugal union, objectively effects an analogous separation of the goods of marriage." Intercourse within marriage, in contrast to artificial reproduction, is not a manufacturing process of making babies but is connected to love. According to this perspective, children are a gift from God and should not be "products" of a reproductive technology industry.

While not all Christians will agree with the Catholic Church's views on marriage and birth control, its arguments against reproduction being turned into a process of manufacture, and more so, a commodity, is helpful. Surprising allies with the Catholic Church on this point are feminists concerned about the medical establishment taking over and profiting from reproduction, eroding the control women have gained. The infertility industry has turned reproduction into a profit-making endeavor, and business is booming. The industry's emphasis on profit over helping all people who suffer from infertility is evidenced by competition for clients who can pay for services and disregard for those who cannot.

While the Catholic Church rightly argues against commodification of reproduction, many Catholic theologians and ethicists do not agree with the natural-law argument that intercourse and conception are inseparable and that a primary goal of marriage is necessarily procreation. It is unclear to many why the church insists on the priority of the physical act of intercourse in begetting children over other means, especially if IVF is being used by married heterosexual couples who value family but suffer from infertility. Other Christian theologians and ethicists challenge the normative conception of family that many Christian denominations continue to hold, that is, the heterosexual nuclear family. They argue that families can come in all shapes and sizes and that human flourishing is more dependent on community acceptance and support than it is on a particular family makeup.

The Catholic Church also takes issue with some of the practices associated with IVF. More than one egg is fertilized in the IVF process, yet not all of the fertilized eggs are implanted. Some are frozen for later use, while others might be discarded. Alison McCrea makes the argument that it is murder to discard fertilized eggs since human life begins at conception.

While not all people agree with Alison's claim that discarding zygotes is murder, some might be uncomfortable with the process of selective reduction that sometimes occurs when a woman ends up with multiple fetuses in her womb and it is clear that they will not all thrive. Most doctors would have advocated for "selective reduction" in Ms. Suleman's case for reasons of safety (for the fetuses and herself) and to promote a quality of life for those fetuses that were the healthiest. For Alison and religious organizations like the Catholic Church, who see life as sacred from conception, these practices that sometimes accompany IVF make the process unethical.

JUSTICE AND A COMMON GOOD

Xavier Suarez illustrates the common belief that a family of fourteen children is excessive in modern America with his comment, "Who in her right mind wants fourteen children?" Liz Sanchez voices the concern that Ms. Suleman was not only having a lot of children, but that she was doing so without sufficient means to raise them, burdening taxpayers by her irresponsibility. Ms. Suleman's situation is the extreme, not the norm. Nevertheless, her situation challenges our Christian commitment to compassion and care, especially if we believe she is seeking some sort of celebrity status.

While there are some who place great emphasis on individual responsibility and would even argue that people who cannot support children ought not to have them, such a stance fails to note the many ways that our society treats people unequally, especially in relation to work and wages. Should people who are in poverty due to oppressive forces in society be further victimized by being told they should not have children? As Phillip argues, even poor people ought to have a right to bear and raise children. Societal supports such as flexible work arrangements, subsidized quality childcare, and affordable health care would go a long way in promoting healthy families no matter their configuration. The oft-cited cliché that it takes a village to raise a child has truth to it.

Promotion of flourishing communities and what some ethicists refer to as the common good requires that we consider the societal implications of reproductive technologies, IVF in particular. Proponents of IVF argue that all people should have the right to reproduction, but in the United States the cost of IVF is prohibitive for many, especially if it is not covered by insurance. Greg Lockyear's sister and her husband were lucky to have insurance coverage for the full process, while Maria pays out of pocket for her cycles of IVF. Several ethical issues arise in relation to cost and coverage.

First of all, some critics decry the amount of money spent on research and utilization of reproductive technologies for a handful of people who can afford them (predominantly upper-middle-class white people) while fifty million people in the United States are without health insurance and basic preventative health care. Advocates of our current health-care system tout the freedom of choice patients have to pick from an array of different medical options and providers. Justice is equated with autonomous choice, yet such access is a reality only for those who are able to pay or who "merit" jobs that provide health-care coverage. While there are plenty of passages in the Bible in which God rewards the righteous and punishes the wicked, many other passages indicate that need, not merit, is the foundation for a biblical conception of justice. The prophets in the Hebrew scriptures were continually calling members of their society to promote justice for the least well off. Jesus was always there for the people on the margins of society, those whom society had deemed "unclean," such as the lepers, the blind, the widows, and the tax collectors. He healed people in need and surely did not ask them if they had the means to cover the costs.

The early Christian communities also shared with one another in terms of need. Access to basic health care is a necessary foundation for individual human flourishing and also central to keeping communities free from disease and other treatable health ailments. In a for-profit system, as much of health care is in the United States, the emphasis is not on basic preventative care for all but on freedom of choice. Yet the claim that everyone has freedom of choice is empty rhetoric when so many people do not have the financial means to access the vast array of choices offered.

Second, the question of what medical procedures should be covered by either private insurance and/or public forms of health care, such as Medicare or emergency room visits funded by taxpayer money, is hotly debated. While there is no end to the number of medical desires (some of them "life enhancement" treatments, as David points out), there are not unlimited funds to pay for them all. This dilemma raises the question of what constitutes a medical need versus a medical want. David mentions Viagra for older people. Is that a medical want or need? What about assisted reproductive technologies? Should all people have a right to reproduction, even if taxpayers foot the bill or if insurance holders are charged higher premiums because of high-cost IVF treatments? And is this right unlimited? In this economic context, how about limiting the recourse to in vitro? And after one live birth, no more insurance access? Limiting the number of embryos per implantation is really a medical safety issue. States are currently dealing with budget deficits and are cutting back on funding for public goods that are necessary for flourishing communities, like education, police, and parks. And every day people opt out of insurance due to too-high premiums. The biblical norm of justice according to need ought to guide public dialogue on health-care rationing, and life-saving medical procedures ought to be given priority over life-enhancing procedures.

Closely related to the question of needs versus wants is a third issue of whether it is ethical to spend so much money on reproductive technologies when there are so many children in need of adoption. Our culture has promoted the desirability of having biological children, and the infertility industry has capitalized on that desire, with people willing to pay thousands of dollars for each IVF cycle, despite a low live-birth success rate. While times have changed, women are still given the message that somehow they are not fully female unless they get pregnant and have children. Yet all children are created in God's image and deserve loving families. Would Ms. Suleman have been so interested in having a large number of children at one time if we as a culture had given as much value to adopting children as we do to biological conception of children? Would she have made the front-page news if she had decided to adopt eight children?

WELL-BEING OF WOMEN

Many of the students thought Ms. Suleman was a publicity hound at best or, as Xavier exclaims, totally "nuts." While we could focus on Ms. Suleman's motivations, the larger question in relation to flourishing lives and the common good is why infertility clinics and doctors who work in them are not adequately regulated. Implanting twelve embryos, as Dr. Michael Kamrava did, was highly dangerous for Ms. Suleman, yet infertility clinics remain largely unregulated. Most regulation is self-imposed and generally only pertains to age limits for women trying IVF with their own eggs. There are no limits, for example, on how many embryos can be implanted at one time, how many rounds of IVF a woman can try, or how much donors can charge for eggs. As David notes, clinics attract paying clients by advertizing a high success rate, and Ms. Suleman clearly boosted Dr. Kamrava's statistics. While many people consider children a blessing from God and IVF has helped many people have children who might not otherwise have been able to conceive, a Christian perspective must also consider the well-being of both women and the potential children that IVF assists people in having.

Recognizing the autonomy of individuals is part of respecting human dignity, yet individual freedom of choice does not always equate with human flourishing. Individuals make choices in social contexts. Without a critical discussion about the ends for which clients of artificial reproductive technologies act, their choices can be influenced in ways that are not conducive to their well-being. For example, Mr. Suleman might have been influenced by patriarchal norms that give primary value to women as mothers, or she might have been caught up in the consumer focus of largely unregulated infertility clinics that seek more clients. Currently women in the United States have much more freedom than women did in biblical times. They are no longer considered property of either their father or husband, and our cultural mores and societal laws support the right of women to reproductive freedom.

ENVIRONMENTAL SUSTAINABILITY

Students in the course also raised environmental concerns with reproductive technologies. In particular, David brings up the issue of overpopulation and the earth's limited carrying capacity. While the Bible says "be fruitful and multiply, and fill the earth and subdue it" (Gn 1:28), the environmental and social situations were quite different in biblical times. Resource depletion, deforestation, pollution, and species extinction were on a limited scale compared to today, and global warming was not a reality. Furthermore, the global population has grown exponentially since then in part due to increased technology that has given people longer lifespans. The dispersed tribes of Israel under Assyrian conquest were generally struggling to keep sufficient numbers to sustain their religion and identity, and so increasing population was an issue of survival. For us, curtailing our fruitfulness is a necessity of survival, for both humans and broader ecological communities. While China's one-child policy might feel extreme to many, it was an effective strategy for curtailing overpopulation and preserving God's creation.

God created the world and declared that it is good (Gn 1:25; 1:31). All of creation is good; humans are but one piece of an intricate whole. Just as God is a sustainer of creation, humans are called to be responsible stewards. The Bible is full of metaphors for stewardship of creation, from the Psalms (104; 145) that celebrate God's sustenance to parables in the Gospels, such as the Good Steward (Lk 12:42) or the shepherd caring for lost sheep (Lk 15:4). Christians are also called to be in covenant with God, with part of the covenant responsibilities including stewardship. The Noahic covenant (Gn 9) illustrated God's sustenance of creation with Noah being instructed to bring two of every animal on the ark. The later Sinai covenant expected reciprocal participation of humans in the stewardship of creation. The Ten

Commandments were geared toward the flourishing of humans in harmony with the earth (Ex 20—24). The prophets continually called the people of Israel back to their covenantal responsibilities of stewardship when they took God's gift of sustenance for granted and dominated the created world and one another for selfish gain. Jesus' emphasis on neighbor love necessarily involves stewardship of creation if we are to be in harmony with one another and not fighting over limited and diminishing resources.

CONCLUSION

There is no one Christian perspective in relation to reproductive technologies. Each student in Dr. Blair's class will find a different issue to be morally central. Values such as human dignity, justice defined by need, a common good, environmental sustainability, and sanctity of life might guide their deliberations. A number of questions can be asked in relation to reproductive technologies: Are we valuing the existing children in our society? Do all people have access to basic medical care? Do we support families adequately? Do we value the autonomy of women to make reproductive decisions? Are reproductive technologies consistent with an emphasis on environmental sustainability? What does it mean to value all life? Paying attention to the larger ends of reproductive technologies will help us to guide our policy decision-making on reproductive technologies toward promoting the flourishing of both humans and the environment in God's community.

SOURCES FOR FURTHER READING

Cahn, Naomi R. *Test Tube Families: Why the Fertility Market Needs Legal Regulation.* New York: New York University Press, 2009.

Callahan, Daniel. *What Kind of Life: The Limits of Medical Progress.* Washington, D.C.: Georgetown University Press, 1990.

Duke, Allen. "Nadya Suleman's Doctor Loses California Medical License." *CNN U.S.* Available on the articles.cnn.com website.

Gervais, Karen G., Reinhard Priester, Dorothy E Vawter, Kimberly K. Otte, and Mary M Solberg. *Ethical Challenges in Managed Care.* Washington, D.C.: Georgetown University Press, 1999.

Harwood, Karey. *The Infertility Treadmill: Feminist Ethics, Personal Choice, and the Use of Reproductive Technologies.* Chapel Hill: University of North Carolina Press, 2007.

Horn, Peter. *Clinical Ethics Casebook*. 2nd ed. Belmont, CA: Wadsworth, 2003.

Johnson, Josephine. "Judging Octomom," *Hastings Center Report* 39, no. 3 (May/June 2009): 23–25.

McKibben, Bill. *Enough: Staying Human in an Engineered Age*. New York: Henry Holt and Co., 2003.

Case

Keeping the Doors Open

Dr. Beatrice Gonzalez, newly appointed CEO of Washington Memorial Hospital, was speaking at her first meeting of the Washington Memorial Public Trust, the board of trustees for the hospital. Washington Memorial is a huge public hospital with an immense downtown complex and two satellite hospitals in the north and south of this south Florida county. The hospital is owned by the county but the Washington Memorial Public Trust is responsible for the administration of the hospital.

"We face an immediate crisis," she announced. "The new auditing firm has informed me that we have the funds to remain open only seven to eight weeks. For next year we face a projected deficit of $200 million. We need at least $50 million simply to keep the doors open until the new fiscal year begins, and by then we will also need to have a deficit-reduction plan in place. The basic problem is that for many years the accounting department has continued to treat unpaid accounts as payable, not writing them off as bad debt, even though it was clear that minimum-wage workers without insurance were never going to be able to pay hundreds of thousands of dollars for extended ICU or surgical care."

The members of the trust looked stunned. "Why are we hearing about this for the first time if this practice has gone on for years?" demanded Peter Migone, a six-year veteran of the trust.

Beatrice replied: "Until very recently there was sufficient income from insurance and paying patients to cover costs. But since the economic crash of 2008, which cost thousands of local people their jobs, more and more of our patients have no insurance. As a result, the situation recently became critical."

This case was prepared by Christine E. Gudorf and the commentary by Laura A. Stivers. The names of all persons and institutions have been disguised to protect the privacy of those involved.

"But why didn't the former auditors tell us about this? We have audits every year!" exploded Peter, whose face was turning red with ire.

Beatrice responded: "When I asked that question of the new auditors, what I heard was that it is not easy to determine which unpaid bills should be written off. The general method involves time—bills that do not involve insurance and are unpaid after a year are either sent to collection agencies, which give us back a proportion of what they collect, or the bills are written off. There is some discretion involved in deciding whether to write them off or send them to collectors. As more and more people lost jobs and insurance over the last two years, the proportion of unpaid bills went up, the staff got behind in handing them to the collection agencies, and the collection agencies' rate of recovery went down. Some of the insurance companies also seem to have delayed payment even more than usual in order to protect their own bottom line during the recession, although they deny it. The combination of these things created our crisis. In addition, all the H1N1 flu admissions last winter didn't help any because many of those who were sick were also too poor to pay their bill."

Elizabeth Walker, a long-term trust member who served on multiple metropolitan boards, asked the question in everyone's mind: "Did Michael Bender [the former CEO] know about this before he retired last month?"

"How could he not have known?" asked Miriam St. Jacques, director of a local education foundation. "He had to know that the three-month and six-month collectibles were increasing since the crash. Surely he was tracking the effect of that on the overall fiscal health of the hospital."

At that, John Bertrucci laughed. "Of course he knew! The man was sixty-seven years old. He had done a good job for years. He did not have the energy to tackle this coming crisis, and so he bailed! Frankly, most of us would have done the same. It's not like he took off with millions. He just retired. We all knew he would in the next year or two. Let's not make him a scapegoat for not solving this problem before it came to us." Other board members who had served with Bender nodded agreement.

The newest member of the trust, Fred Trask, a local businessman, tried to summarize the situation: "So, if I understand it, we need to tighten up the accounting practices, find the emergency funds to tide us over for awhile, and plan to reduce the budget. But surely if the economic downturn caused this crisis, this huge deficit is a short-term thing. The economy will come back—it always does, though it may take a couple of years. And the number of uninsured will go down as the different provisions of the 2010 federal health-care legislation come into effect. Right?"

Beatrice answered him. "None of us has a crystal ball, Fred, but besides not knowing how long the downturn will last, or if the economy will ever come back to where it was before, there are other factors. For decades health-care costs have increased faster than inflation. As we have discussed long before this crisis, our particular situation is going to be greatly affected by our long-term partner, the medical school at the university, which just opened its own hospital right across the street from us. The medical school shows no signs of wanting to end our contract, but how can it both partner with us and compete against us? Our historic advantage in being able to attract insured and even rich self-payers to Washington Memorial instead of local private hospitals has been that our doctors are on the faculty at one of the top medical schools in the nation; they are the best specialists in their fields, the ones who do the latest treatments in transplants, heart surgery, and neonatal care. For that kind of care people have been willing to put up with a shortage of single rooms, old linoleum floors, and sharing corridors and waiting rooms with homeless people. But now these paying patients are hearing the university's ads about getting these very same top specialists in a hospital with only single rooms, all newly decorated, with cable TV and wireless Internet. Why should they come here? The university hospital has only been open two months, so we don't know the economic impact it will have on us, but we have to expect it to be drastic. It is likely that we will at least lose a significant part of our elective surgery patients with insurance coverage."

Elizabeth then asked, "Beatrice, obviously we will need to meet frequently for a while, and will also have to work on committees. How do you want to set them up?"

"The first order of business has to be to look for the support necessary to stay open in the immediate future," stated Beatrice. "We will need one committee to apply for city, county, and state emergency funds. Peter, Miriam, and Fred, you have good political connections. Can you constitute the committee to seek public emergency funding?"

"It would be crazy to think that we will get anything from the city and county, who are facing their own deficit budgets, and are in the middle of big layoff struggles," replied Peter. "We can try, but the state looks like the best bet. It is equally strapped, but it has some rainy-day funds tucked away that we might tap into."

With Peter, Miriam, and Fred agreeing to their assignment, Beatrice turned to John, who had donated two wings to the hospital in the past. "John, you know all the local philanthropists. Can you and Elizabeth form a committee to solicit individual and foundation contributions to our emergency fund?"

John grimaced. "Beatrice, all the 'ordinary suspects' for large donations are not only suffering from losses in the market, but what money Bernie

Madoff didn't scam off them, Scott Rothstein did.[1] Probably 80 percent of the people considered really wealthy in this state have lost much of their surplus and are living on reduced incomes. We can try, but I think we will be lucky to get $5 million, much less the $50 million or more that we need. Every charity and university in the state has been soliciting these same people over the last two years to make up the cuts they took from state budgets. And you know," he said, smiling, "many of us only like to donate when we get our names on buildings or suites—filling in gaps in the operating budget isn't so attractive." The members laughed, knowing that John's name was prominently portrayed around the cancer wing and the paralysis-research wing he had donated.

Beatrice named Steve Garcia—the hospital's chief operating officer—the lead officer in the new accounting firm, and herself to a committee that would come up with options for closing the deficit by the next meeting. They then discussed how to present the crisis at the press conference on the following day. Fred spoke what was on everyone's mind: "Our big problem is going to be with the unions. They will know from the beginning that fixing deficits means cutting jobs, cutting salaries, or cutting benefits, and likely all three. We are in the same fix as the city and county—we negotiated very generous salary and pension contracts that we now can't fund."

Miriam added: "Yes, it will be a hard negotiation. But we will get no place at all with them if we are not perfectly transparent about how bad the situation is. The books must be open to the unions, if they are to be convinced that sacrifice is necessary."

No one responded. Beatrice thanked them all, and the meeting was adjourned.

The announcement of the crisis at the press conference the next day caused a frenzy. The news was full of interviews with indignant county officials and with representatives of the unions demanding explanations. Union officials declared that the problems caused by incompetent management should not be put on the shoulders of their members. Beatrice's subcommittee met the following morning. The initial discussion concerned the news stories, the most disturbing of which were interviews with county officials who demanded that the trust be dissolved and hospital management revert back to the county. Sixteen years ago the trust had been set up as an independent management body in response to mismanagement and corruption on the part of the county in administering Washington Memorial.

---

[1] Madoff ran a Ponzi scheme for large individual and foundation investors, whom he defrauded of about $65 billion. The bulk of his investors were from New York and Florida. In 2009 he was sentenced to 150 years in federal prison. Rothstein, a Fort Lauderdale attorney, ran a Ponzi scheme that bilked Florida investors of over $1.2 billion; he was sentenced in June 2010 to fifty years in federal prison.

Steve Garcia, the chief operating officer, reassured Beatrice that this threat was purely political. "The county commissioners have enough problems on their plate right now with their own deficit and corruption scandals; they do not want to take on Washington Memorial's fiscal problems too. But they will try to focus on our problems in the news as a way to take public attention off their own problems."

The committee went to work, and within a few days it had two initial options to present to the trust members. Beatrice explained to the full body: "We can invoke the fiscal emergency clauses in all the employee contracts—for the residents, interns, staff doctors, nurses, maintenance staff. We will have to defend this in court, but that shouldn't be difficult—to impose a 5 percent cut in all employee wages. That will invalidate present contracts, which we will have to renegotiate in the coming months, but even a 5 percent cut will not be nearly enough to close the gap, which the accountants say continues to widen. We are also suggesting that we close the emergency room at Washington South. Washington South has the highest proportion of uninsured patients, and the majority of these in the medical and surgical wards are admitted from the ER. If we close the ER, these patients will be taken to ERs in other private hospitals in the area—to Baptist Hospital and to Mercy Hospital. This would help stem the losses from Washington South. We are still investigating the situation at Washington North to see if closing that ER would significantly help."

"I can just imagine the protests from Baptist and Mercy," declared John. "They will say, with some justification, that we are the public hospital, funded by a special tax to treat the indigent, and now we are sending the indigent to them. And what about the unions—how many employees would be laid off if we close the emergency room at Washington South?"

"Somewhere between 125 and 160, depending on how many beds it empties in the wards," answered Steve. "Not nearly enough."

Fred demanded to know: "Why isn't the hospital run more like a business? Units that don't take in enough to cover costs should be closed and not be a drain on the rest."

Other members shook their heads. Beatrice responded: "There are lots of reasons why we can't do that, Fred. We can't close down units that have ongoing contracts for research without significant penalties. And every hospital administrator in the nation will tell you that some units, like the ER and maternity wards, never pay for themselves. But if couples can't come to us to have their babies, why would they come here for their kids' ear tubes, tonsillectomies, or appendectomies? How could our cardiology clinic keep patients—or for that matter, physicians—if we didn't have an ER to admit them with heart attacks or strokes? Our range of specializations is our strength; it's what makes us a full-service hospital."

Beatrice asked for a vote on proceeding with the salary cut and a provisional vote on closing the Washington South ER, pending further investigation on the size of the deficit. The vote was almost unanimously in favor of both. But she warned, "The size of the deficit is growing as the accountants dig further. We will certainly have to do more. We might have to close South altogether."

The following week Beatrice and Steve met with Dave Berry, the lead accountant conducting the new audit, and learned that the projected annual deficit was closer to $300 million than to $200 million. As they sifted through the figures, Steve pointed out that the cuts would have to be drastic, perhaps catastrophic. South would not be enough. That afternoon they held the first negotiations with the unions, beginning with the nurses' union. Leona Simpson of the nurses' union pointed out that a 5 percent cut would put the salaries of nurses with less than five years of experience below that of most of the hospitals in the area. Beth Lisandro, director of nurses, volunteered that she would have a difficult time attracting new nurses to fill vacancies if Washington Memorial salaries were not equal to those of surrounding hospitals. Steve responded drily, "I doubt this will be a big problem, Beth. With the kind of cuts we are likely to have to make in nursing staff, at least at the satellite hospitals, there will be sufficient laid-off nurses to fill vacancies for the foreseeable future.

Leona, disturbed, asked, "You think there will be layoffs in addition to imposing a 5 percent salary cut across the board?"

"Leona, at our meeting this morning, we looked at the possibility of closing both satellite hospitals altogether. It might be necessary," insisted Beatrice. "There are no acceptable solutions, Leona. Neither of those buildings is fully paid for, so we might be paying for buildings and equipment that we don't use at all for the next seven or eight years. But the cost of doing that is much lower than paying the salaries of the five thousand employees that work there."

Steve added: "It is unlikely that we could find a buyer for either of those buildings. No other local hospital has the money to buy them, even on generous terms. To reconfigure them for offices would cost a fortune, and in this recession there is almost unlimited office space already standing empty. But if we don't air condition them, even while we don't use them, one summer of South Florida humidity will create a mold problem that will make them good for nothing but demolition."

Leona maintained that she saw no way that the nurses' union would agree to a contract with 5 percent reductions in salary if Washington Memorial was also laying off close to a thousand nurses at the two satellites. That evening the news was full of speculation about how the crisis would be resolved.

As Beatrice and her husband, Bill, ate dinner that night, she rubbed her temples and complained: "I don't know how to find the best solution. The members of the trust are lost and are looking to me for solutions. Nothing I have ever done has prepared me for this kind of disaster. Whose interests should come first? The employees? The patients? The institution itself? The taxpayers? What is best for the institution is to close the two satellites, because that would preserve all of the specializations and allow us to retain the majority of our doctors. But that decision would put five thousand employees out of work with virtually no chance of finding other employment in this economic climate. I just found out today that we transferred some of the supervisors at those satellites from the central complex against their will because we needed their expertise in the new hospitals, and now we would be abandoning them. Many patients would be inconvenienced by having to go farther for care, but emergency care would still only be ten to fifteen minutes farther away by ambulance. It's the employees who would take the hit."

Bill, a professor of philosophy at the local university, asked: "So why not cut salaries more, on a temporary basis, while you find cost savings throughout the system, the country recovers from the recession, and the federal health-care reform kicks in.[2] Would a 10 percent cut do it?"

Beatrice smiled. "That would cover about 85 to 90 percent of what we need. But if I do that, Bill, I suspect that within a year 30 to 50 percent of my physician staff will leave to work at hospitals in other states. We will not be able to attract new interns and residents. I will lose many of the best employees in all the services, because we would be talking about a 10 percent cut for at least three or four years, with no guarantees of ever catching up to where we were. The damage to morale would be tremendous. I am afraid of the consequences of even a 5 percent cut. The deeper the cut, the more likely we are to retain only the lowest-paid employees, those with the least

---

[2] The 2010 federal health-care bill that passed Congress and was signed into law by President Obama has a number of provisions that become effective from three months to five years after passage. The principal effect of the bill on Washington Memorial's crisis would be that over the next five years, employers with more than fifty employees are required to offer their employees health insurance, and those persons without health insurance through employers are required to obtain it individually from health-care pools set up in each state. There are gradually increasing penalties for failure to enroll in a health-care plan. Currently, insurance companies with large enrollments negotiate low charges with hospitals and doctors, and federal Medicare and state Medicaid plans do the same, leaving the individual patient without insurance paying part of the fees for those whose insurance does not cover the entire amount, as well as paying for the indigent without insurance. When virtually everyone has insurance, according to the theory, individual costs per patient will drop a great deal because costs will be equitably distributed among the insurance plans.

professional credentials, who have fewer opportunities in other places. But we can't run a hospital with cooks, cleaning staff, nurses aides, and clerks."

"Normally, that might be true, Bea, but all the other hospitals and states have been affected by the recession, too. There are not that many professional jobs open anywhere these days. How much of a risk is it?"

"I don't know. That's the hard part. Tomorrow the board expects me to make a proposal. One of the nurses stopped me in the hall this afternoon and told me I should think about what Jesus would do in my situation. I wish I knew."

Commentary

Jesus healed people, especially the outcasts—the blind, the leper, and the disabled. Public hospitals have also been places where all people can get medical attention no matter their status or their means. These hospitals have historically served low-income communities, and currently two-thirds of the patients who use public hospitals are minorities. Yet increasingly public hospitals are closing their doors. Public hospitals are critical for addressing societal health disparities, but they are receiving less and less financial support. The recession, governmental budget deficits, the growing number of uninsured people, and increased competition with private for-profit hospitals have threatened the financial viability of public hospitals. Basically, they are experiencing an increased demand for services on their already limited and quickly diminishing resources.

The budget shortfall that Washington Memorial Hospital is facing is not an isolated case. Escalating hospital closures, especially in urban areas, are raising concern about whether low-income people will receive quality health care and, further, whether health care will be seen as a public good in our society or simply an individual privilege. Public hospitals have been closing at a steady rate across the nation. Two major cities with high minority population—Detroit and Philadelphia—now have no public hospital. Public hospitals require state support, but with the recession most have lost much of their funding. These hospitals are often older, and as the safety-net hospitals that care for the uninsured in most counties and/or cities, they have seen heavy use. Thus, they are usually in need of extra funding for infrastructure repair and upkeep.

When a public hospital closes in one area, patients are shifted to other struggling public hospitals or to nonprofit care providers who might or might not take them in. For example, when the Martin Luther King Jr. Hospital in Los Angeles's predominately Latino South Central neighborhood was closed, patient load increased at the four remaining county public hospitals with no increase in their budgets. The result of three hospital closures in Queens, New York, led to an average wait of seventeen hours in the emergency room at the Jamaica Hospital Medical Center. Overcrowding can mean life or death when doctors are overworked and hurried and when ambulances are at a standstill waiting for their stretchers to be returned from the emergency room. The longer distance to access a public hospital also affects the effectiveness of care. While all hospitals must by law provide emergency care, private hospitals can transfer patients to other hospitals once they are stabilized. Furthermore, private hospitals can turn away non-emergency cases, whereas public hospitals have to serve everyone who comes to their doors.

BASIC HEALTH CARE AS A RIGHT

The United States is one of the few developed countries that does not treat provision of health care as a basic human right. It is a wonderful system for those who can pay for services, but health care, apart from emergency medical care, is considered a privilege in US society. Limited access to basic health care is both a class and race issue because about half of the nation's fifty million uninsured are people of color, yet people of color constitute only 35 percent of the US population. Lack of health care compromises human dignity and basic well-being in multiple ways: from elderly people not taking life-saving prescriptions because they cannot afford them, to children not being able to concentrate in school due to abscessed teeth, to families filing bankruptcy over hospital bills. It is a vicious circle: poverty leads to poor health in our country, and poor health negatively affects people's ability to participate fully in school, work, and community endeavors.

Preserving the dignity of the human person, especially the dignity of those who are most vulnerable, is a theme found throughout scripture. The sacredness of every person is grounded in our having been created in the image and likeness of God. This sacredness does not mean that we are entitled to every medical intervention or technological advance in relation to our health, but it does mean that we ought to have a basic right to those aspects of medical care that allow us to participate in the economic, political, and cultural life of our society. We are not isolated individuals; our human dignity can be realized only within communities and in solidarity with one another. The grounding of solidarity necessary for the respect of human dignity is not present in a society where health care is a privilege for those who can afford it. While rights are only guaranteed if society protects them, the right to the basic material needs necessary to live a life of dignity is founded in God, not society. Both the norms of love and justice call us to create social institutions that support the dignity of all people.

God calls us to love our neighbor (Mt 22:39), but what does this concretely entail? Jesus ministered to all people—especially the poor. The poorest and most downtrodden sought him out and, unlike the treatment they got from the dominant society, Jesus always responded to them compassionately. He intentionally directed his ministry to the communities of farmers and fishermen, not to the wealthy communities (Mt 10:5–6). Jesus expected his disciples and all who believed in God to minister to the poor: "Come, you that are blessed by my Father; inherit the kingdom prepared for you from the foundation of the world; for I was hungry and you gave me food, I was thirsty and you gave me something to drink, I was a stranger and you welcomed me, I was naked and you gave me clothing, I was sick and you took care of me, I was in prison and you visited me" (Mt 25:34–46). When Jesus ministered to the sick, he did not determine whose medical needs were more important but instead responded to whatever ailed people.

Love on an individual level is not enough, however. Justice on an institutional level is also required. In the United States health care is a right for some, which comes in the form of Medicaid for the most poor and Medicare for people with some specific disabilities or who are over sixty-five years old. These government-sponsored health plans address the health care needs of many who might be the most vulnerable, but there are still plenty of people whose only access to health care is the emergency rooms at public hospitals or the free health-care clinics run by nonprofit organizations.

That public hospitals like Washington Memorial need to apply for city, county, and state emergency funds or look to philanthropists to stay open is indicative of the low value we as a society have given to social, economic, and racial justice. Rather than having a system of universal health care we have offered a safety net for the most vulnerable and deemed it acceptable for health care to be an arena in which corporations decide what services will be provided to whom based on profits. Would Jesus have sought to profit from the care he gave to people? How do we understand his teaching that when we feed the hungry, welcome the homeless, and visit the imprisoned we have ministered to God? (Mt 25:35–46) Are we to see this teaching as counsel for individuals, or do we apply it to our larger communities and nation?

When hospitals are managed by private, for-profit businesses, society runs the risk that health care will not be universal. Most for-profit health-care centers and hospitals prefer to cater to patients who have insurance and/or can pay for services. These for-profit hospitals can claim to be more economically "efficient" because they do not have to serve those who cannot pay for their care. There are many stories of for-profit hospital staff turning away people without funds and sending them to the nearest public hospital, or even illegally "dumping" homeless and chronically ill persons on the street after providing emergency care.

"Efficiency" in for-profit hospitals is also achieved by cutting back on salaries and benefits for hospital employees or by having employees do more tasks. For example, in many for-profit hospitals today, nurses are expected to serve more patients per shift. According to a recent report issued by the New England Public Policy Center and the Massachusetts Health Policy Forum, lower nurse staffing levels have been linked with patients' increased risk of pneumonia, urinary tract infection, post-operative infection, sepsis, ulcers, gastrointestinal bleeding, cardiac arrest, longer hospital stay, and, in some cases, death. The costs of people without health care, fewer jobs, and overworked and underpaid workers are not borne by the for-profit hospitals but are externalized to the community in the name of efficiency.

Many doctors challenge the claim that the distribution of health care through the free market with corporations and insurance agencies making a profit is actually more efficient. They point to the amount of bureaucracy and extra paperwork demanded by insurance companies that have doubled and tripled the number of office staff that doctors require. Much bureaucratic inefficiency could be eliminated with a single-payer system. Efficiency in hospitals could be achieved by ending the attempt of every hospital to offer the latest and most up-to-date technology in order to attract high-paying customers, and instead strategically locating different hospital services. According to the Connecticut Coalition for Universal Health Care, administrative costs and profit-taking account for 20 to 30 percent of revenues at for-profit hospitals, whereas Medicare only spends 3 percent on administration and has no profit margin.

Government-provided health care is not without inefficiency, however. Medicare and Medicaid lose an estimated $60 billion or more annually to fraud which contributes a great deal to the high per capita cost of health care in the United States compared to other nations. Neither government-sponsored health-care systems nor private insurance systems have been able to implement cost-containment measures that would shift from costly fee-for-service models that reward physicians and hospitals for maximum testing and treatment to rewarding them for maintaining patient health at lower cost.

Proponents of the current fee-for-service system argue that a single-payer universal health care system (government run, with no intermediary insurance companies) would mean a decrease in both the quantity and quality of care and would be too costly. However, the United States spends at least 40 percent more per capita on health care than other industrialized countries that have universal government-sponsored health care. Still, we rank lower than these countries on many health indicators, such as infant mortality, life expectancy, and rates of immunization. In addition, many people do not have access to basic health services. It is clear, historically, that the private sector will not make health care more accessible to those without financial means without being forced to do so.

The Affordable Care Act passed in March 2010 aims to end some of the abuses of the insurance industry and increase health care coverage. It requires everyone to have health insurance by 2014. Large and medium employers will be required to provide health insurance to their employees. Others will be covered by expansion of Medicaid among the poor and a requirement that middle-class people who are self-employed or work for small firms purchase their own policies. This act helps children get health coverage, ends lifetime and most annual limits on care, allows young adults under twenty-six to stay on their parent's health insurance, and gives patients access to recommended preventive services without cost. It also tries to increase coverage even before 2014 by offering tax credits to small businesses that provide insurance for their employees and by offering a preexisting condition insurance plan (PCIP) for those who are denied coverage by private insurance companies. However, this act does nothing to address directly the exponentially increasing cost of health care or insurance coverage in the United States. Universal health insurance coverage is a step forward, but if deductibles and co-pays are too high, health care will continue to be, for many, an elusive privilege. Furthermore, minimally employed people who cannot afford insurance but do not qualify for Medicaid will have a hard time complying with the requirement that they buy insurance. Therefore, this act does not represent universal health care coverage.

HEALTH CARE AS A PUBLIC GOOD

In many ancient cultures hospitals and caring for the sick were associated with religious institutions. In Judaism and Christianity, caring for those who had no one to care for them has been viewed as an aspect of religious duty (Ex 22:22; Is 61:1; Mt 25:35; Lk 7:22; Jas 1:27). The first hospitals in the United States in the 1700s were connected to the church and were originally houses for the poor and elderly—hence, the denominational affiliations still attached to many hospitals. In the early to mid-1900s many of these charities eventually turned into money-making enterprises, and entrepreneurs replaced church workers. Recent studies reveal, however, that 20 percent of hospitals are still controlled by religious organizations, with the Catholic health-care system accounting for 70 percent of the religiously run private nonprofit hospitals. Furthermore, many churches and small nonprofits still run community health clinics today.

Provision of basic health care is not only about respecting individual human dignity, but also is imperative for promoting flourishing communities. The most obvious community benefit of health care as a public good is the prevention of communicable diseases. Sexually transmitted diseases, deadly viruses, and even the flu can affect all community members if not prevented and/or treated. Economic productivity also suffers when there is a lack of adequate health care. Many people without basic health care might not even realize what it would feel like to be in good health. Ill health affects the ability of people to participate fully not only in work but in all facets of community life. It is no surprise, for example, that disability and bad health are found in a higher percentage of people who are homeless than in the general population. Health disparities, exacerbated by the closing of public hospitals, have a negative effect on our communities and on our ideal of being a democratic nation that values equal opportunity.

The dominant thinking in the United States is that we are an association of private individuals, each out for his or her own in competition with others. While Americans historically uphold the value of equal opportunity, we do not consistently ensure that such a reality exists. Rather than seeing the tax system as a way to provide goods and services to all, many tend to see taxation as a burden. The result of this anti-tax sentiment is a much lower rate of taxation than in other developed nations—and a resulting lack of funding for public goods. According to the Tax Policy Center, in 2006 US taxes at all levels of government made up 28 percent of gross domestic product (GDP), compared with an average of 36 percent of GDP for the thirty member-countries of the Organization for Economic Co-operation and Development (OECD). Only Mexico, Turkey, South Korea, and Japan had lower tax percentages.

The communal orientation of the biblical world view is an alternative to our nation's individualistic focus. The biblical people of Israel were told repeatedly that their well-being was a gift from God, not earned. They were brought out of slavery by a God of justice and liberation. While God did not expect repayment, God did expect the people to care for those least well off in their communities, to treat each person with dignity, and to set up systems that ensured the well-being of all. Similarly, Jesus advocated for systems of liberation and justice. He overturned the tables of the moneychangers in the Temple because they were unjustly defrauding the poor. If we want to see a society of equal opportunity, health care coverage for everyone is a moral necessity. The early Christian communities understood this truth: "All who believed were together and had all things in common; they would sell their possession and goods and distribute the proceeds to all, as any had need" (Acts 2:44–45).

In the case, board member Fred Trask asks why the hospital isn't run more like a business. That is, why not close the hospital programs and units that are money losers? Apart from denying basic services to people if emergency rooms or maternity wards are shut down, there is the larger question of whether health care should be run like a business. Should we provide only those services that are money makers? Basic preventative care and public health interventions to prevent and manage diseases, injuries, and other health conditions are not where profit lies, but do we really want to determine what services to provide based on whether they make a profit? The God of justice and liberation expects humans to use the resources of this world wisely. There are justifiable reasons for health care rationing in response to limited resources, but the inability of people to pay for services or the ability of a service to garner profit should not be relevant factors in determining who does or does not get particular health care. God would not condone a system that prioritizes profit over communal flourishing. The merits of rationing particular forms of health care or prioritizing specific groups should be debated publicly. The closing of public hospitals is an invisible way of rationing care in which the poor and people of color are being sacrificed. The larger question for us to ponder is whether health care is to be a public good or a private privilege only for those able to pay?

WORKER JUSTICE

Beatrice, as CEO of Washington Memorial, has negotiated with the unions. She says that in the past Washington Memorial offered generous salaries and pension contracts that it currently cannot fund. The practical answer is to make workers bear a share of the burden associated with the financial straits of the hospital. Clearly, Beatrice has limited options. In most public hospital closures workers were asked to sacrifice pay and benefits until it became clear that even this was not sufficient to keep doors open. According to recent studies only 10 to 12 percent of public-sector workers were unionized in the 1950s and 1960s, compared to one-third to one-half of all private-sector workers. By the mid-1980s there was a reversal, with over one-third of the public-sector work force unionized and only 14 percent of the private sector. While unions have led to many different kinds of worker protections, such as work-place safety, standard work weeks, overtime pay, and child-labor laws, unions have also given workers vital collective bargaining rights with employers. All of these benefits have given workers more security and promoted flourishing communities. Officials of many American states, cities, and counties suffering from lowered tax revenues due to the recession and decreasing payments from the federal government claim that they are unable to fulfill the union contracts they have negotiated in the past. Beatrice's efforts to negotiate with the unions need to be viewed in relationship to this larger picture.

While Beatrice might have few other places to turn, the erosion of worker pay, benefits, and union organizing rights should be limited and short term. It is not right to place the burden for the hospital crisis on the workers; higher paid doctors, administrators, and the taxpayers should all bear a share of the financial burden. Also important to note is that the increasing privatization of public institutions has dealt a heavy blow to unionization because a larger percentage of public-sector jobs are union-ized. Women and minorities are more negatively affected by these changes because they are more heavily represented in public-sector jobs. While unions were not a feature of biblical times, there are biblical stories that point to structuring work to meet the needs of people rather than only to garner profit for the employer. For example, in the parable of Laborers in the Vineyard (Mt 20:1–16), the landowner pays all a wage sufficient to live on, regardless of the number of hours worked. Of course, business owners must be competitive to stay afloat in our economy as it is structured, but such competitiveness should not be at the expense of worker sustenance and security.

The consistent message of the Exodus narrative and the prophetic poetry is that the rich are to act in solidarity with the poor, not only through charity but also through just systems of governance and equitable distribution of resources. Moses taught: "You shall not withhold the wages of the poor and needy laborers, whether other Israelites or aliens [illegal immigrants] who reside in your land in one of your towns. You shall pay them their wages daily before sunset, because they are poor and their livelihood depends on them; otherwise they might cry to the Lord against you, and you would incur guilt" (Dt 24:14–15). Justice distributes power so that people can take care of themselves and participate in community life. Good jobs and just work places are integral to democratic society.

While unions are clearly important for securing worker justice, not all union policies and demands over the last decades have been wise or sustain-able. Many public employees were granted generous benefits during boom times that are hard to sustain today. For example, some public-employee unions have full retirement after twenty to twenty-five years on the job, and so there have been cases of people retiring in their forties, getting a second public job, and then retiring at age sixty-five with two pensions funded from public coffers. While not common for most public employees, some hospital workers have benefited from such unsustainable retirement pack-ages in the past. Public institutions like Washington Memorial might have legitimate reasons for limiting benefits that privilege workers unfairly and lead to inequitable distribution of resources. We should be careful not to forget, however, that union jobs offer a living wage and benefits, especially health insurance, that many jobs do not provide. These good-paying jobs no only help individuals but also support our economy and ensure that fewer people need to use governmental safety nets.

CONCLUSION

Beatrice has several short-term options for saving Washington Memorial Hospital. She will definitely have to tighten up accounting practices and find emergency funds to tide the hospital over for a while, but she will most likely need to take more drastic steps as well, such as cutting salaries and/ or closing satellite hospitals. Addressing the moral issue of health care as a right and as a public good will take longer-term solutions beyond those CEOs of failing public hospitals can enact. Making provision of health care economically efficient will require exploration of cost-containment systems, and making health care universally accessible will entail reconsideration of funding systems, including single-payer schemes. If we are to achieve universal access to health care, the tax burden on the rich and on corporations will undoubtedly need to increase. Jesus' command to love our neighbor and the communal orientation of the biblical world view call us to create systems that ensure the well-being of all, not only those who can afford health coverage. By making health care universally accessible, we would be acting in solidarity to support the dignity of each human person and we would be promoting healthier communities.

ADDITIONAL SOURCES

Berry, Leonard, and Kent Seltman. *Management Lessons from Mayo Clinic: One of the World's Most Admired Service Institutions*. New York: McGraw-Hill, 2008.

Branigan, Michael C., and Judith A. Boss. *Healthcare Ethics in a Diverse Society*. New York: McGraw-Hill, 2001.

Graban, Marc. *Lean Hospitals: Improving Quality, Patient Safety and Employee Satisfaction*. New York: Taylor and Francis, 2009.

Kelly, David F. *Critical Care Ethics: Treatment Decisions in American Hospitals*. Eugene, OR: Wipf and Stock Publishers, 2002.

Staff of the *Washington Post. Landmark: The Inside Story of America's New Health Care Law and What It Means for Us All*. Washington, D.C.: The Washington Post, 2010.

Valbrun, Marjorie. "Hospital Closings Jeopardize Care in Ethnic Communities," America's Wire (January 20, 2011). Available on the newamericamedia.org website.

Walker, Kara Odom, Daphne Calmes, Nancy Hanna, and Richard Baker. "The Impact of Public Hospital Closure on Medical and Residency Education: Implications and Recommendations," *Journal of National Medical Association* 100, no. 12 (December 2008): 1377–83.

Related Website

US Department of Health and Human Services, http://www.healthcare.gov/law/introduction/index.html.

PART VII

SEXUALITY

Case

What Makes a Marriage?

It was the night before the sixtieth-wedding celebration that the five children of George and Lucy Herman were preparing for their parents. The celebration was to be held at the home of the oldest son, and the five siblings and spouses had worked much of the day moving furniture, setting up the rented tables and chairs, buying tablecloths, and making final arrangements to have flowers, a catered meal, and a cake delivered the next day. George and Lucy had just made the rounds, kissing their children and grandchildren goodbye and thanking them for all their work. The grandchildren, ranging in age from the late teens to the mid thirties, had just dispersed, the older married ones to take their children home or to the hotels where they were staying, and the younger ones to a local nightspot.

As George and Lucy and the last of the "young folks" departed, leaving only the siblings and their spouses, the gathering in the kitchen quieted. Maggie, the youngest sister, asked her oldest brother: "Bob, what made you let Cathy bring her boyfriend to live with her in your house? Ted and I were really shocked to hear it." All ears perked up as the siblings waited for a reply, a little anxious that an argument was approaching; Maggie, the most conservative of the siblings, had a history of provoking controversy in the family. Bob, though a lector in his Catholic parish, was known to be independent, a kind of libertarian in most areas. While all the siblings had originally practiced their parents' devout Roman Catholic faith, some were now, like Maggie, entrenched in evangelical or other conservative churches, while others were strongly antireligious. There could well be a storm brewing in the Herman family.

After a short pause Bob answered. "Cathy met Andy in her first week as a freshman at the university. They dated for the next year. She hated the

This case was prepared by Christine E. Gudorf and the commentary by James B. Martin-Schramm. The names of all persons and institutions have been disguised to protect the privacy of those involved.

dorms, even before she moved in that first year, and we had agreed that after the mandatory first year in the dorm we would get her a one-bedroom apartment for her sophomore year. When our daughters were in high school, we asked them to wait for sex until they were at least eighteen, and they agreed. We told them that what was most important to us was that they were safe and that their sexual relationships were respectful. So we made a deal with them that, after they were eighteen, they would tell us before they decided they were ready to have sex, and we would make sure they had contraceptive prescriptions through our health plan. Most of you know that Cathy was a total bookworm in high school, completing a full two years of AP courses. She virtually never dated. At the end of her freshman year of college she came to us and said she and Andy were ready for sex, and Lisa took her to the doctor for a checkup and prescription.

"That summer she lived at home, and I'm sure they had sex here in the house. When she got her apartment in the fall, Andy moved in with her. They used what he saved in rent to outfit the apartment and to fund a couple of ski trips for the two of them that year. In their junior year they moved to a larger apartment in a better area. After two years of living together and a previous year of dating, it was clear that this was a serious relationship. They are both dean's list students headed for graduate school. Frankly, since we have three empty bedrooms with baths, it seemed silly for us to pay Cathy's share of the rent somewhere else in the city, and for Andrew to pay rent, when they could live here and save money for graduate school."

Lisa, Cathy's mother, added: "They were nineteen when they moved in together, and twenty-one when they moved in with us. We would never have agreed if they were fifteen or sixteen, but they were adults. And both of them are straight arrows—no drugs, rarely a beer or two. They are planning a wedding in March or April—you will all get notices of the date next month." There was a murmur of excitement—Herman family weddings were always enjoyable occasions.

Ed, the youngest of the brothers, put in, "But they are only twenty-one, and as you said, Cathy has hardly dated anyone else. Aren't you afraid that they are too immature to make a lifelong commitment?"

"Hold on, Ed!" laughed Ann, the oldest of the girls, who had become engaged to her husband of almost forty years in high school and married him after their freshman year at the university. "Some of you just take longer to grow up than the rest of us." Everyone chuckled.

Maggie responded, "Don't you worry about the example you are setting for your younger kids, implying to Chris and Sean that premarital sex is OK? We all know that Sean has been a little wild." Sean was sixteen, the youngest of Bob and Lisa's three children, and the only son. Over the last year he had more than once come home drunk and had once admitted to using pot. Some months ago his parents had begun breathalyzer tests when he came home and irregular drug tests. Unlike his sisters, he did not apply himself in school; it took regular parental supervision to see that he stayed off academic probation.

Bob stiffened. "Chris is doing just fine at the university—she is also on the dean's list, and you all know she won a first at the nationals in diving last year. She just turned twenty, will be graduating in May, a year early, and plans to do her MBA while still on the last year of her diving scholarship. She brought her boyfriend from school on the family vacation last summer, and seeing him with us for a week made her realize that he wasn't the prize she thought he was. She has been dating another boy for the last six months, and he seems like a nice guy. She just told us she might be ready to get the contraceptive prescription this coming summer if all continues well." Lisa added: "We are proud of our relationships with our daughters—we trust them to make good choices, and they trust us enough to tell us what is going on in their lives. Sean is more difficult."

Another Herman sibling, Rich, laughed, and added, "Boys are always harder. Tom didn't grow up till he was almost thirty, married with kids, and you all know our worries about Brent's drinking. Our boys just don't seem to have any direction compared to the girls." Rich and Carly's daughters, a teacher and an ER nurse, were both married with babies. Their son, Tom, worked construction. He and his wife, Sheila, had two children. The previous year Rich and Carly's youngest son, twenty-year-old Brent, had almost killed himself in a drunken car wreck that left him in a medically induced coma for four months. It was a miracle he survived, but even before his therapy ended, he was back to drinking. This had been hard for Carly, a lifelong Mormon, and Rich, who had converted to the Latter Day Saints and then married Carly in the Temple in Salt Lake City. The Mormon Word of Wisdom prohibits the consumption of alcohol as well as tea and coffee on the grounds that they are not healthy for the body.

Maggie pressed on. "But sex before marriage is not only morally wrong, it is dangerous. And if kids have support in breaking one religious rule, it undermines their respect for all rules. Will you feel the same way if Sean turns eighteen and expects you to provide condoms and sexual health checkups so that he can get drunk and have sex with different girls every week?"

Ed, who was often annoyed with what he called Maggie's self-righteousness, asked, "Who are you to judge? It's not like your kids never had premarital sex."

Maggie recoiled as if bitten. One of her daughters, while in her early twenties, had gotten pregnant in a relatively long-term sexual relationship and given the newborn up for adoption. It had been an open adoption; she regularly visited the child, who was now in school, and had always been very open with the extended family about it. But Maggie had not only been mortified at her daughter's decision, she had also mourned the loss of her first grandchild, since she did not have visitation rights. "I am not saying that kids can be prevented from having pre-marital sex. I am only saying that it is important that we insist that the proper place for sex is in marriage."

Ann replied, "Maggie, I am not so much interested in whether the two are married as I am in the quality of their relationship. As a historian [Ann taught at the major state university in her state], I have to say that even in Christianity, formal marriage and committed, respectful relationships have not often been the same. Because marriages were made for purposes of political power, wealth, and preserving property in families, women and sometimes men were forced into marriages about which they had no say. Consequently, many women were in miserable marriages, frequently abused—and many men loved and treated their long-time mistresses much better than their wives. What is so important about marriage for you, Maggie?"

"That's a pretty strange thing to ask in this crowd. All five of us—except me—are married, and have been for fifteen to forty years now. [Two of the siblings, including Maggie, had been divorced and one had remarried—one of the reasons they were no longer Catholic.] And you all know I hope that Ted and I will work things out and get married. Despite the possibility of divorce, marriage means stability, companionship, fidelity, a partnership for raising children. I want that for myself and my kids. Don't you?" Maggie asked.

"Of course we do," Ann responded. "But what Bob was saying is that Cathy and Andy have put that kind of relationship together, and he and Lisa recognize it and approve. Do you really think couples today would—or even should—get married without ever having sex? You know, Frank [her husband] has a nephew who dated the same girl for seven years without having sex. They got married in the Catholic Church, and then on their honeymoon she decided she didn't like sex; she insisted that she wanted to wait to have sex until it was time to have a baby. The marriage lasted six months, and now the nephew is having a devil of a time getting an annulment. I think if marriages today are going to make it for fifty to sixty years, they have to have a strong dose of sexual attraction." She glanced across the room at Frank, her husband, who added loudly: "Amen to that!"

Maggie asked, "So you are proposing to simply throw out two thousand years of Christian teaching that sex only belongs in marriage?"

Ann responded, "Maggie, two things. First, as a historian, I have to tell you that it is very doubtful that the majority of Christians ever waited until marriage to have sex. This was especially true for men, but also for women and girls of the servant class, whose bodies could be used with impunity by upper-class men. And for centuries in many rural parts of Europe priests were not in residence for long periods, so people lived together until a priest came months or years later to bless their marriage. The teaching may be two thousand years old, but Christian practice was often very different. Second, at a personal level, isn't it more important to ask what values the rule about no sex outside marriage was supposed to protect? I have always thought it was to protect children, whose lives could be forever damaged if they were born outside marriage. While I don't think that the marriage ceremony is as important as you do, I do think that relationships that produce children should at least intend to have the permanence of marriage. That's why I think that unmarried people who have sex have an absolute obligation to use reliable contraception."

Rich's wife, Carly, a nurse who was usually quiet at these rambunctious Herman get-togethers, asked: "I agree that contraception is vital. But under what other conditions do we tell unmarried kids sex is all right? Isn't that the problem—it's so hard to draw the line that we hang onto marriage as the line between the allowed and the forbidden? I know our Jennie fell in love with at least five guys that she dated for six months or more, one after another, before she met her husband. It can't be enough to say that sex is acceptable if you love the guy, or some people like Jennie could have ten or more sexual partners before they are twenty-five. The STD [sexually transmitted disease] risk would be enormous."

Maggie pounced on that idea: "Yes, the issue is not just a religious and moral one now but a health concern. Many of these STDs are incurable, like herpes and genital warts, not to mention HIV/AIDS. Contraceptives don't protect against any of these, except condoms for HIV/AIDS. I just read that the population with the highest rates of new STDs now is people over fifty! Public-health officials think that Viagra and its clones are responsible for that."

Frank added: "Well, I bet it's not just Viagra, but the divorce rate. There are so many more middle-aged and older people without marital partners than there used to be. I worry about Pete [their son, whose wife divorced him two years ago]. He hasn't started dating yet, but after being married for eleven years, he is probably going to be dating divorcees; people who have been married get used to having sex to satisfy arousal. I don't imagine divorced people wait months or years into a new relationship before they have sex. But that doesn't mean that they end up marrying the person they are dating and having sex with."

"Right you are, Frank," said Ed, who, like Maggie, had been divorced. Unlike Maggie, Ed had been remarried for fifteen years; his wife, Sally, had left an hour before to visit her mother, who lived nearby. "I didn't date for four years after Jen left. I was too busy trying to combine care of two little boys and my job. But when I did, I had sex with a couple of the women I dated before I met Sally and eventually persuaded her to move in. You all know it took four years of us living together for me to convince her we should get married. Her experience of holy matrimony had been hell. I think it's ridiculous to ask people to get married before they live together. Marriage is hard, and it takes a lot of different kinds of compatibility that you just can't know until you have lived with someone for a while. But I thanked my lucky stars that I didn't pick up any diseases when I was dating. I have friends who did."

Maggie returned to her theme. "So you're all saying that it's all right to have sex outside marriage if you were married and got used to having sex, or if you arc living with someone you love? When teenage kids want to move their boyfriends or girlfriends into their rooms, sex is fine? Or when they move out and get their own apartments?"

"No," said Lisa impatiently. "They need to have a certain degree of maturity—eighteen is too early for some of them, especially boys, I suspect— but they also need to be committed to the other person, to love that person, and to be willing to compromise on all kinds of things, even important things. Cathy and Andy have been applying to graduate schools, and they are only looking at schools in places that have programs for both of them. They have both nixed their first and second choices because there was no program in that city that worked for the other one. That takes commitment and compromise. I know this isn't a full answer. We are dealing with other problems with Sean now, though we know this one is coming too. He is not mature, not above confusing momentary lust with love, and when he begins to date more, he may well turn from one girl to the next. But he has our example and that of his sisters of responsible sexual relationships. Do you really think that if we had simply told all our kids to wait for sex till marriage, and not had Cathy and Andrew move in, that Sean would be any more responsible with sex in dating?"

A few shook their heads. Some of the couples were preparing to leave for their homes and hotels when Maggie asked one final question: "What will you say to Sean if your fears come true? What if he does sleep around with different girls and makes no commitments to any of them? You didn't object to his sisters having premarital sex, so how can you object to him doing the same? Do you think that teenagers of any age, or even college kids, have the judgment to distinguish the kinds of qualities and relationships that you are all saying should be present for responsible premarital sex?"

Bob retorted: "I know enough of the way Sean thinks to know that he will definitely try to put his own premarital sexual activity in the same category as his sisters, but I think we can deal with that, Maggie. At his level of maturity he is not going to be dating one girl for six to twelve months before he tries to move the relationship toward sex as his sisters have done. Right now he sometimes forgets a date, or just blows it off if something more exciting comes up with his buddies. He doesn't have the maturity for any kind of real relationship with a girl. Yeah, Sean will try to justify his own probably promiscuous premarital sexual activity by pointing to our approving his sisters' premarital sex, but you seem to think that all premarital sex belongs in the same category. We think Cathy's and Andy's relationship belongs in the 'marital' category because of its quality. Are you saying their sex is no different from casual, irresponsible premarital sex because they have not formalized their relationship with a marriage ceremony?"

Maggie was silent. Bob walked over to Maggie and, picking up the box of unused decorations that she had brought from her home, said: "Mags, I'm sorry I don't see this your way. But if all of us look around at all our kids, some of whom were raised strictly, some very liberally, some within actively involved church-going families and some without religion at all, we all have at least one child who has been burned by alcohol, drugs, or sex. I don't know how to get around that, except to say that kids make their own choices." Bob walked Maggie to her car. "Tell Ted we missed him tonight and not to forget to bring his big cooler for the drinks."

As Maggie slipped into the front seat and Bob put the box in the back, she looked up at him and said: "I like rules. They provide structure, and in my experience, kids need structure. The kind of standard that you propose seems to me to require too much thought and judgment for kids to use well. Sean is not alone in being immature and seeking excitement. In fact, he is probably more typical of teenagers than his sisters, certainly more typical of boys. Maybe we need the clear and absolute rules for the majority who are immature." As she turned the key, she smiled and added, "This is a real life issue for me right now, Bob. Ted wants me to give up my apartment and move into his house with him. He sees that—kind of like Ed says—as a trial marriage. All my kids like him. The girls are settled and would be happy for us, but I don't know what effect my moving in would have on Ben. He's only a junior at UCLA, and though he has always been responsible, he has not dated much. I don't want to give him a bad example. Pray for me, please."

Commentary

This case raises several difficult questions that confront many families today. Should Maggie move in with Ted for what he calls a trial marriage? Is Maggie justifiably concerned that doing so might set a bad example for her children, especially her youngest son, Ben? Are Bob and Lisa being unfaithful to the Christian tradition of marriage by supporting their eldest daughter's decision to live with her boyfriend for the past three years? Are Ed and Ann right that it is unwise for couples to get married before they have lived together for a while and had sex together? Does the rapid rise of cohabitation in the United States and around the world mean Christian communities should revise the tradition of marriage and their views about premarital sex?

MARRIAGE, DIVORCE, COHABITATION, AND SEXUALLY TRANSMITTED DISEASES

Fewer American men and women are getting married, but those that do have more education and are older than ever before. According to the US Census Bureau the proportion of the US population that is married dropped from 57 percent in 2000 to 54 percent in 2010. Down from 72 percent in 1960, the percentage is now at the lowest level since the Census Bureau started collecting this information one hundred years ago. The decline has been most precipitous among young adults (ages 25–34). Over 80 percent of young adults were married in the late 1960s; today that percentage has been cut almost in half. From 2000 to 2009 the percentage of young adults who are married dropped from 55 percent to 45 percent. This is the first time in US history that the proportion of unmarried young adults has exceeded the proportion of married young adults. Those with less education are less likely to be married. The proportion of married young adults with a high school diploma or less dropped from 54 percent in 2000 to 44 percent in 2009. In contrast, the percentage of married young adults with a college education and higher dropped only from 56 percent in 2000 to 52 percent in 2009. It sounds as though Cathy and Andy may soon be joining this cohort. The US Census Bureau also reported that the median age at first marriage reached its highest level in

252

2010: for men, 28.2 years compared to 26.8 years in 2000; for women, 26.1 years compared to 25 years in 2000. At the age of 22, Cathy and Andy will be well below the median.

Despite these statistics, the National Center for Health Statistics reported in 2009 that most Americans are likely to get married and that the probability of being married by age forty is nearly 84 percent. A higher proportion of Americans marry at some point in their lives than in most other Western nations. For example, only 70 percent in Sweden and 68 percent in France are married by age 40. Compared to Canadians, Americans have almost twice as many marriages per 1,000 women. After divorce about two-thirds of US women and three-fourths of US men decide to remarry. These statistics are reflected in the case by Ed's and Sally's marriage after both had gone through a divorce.

The only thing that comes close to rivaling US marriage rates are US divorce rates. According to the United Nations *Demographic Yearbook,* the United States has the highest divorce rate in the Western world, with 3.4 divorces per 1,000 people. Only Russia (5.0), Belarus (3.8), Ukraine (3.6), and Moldova (3.5) have higher divorce rates. The US divorce rate has been declining for three decades, however. According to the Centers for Disease Control and Prevention's (CDC's) National Vital Statistics System, the US divorce rate peaked in 1981 at nearly 5.4 divorces per 1,000 people and is now at its lowest level since 1970 at a rate of 3.4 divorces per 1,000 people. There were 840,000 divorces and annulments in the United States in 2009 compared to 2,080,000 marriages. The percentage of divorces compared to marriages per year has hovered around 40 percent for the past decade. The US Census Bureau reported in 2009 that first marriages currently last a median of eight years before they end in divorce. Of currently married couples only 55 percent of the marriages have lasted fifteen years, only 35 percent have lasted twenty-five years, and only 6 percent have lasted fifty years. Divorce rates are lowest among the college educated and substantially higher for the rest of the population. Two of the five Herman siblings have gone through a divorce. Given the high divorce rate three decades ago, US Census data shows that almost half of the US population comes from divorced homes.

While divorce and marriage rates have been declining, the number of Americans deciding to live together has been increasingly rapidly. In 2011 the US Census Bureau reported that cohabitation in the United States has never been higher. The number of opposite-sex couples living together increased 13 percent, from 6.7 million in 2009 to 7.5 million in 2010. Cathy's and Andy's relationship contributed to these statistics. Cohabitation has nearly doubled since 1990. Ed's and Sally's decision to live together for four years before they got married fifteen years ago contributed to this longer trend. In 2010 the Pew Research Center published a study that found 44 percent of adults have cohabited at least once. According to a 2009 study by the National Center on Health Statistics, those who live together after getting engaged have about the same chances of getting a divorce as couples who do not cohabit before marriage. Those who move in together without having any clear plan to marry, however, get divorced more often. This may not bode well for Cathy and Andy, who only recently got engaged. A 2009 federally funded national study of dating and cohabitation revealed that only 9 percent of men and 5 percent of women decided to live together in order to "to test the relationship before marriage." Almost half said they just wanted to be able to spend more time together as a couple. It is clear the economic recession that began in 2008 led to an increase in the number of Americans deciding to live together. Regardless of the motivation, however, most couples who live together either get married or split up after two years.

Researchers are racing to catch up with cohabitation trends. Several studies published in the *Journal of Marriage and Family* over the past two decades have demonstrated that premarital cohabitation has had a negative impact overall on marital quality and marital stability. This is especially true for post-divorce cohabitation, which tends to be associated with lower measures of marital quality and thus contributes to remarriage instability. Thus far, Ed and Sally appear to be beating the odds. A 2010 study in the journal *Demography,* however, demonstrates that premarital cohabitation is associated with greater marital instability only for non-Hispanic white women and not for non-Hispanic blacks and Mexican American women. The study claims that as cohabitation has become more common, fewer divorce-prone individuals are deciding to live together.

Concerns about marital quality and stability are one thing; the impact on children is another. According to a study published by the Population Reference Bureau, 41 percent of all US births in 2008 took place outside marriage. Approximately half of these births were to cohabiting couples, which tend to be less stable and have fewer economic resources than married couples. Andrew Cherlin, professor of sociology at Johns Hopkins University and author of *The Marriage-Go-Round*, claims that more than half of the children born to parents who live together will see their parents separate by the time they are nine, whereas only 25 percent of the children born to married couples will see their parents divorce in this time frame. Given this data, there is good reason to fear that declining marriage rates, high divorce rates, and increased births to cohabiting couples have put more children at risk of growing up poor, which can affect their health and long-term economic prospects.

Maggie does not mention the heightened risk of child poverty in the case, but she does urge her siblings to think about the serious health risks posed by the spread of STDs for the young and old alike. There are at least twenty-five different STDs that are spread through vaginal, anal, and oral sex. The United States only tracks some of these diseases. Reporting for gonorrhea and syphilis began in 1941, but chlamydia has been reported only since 1984. There is also some limited reporting for genital herpes and genital warts. The CDC estimates that 19 million new STD infections occur each year, almost half of them among young people ages fifteen to twenty-four. Cases of syphilis have remained fairly constant over the past decade, and there has recently been a slight downturn in the cases of gonorrhea. Cases of chlamydia, however, have nearly doubled, from 662,647 in 1999 to 1,244,180 in 2009. Bob and Lisa are proud that their daughters have been willing to come to them for access to birth control when they are ready for sexual intercourse, but Maggie is right that contraceptives don't prevent STDs. The only exception is the latex condom, which reduces the spread of HIV, which causes AIDS. The CDC estimates that 1.1 million people are living with HIV and that more than half a million people have died from developing AIDS. Maggie is also correct that people over fifty years of age have the highest rate of new STD infections. In fact, 407,000 of the 1.1 million with HIV are over fifty.

Maggie might take some solace in a 2011 study by the National Center for Health Statistics that found 27 percent of young men and 29 percent of young women ages 15–24 claimed they had never had a sexual encounter, compared to 22 percent for both males and females in a 2002 study. For ages 20–24, 12 percent of women and 13 percent of men said they had never had sexual contact, an increase from 8 percent for both sexes in 2002. For the vast majority who are sexually active, however, the study noted a significant increase in oral sex, which is linked with the growth of genital herpes and other STDs in the United States. Among those ages 15–24, 63 percent of women and 64 percent of men said they had had oral sex. Maggie would likely be disconcerted by this statistic as she thinks about her son, Ben, who is a junior at UCLA.

This review of key statistics associated with marriage, divorce, cohabitation, and STDs reflects important changes in the United States. Increasing measures of gender equality, the impact of globalization on wages and job opportunities, and the arrival of myriad birth control technologies have all had important impacts on US culture and especially on the institution of marriage. Andrew Cherlin points out that "marriage is no longer regarded as the only acceptable arrangement for having sexual relations and for raising children. Marriage is still important, but it is now optional: people can start relationships or have children without it."

A BRIEF HISTORY OF MARRIAGE
AND SUMMARY OF CHRISTIAN VIEWS

The institution of marriage has played an important role in almost every manifestation of human civilization throughout history—in large measure because it has sustained the well-being of related people by providing a framework for care of the young and the old.

Throughout history marriage has taken diverse forms and served several functions. With regard to the latter, marriage has established inheritance lines, reinforced gender roles, and circumscribed sexual activity. With regard to the former, it appears that for much of human history most civilizations practiced polygyny rather than monogamy; that is, men had many wives rather than only one. Certainly the Hebrew Bible reflects this reality at various points. Over time this changed, however, and monogamy became the standard in the Greco-Roman era, though in neither culture was sex confined to marriage. Pederasty, concubinage, prostitution, and sexual intercourse with slaves were all common.

In the case Ann is right that throughout much of Western history marriage was undertaken primarily to preserve property, increase wealth, and achieve greater measures of political power. Many families forced their children, especially girls, into marriages they did not want. Over time, however, the control of marriage shifted away from the families to the individuals involved. Historians point to the seventeenth and eighteenth centuries as an important turning point when marriages came to be viewed less in terms of their benefits to families and more in terms of the experience of love and personal happiness between the two who desired to be married.

At the same time, the state became increasingly involved in sanctioning unions and in this way also shaped gender roles. This was especially true in the United States, where Christian emphases on mutual consent and the couple becoming "one flesh" (Mk 10:8; Gn 2:24) were joined with Anglo-American views regarding contracts and the "legal oneness" of a husband and wife. Since men were the only ones regarded as legal citizens, marriage served to bolster the financial strength of men and reduced the status of women. Husbands were responsible for the economic well-being of the household, and women were responsible for childrearing and homemaking.

This patriarchal model began to break down in the transition to the twentieth century. Noted historian Stephanie Coontz argues in *Marriage, a History* that what emerged was a combination of the "love match" with the "male provider marriage." Gender relations now were based not on male superiority but rather on male/female complementarity. More recently essentialist appeals to masculine and feminine gender roles and gender complementarity have been aggressively critiqued by feminists and others.

Christian views about marriage have also evolved over time. Neither Jesus nor the apostle Paul was married, but many of the early Christians were. While Jesus affirmed a wedding celebration by turning water into wine in Cana (Jn 2:1–11), he also permitted divorce on the grounds of unchastity in the Gospel of Matthew (Mt 5:31–32; Mt 19:3–9). In addition, Jesus challenged the centrality of family life when he declared: "Do not think that I have come to bring peace to the earth; I have not come to bring peace, but a sword. For I have come to set a man against his father, and a daughter against her mother, and a daughter-in-law against her mother-in-law" (Mt 10:34–35). Expecting the imminent return of Christ, Paul urged unmarried and widowed Christians "to remain in the condition in which you were called" (1 Cor 7:8). Paul also harbored a skeptical view regarding sexuality that was common during the Greco-Roman era; this view led him to encourage sexual renunciation for those who could manage it while also encouraging marriage for those who could not quell their sexual passions (1 Cor 7:9). As the first century wore on, Pauline leaders attempted to quell claims that Christian communities were libertine and socially disruptive by promoting patriarchal Greco-Roman household codes that supported slavery and reinforced the domination of husbands over wives (Col 3:18–4:1; 1 Tm 2:8–15; Eph 5:22–33; 1 Pt 2:11–16; Ti 2:2–10).

Stoicism and Gnosticism had important impacts on early Christianity. The Stoics believed sexual passion could divert a person from a life of reason and thought sexual impulses had to be controlled by rational cultivation of the virtues of prudence, temperance, and fortitude. The Stoic focus on the rational purpose of sex in terms of procreation resonated with many early Christian leaders who were also wrestling with Gnostic views about sexuality. Deeply distrustful of the material and bodily world, some Gnostics opposed all sexual intercourse while others permitted it so long as it was not procreative. This led key Christian theologians like Augustine to affirm the goodness of human sexuality while at the same time viewing sexual desire as distorted by original sin. Augustine affirmed marriage as good, though less good than a celibate life. Augustine thought there were three goods associated with marriage. The first is the gift of children through procreation. Augustine believed the structure of marriage helps ensure the well-being of children. The second is the association of the sexes and the experience of unity that marriage provides. The third is the restraint of lust within the bonds of marriage.

Even though Augustine repudiated extreme Gnostic and Manichean views that disparaged the body and discouraged marriage, much of the history of Christianity until the Reformation was marked by a pessimistic view of sex that cast women as sexual temptresses. Martin Luther and John Calvin had both been deeply influenced by the Augustinian tradition.

They shared Augustine's pessimistic view regarding fallen human nature, and they also agreed that marriage was the appropriate location for sexual desire. In contrast to Augustine, however, both extolled the vocation of marriage over and against the primacy of a celibate life devoted to God and lived within the confines of a religious order. Over time Luther focused less on marriage as the context for procreation and as a corral for lust and more on marriage and the family as the locus for character formation where children would be schooled in love for their neighbor. Luther believed marriage was an institution created by God for the benefit of all human beings and that all of creation would be blessed by it. One of the consequences of the Protestant Reformation, however, was that women were left with few alternatives other than serving as wives and mothers. Largely gone was the opportunity for further education in a convent and greater measures of—albeit celibate—independence.

In the case Ann points out that many Christians throughout the centuries have lived together without the benefit of a legally recognized marriage. In remote areas where priests were scarce, some Europeans practiced a form of informal marriage called self-marriage or processual marriage. Prior to the Council of Trent in the mid-1500s, the Catholic Church accepted couples who stated publicly that they considered themselves married, so long as no coercion was involved and their marriages did not violate church laws about who could marry whom. In England, Henry VIII supported self-marriages, and this practice remained common among the poorer classes until the mid-1850s. Many of these marriages utilized the "ritual of the besom," which involved a couple jumping over a broomstick in the presence of their families and friends. If the couple wanted to end the marriage within the first year, they could gather witnesses and jump backward over the besom. Informal marriages also occurred in the American colonies, especially in frontier areas where religious leaders were few and rules were lax. The same was true in slave-holding states. Faced with slave owners who disregarded kinship bonds and existing marriages, slaves also married each other in informal ceremonies.

The rise of modern methods of contraception in the twentieth century influenced Roman Catholic and Protestant views regarding sexual ethics and marriage. In 1930, Pope Pius XI reaffirmed Catholicism's emphasis on the procreative good of marriage, but he also approved of marital intercourse even when conception could not occur. This led Pope Pius XII to publicly approve the rhythm method. As a consequence, Catholic moral theologians began to focus less on the procreative good of marriage and more on sexual intercourse as a means to promote the unity of spouses in a marriage. Nevertheless, Pope Paul VI declared in 1968 that artificial contraception continued to be immoral in the eyes of the church. Today, many lay Roman Catholics and most Catholic ethicists disagree strongly with this stance. Among Protestants the mainline denominations (Methodist, Lutheran, Presbyterian, among others) teach that it is acceptable to use birth control as long as it is not used to encourage or permit promiscuous behavior. Less liberal Protestant denominations (Southern Baptist, Assemblies of God, and others) approve of the use of contraception only for people who are married to each other, and some teach that using contraception to prevent children altogether is not desirable.

PREMARITAL SEX, COHABITATION, AND CHRISTIAN ETHICS

How should Christians come to terms with the increase in cohabitation and high rates of premarital sex? Should sex be confined to marriage? Are there other historical models? Is the content of a sexual ethic more important than its form (marriage)? This commentary concludes by examining three attempts to answer these questions.

A common summary of the traditional Christian stance regarding sexual ethics is the phrase "chastity in singleness and fidelity in marriage." Many conservative Protestants and Roman Catholics have sought to reaffirm this traditional ethic over the past two to three decades. Their efforts have tended to focus on abstinence-only approaches to sex education in public schools and cultivation of the virtue of chastity within Christian communities. According to a 2007 report issued by the Sexuality Information and Education Council of the United States (SIECUS), Congress has spent over $1.5 billion on abstinence-only programs over the past twenty-five years. The SIECUS report claims "no study in a professional peer-reviewed journal has found these programs to be broadly effective." As evidence, some opponents point to a 2010 Guttmacher Institute report that found pregnancy rates for teens 15–19 increased 3 percent in 2006, which was when abstinence-only campaigns were near their peak in the nation. On the other side, supporters of abstinence-only approaches point to the 2011 study by the National Center for Health Statistics noted above, which found a significant increase in the number of young men and women ages 15–24 who claim they have never had a sexual encounter. A study the same year in the journal *Pediatrics* found that 10 percent of young people with a sexually transmitted disease would not admit to prior sexual activity.

Many Christians base their support for abstinence-only programs less on effectiveness or obligation and more on a desire to cultivate the virtue of chastity. This is especially true within the Roman Catholic community. Chastity is promoted as a positive invitation to cultivate virtue rather than a negative injunction to "just say no." At its core, chastity seeks freedom from sexual impurities but not necessarily freedom from sexual activity, because God created sex and everything God created is good. Chastity is the virtue of understanding and respecting sex by reserving it for its proper time and place—marriage. By cultivating the virtue of chastity a person seeks to be free from all sexual impurities in both the mind and heart. Chastity encourages an understanding of our own sexuality, a deep appreciation of the emotional, physical, mental, and spiritual aspects of sex, and a sincere respect and love for others, including those we date or marry. Chastity encourages a healthy understanding of sexuality, not a repression until marriage. So what makes for a good marriage? Champions of this view believe the virtue of chastity is key.

While some Christians have sought to reaffirm traditional understandings of chastity, others have sought to recover the "betrothal tradition," once relatively common in the history of European Christianity. The most prominent proponent of this view is Adrian Thatcher, a research fellow in applied theology at the University of Exeter in England. In *Living Together and Christian Ethics* Thatcher notes that there have been *two* traditions regarding the beginning of marriage. The conventional and contemporary view is that a marriage begins with a wedding. For many centuries, however, Christians believed that a marriage began with a betrothal, which was followed later by a wedding ceremony. During the betrothal period couples would cohabit and begin to develop the skills they needed to ensure a good marriage. Since sexual intercourse is part of marriage, betrothed couples would not refrain from sex but engage in it. At some point in the future a marriage ceremony would solemnize the union already operative in the lives of the couple.

Thatcher argues that Christian communities should respond to the increase in cohabitation by recovering the betrothal tradition. While it is true that few today say they are testing their relationship to see if it could withstand the rigors of marriage by living together, perhaps more would do so if the Christian communities to which they belonged encouraged them to view cohabitation in this light. In order to do this Thatcher argues that Christian communities need to place greater emphasis and moral weight on the engagement. Once engaged, Christian communities would no longer frown on premarital sex because the betrothal period would be inaugurated with a publicly stated desire to wed. Thatcher urges Christian communities to view the time a couple is engaged and living together as a "catechumenate" that would restore some of the processive, pedagogical, public, and sacramental dimensions of marriage. Just as catechumens prepare for baptism, which ushers them into membership in the church, the betrothal would prepare partners for their wedding, which ushers them into a marriage relationship. From Thatcher's perspective, a marriage is made over time and includes the period between the betrothal and the public celebration of the wedding.

Another way to answer the question that serves as the title of this case is to focus less on the form of a Christian sexual ethic and more on its substance. The renowned moral theologian, Margaret Farley, develops such an approach in her award-winning book *Just Love*. As the title implies, the foundations for this ethic are the principles of justice and love. Farley writes: "It will not do, as some wish, to end all ethical discernment by simply saying that sexual relations and activities are good when they express love; for love is the problem in ethics, not the solution." For Farley, "love is true and just, right and good, insofar as it is a true response to the reality of the beloved, a genuine union between the one who loves and the one loved, and an accurate and adequate affective affirmation of the beloved." Farley acknowledges that justice can mean many things and take different forms, but she focuses on the classical Latin definition, *suum cuique,* which means to render to each his or her due. While it is hard to determine fairly what is owed to whom, Farley believes justice requires respect for the autonomy and relationality of all individuals as ends in themselves and not merely as means to the ends of others.

Farley goes on to identify seven other moral norms that flesh out "just love." On the basis of the first norm, "do no unjust harm," Farley precludes all forms of violence, as well as pornography, prostitution, sexual harassment, pedophilia, and sadomasochism. The second norm, "free consent," requires truth telling, respects privacy, and rules out rape, sexual intimidation, and anything else that does not respect a person's autonomy and relationality. The third norm, "mutuality," makes for "good sex" because it requires sexual partners to respect each other in terms of desire, action, and response. The fourth norm, "equality," rules out sexual relations that reflect major inequalities of power in terms of age, maturity, gender roles, social and economic class, and so forth. The fifth norm, "commitment," acknowledges that sexuality is so important to human life that "it needs to be nurtured, sustained, as well as disciplined, channeled, controlled." The sixth norm, "fruitfulness," extends beyond the traditional focus on the procreative good of marriage to focus on a life that contributes to the flourishing of others. The seventh norm, "social justice," requires sexual partners to take responsibility for their offspring and to oppose all forms of violence in the world.

Thus, what makes a marriage? Farley summarizes her ethic of "just love" in some comments about the institution of marriage:

All of the goals and the realities of marriage as a social framework for love and for life depend, however, on whether the relationship it frames is just. This in turn depends to a great extent on whether the structures of the framework are just. Free choice, mutuality, equality, commitment, fruitfulness, and a responsibility for the wider world can be the measures of this justice.

One wonders how Maggie would respond to Margaret Farley's new framework for sexual ethics, especially as a source of guidance for young men and women. Toward the end of the case she says to her brother Bob: "I like rules. They provide structure, and in my experience, kids need structure. The kind of standard that you propose seems to me to require too much thought and judgment for kids to use well." Maggie's sentiments are shared by a leading Christian ethicist, Stanley Hauerwas. In *A Community of Character* Hauerwas notes that many Christian ethicists (like Margaret Farley) think genital sexual behavior should be evaluated with regard to whether the motivations, intentions, consequences, and the nature of the act itself are motivated by love. Hauerwas thinks this would all be good, "but [it] is a lot for teenagers in the back seat of a car to remember." Hauerwas thinks "any ethic of sex that does not provide direction for how adolescents should learn to understand and govern their sexual behavior cannot be sufficient."

What sexual ethic should Christians commend within the church and to the broader society? Should there be one ethic for adolescents and another for adults? Are appeals to chastity and the tradition of marriage sufficient? Should Christians like Maggie reconceive cohabitation through the lens of the betrothal tradition? Is a "just love" framework sufficiently expansive to provide helpful normative guidance for the various characters in the case? What kinds of moral guidance can the church give Cathy and Andy, Maggie and Ted, and all of the other members of the Herman family?

ADDITIONAL RESOURCES

Amato, Paul, Alan Booth, David R. Johnson, and Stacy J. Rogers, *Alone Together: How Marriage in America Is Changing*. Cambridge: Harvard University Press, 2009.

Cherlin, Andrew J. *The Marriage-Go-Round: The State of Marriage and the Family in America Today*. New York: Alfred A. Knopf, 2009.

Coontz, Stephanie. *Marriage, a History: From Obedience to Intimacy or How Love Conquered Marriage*. New York: Viking Press, 2005.

Farley, Margaret. *Just Love: A Framework for Christian Sexual Ethics*. New York: Continuum, 2006.

Grenz, Stanley J. *Sexual Ethics: An Evangelical Perspective*. Second edition. Louisville, KY: Westminster/John Knox Press, 1997.

Gudorf, Christine. *Body, Sex and Pleasure: Reconstructing Christian Sexual Ethics*. Cleveland: Pilgrim Press, 1994.

Hauerwas, Stanley. *A Community of Character: Toward a Constructive Christian Social Ethic*. Notre Dame, IN: University of Notre Dame Press, 1988.

Lawler, Ronald, Joseph M. Boyle, and William E. May. *Catholic Sexual Ethics: A Summary, Explanation, and Defense*. Huntington, IN: Our Sunday Visitor Press, 2011.

McManus, Mike. *Living Together: Myths, Risks, and Answers*. New York: Howard Books, 2008.

Ruether, Rosemary Radford. *Christianity and the Making of the Modern Family: Ruling Ideologies, Diverse Realities*. Boston: Beacon Press, 2000.

Stanton, Glenn T. *The Ring Makes All the Difference: Consequences of Cohabitation and the Strong Benefits of Marriage*. Chicago: Moody Publishers, 2011.

Thatcher, Adrian. *Living Together and Christian Ethics*. New York: Cambridge University Press, 2002.

Thornton, Harland, William G. Axinn, and Yu Xie. *Marriage and Cohabitation*. Chicago: University of Chicago Press, 2010.

Wheat, Ed, and Gaye Wheat. *Intended for Pleasure: Sex Techniques and Sexual Fulfillment in Christian Marriage*. Grand Rapids, MI: Baker Publishing, 2010.

Related Videos

"Single: A Documentary Film." 73 minutes. Osiris Entertainment. 2009.

Related Websites

Alternatives to Marriage Project, http://www.unmarried.org/.

Centers for Disease Control and Prevention, National Marriage and Divorce Rate Trends, http://www.cdc.gov/nchs/nvss/marriage_divorce_tables.htm.

The National Marriage Project, http://www.virginia.edu/marriageproject/.

US Census Bureau, http://www.census.gov/.

Case

Mixed Blessing?

I

It was a glorious day in May—perfect for Melanchthon College's commencement ceremony. Afterward, Pastor Nathan Moe was approached by Sarah Anderson and Kjersten Lundy. They had both graduated from Melanchthon two years earlier and were on campus to celebrate the graduation of Sarah's brother.

Sarah and Kjersten had been active in campus ministry when they had been students at Melanchthon, and both had served in different cities for the Lutheran Volunteer Corps for a year after graduation. Nathan thought very highly of both of these young women. In his mind they embodied the mission of Melanchthon College. Sarah had just completed her first year in seminary, and Kjersten was teaching mathematics at an inner-city high school in Chicago.

"Hi, Nathan. It's so great to see you," said Sarah. "Kjersten and I were going to call to set up an appointment to talk, but we were also hoping we might bump into you today. Could we find a place to visit?" They found a nice spot on some benches in the shade, and after getting caught up on each other's lives, Sarah came to the point: "Pastor Nathan, Kjersten and I want to get married, and we very much hope you will be able to help us plan the service and officiate at our wedding. As you know, we have been together for almost four years now, and we feel these past two challenging years have confirmed that we really do love each other and want to spend the rest of our lives together. We are also incredibly pleased that the Churchwide Assembly voted last summer to recognize gay relationships, and more important to us, to allow partnered gay pastors to serve our church. As a result, it seems

This case and commentary were prepared by James B. Martin-Schramm. The names of all persons and institutions have been disguised to protect the privacy of those involved.

265

to us we should get married before I start my parish internship a year from now. Are you willing to do this for us?"

Nathan said: "I'm so happy for you two! I'm sure you've thought long and hard about this. I had an inkling this day might come. Do you plan to get married in one of your home congregations?" Sarah said: "We've talked about it with our parents and with both of our pastors, but it's pretty clear our wedding service could cause problems in both congregations. This is hard for both of us, because Kjersten and I have been baptized and confirmed in our churches, but it sounds as though marrying us at the altar has the potential to divide both congregations. We don't want to cause problems, and we don't want to be married under a cloud of controversy."

"So where do you want to get married?" asked Nathan. Sarah and Kjersten looked at each other and then replied in unison, "Here." Sarah said: "We met each other here, and it was this community that really accepted us for who we are and nurtured our sense of vocation." Kjersten added, "You know us better than either of our pastors really do. Plus, the campus is sort of midway between both of our homes." Sarah asked: "What do you say, Nathan? Are you willing to marry us?"

"I would be honored," said Nathan, "but this is not a decision I have the authority to make by myself. As you know, the Evangelical Lutheran Church in America (ELCA) doesn't have a rite for same-sex marriage or the blessing of civil unions. I will have to ask my bishop what she thinks. In addition, the college has a wedding policy, but we haven't addressed the question of same-sex ceremonies on campus. I'm afraid I can't give you an answer right now, but would it be all right if I shared this news with Pastor Nancy? She'll be very happy for you as well."

Sarah replied: "That would be fine, Nathan. We understand. We figured you'd have to talk this over with others and clear it with the administration. That's one of the reasons we are thinking we would not have the service until a year from now. Let us know what they say. We don't know where else to turn. We know we can just go down and get married by a justice of the peace at any court house here in Iowa, but our faith commitments form the foundation of our relationship with each other. We want this to be a religious service, just like any other wedding." Kjersten added, "As far as we're concerned you can just use the marriage service right out of the hymnal. Obviously we will have to find some alternative to 'husband and wife,' but there is nothing else about the service we want to change. We are ready and eager to make the same commitments heterosexual couples make when they get married." Sarah concluded, "We have some gay friends who think we are nuts to buy into the institution of marriage. They think it is hopelessly patriarchal and thoroughly associated with heterosexism, but

Kjersten and I tell them traditions can change, and we want to contribute to that change."

Nathan was impressed by the poise and thoughtfulness of these two young women. He felt called to bless faithfulness wherever he found it, but he did not feel responding to their request was his call alone to make. In some ways this was a mixed blessing. Here were two young women who wanted to make a lifelong commitment to each other, but their request had the potential to ignite a firestorm of controversy at Melanchthon. Nathan promised to get back to them as soon as possible.

II

The next day Nathan shared Sarah's and Kjersten's request with his colleague in campus ministry, Nancy Harris. They talked about it for most of the morning. After lunch, Nathan picked up the phone to talk about the situation with his bishop, Rebecca Jacobsen.

"These are interesting times," said Bishop Jacobsen. "Like you, Nathan, I was pleased when the Churchwide Assembly voted last summer to encourage congregations in our church to recognize and support gay couples in committed relationships. The problem is that we don't have a rite to sanctify these relationships, and a lot of the congregations in our church have no desire to see them performed. We have already had half a dozen congregations in our synod vote to leave the ELCA, and there are another dozen or so that are talking about doing the same. I know you've seen the news reports in *The Lutheran* about the ELCA budget shortfalls within synods and at national headquarters. While a few are voting with their feet, a lot of our congregations are voting with their dollars. There are certainly plenty of our members who fully support the Churchwide Assembly's actions of last summer, but there are also plenty of others who do not."

"I know," said Nathan. "I certainly don't envy you. These are hard times for our church, but do I have your support to do this wedding for Sarah and Kjersten?"

"There are really two aspects to your question," said Bishop Jacobsen. "The first part regards my support; the second part regards how you refer to this service. As far as I am concerned, you do not need my permission. The Churchwide Assembly has spoken. It is the highest decision-making body in our church. It is up to individual congregations to decide whether they want to call gay pastors who are in committed relationships. I doubt many delegates realized their decision last summer would open the door to the broader matter of blessing same-sex unions, but those requests are now going to emerge—as this one certainly has for you. The support you need to secure is not my own but that of the college's administration."

Bishop Jacobsen continued: "The only service we currently have to bless lifelong, monogamous relationships is the rite of marriage found in our hymnal. That liturgy assumes and refers to the marriage of a male and female who will become husband and wife. I personally have no objection to you using the main elements in that rite to bless the union of these two former students, but I think you and Melanchthon College may want to consider carefully whether it is wise or appropriate to refer to the service as a marriage since so many of our members clearly have difficulty with the issue of homosexuality. In the minds of many, marriage is an institution that is reserved exclusively for heterosexuals."

After a brief pause, Nathan replied. "Thank you, Bishop Jacobsen. I appreciate your support and respect your concern about naming their union a marriage. I think it would be odd, however, for the church to call the blessing of a same-sex union something other than marriage when the State of Iowa now issues the same marriage license to all couples regardless of their sexual orientation. If we call these weddings something other than marriages I fear we will set them up to be second-class unions. I think that would be grossly unfair." Nathan looked at the phone and couldn't believe he had just said that to his bishop.

Bishop Jacobsen laughed. "There you go, Nathan. That's one of the points I fully expect to hear when we debate this issue more fully as a church. I'm just saying we have not really had that debate yet, so I advise you to proceed cautiously. That said, you do not need to fear any disciplinary action from me. To the contrary, I will support you as best I can. Take care."

Nathan next called the president's office and was connected with President Ed Olson. Nathan explained why he was calling. There was a long pause before the president replied. He thanked Nathan for bringing this matter to his attention and invited him and Nancy to the next meeting of the president's cabinet to discuss it further. As Nathan hung up the phone he reflected on the wary tone of the president's voice. Or perhaps it was just weariness.

III

One week later Nathan and Nancy sat around a table with President Olson and the vice presidents of the college. They knew one another well. Melanchthon was a relatively small liberal-arts college. It prided itself on being a community that cared about the welfare of its students, faculty, and staff. In Nathan's experience that sentiment was genuine, and it helped explain the great fondness alumni had for the college.

President Olson called on Nathan to summarize his impromptu meeting with Sarah and Kjersten after graduation and to share the content of his conversation with Bishop Jacobsen about the couple's request to be married at Melanchthon. After Nathan shared this information, President Olson opened the floor for discussion.

Bob Marquard, vice president for student life, asked Nathan and Nancy to review Melanchthon's policy about weddings. They explained that the college typically hosts only two or three weddings a year in the main worship space on campus because that multi-use facility is heavily scheduled and thus seldom available for weddings. Nancy noted that sometimes wedding services are held outside on the campus grounds or in smaller venues on campus. Nancy pointed out that she and Nathan actually encourage most couples not to get married at the college but rather in their home congregations or in the congregation where the married couple intends to worship after the marriage.

This led Solomon Hughes, vice president for enrollment management, to ask why Sarah and Kjersten were not getting married in a congregation. Nathan explained that they were pretty sure that their wedding would ignite substantial controversy in their respective congregations. At this point Solomon sat up straight and asked, "But don't they realize that having their wedding at Melanchthon is going to produce a similar firestorm of controversy here? I'm all for making Melanchthon a safe and welcoming place for all people, but blessing same-sex unions on our campus is only going to reinforce the view that we are a gay college."

Before either Nancy or Nathan could respond, Solomon posed a question to George Sullivan, vice president for marketing and communications. "George, what do you think would happen if we let gay couples get married on our campus? Don't you think this would really stir up a hornet's nest?"

George paused before he replied, "We certainly do deal with various matters related to homosexuality. It goes in spurts. We'll get angry letters from alumni and parents after the annual Drag Ball and Coming Out Week activities. As you know, we recently got raked over the coals in the local paper by some alums when we hired an openly gay professor in the religion department. Of course, the fact is that many valuable members of our faculty and staff are gay. That is nothing new. Our response has been that we want Melanchthon to be a safe and welcoming place for all people. We also emphasize that a college is perhaps the best place in our society to discuss controversial subjects like homosexuality. I confess, however, that these responses seldom placate our critics because they believe this issue should not be open for debate. They often accuse us of turning our back on our Christian heritage and of not taking a stand against immoral and sinful behavior."

Sharon Drewes, vice president for academic affairs, spoke next: "I know we would be a weaker academic institution without the valuable contributions of the gay members of our community. I don't live in an ivory tower, however. I know there have been financial repercussions because we have been such an open and welcoming place." Sharon turned to Karen Armstrong, vice president for development and alumni relations. "Karen, how big of a hit are we taking on this issue already?"

Karen replied, "We have lost a few big donors and several small donors over the last ten years due to complaints about homosexuality. I wish I could say we have gained some big donors because we are so open and welcoming, but that is not yet the case. This appears to be very much a generational thing, though not entirely so. Though some young alums have refused to give money because of this issue, most of the angry letters and dropped pledges have come from older alumni and donors. Given the current recession and the related drop in Melanchthon's endowment, I don't need to tell you how valuable each donation is to the ongoing life of this college. As Bishop Jacobsen told Nathan, those opposed to the decisions of the ELCA Churchwide Assembly are starting to vote with their dollars. We have certainly seen that here, and my guess is that we would take a further hit if we approve same-sex weddings on our campus."

"Yes, I suppose that's true," replied Nancy, "but I bet this college took a hit back in the 1930s when we let women in and became a coed school, and yet here we are—going strong and doing fine. Or think about race relations in the United States during the 1950s and 1960s. I wasn't here, but I bet some members of the Melanchthon community expressed outrage at the prospect of interracial dating on campus and interracial marriage. Change is hard, but we can get through it, especially when that change is built on the foundations of love, justice, and equality."

At this point President Olson looked up and addressed Nathan and Nancy. "That was very eloquent, but why should Melanchthon College do something the ELCA has not yet decided is appropriate? The ELCA doesn't even have a service to bless gay marriages."

Nathan replied, "That is true, but the Churchwide Assembly last summer called upon our church 'to recognize, support and hold publicly accountable lifelong, monogamous, same-gender relationships.' We are one of the colleges of the church. This call pertains as much to us as it does to the congregations in the ELCA. Nancy and I realize we are not responsible for bringing in the students or donations we need, but in our view we think Melanchthon College needs to be a leader and not a follower on this issue."

"Well, I *am* responsible for bringing in new students," said Solomon Hughes, "and I'm really worried about the potential fallout here. You said that Melanchthon only hosts two or three weddings a year in our worship space. I think we should just say no weddings can be held at Melanchthon because it is difficult logistically and now it is problematic ethically. People get married in parks and Elks Lodges all the time. Why do they have to get married here? Any gay couple can go to any court house in Iowa and get married by a justice of the peace. If we develop a new policy that precludes any weddings at Melanchthon, then this problem goes away."

Bob Marquard spoke next. "Another alternative might be for us to empower our campus pastors to bless same-sex unions in a manner that is in accordance with ELCA policies and the laws of Iowa, but to hold those services off campus out of respect for members of our campus community who would not support this practice."

Sharon Drewes responded. "I see some merit to that, Bob, but don't you think that those who oppose these services will be angry regardless of where they are held? We are going to take it on the chin no matter what we do, so let's do the right thing and have these services on our campus."

Karen Armstrong asked, "Do we *have* to make this official? Why can't we just let our pastors do these services below the radar?"

President Olson surveyed the room and considered the discussion thus far. It was not clear to him that a majority of his vice presidents favored one position more than another. They had certainly not reached any consensus, which was their typical practice. They had already taken more than half the meeting on this issue alone and still had other business to conduct. In the end the decision would be up to him anyway, and he fully intended to talk to the executive committee of the board of regents beforehand about the matter.

President Olson thanked Nathan and Nancy and said that the cabinet would continue the discussion and aim to arrive at some resolution at its next meeting in two weeks.

IV

The two weeks flew by. Nathan and Nancy prayed for President Olson and the vice presidents. Nathan also prayed daily for Sarah and Kjersten, whom he had briefed after the meeting with the cabinet. He was struck by how gracious they were.

Nancy found herself thinking this was really a test of the moral character of the Melanchthon College community. She kept thinking about the four cardinal virtues: prudence, justice, moderation, and courage. She acknowledged that Christians need to make wise and judicious judgments that take consequences seriously, but courage and justice are also vital to the Christian moral life. She felt Melanchthon needed to find the courage to do what is just.

Nathan wondered what sort of collective moral wisdom the cabinet would arrive at. He tried to look at the situation from the perspective of President Olson. What would he do if he were charged with advancing the faith and learning mission of the college while also maintaining its financial stability? Major ethical changes take time, but when, where, and how do they begin?

Commentary

There is perhaps no issue more hotly debated in the church today than homosexuality. Over the past two decades virtually every major Christian denomination has grappled with this issue in one way or another. Regrettably, debates about blessing same-sex unions, ordaining homosexual pastors, and protecting the civil rights of homosexuals have tended to produce more heat than light. These contentious discussions are not receding because, as we see in the case, they are being prompted in part by members of Christian families who have been baptized in the fonts and confirmed at the altars of congregations in these denominations. Many of these men and women are asking to be affirmed and held to the same moral standards as their heterosexual counterparts so that they can faithfully render service both to the church and to society. In addition, homosexual persons inside and outside of the church are pleading for the same rights and privileges heterosexuals enjoy in society.

This case focuses on same-sex marriage. The most immediate and pressing ethical question in this case is whether Melanchthon College should allow homosexuals to get married on campus. In order to answer this question, it is necessary to explore the concept of sexual orientation, biblical passages that refer to same-sex behavior, and support for same-sex unions in church and society.

SEXUAL ORIENTATION

What attracts one person to another? Why are most people attracted to individuals of the opposite sex, while some are attracted to those of the same sex? Why are a few attracted to both sexes? We don't really know the answers to these questions. Scientists are exploring answers by studying genetic, hormonal, and environmental factors, but the basis for emotional, romantic, and sexual attraction remains an intriguing mystery to modern science. Human sexuality is complicated. For example, scientific studies of twins have shown that there is some genetic predisposition—not determination—involved in homosexuality. Studies have shown that the chances of the identical twin of a homosexual male being homosexual are many times higher than the rate found in the general population, even when those twins have been raised apart. Nevertheless, there is clearly some environmental factors as well, because the adopted siblings of homosexual males are also more likely to be homosexual than the general population, though the correspondence is much lower than for identical twins. These research findings demonstrate that genetics and environment both appear to play a role in sexual orientation and may influence each other.

Genital sexual activity between persons of the same sex has been recorded throughout human history. In most eras and in many Western societies same-sex behavior has been viewed religiously as a sin and legally as a crime. These views began to change in Western nations, however, in the latter half of the nineteenth century as modern scientists began to develop distinctions between heterosexuality and homosexuality and the related concept of sexual orientation. Initially, homosexuality was regarded as a pathological illness, but by the turn of the twentieth century a few scientists argued it was merely a variant of human behavior like left-handedness. In the middle of the twentieth century Alfred Kinsey published a groundbreaking study about human sexuality that revealed that homosexual behavior was far more prevalent than most had thought. At the same time another group of researchers documented evidence of same-sex behavior in other animal species and in other eras of human history. Nevertheless, homosexuality was included as an illness in the first *Diagnostic and Statistical Manual* of the American Psychiatric Association in 1952. It wasn't until 1973—after two decades of further research—that the organization reversed its decision. The American Psychological Association endorsed this decision shortly thereafter and urged its members to eradicate the stigma associated with a homosexual orientation.

Today, the American Psychological Association website says the following about sexual orientation:

> Sexual orientation refers to an enduring pattern of emotional, romantic, and/or sexual attractions to men, women, or both sexes. Sexual orientation also refers to a person's sense of identity based on those attractions, related behaviors, and membership in a community of others who share those attractions. Research over several decades has demonstrated that sexual orientation ranges along a continuum, from exclusive attraction to the other sex to exclusive attraction to the same sex. However, sexual orientation is usually discussed in terms of three categories: heterosexual (having emotional, romantic, or sexual attractions to members of the other sex), gay/lesbian (having emotional, romantic, or sexual attractions to members of one's own sex), and bisexual (having emotional, romantic, or sexual attractions to both men and women). This range of behaviors

and attractions has been described in various cultures and nations throughout the world. Many cultures use identity labels to describe people who express these attractions. In the United States the most frequent labels are *lesbians* (women attracted to women), *gay men* (men attracted to men), and *bisexual* people (men or women attracted to both sexes). However, some people may use different labels or none at all.

Sexual orientation is distinct from other components of sex and gender, including biological sex (the anatomical, physiological, and genetic characteristics associated with being male or female), gender identity (the psychological sense of being male or female), and social gender role (the cultural norms that define feminine and masculine behavior).

This distinction between sexual orientation and behavior has been important in debates about homosexuality within Christian communities. Since many have perceived sexual orientation as a given and not easily changed, they have argued that there is nothing inherently sinful about a person's sexual orientation. That has not stopped others, however, from claiming that choosing to engage in same-sex sexual behavior is sinful and morally wrong. Scientific studies have revealed that most people *can* experience sexual arousal by a person of either sex but choose to block one of these dual sexual capacities to develop the other. These choices are made in response to familial and cultural messages first received in childhood and continuing into adulthood. Thus it appears that sexual orientation, like gender, is not fixed in advance of social interaction, but rather is constructed through that interaction. This means the line between sexual orientation and behavior becomes blurred. Individuals act or perform their gender and sexual orientation and thus establish and demonstrate their identity. Drawing a neat line between sexual orientation and behavior is not possible. While at first glance this appears to complicate issues, it has the effect of focusing ethical scrutiny on the moral character of sexual relationships and opens the door to the development of a sexual ethic that pertains to all people, regardless of sexual orientation.

THE BIBLE AND HOMOSEXUALITY

At the heart of most discussions about the morality of homosexuality is the interpretation of scripture. Invariably, debates quickly focus on a handful of texts that offer a negative assessment of sexual activity between members of the same sex. Those opposed to homosexuality claim these texts should be taken at face value and are sufficient to settle the matter ethically. Others do not think these biblical texts address the issue Christian communities face today; namely, how to respond to homosexuals who want to enter into publicly accountable, monogamous, lifelong relationships. Given the importance of the Bible in Christian ethics, it is necessary to examine these texts in some detail.

The stories of Sodom (Gn 19:1–11) and Gibeah (Jgs 19:16–30) are similar. In the first story two men—whom the text says are really angels—are invited by Lot to spend the night in his home. Shortly thereafter all of the men of the city surround the house and demand that Lot make the men come out so that they may "know" them (Gn 19:5). Lot realizes that the men of the city want to rape his male guests, and so he offers his two daughters instead. The men of the city refuse and try to break into Lot's house, but the angels strike the men blind. A few verses later the inhabitants of Sodom, plus Gomorrah, are destroyed by "sulphur and fire from the Lord out of heaven" (Gn 19:24).

In the second story, in Judges, an elderly man invites a traveler along with his concubine and servant to spend the night at his home in Gibeah. As in the Sodom account, the men of the city surround the home and demand that the traveler be brought out so that they may "know" him (Jgs 19:22). Like Lot, the elderly owner of the home says this would not be hospitable to his guest and offers his virgin daughter and the traveler's concubine instead. When the men of the city refuse, the traveler seizes his concubine and gives her to the men of the city who "abused her all through the night until the morning" (Jgs 19:25).

It is hard to see what these texts of terror have to do with discussions about homosexuality today. In both cases these are stories of gang rape and domination. They have nothing to do with the morality of consensual, monogamous, and lifelong sexual relationships between persons of the same sex. When the "sin of Sodom" is referred to elsewhere in scripture it is primarily a condemnation of the general disorder of a society opposed to God. In the Hebrew scriptures the prophets view Sodom as a city of unjust people who were prideful, adulterous, gluttonous, and indifferent to the needy and vulnerable (Is 1:10; 3:9; Jer 23:14; Ez 16:49). In the Christian scriptures the Epistle of Jude refers to the sexual immorality of Sodom and Gomorrah (Jude 7), but the other passages do not specify the sin in question and focus instead on God's destruction of those who disobey God's will (Lk 17:28–29; Romans 9:29; 2 Peter 2:6; Revelation 11:8) Perhaps most importantly, when Jesus refers to Sodom and Gomorrah he does not focus on same-sex activity but rather casts the sin in terms of their refusal to offer hospitality to the stranger (Mt 10:1–15; 11:23–24; Lk 10:1–12).

The two condemnations of male same-sex activity in the Book of Leviticus appear to be more directly relevant because they are not associated with gang rape. Leviticus 18:22 proclaims, "You shall not lie with a male as with a woman; it is an abomination." Leviticus 20:13 stipulates that "if a man lies with a male as with a woman, both of them have committed an abomination; they shall be put to death; their blood is upon them." Both of these verses are part of the Holiness Code in the Book of Leviticus, which prescribes ways of living intended to distinguish the followers of Yahweh from the people of Canaan. Many of these laws, especially in chapter 18, focus on various forbidden sexual relationships like incest, intercourse during a woman's menstrual period, adultery, and bestiality. Other laws prohibit the sacrifice of children to Molech (18:21; 20:2–5), the eating of shellfish (11:11), breeding animals of different kinds, sowing fields with two kinds of seed, and wearing a garment made with two different kinds of fiber (19:19).

Scholars disagree about how the two prohibitions against male same-sex activity in Leviticus should be interpreted today. Some have asserted that the texts refer to cultic temple prostitution and thus dismiss them as irrelevant to contemporary discussions about homosexuality focused on lifelong committed relationships rather than prostitution and promiscuity. Others believe the laws assume a flawed Hebraic understanding about procreation—that the male seed is planted in passive female soil—and thus are irrelevant in light of what we know today about reproductive biology. Another group of scholars makes a distinction between ceremonial and ethical laws in Leviticus and argues that the prohibition of male same-sex activity is simply a cultural aspect of the Holiness Code law that no longer pertains in modern culture. There are well-regarded biblical scholars who support and refute all these views.

The interpretation of scripture is not easy. While some Christians might be tempted to disregard the peculiar mix of cultural taboos and purity regulations in Leviticus, they must remember that Jesus' command to "love your neighbor as yourself" (Mt 19:19; Mk 12:31; Lk 10:27) is drawn directly from the Holiness Code (Lv 19:18). The challenge in Leviticus is to determine which passages contain enduring ethical counsel and which reflect matters that were more directly relevant to the ancient people of Israel and thus are not morally normative today. The early church began that process by setting aside some of the Jewish purity laws as well as male circumcision in order to accept Gentiles who followed Jesus into the Christian community (Acts 10:9–29). The Holy Spirit led the early church to accept these Gentiles, who previously had been viewed as both immoral and unclean. Much of the debate today is about whether Christians should set aside the biblical prohibitions against same-sex activity because they are being used to exclude Christian homosexuals from full participation in the church.

There are three other passages in the Christian scriptures that are most directly relevant to contemporary discussions about homosexuality. The most important may be Paul's apparent condemnation of male and female genital same-sex activity in his letter to the church in Rome. At the outset of the letter Paul condemns the idolatry and failures of the Gentile world. Paul concludes:

> For this reason God gave them up to degrading passions. Their women exchanged natural intercourse for unnatural, and in the same way also the men, giving up natural intercourse with women, were consumed with passion for one another. Men committed shameless acts with men and received in their own persons the due penalty for their error. (Romans 1:26–27)

On the face this text appears to be an unambiguous condemnation of male and female homosexual sexual activity. Some scholars warn, however, that the interjection of the modern notion of sexual orientation on an ancient text would be an anachronism. Key to understanding this text is deciphering what Paul meant by degrading passions and unnatural acts. In Paul's Greek-speaking world, passion *(pathos)* was viewed as a disease of the mind and a defect in the self that could only be cured by the application of reason. For a man, loss of control over the body was shameful. Passion was associated with females and irrationality. The mark of a real man was to control the slavish impulses of passion and to act according to the dictates of reason.

Paul's argument in Romans 1 is that God handed Gentile idolaters over to passion so that they might experience the shame they had caused God. He claims this led them to exchange natural for unnatural sexual relations, but what did Paul mean by "natural" sexual relations? For the Greeks, the natural use of something was to use the object *without* passion. For example, the natural use of food was to eat enough to satisfy hunger and to stay well. It would be unnatural to be gluttonous. Similarly, the natural use of clothing was to maintain modesty and to protect oneself from the elements. It would be unnatural to dress extravagantly in order to call attention to oneself. Thus, the natural use of sex was equally measured. People should only engage in sex occasionally, without enthusiasm, and only for the purpose of procreation. It would be unnatural to have sex solely in order to experience pleasure.

So what are we to make of Romans 1:26–27? Some scholars describe the past as a foreign country. Immersed in the Greco-Roman culture of his day, Paul did not have access to or operate with our modern notion of sexual orientation. Some scholars think Paul was denouncing married Gentile women who were taking too much pleasure in marital relations rather than denouncing lesbian relationships. While Paul does condemn same-sex activity between men, this appears to be a condemnation of unbridled and irrational passion rather than an unqualified rejection of mature, consensual, and committed sexual relationships between men.

The last two texts that address same-sex activity in the Christian scriptures are normally discussed together because they are viewed as "vice lists." Paul writes to the church in Corinth:

> Do you not know that wrongdoers will not inherit the kingdom of God? Do not be deceived! Fornicators, idolaters, adulterers, male prostitutes, sodomites, thieves, the greedy, drunkards, revilers, robbers—none of these will inherit the kingdom of God. (1 Cor 6:9–10)

It is an interesting study in the history of biblical translation (and interpretation) to review the various translations of the Greek words *malakoi* and *aresenokoitai* that are respectively translated above as "male prostitutes" and "sodomites" in the New Revised Standard Version (NRSV). The first edition of the Revised Standard Version (RSV) released in 1946 collapsed the two terms *malakoi* and *aresenokoitai* together into one term, "homosexuals." In 1971 the editors of the RSV replaced "homosexuals" with "sexual perverts." Other translations of the Bible render these two Greek words respectively as "effeminate" and "abusers of themselves with men" (American Standard Version), "male prostitutes" and "homosexual offenders" (New International Version), and "boy prostitutes" and "practicing homosexuals" (New American Bible). Clearly these translations differ markedly, and there are important things at stake in these differences.

Similar issues arise in the translation and interpretation of the first letter to Timothy, which has been attributed to Paul:

> This means understanding that the law is laid down not for the innocent but for the lawless and disobedient, for the godless and sinful, for the unholy and profane, for those who kill their father or mother, for murderers, fornicators, sodomites, slave-traders, liars, perjurers, and whatever else is contrary to the sound teaching that conforms to the glorious gospel of the blessed God, which he entrusted to me. (1 Tm 1:9–11)

In this passage scholars have focused on the sequence of "fornicators, sodomites, and slave traders," which are translations of the Greek words *pornoi, arsenokoites,* and *andrapodistes.* While some scholars think these terms are independent, another group of scholars think the three terms are related and pertain to the ancient Greek practice of pederasty, which involved a sexual relationship between an adult male and a young boy, normally in his early teens. From this perspective the young boys are the *pornoi,* the adult men who penetrate the boys are the *arsenokoites,* and the men who enslave the boys and sell them to the adult males are the *andrapodistes.* If the view represented by the second group of scholars is true, then it is pederasty that is being condemned in 1 Timothy and not all homosexual relationships. Regardless, many Christians who are homosexuals feel it is hurtful and unjust for them to be lumped together with murderers, liars, perjurers, and thieves. They do not see their lives reflected in these vice lists, and those who know and love them do not either.

In summary, it is clear that many Christian scholars and laypeople believe that the texts discussed above form the biblical basis for the immorality of homosexuality. While many are willing to set aside the relevance of the passages in Genesis 19 and Judges 19, they believe the remaining passages clearly indicate that same-sex sexual activity is forbidden and punished by God. From their perspective, same-sex sexual relationships are "against nature" and contrary to the will of God expressed in creation. As some say, Genesis focuses on the creation of Adam and Eve, not the creation of Adam and Steve. They argue that normative heterosexual complementarity has been the consistent stance of the church throughout the centuries and that any departure from this tradition will divide the church.

On the other side of the spectrum stand a group of scholars and laypeople who also respect the authority of scripture as a source in Christian ethics. Their examination of these passages leads them to conclude that these texts do not really address modern conceptions of homosexual orientation in general or the particular issue in this case, which is how to respond to Christian homosexuals who want to enter into publicly accountable, monogamous, lifelong relationships. Many point to the inclusion of Gentiles in the early Christian community as a biblical precedent that can empower the church today to welcome homosexuals who want to live by the same ethical standards as heterosexuals. Members of this group also emphasize that the Holy Spirit has led many Christian denominations to reinterpret scripture and change their previous views on the morality of slavery, the permissibility of divorce, and the ordination of women.

SUPPORT FOR SAME-SEX UNIONS
IN CHURCH AND SOCIETY

The fictional Melanchthon College in the case is related to the Evangelical Lutheran Church in America (ELCA). The ELCA was formed in 1988 when three preexisting Lutheran denominations merged into one church. In 2011 the ELCA was the fourth-largest Protestant denomination in the United States with over 4.6 million members and more than 10,300 congregations. There are twenty-six colleges and universities affiliated with the ELCA.

Debates about human sexuality emerged within the ELCA almost from the day it was formed. An initial attempt to pass a social statement on the topic was postponed in 1995 because of intense disagreements within the church over homosexuality. The denomination continued to wrestle with the issue in various ways during the rest of the decade. In 2001 the largest and most powerful decision-making body in the church, the Churchwide Assembly, called for a new study to be completed by 2005 that would address sexuality in general, homosexuality in particular, and would include recommendations for how to deal with homosexuals who want to serve the church in an ordained capacity. At that time only homosexuals who promised to be celibate could be ordained and called to be pastors in the ELCA. Those who violated this expectation could be removed from the clergy roster and congregations that called them could be expelled from the denomination.

It should come as no surprise that it took longer than expected to develop the materials requested in 2001. In 2009, the ELCA Churchwide Assembly adopted a new social statement, "Human Sexuality: Gift and Trust," which was approved by the necessary two-thirds majority. While the statement emphasizes the goodness and complexity of human sexuality, it does not take a definitive position on the morality of homosexuality. After an extensive reaffirmation of marriage, however, the statement discusses lifelong, monogamous, same-gender relationships:

> We in the ELCA recognize that many of our sisters and brothers in same-gender relationships sincerely desire the support of other Christians for living faithfully in all aspects of their lives, including their sexual fidelity. In response, we have drawn deeply on our Lutheran theological heritage and Scripture. This has led, however, to differing and conscience-bound understandings about the place of such relationships within the Christian community. We have come to various conclusions concerning how to regard lifelong, monogamous, same-gender relationships, including whether and how to recognize publicly their lifelong commitments. . . . Although at this time this church lacks consensus on this matter, it encourages all people to live out their faith in the local and global community of the baptized with profound respect for the conscience-bound belief of the neighbor. (pp. 20–21)

Despite this lack of consensus the ELCA Churchwide Assembly passed a series of important recommendations on ministry policies. One of these recommendations, which was approved by 60.6 percent of those voting, resolved "that the ELCA commit itself to finding ways to allow congregations that choose to do so to recognize, support, and hold publicly accountable lifelong, monogamous, same-gender relationships." Pastor Nathan refers to this resolution in the case. Another recommendation, which was approved by 55.3 percent of those voting, resolved "that the ELCA commit itself to finding a way for people in such publicly accountable, lifelong, monogamous, same-gender relationships to serve as rostered leaders of this church."

With these votes the ELCA became the largest Christian denomination in the United States to withdraw the requirement of celibacy from homosexual pastors as long as they can demonstrate that they are in a publicly accountable, lifelong, monogamous, same-gender relationship. The smaller United Church of Christ became the first mainline Christian denomination officially to support same-sex marriage when its general synod passed a resolution in 2005 affirming "equal marriage rights for couples regardless of gender." In addition, Episcopal Church delegates voted in 2009 not to stand in the way of dioceses that choose to bless the unions of same-sex couples. In 2011 the Presbyterian Church (U.S.A.) voted to change its constitution in order to allow homosexuals in same-sex relationships to be ordained as ministers, elders, and deacons. Also in 2011 the Evangelical Lutheran Church in Canada voted to allow same-sex marriages and the ordination of gays and lesbians.

Not surprisingly, the decisions by the ELCA provoked an outcry from conservative members and congregations who voted with their dollars and their feet. A year after the Churchwide Assembly vote the ELCA had to fire sixty-five employees and restructure the national church staff because mission support from congregations had dropped by almost 30 percent, from $62.5 million to $45 million. In addition, by the end of 2010, 666 ELCA congregations had taken a first vote to leave the denomination, and over 72 percent received the required two-thirds majority. Among these congregations, 327 held a second required vote 90 days after the first, and over 94 percent of these votes passed with a two-thirds majority. Some of these congregations joined the new North American Lutheran Church, which was established in August 2010.

These serious financial and demographic repercussions are real concerns for the administrative leaders of Melanchthon College who are faced with a request from two gay alumni who want to get married on campus. It was probably only a matter of time before the college would receive such a request because Iowa's Supreme Court ruled unanimously in 2009 that a state law limiting marriage to a man and a woman violated the equal protection clause in the state's constitution. At the time this case and commentary were written same-sex couples could receive marriage licenses only in Connecticut, Iowa, Massachusetts, New Hampshire, New York, Vermont, and in the federal district of Washington, D.C.

While several states offer civil unions or domestic partnerships that grant all or part of the state-level rights and responsibilities of marriage, thirty-one states have constitutional restrictions that limit marriage to the union of one man and one woman. Most of these states made these amendments to their constitution after Congress passed the Defense of Marriage Act in 1996. This federal legislation defines marriage exclusively as a union between a man and a woman. The fate of the Defense of Marriage Act is now unclear, however. President Obama directed the Department of Justice in February 2011 to stop defending the legislation because it violates the rights of same-sex couples to equal protection under the law.

CONCLUSION

This case raises several interesting ethical questions. One comes at the beginning of the case when Pastor Nathan tells Bishop Jacobsen he thinks it would be odd to call the blessing of a same-gender union something other than marriage, given that the State of Iowa issues the same marriage license to all couples regardless of sexual orientation. There is some merit to Pastor Nathan's fears that such blessings would result in second-class or less-than-equal unions that would not have the same legitimacy or powers as heterosexual marriages. Many who advocate for same-sex marriage do so because the legal institution of marriage confers over a thousand legal rights and privileges, many of which are not included in various state laws that permit civil unions and domestic partnerships. In Iowa, however, this issue is moot; the issue now rests with the church in general, and, in this case, with the ELCA in particular.

The ELCA's 2009 social statement on human sexuality calls the church "to build social institutions and practices where trust and trustworthy relationships can thrive." It emphasizes that "relationships flourish according to the depth and trustworthiness of commitments." The social statement goes on to discuss the way Lutherans believe God works through social structures like marriage for the good of society:

> Marriage is a covenant of mutual promises, commitment, and hope authorized legally by the state and blessed by God. The historic Christian tradition and the Lutheran Confessions have recognized marriage as a covenant between a man and a woman, reflecting Mark 10:6–9:

"But from the beginning of creation, God made them male and female. For this reason a man shall leave his father and mother and be joined to his wife, and the two shall become one flesh. So they are no longer two, but one flesh. Therefore what God has joined together, let no one put asunder." (Jesus here recalls Genesis 1:27 and 2:23–24.)

Lutherans long have affirmed that the public accountability of marriage, as expressed through a legal contract, provides the necessary social support and social trust for relationships that are intended to be sustained throughout life and within changing and often challenging life situations. In this country, pastors carry both legal and religious responsibilities for marriage. In carrying out these responsibilities, pastors hold and exercise pastoral discretion for the decision to marry in the church. In the community of the church they preside over the mutual promises made between a couple seeking the lifelong, monogamous, and faithful relationship of marriage.

Marriage requires constant care and cultivation. It is intended to protect the creation and nurturing of mutual trust and love as one foundation of human community. It is a binding relationship that provides conditions for personal well-being, the flourishing of the partner, and the possibility of procreation and the nurturing of children. It also is intended to be a blessing to the community and the world. Because of promises of fidelity and public accountability, marriage provides a context of love, trust, honesty, and commitment within which a couple can express the profound joy of relationship as well as address the troubles they encounter throughout life.

The social statement's section on marriage ends by acknowledging that some members of the ELCA and the broader Christian community "conclude that marriage is also the appropriate term to use in describing similar benefits, protection, and support for same-gender couples entering into lifelong, monogamous relationships." The social statement goes on to note, however, that other contractual agreements, like civil unions, also seek to provide some of these protections and commitments.

This brings us to another interesting ethical question posed by the case: What does it mean for ELCA congregations "to recognize, support, and hold publicly accountable lifelong, monogamous, same-gender relationships"? While the ELCA ministry recommendation does not explicitly encourage ELCA congregations (or its colleges, universities, and seminaries) to perform gay marriages, there are certainly some lay and ordained members of the church—like the two campus pastors in this case—who think the door has been opened to do so. There is no question, however, that the rite of marriage in the Lutheran hymnal refers explicitly and exclusively to the union of a man and a woman. In addition, the ELCA's *Occasional Services* resource for pastors includes a "Prayer and Blessing for a Civil Marriage," but this too assumes a heterosexual union. Could both be revised to bless same-sex unions? Certainly. New liturgies, like new hymns, are normally developed at the grassroots and are later adopted on a broader basis. One way to read the ELCA's recommendation is to view it as an invitation to experiment with such liturgies. Of course, another way to read it is to view it as an invitation that can be rejected.

That brings us to the primary ethical question in this case: Should Melanchthon College allow homosexuals to get married on campus? The members of the president's council discuss four options. One is to permit gay weddings on campus, and another is to ban *all* weddings on campus because they are difficult logistically and problematic ethically. Another pair of options would authorize the campus pastors to conduct these services in an unofficial and quiet way on campus, or to do so in an officially sanctioned way but off campus out of deference to those in the Melanchthon College community who would not approve. On the one hand, given the uproar in the ELCA, it is reasonable for Melanchthon's administration to fear that permitting gay weddings on campus could have serious repercussions for the college. On the other hand, given the number of homosexual students, faculty, staff, and alums in the Melanchthon College community, it is not likely that this issue is going to go away. What should they do?

Pastor Nancy finds herself thinking at the end of the case that Sarah's and Kjersten's request is really a test of the moral character of the Melanchthon College community. She reflects on the four cardinal moral virtues: prudence, justice, temperance, and fortitude. She believes justice sanctions the blessing of gay weddings on campus, and that fortitude (courage) will be required to carry through with such a change in the tradition of marriage. Viewing the case from the perspective of President Olson yields a different assessment of the virtues to be cultivated. Given the potential for significant repercussions, and out of a desire to maintain the long-term well-being of the whole Melanchthon community, President Olson might argue that prudence and temperance should lead the college not to allow gay couples to have their weddings on campus until the ELCA has developed a more definitive position on the matter. Finally, had they a greater voice, Sarah Anderson and Kjersten Lundy might offer a reminder that Christian theologians since Aquinas have emphasized that the four cardinal virtues need to be combined with the three theological virtues of faith, hope, and love. Which option in this case would best embody these virtues?

ADDITIONAL RESOURCES

American Psychological Association. "Sexual Orientation and Homosexuality." Available on the apa.org website.

Boswell, John. *Christianity, Social Tolerance, and Homosexuality: Gay People in Western Europe from the Beginning of the Christian Era to the Fourteenth Century.* Eighth edition. Chicago: University of Chicago Press, 2005.

————. *Same-Sex Unions in Pre-Modern Europe.* New York: Vintage Press, 1995.

De La Torre, Miguel A., ed. *Out of the Shadows into the Light: Christianity and Homosexuality.* St. Louis: Chalice Press, 2009.

Ellison, Marvin M. *Same-Sex Marriage? A Christian Ethical Analysis.* Cleveland, OH: The Pilgrim Press, 2004.

Evangelical Lutheran Church in America. *Human Sexuality: Gift and Trust.* 2009. Available on the elca.org website.

Fredrickson, David E. "Natural and Unnatural Use in Romans 1:24–27: Paul and the Philosophic Critique of Eros." In *Homosexuality, Science, and the "Plain Sense" of Scripture,* ed. David Balch. Grand Rapids, MI: Eerdmans, 2000.

Glazer, Chris. *As My Own Soul: The Blessing of Same-Gender Marriage.* New York: Seabury Books, 2009.

Hill, Wesley. *Washed and Waiting: Reflections on Christian Faithfulness and Homosexuality.* Grand Rapids, MI: Zondervan Press, 2010.

Hultgren, Arland J., and Walter F. Taylor, Jr. *Background Essay on Biblical Texts for Journey Together Faithfully, Part Two: The Church and Homosexuality.* Chicago: ELCA, 2003.

Marin, Andrew, and Brian McLaren. *Love Is an Orientation: Elevating the Conversation with the Gay Community..* Downers Grove, IL: InterVarsity Press, 2009.

Myers, David G., and Letha Dawson Scanzoni. *What God Has Joined Together: The Christian Case for Gay Marriage.* New York: HarperOne, 2006.

The New York Times. "Same-Sex Marriage, Civil Unions, and Domestic Partnerships." Available on the topics.nytimes.com website.

Rogers, Jack. *Jesus, the Bible, and Homosexuality: Explode the Myths, Heal the Church.* Revised and expanded edition. Louisville, KY: Westminster John Knox Press, 2009.

Scharen, Christian Batalden. *Married in the Sight of God: Theology, Ethics, and Church Debates over Homosexuality.* Lanham, MD: University Press of America, 2000.

Related Videos

"For the Bible Tells Me So." 98 minutes. First Run Features. 2008.
"Prayers for Bobby." 86 minutes. A&E Home Video. 2010.
"Through My Eyes." 46 minutes. The Gay Christian Network. 2009.

PART VIII

LIFE AND DEATH

Case

A Matter of Life or Death

The antiseptic smell of clinics and hospitals had always made Sue Ann Thomas feel sick to her stomach. As she waited alone in the cold reception room, her mind flashed back to two weeks ago when she had told Danny she thought she was pregnant. He wasn't so much angry as he was confused and kind of dazed. They talked about what she could do.

Sue Ann was eighteen, a freshman at South Central Community College, and she was afraid to tell her parents that she was pregnant. Danny had also finished high school last year and had a job in a garage in South Chicago. She felt that Danny had been honest about how he felt. "You are really important to me, Sue Ann, but I don't think either of us is ready to get married right now. I guess we have to figure out what to do." They decided that by pooling their savings they could get together the $400 for an abortion.

Sue Ann remembered the name of Dr. Engles. Her mother had gone to him a couple of times. Making an appointment under another name, Sue Ann told him she that she wanted an abortion. Dr. Engles talked to her after her examination when the pregnancy tests proved positive. He told her about what he thought was the best health clinic in Chicago for pregnancy termination. While Sue Ann was still there, he called the clinic for a counseling date and a surgery date the next day, wrote out the papers for her to take in, and asked her to make an appointment with the nurse to see him three weeks after the abortion to make sure everything was all right. As Sue Ann walked out of the office, she thought that Wednesday—one week away—would never come soon enough.

The next week of waiting had been hell. Sue Ann was only seven weeks along, but she was sure she would begin to show. When Wednesday came,

This case was prepared by Alice Frazer Evans and the commentary by Christine E. Gudorf. The names of all persons and institutions have been disguised to protect the privacy of those involved.

Sue Ann told her mother she was going over to a girlfriend's house for supper so she would be home late. When Danny came by early that morning in his old Ford to take her to class on his way to work, Sue Ann was sure her parents would never know.

Both her mother and her father had been bugging her for a couple of weeks now. She had been able to hide her nausea, but her mother said she didn't look well. Sue Ann knew they were worried about her. She also felt their pressure and their pride. She was the first member of the family who had ever attended college. Sue Ann thought that having a younger brother and sister who really looked up to her didn't help either. She knew her dad got pretty good wages working for a construction company, but her mom had started working part-time to help pay for her books and school fees.

Danny and Sue Ann didn't say much on their way into the city. Danny was already going to be late for work, so he let her out at the clinic door and said he'd pick her up after he got off work about 5:30. She had seemed so confident, so sure of herself last week, and even this morning, but as she handed the papers to the receptionist and paid the clinic cashier, she was aware of how cold and clammy her hands felt. She jumped when the nurse called her into a small office to take her blood pressure and temperature.

Dr. Engles had told Sue Ann what would happen during those two days. Today was for a checkup and counseling. She was healthy and still in her first trimester, so the clinic doctor would do something called a "vacuum aspiration" tomorrow. This would take about fifteen minutes. Then she would have to wait at least an hour before she could leave.

Sue Ann was taken into a large room with four other women for a group counseling session with a social worker. Three appeared to be in their early to late twenties, and one looked to be in her mid-to-late thirties. She had known that at some time during the day before the abortion there would be a group counseling session. She remembered a couple of weeks ago telling her closest friend, Sharon, that she was pregnant. Sharon had blurted out that she could never have an abortion, that it was wrong and that she would feel too guilty. Sue Ann realized that Danny was the only other person she had told about her pregnancy. She was already afraid of having to talk with these women about it. Sue Ann chose a corner chair and stared out the window as she waited. It had begun to snow.

For the first time Sue Ann let herself think about Paul Reynolds. She hadn't dated anyone else during her last two years of high school. Paul was older, he went into the army, and they wrote to each other nearly every day. They planned to be married as soon as Sue Ann finished high school. But last summer the army found that Paul had a heart defect. He came home on an extended leave, and he died in June. Sue Ann still couldn't really believe it. She had cried for weeks. Her friends and her mother said that she needed to move on and that she had to think about her own life. They all said that beginning college in September would be the best thing for her.

Sue Ann had known Danny since grade school and started dating him not long after her classes began in the fall. He was good company but nothing like Paul. She and Danny had a good time together; he made her laugh. When Danny said he loved her, Sue Ann thought that having sex with him would help her forget Paul, but it didn't. Paul had been a Roman Catholic. They had talked about sex a long time before they went to bed together. This was after they had decided to get married. Paul said that this meant having sex was okay with the church, but she wasn't sure he was right. She remembered reading that the Catholic Church was against premarital sex and also said abortion was murder. Sue Ann didn't want to think about what Paul would have said about her pregnancy. Getting an abortion had seemed the only thing to do.

The social worker came in and introduced herself. The women began to talk, to tell their ages, and to give their reasons for choosing to have an abortion. A girl in her twenties, who introduced herself as Mary, laughed uneasily and asked if anyone had ever backed out this far along. Connie Davies, the social worker, responded very seriously. "Yes, over the past six months of this particular program there have been a few women who chose at the last minute not to terminate their pregnancies. A couple of them said they had decided to give their babies up for adoption. That's one of the reasons I'm here to talk with you, to make sure you are clear about what you are doing."

Sue Ann dug her nails into her palms and began to feel the tears well up in her eyes. She had come this far. What could she do if she backed out? Sue Ann was the only one who had not spoken. Connie Davies turned to her and waited.

Commentary

Sue Ann Thomas, with her friend Danny, faces an agonizing decision: whether to terminate with medical assistance an unwanted pregnancy in its early stages. With her decision Sue Ann enters the arena of fierce public debates over the definition of human life, the meaning of motherhood, the issue of who should control the abortion decision, and the role of sacrifice in Christian life. If all this were not enough, she must also work through how she will relate to her parents.

In facing this decision Sue Ann needs to consider the facts about abortion in her society; the resources of scripture and Christian tradition regarding abortion, definitions of human life, and parenting roles; and the choices and roles open to her and other women in contemporary society.

FACTS ABOUT ABORTION IN THE UNITED STATES

Sue Ann's option to elect to have a legal abortion is provided in the United States under the landmark 1973 Supreme Court decision Roe v. Wade, which ruled that in the early stages of pregnancy prior to the viability of the fetus, the decision to have an abortion must be left to a woman and her doctor. Only after viability may the state prohibit abortion, and then not when the woman's life is in danger. This ruling threw out the laws of most states enacted in the second half of the nineteenth century prohibiting abortion unless a physician could claim compelling medical indications.

According to a 2011 report by the Alan Guttmacher Institute, just over 1.2 million legal abortions were performed in the United States in 2008. This number has declined from a peak of 1.6 million in 1990. Almost one-half of US pregnancies are unintended. Approximately 50 percent of unintended pregnancies are terminated by abortion. Thus, about one in four pregnancies ends in legal abortion, with over 90 percent of these being in the first trimester. Another 15 percent end in spontaneous abortion (miscarriage).

Of women who get abortions about 85 percent are unmarried, 61 percent are already mothers, and 17 percent are teenagers. According to a 2010 National Vital Statistics Report by the Centers for Disease Control and Prevention, the birth rate for US teenagers ages 15–19 reached a record low in 2009 (39.1 per 1,000). The rate for 2009 was 37 percent lower than in 1991 (61.8 per 1,000). Abortion statistics lag behind records of live births. According to the Alan Guttmacher Institute, 32 percent of the 750,000 teens who got pregnant in 2006 got an abortion, which was down from 46 percent in 1986. The abortion rate is much higher for teens from affluent families than it is for those from poor families. This may be related to the fact that many abortion providers have shut down over the last two decades in response to opposition, including bombings and assassinations; in some states women must travel hundreds of miles to the nearest hospital or clinic that provides abortion services. Of the 68 percent of teens who chose to give birth in 2006, an overwhelming number (more than 98 percent) decided to keep their child and to not relinquish the child for adoption.

Abortions are relatively safe for the women involved, especially if they are done early in the pregnancy. Less than 1 percent experience complications. The maternal death rate due to abortion-related causes is 0.6 per 100,000. The figure for live births is 7.1 per 100,000, which does not include miscarriages or ectopic pregnancies.

Women seek abortions for many reasons. The top three, according to the Guttmacher Institute research, are "concern for or responsibility to others" (74%), "cannot afford a baby now" (73%), and "a baby would interfere with school, employment, or the ability to care for dependents" (69%). Contraceptive failure was not mentioned in this case, although women frequently cite it when seeking abortions.

In the United States, opinion polls indicate substantial acceptance of abortion in cases of rape, incest, danger to the mother's life and mental health, and a deformed fetus. Most polls indicate majority approval of the *Roe v. Wade* decision, although a few polls indicate a fairly even split. Disapproval of abortion is greatest when it is viewed as a form of family planning.

The American Psychological Association published a report in 2008 that examined the relationship between mental health and abortion. It concluded that adult women who have an unplanned pregnancy have no greater risk of mental health problems if they have a first-trimester abortion than if they give birth to the child. The report went on to note, however, that "it is clear that some women do experience sadness, grief, and feelings of loss following termination of a pregnancy, and some experience clinically significant disorders, including depression and anxiety."

SCRIPTURE AND TRADITION

As one surveys Christian traditions, scripture, and the contemporary views and roles of women, five central issues rise to the fore. These are the goodness of life, natural law, self-sacrifice, freedom, and the well-being of women. In the rest of this commentary these issues will come up again in varying combinations and will be viewed from various perspectives.

Historically, abortion has not been a major issue in Christian traditions. For centuries it was unsafe; children were considered an economic benefit; and underpopulation, not overpopulation, was the problem. The Bible itself has nothing directly to say about the morality of abortion. Although the Bible does not legislate about abortion, the Hebrew scriptures do indirectly provide some insight. Within the Mosaic Law, fetal life was held to have value. Anyone who caused the loss of fetal life was held guilty and subject to sanctions. But the loss of fetal life was not of equal weight with the death of the already born. Responsibility for loss of fetal life was not considered murder but a lesser crime for which payment in coin was to be made in restitution. It is perhaps most accurate to say that the Mosaic Law regarded fetal life as potential human life and therefore of value. The Christian scriptures do not directly deal with abortion or the value of fetal life.

The Christian theological tradition has been rather consistently against abortion since the early church. Some describe this as continuity within the tradition, but others make two points that undermine the value of the tradition's consistency. It may be useful at this point briefly to discuss those two points, for that discussion will help bring the key issues in the debate into focus.

The first point is that although abortion has been denounced within the theological tradition of the church, until relatively recently the term was understood to describe the deliberate termination of pregnancy after the infusion of the soul (ensoulment), which was generally held to occur anywhere from six weeks to four months after conception. Thomas Aquinas, the Scholastic thinker whose philosophy and theology were made normative for the Catholic Church in 1878, adopted Aristotle's teaching on fetal animation and held that God infused the soul into the fetus at forty days after conception for males and eighty days after conception for females. In fact, popular folk practice for over a thousand years in Christian Europe, until after the Reformation, was to regard quickening (first fetal movement) as the definitive evidence of ensoulment, which was understood to be the cause of animation. Quickening usually occurs about the fifth month. Until that time midwives consulted by desperate women regularly practiced various methods of terminating pregnancy, most of them dangerous to the woman.

Tradition carries great weight in theological and moral thought, especially when it has been consistent. This is based on the recognition that the Holy Spirit not only enlightens the present generation but has also enlightened past Christian communities who passed this tradition on. But if all

Christian communities condemned abortion but permitted termination of pregnancy for weeks to months after conception, does this really constitute a consistent tradition for banning all termination of pregnancy?

A second issue raised concerning the critical views of the Christian tradition on abortion is the fact that at least some of the tradition's opposition to abortion rested upon false understandings about the biology of conception and the natures of men and women. Many of these beliefs are no longer accepted by Christians. In the past there was widespread agreement in the theological tradition that the primary purpose of marriage was procreation; that the only purpose of sexuality was procreation; that women as a sex had been created by God solely for motherhood (although they could renounce sexuality through religious vows of celibacy); and that a woman's sole contribution to the process of procreation was acceptance in her body of the self-contained seed of her husband, which it was her role to shelter and nourish. Christian churches have modified or abandoned all these beliefs.

Today, Roman Catholics and almost all Protestant churches agree that procreation is but one purpose of marriage and that the covenant of love between the spouses is equally or more important. There is similar agreement that sexuality is not an evil or near evil tolerated for the sake of children, and that sexual pleasure is itself legitimate and valuable for its role in bonding spouses to each other in love. All Christian churches accept the findings of biological science regarding the equal genetic contribution of parents in conception. All Christian churches recognize the equality of women, at least in theory, although there are tremendous divisions among and within denominations over whether women's nature is ordained for motherhood or is open to other roles that women might choose.

Those who oppose abortion are quick to point out that the above issues are not sufficient to reverse a centuries-old tradition. The heart of the issue, they say, is the preservation of human life. This is why much of the discussion within and outside the churches is about when in the process of gestation fetal life becomes human and should be protected by the law and about how much to emphasize the life of the fetus in relation to the life of the mother and others affected by a birth.

Finally, regarding the tradition as a whole, there is the matter of conscience. All churches, including the Catholic Church, which takes a definite and rigorous stance against abortion, have longstanding teaching regarding the moral necessity of developing and following individual conscience. There are very complex relations among one's individual conscience, the teachings of one's church, and the values of the society in which one lives, but all churches agree that the conscience is a linchpin of the process of making important decisions.

This would mean that Sue Ann should not make her decision based on the fact that the majority believes that abortion can be moral, or that those who approve abortion tend to be more educated and middle class. Nor should she make her decision based solely on the teachings of a religious tradition or authority. She must consult all sources and judge for herself. Religious traditions can furnish arguments that Sue Ann may find ultimately convincing. Sociological data about the opposing sides in the abortion debate can illuminate the reasons individuals are more influenced by some reasons than others. But it is never legitimate to shortcut the formation of personal conscience and blindly accept the conclusions of others.

GROUNDINGS OF CATHOLIC AND PROTESTANT POSITIONS

In the ethical treatment of abortion in Christianity today great division appears at a number of levels. As was touched upon above, a primary division occurs over the definition and value given to fetal life.

The Roman Catholic Church has defined all fetal life as full human life, while most Protestant churches are unwilling to define any specific point at which the fetus becomes fully human. Pope Pius IX in 1869 stipulated excommunication for abortion and fixed conception as the moment when the fetus, in technical terms at this stage a *zygote,* becomes a person, and, religiously speaking, ensoulment occurs. In so doing he closed the door on the hitherto prevailing views that: distinguished between an animate and an inanimate fetus; fixed the moment of ensoulment at quickening; and by implication, permitted abortion before quickening. Protestants in the United States, influenced like Catholics by more than a century of opposition to abortion by physicians attempting to take over the birthing process from "unscientific" and "untrained" female midwives, generally followed suit with the pope. From the 1870s to the 1960s the matter was settled and debate virtually closed.

Today, the Catholic Church's strong opposition to the practice of abortion as well as to allowing women the legal option of abortion is based primarily on two moral principles. The first is that according to the natural-law tradition, God's will is embedded in the patterns of creation and can be apprehended by the human mind. According to the Catholic interpretation of this tradition, a rational investigation of sexuality reveals that its innate purpose is twofold: procreation and mutual love. Therefore every sexual act must be open to the possibility of conception and should express love.

Anything that interferes with either thwarts God's intent. This perspective has been the backbone of Roman Catholic proscription of both abortion and artificial contraception for over a century. It is for this reason that abortion is understood as a sexual sin as well as a form of murder.

The second moral principle used by the Catholic Church in its rejection of abortion is one that absolutely forbids the direct taking of innocent life. This is not a prohibition against all taking of life. Not all life is innocent. It is not forbidden for the state to take the life of the guilty in capital punishment, or for soldiers to kill other soldiers who are presumed to be trying to kill them, or for anyone to kill in defense of self or others under attack. Further, under this principle it is possible that one would not be held responsible even for killing an innocent, if that killing were indirect. For example, indirect abortions can be permitted under this principle. If a pregnant woman has a cancerous uterus, a hysterectomy to remove the cancerous uterus is permitted if the delay until delivery poses a threat to her life. The purpose of the hysterectomy is to remove the diseased body part that threatens the woman's life. The loss of the life of the fetus is indirect and not intended, for the hysterectomy would have been performed had she been pregnant or not.

Most Protestants are not convinced by these Catholic arguments because they do not share Catholic biological interpretations of natural law or Catholic assumptions about full human life existing from conception. While virtually all Protestants accept the ban on direct taking of innocent life, many deny that fetal life is fully human and therefore protected by the ban. Nor have Protestants relied on natural law as a moral grounding. Historically, Protestant churches have understood the Fall to have corrupted human reason to such an extent that humans are without any natural capacity to comprehend God's will. They are instead dependent on God's grace for understanding.

Today natural law is receiving more Protestant attention than in the past largely because of its role in civil morality. But the biologically based model of natural law used by the Catholic Church is rejected in favor of models that draw upon other human capacities as well. For example, one might find that numerous actions and goals—preservation of human life by avoiding overpopulation or the use of abortion when family income is minimal or a mother's health is in danger—rest on equally compelling interpretations of natural law, based on the belief that God gives human beings the desire to preserve the species with dignity.

A further problem with natural law for Sue Ann is the finiteness of human rationality. God's will can be intentionally or unintentionally misread and is always discovered through the eyes of a specific culture.

What in one culture or historical period seems natural or clear does not in others. There is no way to decide what is natural for all short of imposing authority.

CONTEMPORARY ATTITUDES
TOWARD WOMEN AND MOTHERHOOD

Other religious arguments that favor or condemn abortion depend heavily upon the two issues discussed above: whether the fetus is a fully human life, and whether God's will can be determined through investigation of biological processes. How these two issues are interpreted not only shapes much of the basis for the way abortion is viewed but also affects our view of motherhood and the role of women in our society. As stated above, in Christianity much debate around the issue of abortion focuses upon nuances and inconsistencies in the Christian tradition's position on the nature of fetal life. Those positions and debates have been spelled out in the previous sections because they form part of the backdrop of and resources for Sue Ann's and Danny's decision. Without losing sight of those issues, this section will shift the focus to the varying conceptions of women and motherhood that are powerful aspects of Sue Ann's context as she strives to reach a decision about her pregnancy. A cornerstone in the debate about motherhood and women's roles is the norm of well-being, with its attendant norms of self-sacrifice and self-development, freedom, and justice and equality. The emphasis in this section is upon the perspective that stresses freedom, justice, self-development, and equality for women. The reason for emphasizing this perspective is that it has been a catalyst for the current debates about abortion.

Well-being

At the heart of the clash over abortion and what constitutes the well-being of women are two quite different views of motherhood and the role of women in society. Sue Ann is caught between these views, and her struggle runs much deeper than the decision of whether or not to abort. It involves how she understands herself as a woman and mother. There is, of course, a great variety of views on women's roles and what constitutes their well-being. Without doing too much injustice to these views and for the sake of clarity and discussion, these many views will be arranged under two opposing headings, the *traditional view* and what we will label a *late modern view*.

The traditional view stresses that a woman's well-being is fulfilled through her service to her children and husband. Such service is what truly frees. This traditional view is held by many of the most ardent opponents of legalized abortion. In part rooted in the natural-law position discussed above, this view holds that there are intrinsic differences between men and women, differences that lead to dissimilar roles. Men work in paid jobs and provide for women, whose primary role is childbearing and childrearing. Male leadership, exercised in a benevolent way, is considered normal and right. Freedom for women to work outside the home or to control the birth of children may even be a threat because it appears to upset the natural pattern and downgrade traditional roles. Thus at one end of the spectrum of what constitutes women's well-being is the position which stresses self-sacrifice and honorable service to children and husband.

Opposed to the above position is a view that women's well-being is fostered through equality with men and through the freedom to make choices about a host of issues—from careers to motherhood to the structure of relationships between men and women. Those who advocate this position hold that the context of women's lives today is radically different from the context in which the traditional view of women's roles developed. They point out that, for instance, dramatic changes are now occurring in the relation between men and women, changes partially indicated by the great increase of women in the work force. In 1970, 43 percent of all women age sixteen or over were in the work force. By 1980, that figure had increased to over 50 percent, in 1990 to 57.5 percent, and in 2000 to over 60 percent. In 2010, the percentage of women over the age of sixteen in the work force declined to 58.6 percent due to the recession. According to the Bureau of Labor Statistics, however, in January 2010 the number of women on America's payrolls for the first time outnumbered the number of men. This is not a mere change in numbers. This shift reflects a new concept of women as free and equal partners in society, capable of doing what men do and having the right to pursue nontraditional roles.

This new understanding of women, dominant among those who advocate women having a choice about abortion, sees men and women as substantially equal. Traditional roles are seen as reflecting not the order of nature but the ideology of a male-dominated society. The combination of male domination and oppressive ideology inhibits the full development and well-being of women. Being a mother is important, and many will elect it, but it is not the only role for women. According to this view, women must have choices about service and sacrifice, two central Christian affirmations we would do well to explore in greater depth before moving on to the critical issues of choice and equality.

Self-sacrifice

Within the Christian tradition there are various views of self-sacrifice, all largely stemming from interpretations of the words and actions of Jesus. One powerful image that is frequently raised here is that of Jesus on the cross and the implied mandate to sacrifice self for others. In very broad terms, many who stress this interpretation of Jesus urge a woman such as Sue Ann to choose against having an abortion and opt to sacrifice for the fetus she carries. But here the discussion returns to the questions raised above: Is the fetus fully human? Does it constitute one of the "others" for whom Sue Ann is called to sacrifice?

There are also questions about the understanding of self-sacrifice. Counter to the more traditional position is one that stresses a different interpretation of Jesus' sacrifice on the cross. In this interpretation Jesus did not go to the cross for the sake of self-sacrifice but to bring others a full and new life in the realm he announced. Self-sacrifice was a means, not an end; the end is entrance into the realm of God. Thus what is normative is bringing others to this realm. Still, self-sacrifice, or, in less extreme terms, service to others, is often a good means to this end, so much so that in certain circumstances it is legitimately normative. The legitimacy of self-sacrifice depends on whether there is a self to sacrifice or to give in service freely. The self in its fullest realization is a gift given by God through Jesus Christ and received in mutual love and community. Under conditions of oppression or under the influence of repressive ideologies, the self in its fullest realization is often not possible and is replaced by false consciousness. In a sense, there is no self to give. It cannot therefore be commanded or exhorted from individuals. This is crucial. Calling for self-sacrifice from someone under such conditions, for example, a slave or an abused and passive woman, is not a call to new life but to further slavery and oppression because it does not produce but impedes the mutual love and community to which the realm of God calls us.

These crosscurrents over self-sacrifice are, or at least should be, affecting Sue Ann and the decision she faces. Sue Ann must carefully evaluate her personal situation. She must try to understand what kind of relationship she and the child would have and whether it ultimately could be one that supports the mutual growth of each. She must, in short, try to come to conclusions about the relative values of fetal life, her life and personal choices and development, and the life within the communities of which she is a part.

Freedom of Choice and Equality for Women

As has been discussed, the decision Sue Ann faces is in large measure left to her conscience. Hers is the freedom to exercise conscience, although the responsible use of conscience means consulting the wisdom available from the larger community, including her religious tradition, if any, and her society. Sue Ann must decide whether the use of her freedom to abort in this situation is a legitimate exercise of her power to control her own body or a misuse of her power to control her body by denying life to the fetus she carries.

Freedom is part of the biblically based understanding of justice that has evolved in Western thought. In the United States the legal system provides for individual freedom unless democratically determined laws are broken. The norm of freedom places the burden of proof on those who would restrict the control that Sue Ann and other women have over their bodies. Opponents of legalized abortion are convinced they have satisfied this burden. They argue that just as society rightly denies freedom to a murderer, so it should deny a woman the right to abort a fetus, which in their view has full rights as a person. Proponents of legalized abortion counter by denying full legal status to fetal life in the early stages of pregnancy and point to the injustice of the state or any other body compelling Sue Ann to bear a child. They argue that women should have the freedom to control conception in order to control their bodies and their lives. At issue is whether the power to control conception includes the right to abort a fetus, and whether this power to control fertility is essential to women's well-being.

Obviously, this notion of the right to control one's own body is a key element in the position that sees abortion as an option. Those who hold this position argue that in order for women to take control of their lives and to construct a meaningful life plan, they must have the capacity to break the link between sex and procreation. Otherwise their bodies, or whoever controls their bodies, will control them, and pregnancy will interrupt all possible plans except mothering. Statistically effective contraceptives and safe, affordable abortions make breaking the link possible for the first time in history. For many who support choice, the right to choose is more than just a symbol of the newfound freedom and equality of women. For those who hold this view, the freedom to choose is fundamental to all other justice claims of women. They argue that without the right to choose contraception to prevent pregnancy, or abortion to terminate an undesired pregnancy, women will be discriminated against. Employers, for example, may be reluctant to train women for or employ them in significant positions because those employers will anticipate that women will be in and out of the work force. There can be no equality in the work place when women and men function under the assumption that a woman's occupation will be subordinated to each and every pregnancy.

In essence, then, those who stand for women's choice argue that, for women, the capacity to choose is the capacity to gain equality, new identities, and new avenues for vocation. The very well-being of women is at stake, and society has a moral obligation to further this well-being. Part of the well-being of women includes openness to the growth possibilities inherent in childrearing and homemaking. If women are to be free to choose how to pursue their lives, then obviously they must be free to choose childrearing and homemaking as focal points of their lives. It does no one good to draw the options as a choice between passive, dull housewives and active, responsible career women. There are many paths between these stereotypes.

SEX BEFORE MARRIAGE

Sue Ann and Danny by mutual consent engaged in sexual relations outside of marriage. Sue Ann also had sexual relations with Paul Reynolds. These relationships raise the ethical issue of premarital sex.

Christian reflection on the ethics of premarital sex is in a state of flux and has become part of the cultural wars that now rage over the family and sexual relations in general. On the one end of the spectrum are those who say the norm is clear and leads to only two moral outcomes: chastity outside of marriage and fidelity within marriage. This traditional view is still the official one in most churches, although adherence is hardly universal. Sexual relations outside of marriage are commonplace today, as they have been in other historical periods.

On the other end of the spectrum is the view that sex outside of marriage is appropriate for consenting adults. While not endorsed by many churches, this view is widespread both among Christians and in secular quarters as evidenced by the increasing number of couples living together and even raising families without marrying.

In between these two ends of the spectrum are a number of other perspectives. There is no consensus.

The more traditional perspective with its legal approach has certain attractions. Sexual relations are far more than physical intercourse that satisfies a strong instinct. They involve great emotion and go to the core of a person's being. They involve the giving and the receiving of the self that can lead to a deep sense of inner wholeness. They are one of God's greatest gifts, and it is not too much to say that humans may even experience God through them.

The same vehicle serves sin, however. Some do not love but seduce. They take advantage of a vulnerable other person in order to serve their own selfish purposes. Hurt and alienation follow, and this is one reason why Christian traditions have put up so many warning signs around sex. "Proceed with caution," they seem to say.

Even if seduction is not conscious, physical sex is easily mistaken for love. Momentary sexual attraction can give the illusion of deeper intimacy. Love is easily trivialized. Sexual relations should therefore be part of a deeply loving and committed relationship, and normally such relationships take time to mature.

Another critical reason for caution has to do with children. Marriage, or at least two-parent families, is still the best context for raising children. Social scientists are in fundamental agreement that children of single-parent families, especially those in poverty, face heightened risk. They drop out of school at a much higher rate. They have higher unemployment rates and are more likely themselves to have a child before age twenty.

On the other side of the issue, many single parents do admirable jobs. Marriage is no guarantee of love or well-raised children. Marriage relationships are often unloving, some even involving spouse and child abuse. Loving relationships can be found outside of marriage. The prohibition on sex outside of marriage is part of a patriarchal tradition that has been oppressive to both men and women.

Today's more open sexual relations are also a breath of fresh air in the catacombs of prudery where sex is dirty and the inferior cousin of celibacy. They bring a measure of joy back to sex. For these and other reasons a rigid legalism is misplaced. But so is the contrasting perspective that offers no normative guidance, often trivializes sex, and is not nearly as "open" as it purports.

THE CHOICES

Sue Ann apparently has not reflected in any depth about her future role as a woman. She had planned to marry Paul Reynolds as soon as she finished high school. This suggests that she envisioned a more traditional role. After Paul's death and her graduation, however, she enrolled in a community college, the first in her family to do so. This suggests she may have other plans for her life that giving birth and mothering may change, especially if she becomes a single mother.

Her options appear to be to give birth or to have an abortion. If she gives birth, she may keep the baby or allow someone else to adopt it. Adoption may be an attractive alternative, but she should be prepared for the bonding that develops between the mother and the unborn child that makes giving the baby away difficult. The National Adoption Council tracks the number of adoptions in the United States. In 2011 it published its most recent Adoption Factbook V, which reports 2007 data. In that year less than one-half of 1 percent of all live births in the United States resulted in children being relinquished for adoption as infants. In addition, less than 1 percent of unmarried mothers chose adoption for their infants; over 99 percent decided to parent the baby. Statistics like these are sobering. The reality is that virtually all mothers decide to keep their infant children after birth.

The Mosaic view that regarded fetal life as potentially human and therefore of value, the norm of the goodness of life, and considerations of legitimate self-sacrifice would lead Sue Ann in the direction of preserving the fetus. The norm of freedom makes her morally responsible for the decision.

If abortion may be read as too "pro-self," then in contrast the decision to go to term and reject abortion may seem to her too "pro-birth." The norm of self-giving and self-sacrifice may be perceived as an alien demand forcing her to negate herself endlessly for childbearing and childrearing, unless she chooses the path of adoption.

Her choice between these options should be influenced by Danny's response. Danny seems to be dumbstruck by the pregnancy, and there is no indication what he intends to do. He is not pressing her to marry him at this time in their lives. Sue Ann does not say how she feels about marrying Danny but does not object to Danny's reading of the situation. Sue Ann is on the rebound from Paul Reynolds and probably had sex with Danny more in response to her grief than love for him. Danny says, "You are really important to me." This is a lukewarm statement of affection. He does, however, pay his share of the $400 for the abortion. This may be an indication he will provide further support, but the job he holds probably does not pay very well.

Should Sue Ann and Danny marry now that she is pregnant? Marriages under these circumstances are at risk. There was a day when both church and social norms would have put pressure on them to marry. These norms have weakened in recent years for a variety of reasons, including the high divorce rates of teens that marry without much love under pressure from family, church, and society. Perhaps the best advice is to proceed with caution.

Danny does have responsibilities to Sue Ann, however. If she decides to have the baby, he is responsible for providing support, as he is able. He should participate in the birth and the care of the child and act as a loving father. He should also care for Sue Ann by giving her emotional as well as financial support. Who knows, their love may grow into a mature, stable relationship where God is present. Or it may not.

Rather than facing alone an impossible choice between the potential life within her and her own needs, Sue Ann may be freed by considering her interdependence with other persons. She might ask how her decision would enhance not only her well-being, but also the well-being of her family and those in the wider community.

The place to start is probably with her own parents, whom she has not consulted. Her parents are concerned about her health, but Sue Ann is reluctant to tell them she is pregnant. Normally, young women in her situation are wise to seek their parents' help. Most parents are understanding, however disappointed they may be. Whether she is afraid of letting them down or being criticized by them, the case does not say. In some situations past abuse by parents may justify not telling them, but there is no indication of that here. Sue Ann's parents may also have different views about abortion than she does and could possibly put heavy pressure on her at a time when she is already under stress. Sue Ann certainly is not the first young woman to be reluctant to tell and seek help from her parents.

Whatever the decision, Sue Ann's seeming choice between an agonized decision to abort and resentful surrender to having a child, even if only temporarily should she opt for adoption, must be faced. Perhaps both Danny and Sue Ann know the healing power of grace that comes through faith in Jesus Christ. The task will be to unite head and heart so that this power can do its work.

ADDITIONAL RESOURCES

Baird, Robert M., and Stuart E. Rosenbaum, eds. *The Ethics of Abortion: Pro-life vs. Pro-choice.* Third edition. Amherst, NY: Prometheus Books, 2001.

Farley, Margaret. *Just Love: A Framework for Christian Sexual Ethics.* New York: Continuum, 2006.

Harrison, Beverly Wildung. *Our Right to Choose.* Boston: Beacon Press, 1983.

Kaczor, Christopher. *The Ethics of Abortion: Women's Rights, Human Life, and the Question of Justice.* New York: Routledge Press, 2010.

Maguire, Daniel C. *Sacred Choices: The Right to Contraception and Abortion in Ten World Religions.* Minneapolis: Fortress Press, 2009.

O'Brien, George Dennis. *The Church and Abortion: A Catholic Dissent.* Lanham, MD: Rowman and Littlefield, 2010.

Riddle, John. *Contraception and Abortion from the Ancient World to the Renaissance.* Cambridge: Harvard University Press, 1994.

Stallsworth, Paul, ed. *The Church and Abortion.* Nashville, TN: Thomas Nelson, 1998.

Stassen, Glen H., and David P. Gushee. *Kingdom Ethics: Jesus in Contemporary Context.* Westmont, IL: InterVarsity Press, 2003.

Tooley, Michael, Celia Wolf-Devine, Philip E. Devine, and Alison M. Jaggar. *Abortion: Three Perspectives*. New York: Oxford University Press, 2009.

Related Websites

Allan Guttmacher Institute. Abortion. http://www.guttmacher.org/sections/abortion.php.
National Adoption Council. https://www.adoptioncouncil.org/.

Related Videos

HBO Home Video. "The Cider House Rules." 125 Minutes. 2000.
Miramax. "Unborn in the USA." 105 minutes. 2007.
National Geographic Video. "In the Womb." 120 minutes. 2005.
National Geographic Video. "Soldiers in the Army of God." 70 minutes. 2006.

Case

Death, Duty, and Dignity

Professor Theresa Christiansen gazed out her office window after reading the letter for a second time. A large ecumenical organization had invited her to give the keynote address at a conference that would be held in the state capital in six months. The conference—Death, Duty, and Dignity— had been prompted by a new proposal in the state legislature to pass a bill identical to Oregon's Death with Dignity Act. As in Oregon, the proposed legislation would make it legal for a person in the last stages of a terminal illness to hasten his or her death with the assistance of a physician.

Theresa assumed she had been invited to give the keynote address because she had been an outspoken critic of the Oregon law when it was first debated in 1994. Drawing on her training as a historian of the Reformation, Theresa had contrasted the *ars moriendi* (the art of dying) in the medieval and modern eras. She had opposed physician-assisted suicide because she felt it reflected an individualistic world view grounded in appeals to rights and autonomy that is foreign to a Christian world view that emphasizes subservience to God and duties to others. Theresa had reminded her audiences in print and in person that religious leaders like Martin Luther had viewed their deaths as an opportunity and an obligation to witness to their faith—to use their deathbeds as teaching moments. In contrast to those who appealed to the rights of privacy and autonomy as the legal foundations for access to physician-assisted death, Theresa had emphasized that Luther viewed his death as a public affair in which he had a moral obligation to testify to his faith in the resurrection despite his suffering. To die well is one's final responsibility to others in the community. Dependence on God—not independence from others—is one of the hallmarks of a Christian world

---

This case and commentary were prepared by James B. Martin-Schramm. The names of all persons and institutions have been disguised to protect the privacy of those involved.

309

view. It is precisely because Christ's suffering had been redemptive that our suffering should not be avoided.

Theresa was disappointed when Oregon's public referendum on the Death with Dignity Act passed in November 1994 by a slim majority, 51 percent in favor to 49 percent opposed. After the US Supreme Court ruled in June 1997 that there is no constitutional right to die and that this issue is best addressed by the states, she was a bit surprised when the citizens of her home state defeated a ballot measure to repeal the Death with Dignity Act by a 60 percent to 40 percent margin. By then Theresa had left Oregon to take up a new teaching position and had not been able to participate much in the second round of debate. Nearly fifteen years had passed, and Theresa had not thought much more about the issue until last year, when her father called from the home Theresa had grown up in back in Portland, Oregon. Theresa remembered the call all too well. She had been totally unprepared for it.

Theresa's father, Ted Christiansen, had been a dentist for forty years when he retired at the age of sixty-five. Theresa's mother, Mary, had married Ted the year he graduated from dental school. Their two children, Theresa and Peter, followed in short order. They were a close family and loved one another very much. After the children went off to middle school, Mary went back to work as a teacher. She retired at the same time Ted retired from his dental practice. They had thoroughly enjoyed retirement. The couple had visited family in Scandinavia and had seen many spots in the world they had long wanted to visit but had been unable to do so while they had both been working. In Portland they were active in their church, and both belonged to different civic organizations like the Rotary Club and the League of Women Voters. Their three grandchildren absolutely adored Grandma and Grandpa. Ted and Mary had been blessed in many ways, and they had also been a blessing to others. One of these blessings had been the gift of good health for over a decade of their retirement.

A couple of years ago, however, her dad had not been feeling well. He had been having trouble with his vision and was increasingly nauseated and forgetful. The initial consult with his doctor led to an appointment with a brain specialist, an MRI, and finally a biopsy. Ted called his son and daughter after the specialist informed him that the result of the biopsy was brain cancer. More specifically, he had a grade IV glioblastoma multiforme (GBM), which is an extremely fast-growing and lethal form of brain cancer. The doctor had informed him that without any treatment the median survival time from diagnosis was three months. With surgery and perhaps radiation and chemotherapy, the median survival time was about eleven months. Theresa remembered hearing her mother sobbing in the background on the other phone.

After a week of prayer and reflection, Ted called Theresa and Peter to tell them he had decided to have the surgery to remove as much of the tumor as possible. The surgery took place about two weeks after that and went well. The brain surgeon set Ted up with regular doses of radiotherapy because studies showed that these treatments almost doubled the post-surgical survival time. Ted recovered fairly quickly from the surgery and was able to communicate and walk quite well. After about six months, however, his nausea and blurred vision increased significantly, and he began to experience increasingly severe headaches. Ted discussed the matter with his specialist, who sent him to a colleague for a second opinion. Both concurred that Ted had less than six months to live.

That night Ted and Mary shared this news with Theresa and Peter. About a month later they called both children and asked them to come home the following weekend so that they could tell them how they intended to handle the last stages of Ted's disease. Theresa had not anticipated what would follow. Seated around the kitchen table, Ted told his children that he had asked his lifelong friend and their family physician to assist him in hastening his death. With Mary holding his hand, Ted explained that he saw no point in dragging this on to the inevitable end. As the disease progressed he would experience more and more pain, and while his doctors assured him they could keep the pain to a minimum, they could not guarantee how long he would retain his memory and cognitive powers. Ted explained that he did not want to die unable to recognize his family and friends gathered around his deathbed.

Ted reached into a folder and pulled out an article that Theresa had published almost fifteen years earlier during the height of the debate about the Death with Dignity Act in Oregon. He looked directly at Theresa and said that he could not be more proud of her and her work. He agreed that as a Christian he should testify to his faith at the end of his life. He explained, however, that he thought he could be a better witness while he retained the cognitive abilities he had left. With tears in his eyes he told Theresa and Peter he loved them with all his heart. He added that this decision was made easier by his sure and confident faith in the resurrection. He concluded by saying he could never do this without the unqualified support of Mary, who nodded her sure assent through the tears streaming down her face. It was a moment Theresa would never forget, nor could she forget the actual day about two months later when Ted's life came to an end.

Ted decided to end his life on Reformation Sunday. Their pastor had agreed to come to their home, where Ted was now in hospice care, to lead a worship service for the family, friends, and members of their congregation that Ted had invited. Peter's wife, Faith, had refused to come, however, and had insisted that Peter not take their three children. While she loved her father-in-law, she thoroughly disagreed with his decision. As a Roman Catholic she firmly believed that suicide was a sin. She thought it would be sinful to participate in the service in any way because, in her mind, the service was sanctioning the sinful act that would follow. She said physician-assisted suicide was just the first step down a slippery slope that in the future could lead to a host of human rights abuses. She had urged Peter and Theresa to talk their father out of his decision, but they knew his mind was made up.

During the service Mary read Romans 14:7–8: "None of us lives to himself, and none of us dies to himself. If we live, we live to the Lord, and if we die, we die to the Lord; so then, whether we live or we die, we are the Lord's." Theresa's father followed with John 11:25–26, which he read haltingly: "'I am the resurrection and the life,' says the Lord; 'he who believes in me, though he dies, yet shall he live, and whoever lives and believes in me shall never die.'" The pastor gave a short homily giving thanks for Ted's ministry to others through his dental practice and in his service to the congregation and the wider community. The pastor also emphasized that each Christian has been baptized into the death and resurrection of Jesus Christ and thus can fully embrace life on earth as well as eternal life in heaven. During the prayers that followed Ted's and Mary's friends surrounded him with love as they offered prayers of thanks and reassurance. Afterward the pastor celebrated the Eucharist. Mary dipped the small portion of the host in the cup and gave it to her husband, saying, "This is the body and blood of our Lord Jesus Christ given and shed for you." At the end of the service the pastor offered a closing prayer: "Lord Jesus, by your death you took away the sting of death. Grant to us, your servants, so to follow in faith where you have led the way, that we may at length fall asleep peacefully in you and wake in your likeness; to you, the author and giver of life, be all honor and glory, now and forever. Amen."

After the service ended Mary invited their friends to say their last goodbyes to Ted. About an hour later Peter, Theresa, and Mary gathered in Ted's bedroom with their pastor and their family physician. It was all Theresa could do to walk back into the bedroom. Mary asked Ted if he was ready. Brimming with emotion Ted quietly said, "Yes." He reached out and grasped the hands of Theresa and Peter and told them how much he loved them. Finally, he did the same with Mary. Still holding her hand, he used his other hand to lift the small cup that held the liquid opiates that had been prescribed for this purpose. Fully aware of his actions, context, and surroundings, Ted pointed to the Dag Hammarskjöld quotation on a poster across from his bed: "For all that has been—Thanks. For all that will be—Yes." Shortly after Ted drank from the cup, he lost consciousness. About ten minutes later his friend and physician pronounced him dead.

Theresa sat in her office weeping quietly. It had not yet been a year since her father had died. Her emotions were still raw. She held the invitation in her hand. She felt she should accept the invitation, but what should she say about death, duty, and dignity? Her father had chosen to end his life while he still had the ability to testify to his faith with his loved ones around his deathbed. Had this profound experience led her to change her views about physician-assisted death and the *ars moriendi* in the twenty-first century? Are laws like Oregon's Death with Dignity Act compatible or incompatible with a Christian world view?

Commentary

This case grapples with the topic of euthanasia, which, in Greek, refers to a "good death." For many, it is impossible to separate a good death from what constitutes a good life. While modern medicine has worked wonders and extended the length of human life, it has not always improved the quality of human life—especially in the last few years before death. In addition, while modern palliative care has made it possible to relieve virtually all physical pain for those who have access to these services, drugs do not necessarily relieve the emotional and psychological pain associated with losing control of one's physical and mental abilities as well as the loss of one's independence. Both of these factors have given rise to what has come to be called the death-with-dignity movement around the world.

Ethical discussions about this topic draw upon important distinctions between passive and active euthanasia as well as voluntary and involuntary forms of euthanasia. Passive euthanasia is typically described as not preventing death but rather allowing nature to take its course, whereas active euthanasia is typically described as taking a deliberate action to hasten and cause death. Voluntary euthanasia occurs when a person consciously decides no longer to fight death or takes steps to end his or her life. Involuntary euthanasia occurs when others decide either to let a person die or to hasten death without that person's explicit consent.

Voluntary, passive euthanasia is widely accepted legally and morally. All fifty US states permit individuals by themselves or through others named in a living will or advanced health-care directive to refuse or to withdraw futile medical treatments or interventions. Typical examples involve refusing surgery, ceasing medications, and turning off ventilators. Involuntary, passive euthanasia takes place when others authorize steps like these or otherwise allow someone to die—but without the patient's explicit consent. Similarly, involuntary, active euthanasia takes place when a loved one or physician takes steps to hasten a person's death without their consent. These "mercy killings" take various forms. Sometimes they involve a physician prescribing so much pain medication that it causes sedation and then shallow respiration to the point of death. On other occasions they involve parents, spouses, and friends euthanizing loved ones they can no longer bear to watch die a lingering and painful death. For obvious reasons active and passive forms of involuntary euthanasia are not morally accepted. Normally they are legally prosecuted, although often without severe punishment.

This case involves voluntary, active euthanasia, in which a person takes deliberate steps, with or without the assistance of others, to hasten the end of his or her life and to ensure a certain death. For example, a patient could choose voluntarily to stop eating and drinking in order to hasten death. This requires enormous strength of will, however, to overcome the natural desire to eat and drink. A person could also try to commit suicide, but these attempts often fail because people either do not know how to kill themselves, lack access to sufficient means, or simply are physically incapable of doing so because they are bedridden and immobile. It is precisely for this reason that many terminally ill patients like Ted Christiansen have asked their physicians or loved ones to assist them in their death.

Active, voluntary euthanasia has been legal in the Netherlands since 1995, in Belgium since 2002, and in Luxembourg since 2008. While confined to competent persons suffering from a terminal illness, laws in these countries permit physicians to assist patients with their deaths, but they also permit physicians to administer the means if the patient is unable to do so but has requested to end his or her life in this manner. Assisted suicide has been legal in Switzerland since the 1940s, but it does not have to involve a physician. Under Article 115 of the Swiss penal code an assisted suicide is only a crime if the motive is selfish. In order to establish the motive, assisted suicides in Switzerland are typically video-taped and then reported to the police who interview the family and others involved. If the police do not establish a selfish motive, the assisted suicide is not deemed a crime.

As the case explains, by two public referendums in the 1990s Oregon became the first US state legally to permit physician-assisted suicide. After various legal challenges that reached as high as the US Supreme Court, the state's Death with Dignity Act became law on January 1, 1998. A little more than a decade later, the state of Washington passed a ballot initiative in November 2008 establishing a similar law modeled on Oregon's initiative. Most recently, Montana's Supreme Court ruled in a narrow 4–3 decision on December 31, 2009, that physicians in Montana need not fear criminal prosecution if they write lethal prescriptions for mentally competent patients with terminal illnesses. The court chose not to address whether physician-assisted suicide is a right guaranteed under the state's constitution, and thus left this decision in the hands of the state legislature.

Given the location of Ted Christiansen's death—in the state of Oregon—this commentary first provides more information about the state's Death with Dignity Act before turning to discuss Christian views about the morality of euthanasia in general and physician-assisted euthanasia in particular.

OREGON'S DEATH WITH DIGNITY ACT

Enacted on October 27, 1997, Oregon's Death with Dignity Act (DWDA) allows terminally ill Oregonians to end their lives through the voluntary self-administration of lethal medications, expressly prescribed by a physician for that purpose. A 2007 article in the journal *Bioethics* provides a valuable summary of the key provisions of the program:

> Any resident of Oregon who is at least 18 years old, is capable of making and communicating health care decisions, and has been di-agnosed with a terminal illness with less than 6 months to live can request a prescription for lethal medication. The request must be made to a licensed Oregon physician.

> The following provisions are written into the Oregon law:

> - The patient must make two oral requests to his or her physi-cian, separated by at least 15 days.
> - The patient must provide a written request to his or her phy-sician, signed in the presence of two witnesses.
> - The prescribing physician and a consulting physician must confirm the diagnosis and prognosis.
> - The prescribing physician and a consulting physician must determine whether the patient is capable.
> - If either physician believes the patient's judgment is impaired by a psychiatric or psychological disorder, the patient must be referred for a psychological examination.
> - The prescribing physician must inform the patient of feasible alternatives to assisted suicide, including comfort care, hos-pice care, and pain control.
> - The prescribing physician must request, but may not require, the patient to notify his or her next-of-kin of the prescription request.

> If all steps are followed and a lethal prescription is written, the prescribing physician must file a report with the Oregon Department of Human Services. Physicians are not required to participate in [physician-assisted suicide] PAS, nor are pharmacists or health care systems.

From 1998 to January 7, 2011, 525 patients have died from ingesting medications prescribed under the Death with Dignity Act. These deaths constitute 0.132 percent of the 398,180 deaths in Oregon from 1998 through 2010. (The websites listed at the end of this commentary provide access to the most recent annual reports and additional information about the Death with Dignity Act in Oregon and the one in Washington.)

While the number of DWDA deaths represents a tiny fraction of deaths in the state of Oregon, the number of persons requesting and dying from lethal prescriptions has been growing over time. The following information is excerpted directly from the state's 2011 annual report:

- As of January 7, 2011, 96 prescriptions for lethal medications had been written under the provisions of the DWDA during 2010, compared to 95 during 2009. Of the 96 patients for whom prescriptions were written during 2010, 59 died from ingesting the medications. In addition, six patients with prescriptions written during previous years ingested the medications and died during 2010 for a total of 65 known 2010 DWDA deaths at the time of this report. This corresponds to 20.9 DWDA deaths per 10,000 total deaths [0.209%].
- Of the 65 patients who died under DWDA in 2010, most (70.8%) were over age 65 years; the median age was 72 years. As in previous years, most were white (100%), well-educated (42.2% had a least a baccalaureate degree), and had cancer (78.5%).
- Most (96.9%) patients died at home; and most (92.6%) were enrolled in hospice care at time of death. Most (96.7%) had some form of health care insurance, although the number of patients who had private insurance (60.0%) was lower in 2010 than in previous years (69.1%), and the number of patients who had only Medicare or Medicaid insurance was higher than in previous years (36.7% compared to 29.6%).
- As in previous years, the most frequently mentioned end-of-life concerns were: loss of autonomy (93.8%), decreasing ability to participate in activities that made life enjoyable (93.8%), and loss of dignity (78.5%).
- In 2010, one of the 65 patients was referred for formal psychiatric or psychological evaluation.

These statistics and others reveal that Ted Christiansen's case is in many ways typical, though his death is still quite exceptional. For example, his case is typical because males have constituted 53 percent of all DWDA deaths over the life of the program. In addition, he is among the vast majority who have been diagnosed with cancer and who have died while enrolled in hospice care. Ted's death is exceptional, however, insofar as DWDA-related deaths represent just over one-tenth of 1 percent of all deaths in the state of Oregon since 1998. Nevertheless, this tiny fraction of deaths has been part of a large debate within Christian communities about the morality of euthanasia and physician-assisted death.

CHRISTIAN VIEWS
REGARDING PHYSICIAN-ASSISTED EUTHANASIA

Christian opposition to euthanasia and physician-assisted suicide has been relatively widespread across denominations. For various reasons the Roman Catholic Church has tended to be at the forefront of public opposition and thus receives substantial discussion in this commentary.

Deontological Arguments

At the heart of a deontological argument is the claim that moral agents have obligations to obey authorities that are extrinsic to themselves. These authorities can be sacred scriptures like the Bible, the teachings of religious leaders and councils, the laws or principles that govern a community, or the rules of a home and accountability to one's parents. Deontological perspectives offer greater assurances of moral consistency over time, but deontologists also find it hard to compromise because certain options are precluded by the authorities they are obligated to respect. What follows is a discussion of five deontological arguments related to physician-assisted euthanasia. This is not the term that is typically used in public debates, however. Opponents to this practice normally refer to it as physician-assisted *suicide,* whereas proponents prefer to call it physician-assisted *death.* These different terms are used below depending on whether the argument supports or opposes physician-assisted euthanasia.

1. Physician-assisted suicide transgresses God's commandment not to kill innocent life (Ex 20:13), it usurps God's sovereignty over our lives, and it violates our obligations to serve others and the common good.

Ted Christiansen's daughter-in-law, Faith, appears to agree with this argument because it is consistent with her Roman Catholic tradition. In 1980 the Vatican's Sacred Congregation for the Doctrine of the Faith issued the "Declaration on Euthanasia." The statement emphasizes that "no one can make an attempt on the life of an innocent person without opposing God's love for that person, without violating a fundamental right, and therefore without committing a crime of the utmost gravity." The statement also stresses that

> everyone has the duty to lead his or her life in accordance with God's plan. . . . Intentionally causing one's own death, or suicide, is therefore equally as wrong as murder; such an action on the part of a person is to be considered as a rejection of God's sovereignty and loving plan. . . . Suicide is also often a refusal of love for self, the denial of a natural instinct to live, a flight from the duties of justice and charity owed to one's neighbor, to various communities or to the whole of society.

Given this wide-ranging condemnation it is interesting to note that suicide is not uniformly condemned in the Bible, and where it is discussed, it is often associated with an act of sacrifice or a death with dignity. For example, in the Hebrew scriptures Saul and his armor-bearer fall on their swords rather than be captured by the Philistines and subjected to a humiliating death (1 Sm 31:1–7). In addition, Samson prays to God to renew his strength so that he can pull down the house of Dagon and thus bring death to himself but also to his enemies (Jgs 16:23—17:2). In the Apocrypha, Eleazar stabs a war elephant from underneath knowing that it will crush him, but he thinks it will help his compatriots win their battle (1 Macc 6:43–47). Like Saul, Razis falls on his sword and tears out his entrails rather than be captured by the enemy (2 Macc 14:41–42). In the Christian scriptures Jesus emphasizes that "no one has greater love than this, to lay down one's life for one's friends" (Jn 15:13).

Texts like these reflect the fact that biblical authors did not view life as an ultimate good that must be preserved at all costs. As a result, they could sanction acts in which persons gave up their lives for the benefit of others. While suicide motivated by despair violates God's sovereignty over one's life, the Vatican's Sacred Congregation for the Doctrine of the Faith acknowledges that "one must clearly distinguish suicide from that sacrifice of one's life whereby for a higher cause, such as God's glory, the salvation of souls or the service of one's brethren, a person offers his or her own life or puts it in danger (cf. Jn 15:14)." In the case presented here it does not appear that Ted Christiansen's decision is motivated by despair. Instead, he testifies to his faith in the resurrection, he trusts in God's goodness, and he wants his death to be edifying both for his family and for others in his faith community.

2. Physician-assisted death is justified by the Golden Rule that implores us to treat others the way we would want to be treated.

Paul Badham makes this argument in *Is There a Christian Case for Assisted Dying?* Badham is a professor of theology and religious studies at the University of Wales and an ordained Anglican priest. He believes Jesus summarized the essence of Christian theology and ethics when he was asked by the Pharisees to identity the greatest Jewish commandment. Jesus replied: "'You shall love the Lord your God with all your heart, and with all your soul, and with all your mind.' This is the greatest and first commandment. And a second is like it: 'You shall love your neighbor as yourself.' On these two commandments hang all the law and the prophets" (Mt 22:37–40). Badham draws two important points from this key biblical passage. First, that Christians who love God with their heart, soul, and mind do not fear death but rather view it as "the gateway to eternal life." Second, denying our neighbors and loved ones their repeated requests to die lacks compassion and violates Jesus' injunction to "do to others as you would have them do to you" (Mt 7:12). Badham asks, "If we truly love our neighbor as ourselves how can we deny them the death we would wish for ourselves in such a situation?" Badham implies that Jesus would support a humane, physician-assisted death because Jesus broke the law to heal on the Sabbath (Mk 2:27). That is, Jesus was willing to break the law and violate social custom in order to do what was humane for a person who was suffering.

There are two primary responses to this argument from conservative Christians. The first is that some human actions, like murder, are always objectively wrong regardless of the motivations or circumstances. After all, Jesus heals the man on the Sabbath; he does not kill him out of mercy. The second is that compassion is best expressed when it leads Christians to bear one another's sufferings rather than terminate them. Pope John Paul II summarizes both views in his 1995 papal encyclical, *Evangelium vitae.* He writes, "Suicide is always as morally objectionable as murder. The Church's tradition has always rejected it as a gravely evil choice." Regarding assisted suicide he writes, "To concur with the intention of another person to commit suicide and to help in carrying it out through so-called 'assisted suicide' means to cooperate in, and at times to be the actual perpetrator of, an injustice which can never be excused, even if it is requested." Regarding compassion the pope states, "True 'compassion' leads to sharing another's pain; it does not kill the person whose suffering we cannot bear." Anticipating involuntary euthanasia, Pope John Paul II concludes: "The height of arbitrariness and injustice is reached when certain people, such as physicians or legislators, arrogate to themselves the power to decide who ought to live and who ought to die. Once again we find ourselves before the temptation of Eden: to become like God who 'knows good and evil' (cf. Gen 3:5). God alone has the power over life and death: 'It is I who bring both death and life' (Dt 32:39; cf. 2 Kg 5:7; 1 Sam 2:6)."

While it is true that human beings have sought to become like God in their quest for the knowledge of good and evil, it is also true that modern medicine has been able to bar the doors to death for well beyond what has been viewed as a natural or normal lifespan. Badham and other proponents of physician-assisted death think it is odd to ignore the way modern medicine seems to arrogate or deny God's powers over life and death, while at the same time we find fault with those like Ted Christiansen who are ready to embrace their mortality and welcome death as the gateway to eternal life.

3. Physician-assisted suicide rejects the power of redemptive suffering and the Apostle Paul's promise that "God is faithful, and he will not let you be tested beyond your strength" (1 Cor 10:13).

The Christian gospel message is often summed up in John 3:16, "For God so loved the world that he gave his only Son, so that everyone who believes in him may not perish but may have eternal life." Isaiah 53:3–5 emphasizes that the suffering servant was "wounded for our transgressions" and "bruised for our iniquities." Jesus connects the cross to suffering and discipleship in all three of the synoptic gospels (Mk 8:34; Mt 10:38; Mt 16:24; Lk 9:23). Christians refer to the anniversary of Jesus' crucifixion as *Good* Friday. Central to the Christian gospel is the belief that suffering can be redemptive.

It is precisely for this reason that the Vatican's Sacred Congregation for the Doctrine of the Faith says in its "Declaration on Euthanasia" that "suffering is not pointless. . . . The Catholic church holds that 'suffering, especially suffering during the last moments of life, has a special place in God's saving plan; it is in fact a sharing in Christ's passion and a union with the redeeming sacrifice which he offered in obedience to the Father's will." Pope John Paul II qualifies this stance later in *Evangelium vitae* in a section devoted to palliative care and pain relief: "While praise may be due to the person who voluntarily accepts suffering by forgoing treatment with pain-killers in order to remain fully lucid and, if a believer, to share consciously in the Lord's Passion, such 'heroic' behavior cannot be considered the duty of everyone." Pope John Paul II did accept the "vocation of suffering" in his own life, however, choosing to live out his last days with minimal pain relief in the public eye.

While Pope John Paul II emphasized that the "vocation of suffering" is voluntary, some evangelical Christians firmly oppose this view because, from their perspective, the whole point of Christ's death on the cross is that it, by itself, achieves reconciliation with God apart from any actions on the part of humanity. Christ's sacrifice on the cross is sufficient for atonement; no additional human suffering is required. More liberal Christians are repulsed by the very notion that a good and gracious God could only achieve reconciliation by the torturous death of a crucifixion. Some Christian pacifists also encourage caution with regard to "taking up one's cross" because they believe the related suffering stems from persecution for following Jesus and living out the values of the kingdom of God in a hostile world. While Jesus certainly has compassion for those who suffer from painful diseases like stomach cancer, some pacifists would not describe this as one's "cross to bear." Finally, even though suffering related to illness is often born bravely and can provide occasions for one to bear witness to his or her faith, there are also times when this form of suffering no longer seems to bear any redemptive or salutary purpose and can jeopardize faith.

4. Physician-assisted death is justified by the same rights to privacy, autonomy, and self-determination that enable a person to refuse or withdraw medical treatments.

Pain is not the only thing that produces suffering. While palliative care can treat physical symptoms of suffering, drugs are far less effective at alleviating the suffering people experience as they experience the loss of their freedom, cognitive faculties, and control over their bodily functions. The statistics from Oregon and Washington bear this out. The reasons most frequently given by those who have chosen to utilize physician-assisted death are loss of autonomy, decreasing ability to participate in activities that made life enjoyable, and loss of dignity. While many fear that the legalization of physician-assisted death may lead to the euthanizing of vulnerable populations, the statistics in Oregon and Washington reveal that those who value responsibility, independence, and personal autonomy are most likely to want to exercise these capacities in relation to the manner and timing of their deaths. It is important to note that these are not merely secular values. Ted Christiansen, in the case, utilizes his autonomy and self-determination to bear witness to his Christian faith upon his deathbed, albeit in a very untraditional way.

Opponents to this view challenge it on both legal and ethical grounds. Legally, they point out that courts have based the right to withdraw or refuse medical treatment not on the right to autonomy but rather on the right to self-defense and protection from assault. In 1977 the US Supreme Court ruled in *Vacco v. Quill* that the negative legal right to refuse medical treatment on the basis of freedom from abuse does not translate into a positive legal right to freely choose physician-assisted suicide, though the court did leave this up to the states to decide. Ethically, the Roman Catholic Church establishes a moral foundation for refusing or withdrawing medical treatments by distinguishing between proportionate or ordinary care and disproportionate or extraordinary care. These key terms are defined in the most recent edition of *Ethical and Religious Directives for Catholic Health Care Services* published by the US Conference of Catholic Bishops. Proportionate means "are those that in the judgment of the patient offer a reasonable hope of benefit and do not entail an excessive burden or impose excessive expense on the family or the community." Disproportionate means "are those that in the patient's judgment do not offer a reasonable hope of benefit or entail an excessive burden, or impose excessive expense on the family or the community." Catholic patients are obligated to pursue proportionate health-care services and to reject disproportionate and futile services.

The Roman Catholic tradition also draws upon the *principle of double effect* when faced with life and death decisions, including those associated with medical treatment in the last stages of a terminal illness. The reality is that many actions have more than one effect. For example, the use of morphine as a form of palliative care is intended to relieve pain, but at certain levels it can also cause shallow breathing and respiratory failure. Intentions matter. If a physician prescribes a level of morphine with the intention of hastening the death of his or her patient, then this would constitute euthanasia in the eyes of the Roman Catholic Church. If the intent of the physician is merely to relieve the patient's pain, but the morphine does hasten the patient's death, then the bad effect of hastening death, while foreseen, is not unethical because the primary intention and good effect were to relieve the patient's pain.

5. Physician-assisted suicide forces doctors to violate the Hippocratic Oath and can force church-affiliated health-care institutions and their employees to violate their codes of ethics.

This argument appears to be quite persuasive on its face but upon closer examination has less moral force. What follows are two important provisions in the Hippocratic Oath: "I will prescribe regimens for the good of my patients according to my ability and my judgment and never do harm to anyone. To please no one will I prescribe a deadly drug nor give advice which may cause death." The reality, however, is that the American Medical Association does not espouse the Hippocratic Oath in its current principles of medical ethics. In fact, very few medical schools in the United

States and Europe use the Hippocratic Oath at graduation, and almost none requires students to swear by it. Instead, the World Medical Association emphasizes the Geneva Declaration, which requires a physician more generally to "consecrate my life to the service of humanity" and to "maintain the utmost respect for human life." Thus, the vast majority of physicians would not face a moral dilemma due to the Hippocratic Oath if one of their patients asked them to assist them with their death. In addition, one of the key provisions in Oregon's and Washington's Death with Dignity Act is that physicians, health care workers, and health-care facilities are legally exempted from any obligation to participate in the program if they believe it violates their conscience or ethical commitments.

Teleological Arguments

At the heart of a teleological argument is the desire of the moral agent to reach an end or goal *(telos)*. These goals can vary, but within the context of this case relevant goals might be to relieve suffering, promote human dignity, and proclaim the gospel. Certainly Ted Christiansen wants to maximize his opportunity to witness to his Christian faith at the point of his death. A teleologist weighs various alternatives and chooses the alternative that best achieves the desired end or goal. Consequences matter. One advantage of a teleological approach to ethics is that it can tolerate compromise in order to draw closer to the goal. While ideals are important, teleologists don't want the perfect to become the enemy of the good. The danger, however, is that the desire to achieve the end may lead one to justify virtually any means. This is typically what produces conflicts with deontologists; both groups can agree on the ends, but they often do not agree on the means.

What follows are four teleological concerns that have been raised in opposition to physician-assisted suicide. Arguments in favor of physician-assisted death are almost always framed around deontological appeals to a person's individual rights to autonomy, privacy, dignity, and self-determination or to a principle like the Golden Rule. These arguments have been discussed above. While it is possible to convert these rights or principles to values and then to seek the teleological maximization of autonomy, privacy, dignity, self-determination, and humanitarianism, this is not normally done, and thus no teleological arguments in favor of physician-assisted death are discussed below. Unlike deontological arguments, teleological arguments can be substantiated or refuted with empirical evidence. Insofar as the explicit arguments below are refuted on the basis of empirical evidence, implicit teleological arguments that support physician-assisted death do emerge.

1. Physician-assisted suicide will weaken the prohibition on killing and be the first step down a slippery slope that ultimately will end with involuntary euthanasia of persons with disabilities and others that society does not value.

Nigel Biggar, professor of pastoral theology at Christ College in Oxford, England, addresses this concern in his book *Aiming to Kill*. Biggar discusses the Nazi euthanasia campaign that systematically ended the lives of sixty thousand to eighty thousand physically or mentally ill people the Nazis thought did not deserve to live. He argues that this early euthanasia campaign cleared the path for the Holocaust, which took the lives of over six million people:

> Whatever proportion these [Nazi euthanasia] crimes finally assumed, it became evident to all who investigated them that they had started from small beginnings. The beginnings at first were a subtle shift in the emphasis in the basic attitude of physicians. It started with the acceptance of the attitude, basic in the euthanasia movement, that there is such a thing as a life not worthy to be lived. This attitude in its early stages concerned itself merely with the severely and chronically sick. Gradually the sphere of those included in this category was enlarged to encompass the socially unproductive, the ideologically unwanted, the racially unwanted and finally all non-Germans. But it is important to realize that the infinitely small wedged-in lever from which this entire trend of mind received its impetus was the attitude towards the non-rehabilitable sick.

Could this happen in the United States? Will physician-assisted death in Oregon and Washington lead inevitably to horrible human rights abuses akin to those perpetrated by the Nazis? Will these laws undo all of the good work the disability rights movement has done to present a view of people with disabilities as different, not less valuable? Anything is possible, and history does have a way of repeating itself, but it is worthwhile to remember at least two things. First, physician-assisted death has been approved by democratic majorities in two US states, and it is regulated strictly by several specific and limiting legal provisions. The Nazi euthanasia campaign was conducted only after the Nazis had seized power, and the Holocaust was perpetrated only after Adolf Hitler had secured complete totalitarian control. Second, none of the statistics from Oregon or Washington indicates that involuntary acts of euthanasia are on the rise. Since the legal option of physician-assisted death has been made available, the contrary appears to be the case. In addition, while the statistics from Oregon and Washington do not indicate whether DWDA patients have disabilities, it is clear that in both states approximately 98 percent of those dying do not perceive their illness as a disability that might lead them to value their lives less and end their lives prematurely.

2. Physician-assisted euthanasia will lead vulnerable groups like women, minorities, the poor, and the elderly to be encouraged or coerced to end their lives prematurely.

The statistics from Oregon and Washington do not support this claim. For example, more men than women in these states have chosen to end their lives with the assistance of a physician. In Oregon, males have represented 53 percent of all DWDA patients from 1998 to 2010; in 2010, males represented 58.5 percent of the state's DWDA patients. In Washington, males represented 55 percent of all DWDA patients in 2009, the first year the state's law went into force. In 2010, women and men each represented 50 percent of the DWDA deaths in Washington. If women were being encouraged or coerced to end their lives prematurely, one would expect to see female DWDA deaths outnumber male DWDA deaths. That has not been the case. It would be helpful to know, however, whether women disproportionately decide to pursue physician-assisted death out of a concern that they are a burden on family, friends, and caregivers. While Oregon and Washington do track this end-of-life concern along with several others, neither state breaks down its data by gender. In both states, however, fear of being a burden to others ranks low (25–35 percent) in comparison to concerns like loss of autonomy, loss of dignity, and being less able to engage in activities that make life enjoyable (84–91%).

The claim that minorities, the poor, and the elderly will be encouraged or coerced to end their lives prematurely also is not substantiated by the data from Oregon and Washington. In Oregon, whites represented 97.6 percent of all DWDA patients from 1998 to 2010, and in 2010 whites represented 100 percent of those who ended their lives in this manner. In Washington, whites represented 98 percent of all DWDA deaths in 2009 and 95 percent in 2010. If health-insurance coverage and level of education are used as proxies for degrees of wealth and poverty, neither measure lends credence to the claim that the poor are being coerced to end their lives prematurely. Over the life of the Oregon program only 1.6 percent of all DWDA patients have lacked health insurance. In Washington no DWDA patients lacked access to health insurance in 2009, and only 3 percent lacked access in 2010. In addition, only 7.2 percent have had less than a high school education in Oregon, and only 5.8 percent have had less than a high school education in Washington. Data regarding the elderly are less conclusive. In Oregon, the median age of DWDA patients went up from the 1998–2009 average of seventy-one years of age to seventy-two years of age in 2010. Nevertheless, approximately 44 percent of all DWDA patients in Oregon from 1998 to 2009 have been under the age of sixty-five. Similarly, in Washington, 46 percent of all DWDA patients in 2009–10 have been under the age of sixty-five.

3. Physician-assisted suicide will reinforce the solitary nature of death and diminish improvements in palliative and terminal care.

According to the most recent National Vital Statistics Report issued by the US Centers for Disease Control and Prevention, nearly 57 percent of all deaths in the United States still take place in hospitals. The reality of death in the United States is that it tends to be highly institutionalized and very expensive. Given these facts it is interesting that nearly 89 percent of all DWDA patients in Oregon and over 79 percent in Washington have died while enrolled in hospice care. The executive director of the Oregon Hospice Organization initially opposed the law but later acknowledged that fears were unfounded and that the program has resulted in an increase in hospice and palliative care in the state. In the case presented here Ted Christiansen dies at home while in hospice care surrounded by his family and friends.

4. Physician-assisted suicide will increasingly lead the dying to feel they not only have a right to die but also a duty to die.

There is no question that the annual number of persons requesting a lethal prescription under Oregon's Death with Dignity Act has more than tripled since the program was initially made legal in 1998. In addition, even though only 0.132 percent of all Oregon deaths from 1998 to 2010 are due to physician-assisted death, it is true that 0.209 percent of all deaths in 2010 were attributed to the DWDA program, which is a 63 percent increase over the historical average. Such a large percentage increase is significant, but the actual numbers reveal that Oregonians are not flocking in droves to end their lives in this manner. Only 65 of the 31,059 deaths in 2010 were due to the Death with Dignity Act. While Oregonians do possess the right to an assisted death, it does not appear that many perceive this as a duty to die. The same is true in the state of Washington.

CONCLUSION

Theresa Christiansen is trying to decide what she will say if she accepts an invitation from a large ecumenical organization to speak at the Death,

Duty, and Dignity conference. In many respects her previously articulated views about physician-assisted suicide were more areteological in nature and not as focused on the deontological and teleological arguments reviewed above. In Greek, *arête* refers to the excellence of one's moral character. An areteologist does not focus on whether a decision will maximize the good (like a teleologist) or reflect obedience to an authority (like a deontologist). Instead, an areteologist is concerned about whether an action or decision will reflect a good moral character or diminish it. Areteologists want to cultivate various virtues and minimize related vices.

In the case, Theresa focused on the moral and religious character of those who are dying and of the people who should be there to support those who are dying. Theresa argued fifteen years ago that Christians have an obligation to die well—witnessing to their faith upon their deathbeds. She offered these views, however, prior to experiencing her father's physician-assisted death and the religious service that preceded it. As a result, several questions have emerged. Has this experience changed her views? Can physician-assisted death be supported on Christian areteological grounds? Is it consistent with the classic theological virtues of faith, hope, and love, or does it undermine and erode these virtues? Should Christians affirm physician-assisted death on the basis of compassion, care, and love? How might Theresa appropriate or reject related deontological and teleological arguments as she works through her areteological position on the issue?

Finally, should Theresa draw a distinction between her moral views and what constitutes wise public policy? That is, could she remain opposed to physician-assisted suicide for various ethical and religious reasons while not opposing its legalization if it is carefully regulated, as it appears to be in Oregon? Given the gradual aging of populations in industrialized societies, and the value given to freedom and self-determination in nations like the United States, questions related to physician-assisted euthanasia are likely to increase in coming years.

ADDITIONAL RESOURCES

Badham, Paul. *Is There a Christian Case for Assisted Dying? Voluntary Euthanasia Reassessed.* London: SPCK, 2009.

Battin, Margaret Pabst. *Ending Life: Ethics and the Way We Die.* New York: Oxford University Press, 2005.

Biggar, Nigel. *Aiming to Kill: The Ethics of Suicide and Euthanasia.* Cleveland: Pilgrim Press, 2004.

Boer, Theo A. "Recurring Themes in the Debate about Euthanasia and Assisted Suicide," *Journal of Religious Ethics* 35, no. 3 (Summer 2007): 529–55.

Carr, Mark F., ed. *Physician-Assisted Suicide: Religious Perspectives on Death with Dignity.* The Jack W. Provonsha Lecture Series 2006. The Center for Christian Bioethics: Loma Linda University. Tucson, AZ: Wheatmark, 2009.

Dieterle, J. M. "Physician-Assisted Suicide: A New Look at the Arguments," *Bioethics* 21, no. 3 (2007): 127–39.

Dowbiggin, Ian R. *A Merciful End: The Euthanasia Movement in Modern America.* New York: Oxford University Press, 2003.

Engelhardt, H. Tristam Jr., and Ana Smith Iltis. "End-of-Life: The Traditional Christian View," *The Lancet* 366 (September 17, 2005): 1045–49.

Gorsuch, Neil M. *The Future of Assisted Suicide and Euthanasia.* Princeton, NJ: Princeton University Press, 2006.

John Paul II. *Evanglium vitae.* Available on the vatican.va website.

Küng, Hans, and Walter Jens. *Dying with Dignity: A Plea for Personal Responsibility.* New York: Continuum International Publishing Group, 2005.

Quill, Timothy E. "Physician-Assisted Death in the United States: Are the Existing 'Last Resorts' Enough?" *Hastings Center Report* 38, no. 5 (September-October 2008): 17–22.

Sacred Congregation for the Doctrine of the Faith. "Declaration on Euthanasia." Available on the vatican.va website.

Warnock, Mary, and Elisabeth Macdonald. *Easeful Death: Is There a Case for Assisted Dying?* New York: Oxford University Press, 2008.

World Medical Association. Declaration of Geneva. Available on the wma.net website.

Young, Robert. *Medically Assisted Death.* New York: Cambridge University Press, 2007.

Related Websites

American Medical Association, available on the WMA website at wma.net (search "Medical Ethics").

Death with Dignity National Center, http://www.deathwithdignity.org/.

Oregon Department of Public Health, http://public.health.oregon.gov (search "Death with Dignity Act").

Washington State Department of Health, http://www.doh.wa.gov/dwda/.

Appendix

Teaching Ethics
by the Case Method

The authors' use of the case method to teach Christian ethics is conscious and deliberate. The method is problem posing and dialogical in contrast to traditional teaching approaches of the teacher/expert transferring information to the student/novice. Traditional methods, although well suited for some purposes, do not explicitly invite students to think for themselves, learn by discovery, and engage the teacher and other students.

The discipline of Christian ethics involves the transfer of information, of course. Students need, among other things, to know facts, theories, and contexts of situations. They need to be acquainted with Christian theology and ethical traditions. They need to understand how to apply Christian insights to the analysis of situations.

The discipline, at least in the minds of the authors, involves more, however. It finds its basis in faith, which, in Paul Tillich's understanding, includes reason, emotion, and will. The relationship of faith is a centered act of the whole person, something to be experienced, not just thought about. Information is only one part of its dynamic. The case approach encourages students to become part of the situation, willingly to suspend belief, to act as if they were one of the characters, and to make decisions that engage mind, will, and emotion.

In addition, one aim of teaching ethics is to enhance the limited freedom each person possesses to make choices. By freedom the authors mean freedom *from*, that is, freedom from ignorance, prejudice, paralysis of decision, oppressive ideology, and ultimately, sin. Freedom *from* opens the door to freedom *in* and freedom *for*. Freedom *in* is the freedom that comes through God and others and frees the self to be *for* others.

The authors think that a problem-posing, dialogical method is well suited to help people of faith learn to enhance the limited freedom they possess to make choices. Cases in this volume are not intended to give answers. Rather, they pose problems and encourage students to go through a relational process and experience their own freedom to decide. Cases taught in a dialogical style encourage this relational process. Whether in classes or discussion groups, the case approach allows students and teachers to learn from each other. Everyone participates in a process of discovery. The use of cases over time frees students to discover how to go about making ethical decisions so they are not stymied at the start by lack of direction and at the end by indecision. They become accustomed to making choices, even tough ones.

Finally, cases are useful in character formation. Students discussing cases unavoidably find themselves evaluating the characters, comparing themselves, and, one hopes, adjusting their own characters in accordance with the discoveries they make. They develop their own "habits of the heart" by putting themselves in the shoes of others.

The case approach opens doors to freedom, but it also opens other doors. First, it introduces students to contemporary ethical issues. The authors contend that thorough knowledge of issues is one of the first steps in a liberating education. Parenthetically, teachers may have to provide background in advance of case discussions using more traditional methods, especially in complex cases.

Second, cases are a way of entry into Christian traditions. At some point both teachers and students need to ask how the Bible, theology, and the church inform issues. The cases on life and death, for example, raise questions about abortion, euthanasia, the nature of God, the purposes of human life, and the meaning of death. Similarly, the cases on violence lead to an investigation of the church's different historical stances regarding punishment, peacemaking, and coercive force. At the same time that students are addressing issues and making decisions, they are in a position to learn the content of Christian tradition and how to apply it.

Knowledge of traditions is liberating if it helps students detect selective and self-serving attempts to manipulate authority for the purpose of supporting conclusions arrived at on other grounds. Traditions provide alternative perspectives from which to understand and challenge cultural myopia. Traditions provide the wisdom of experience, lend authority, offer general guidance, set limits, and designate where the burden of proof lies—all helpful in finding ways through the maze of experience and conflicting opinion and on to appropriate moral choices.

Third, repeated use of case studies encourages students to economize in the way they approach ethical problems. That is to say, cases teach ethical method. The more cases are used and the more explicit methodological awareness is, the more indelible a pattern for making choices becomes.

However little students retain of the content of a given issue or the theology that informs it, the authors are convinced they should leave a course in ethics knowing how to address ethical problems and how to avoid the confusion of too many options and conflicting guidelines.

The authors also believe that an essential component of any pattern of learning is drawing on the insights of others. Discovery of the limitations of individuals acting alone and of the liberation in learning to trust others in community is an important benefit of this dialogical approach. The case setting calls on participants to listen to one another, to challenge their own and others' perceptions, and to build on one another's insights and experiences.

Fourth and last, the case approach is an experience-based form of education. As one veteran case teacher put it: "Cases are experience at a fraction of the cost." The cases in this volume represent the experiences of others that students can make their own without going through all the turmoil. The cases encourage students to express and apply their own experience. Finally, the cases push students to practice resolving complex dilemmas such as parenting, personal responsibility, individual and community rights, and thus to add to their own experience.

CASES FOR GROUP DISCUSSION

As stated in the Introduction, there are numerous types of cases used in contemporary education. These range from a hypothetical problem to a one-page critical incident or verbatim report of an actual event, to a four-hundred-page case history describing a situation. The type of case employed in this volume is modeled after those used by the Harvard Law and Business Schools and the Association for Case Teaching; that is, each case consists of selected information from an actual situation and raises specific issues or problems that require a response or decision on the part of one or more persons in the case. The problem should be substantive enough and so balanced in its approach that reasonable people would disagree about the most effective or appropriate response. As a pedagogical tool the case calls for a response not only from the case characters but also from those studying the case.

Although cases can be extremely useful for inducing reflection by an individual reader, they are specifically designed for group discussion. They might be used in classrooms, retreat settings, community gatherings, or with any group seeking to gain new perspectives.

As this is a distinctive educational approach, the authors feel it is important to offer suggestions for guiding a case discussion. To begin with, while it is possible to hand out copies of shorter cases—for example "Rigor and

Responsibility"—and ask participants to read them immediately prior to discussion, the quality of discussion is heightened by careful advance reading. The case leader might suggest ahead of time that participants (1) read through the case at least twice; (2) identify the principal case characters; (3) develop a time line to indicate significant dates or events; (4) list the issues that surface; and (5) think through a number of creative alternatives to the dilemma posed.

The case leader functions primarily as organizer, catalyst, probe, and referee. Good case leaders know where they want to go with a case and what they want to teach. They highlight insights and assist in summarizing the learning from the discussion. As a facilitator, case leaders are responsible for clear goals and objectives for each discussion session and for guiding the quality and rhythm of the discussion. Many who have worked with cases suggest that the most crucial factor for a rewarding case experience is the leader's style. Openness, affirmation, and sensitivity to the group create the climate in which genuine dialogue can occur. Second in importance is that the case leader thoroughly master the case facts and develop a discussion plan or teaching note.

It is important to keep in mind that there is no single way to approach a case. The Introduction to this volume highlights the elements of making an ethical decision, and the commentaries offer authors' analyses of more specific issues. Case leaders might order the discussion of cases by proceeding from analysis to assessment to decision, suggesting that students not read the commentaries until after the initial case discussion. Alternatively, leaders might integrate the material in the commentaries and the discussion. Neither the Introduction nor the commentaries should constrain teachers or students from taking different entry points or addressing different topics or issues.

Whatever approach is taken should draw participants into dialogue, uncover what is needed to make an informed ethical decision, and push students to a critical consciousness and finally to a decision that will help them when they encounter similar situations in their own lives.

There are no right answers to the dilemmas presented in this volume. This means that the problems posed are open to a number of creative alternatives. This approach stands in contrast to a closed, problem-solving approach in which the right answer or solution, known only to the teacher, can be found in the back of the book. In contrast, the case approach calls for participants to become active subjects in the learning process, to consider various responses, and to analyze the norms that inform their decisions.

Experienced case leaders report that recording the essence of participants' contributions on newsprint or on a board gives order and direction to the discussion. A skilled instructor is able to help participants show relationships among contributions. The leader should be willing to probe respondents for additional clarification of points.

Honest conflict of opinion is often a characteristic of case discussions and can be quite constructive. The case leader may need to assume the role of referee and urge participants to listen to one another and to interpret the reasoning behind their conclusions. It is often helpful to put debating participants in direct dialogue by asking, for example, "Laura, given your earlier position, how would you respond to Mark's view?" The leader's role as mediator is also significant, especially as a discussion nears conclusion. It is helpful to encourage group members to build on one another's suggestions. One constructive process for closing a case discussion is to ask participants to share their insights from the discussion.

Case leaders employ two additional techniques. Leaders might focus and intensify discussion by calling participants to vote on a more controversial issue. For example, in a discussion of the "Sustaining Dover" case, one might ask, "If you were a member of the Dover City Council, would you vote to approve Walmart's request to fill in the flood plain and rezone the property?" The dynamics of case teaching reveal that once persons have taken a stand, they frequently assume greater ownership of the decision and are eager to defend or interpret their choice. Voting provides an impetus for participants to offer the implicit reasons and assumptions that stand behind a given decision. It can also be a test of the group's response, especially if one or two outspoken participants have taken a strong stand on one particular side of an issue. If a vote is taken, it is important to give participants an opportunity to interpret the reasons behind their decision.

Another way to heighten existential involvement in a case is to ask participants to assume the roles of characters in the case for a brief, specified period of the discussion. When individuals are asked to assume roles before a group, they can either be asked ahead of time or invited on the spot from among those who have shown during the discussion that they identify with the characters and understand the issues. It is often most helpful for individuals in a role play to move into chairs visible to the entire group. Case leaders can guard the personal integrity of those who assume roles by giving them an opportunity to "de-role." This is easily done by asking them how they felt during the conversation and by asking them to return to their original seats. Then group members can be called on to share what they learned from the experience.

Notwithstanding the preceding suggestions for case teaching, the authors wish to acknowledge that a good case discussion is not ultimately dependent on a trained professional teacher or a learned group of participants.

A gifted leader is one who listens well, encourages participants to do the same, and genuinely trusts the wisdom, insights, and personal experiences of the group. To benefit significantly from the cases a reader needs to be willing to wrestle honestly with the issues in the cases and to evaluate with an open mind the insights of the commentaries.

SAMPLE TEACHING NOTE

Most case teachers prepare in advance a teaching note with suggestions for the general direction of the discussion as well as clear, transitional questions to move from one topic to the next. The following note is intended as an illustration of how the first case in this volume, "Rigor and Responsibility," might be taught in a short session.

A. Read the case if not pre-assigned. (ten minutes)

B. Have the class sketch a biography of each character. (ten to fifteen minutes)

C. Identify the basic questions: How is a family to live in a poor and environmentally degraded world? Alternatively, should an affluent family follow the rigorous holy poverty of Jesus or another option, which might be called responsible consumption, stressing right use and good stewardship? (one to two minutes)

D. Identify alternative issues. (five minutes) This category could be eliminated if the basic question is the focus. Or one of the following issues could become the main issue:

    1. Stewarding an inheritance

    2. Living in an impoverished, malnourished, and environmentally degraded world

    3. Discovering the biblical and theological witness on justice, wealth, poverty, possessions, and consumptions

    4. Overworking in modern society

    5. Making a family decision

    6. Dealing with guilt

    7. Acting as an individual in a world dominated by mass consumption

    8. Distributing income and wealth

    9. Raising children

E. Ask each student to identify with one of the following: (ten minutes)

    1. Nancy or Clea

    2. Nathan

    3. Al

    4. The children

F. Adjourn to four separate groups. (twenty minutes)

1. Discuss what is and what should be the normative position of the character selected. Point to:
   a. Biblical and theological views of justice, wealth, poverty, and consumption
   b. The two normative positions identified in the title of the case
   c. The norms of justice and sustainable sufficiency

OR

2. Discuss the family relationships and how they should be worked through to arrive at a decision. Point to:
   a. The involvement of the Trapp family in a number of issues, the extent of its giving, and the crisis of the family in the United States
   b. Cultural attitudes in the local community
   c. Poverty, malnutrition, and environmental degradation in the world community
   d. Traditional patriarchal family patterns

OR

3. Discuss the method question. How is a Christian family to decide?
   a. Point to the alternatives of using deontological, teleological, or areteological approaches
   b. Apply each to the case and note the differences

OR

4. Discuss the character question. What are the characteristics of a person who responds well to the main problem? Point to:
   a. Basic character orientation, loyalties, and world views
   b. Character-building aspects of this situation

G. Conduct a role play, selecting one person from each group. Add David as an option. (ten to fifteen minutes)

1. Role players discuss what the Trapps should do and how it relates to the main issue and to the alternative issues selected in "D" above.

H. Debrief and generate discussion. (ten minutes)

1. "De-role"
2. Ask students to identify what they have learned
3. Open a general class discussion of the main issue

If time allows, the case leader can provide background in lectures, readings, films, small study groups, and so on. The more background, the more open-ended the small group discussions can be.

CASES AND COURSE DESIGN

How might cases be used in a course in Christian ethics? For starters the authors recommend using the case approach in conjunction with other teaching methods. Cases can be overworked, and the freshness they bring lost.

In terms of overall design the teacher might select one of the cases with high student interest and open with it the first day of class. Cases are good discussion starters, and early use can introduce students to the method, to the use of critical consciousness, and to the goal of liberating education.

Following this, several general sessions on ethics would be appropriate, including the elements of making an ethical decision discussed in the Introduction and how to use Christian sources to derive norms. Use of a case or two to illustrate specific aspects of the ethical discipline would also be appropriate.

The remainder of the course could be devoted to the specific issues in this volume. Using all of the cases in a single semester might be ill advised. Selectivity on the basis of student interest and teacher expertise would be more suitable.

The authors recommend that students write briefs, that is, a four- to five-page analysis of a case. This process accomplishes several things. First, it brings writing into a course. Second, particularly if graded, briefs heighten interest by increasing the stakes. Discussion is more intense because preparation is more thorough. Third, briefs offer less vocal students another avenue of expression. Fourth, briefs are a vehicle for method, since method is implicit in any act of organization. Methodological awareness is more pronounced if the teacher requires a certain approach, or better, if the teacher insists that the students be cognizant of the approach they are taking. Finally, briefs may serve as the first draft of a term paper.

If briefs are used, students must be selective in what they cover. Four to five pages are not sufficient to analyze fully any case in this volume. In organizing their briefs students might follow the order of analysis, assessment, and decision outlined in the Introduction. Somewhere in the brief the "problem" should be clearly stated. The larger part of the brief should be devoted to ethical assessment, that is, to the derivation of norms, to the relating of norms to situations using one or more method, and to the relationships involved in the case. Briefs may be expository and present the various sides in a case, or they may be persuasive and argue one side in depth. While the commentaries in this volume avoid arguing for a particular side of an issue, the teacher may ask students to make a decision and justify it

Lack of time makes selectivity a cardinal virtue in a workshop setting. The typical one-hour adult class is long enough for a good discussion of a single case, especially if it has been read prior to the session. Needless to say, the teacher should have a very clear idea of what he or she wants to accomplish and try to keep the class on task. An alert teacher, picking up on points in the discussion, can even insert background material through mini-lectures or asking students to elaborate. Small groups and role plays are especially helpful in stimulating discussion and breaking complex cases into manageable units.

LIMITATIONS OF THE CASE APPROACH

The case approach is not without limitations. First, case material must go through the personal filter of a writer. The situation is seen through the eyes of a single character with all the limitations of perspective. Seldom is enough information provided to satisfy participants. Crucial signals can be misread or misunderstood.

A second drawback is that the success of this form of education and presentation of material is dependent on the critical thinking and participation of students. This can be quite disconcerting, even threatening, for those who are accustomed to a process in which they are handed a complete analysis from the lectern. For most learners tutored in an educational system that fosters uncritical acceptance of the teacher's wisdom and authority, passive reception of information is the comfortable norm. This is, however, also the pattern of uncritical acceptance of the world as it is and contributes to a loss of vision. Case leaders need to develop a mode of open rather than closed questions to induce critical thinking and genuine dialogue.

Third, case discussion can consume more time and emotional energy than the direct communication of information. Intelligence is imperfectly correlated with the propensity to speak. Some participants are bent on dominating the discussion rather than learning from others. Tangents can carry the discussion into dead ends. These limitations call for good referee skills from the case leader.

Fourth, the forest can be lost for the trees, the macro for the micro, and the social for the individual by focusing on the particulars of a given situation to the exclusion of the context. For example, to reduce the discussion of abortion to a personal moral decision in the case "A Matter of Life or Death" is to lose sight of a critical social question about who should control the decision, the woman or the state. The cases, and in particular the commentaries, have been written to help avoid this problem, but it is well to keep it in mind. Teachers can easily do this by including these elements in their background material and case plans.

Finally, relative to other methods the case approach is limited in its capacity to convey large blocks of factual information. This drawback does not mean teachers need to revert automatically to lectures. There are alternatives to "depositing" information, and even the lecture style can be approached with a different spirit. Many case teachers, for example, use mini-lectures in case discussion to introduce relevant material when it is needed.

The case approach is no panacea and must be seen as only one of many effective educational instruments. The authors have attempted to respond to the limitations of the approach. They have not removed them. They trust, however, that the cases in this volume and the approach itself can lead to constructive, liberating engagements with what they think are critical contemporary issues. Their trust is based on many years of experience with the approach. They are convinced that the approach is not only a valuable and liberating pedagogical instrument, but also a way to build community in the classroom.

Related Websites

Harvard Law and Business Schools, www.hbr.org/case-studies.
Association for Case Teaching, caseteaching.org.

List of Authors and Contributors

AUTHORS

Christine E. Gudorf is professor of religious studies at Florida International University, the state university in Miami. She holds a doctorate in Christian ethics from Columbia University in a joint program with Union Theological Seminary in New York City. Her publications have been concentrated in religious social ethics, especially in sexual and environmental ethics. Her last book, co-authored with James Huchingson, is *Boundaries: A Casebook in Environmental Ethics*; her forthcoming book is in comparative religious ethics.

James B. Martin-Schramm is professor of religion at Luther College in Decorah, Iowa. He is an ordained member of the Evangelical Lutheran Church in America and holds a doctorate in Christian ethics from Union Theological Seminary in New York City. Most of his scholarship has focused on issues related to ethics and public policy. He is the author of *Population Perils and the Churches' Response* and co-author of *Christian Environmental Ethics: A Case-Method Approach*. His most recent book is *Climate Justice: Ethics, Energy, and Public Policy*.

Ramona Nelson is professor of accounting and management and chair of the Department of Economics and Business at Luther College in Decorah, Iowa. She is a certified public accountant and recently completed fifteen years of service on the Decorah School Board.

Laura A. Stivers is associate professor of ethics and chair of the Religion and Philosophy Department at Dominican University of California. She holds a doctorate in ethics and social theory from the Graduate Theological Union in Berkeley, California. Most of her scholarship has focused on economic and environmental ethics. She is the author of *Disruptive Christian Ethics: Alternative Christian Approaches* and a co-editor of *Justice in a Global Economy: Strategies for Home, Community, and World*.

341

Albert Wuaku is assistant professor of religion at Florida International University. His scholarship has focused on African/African Diaspora religious cultures and Hindu traditions currently taking root in Ghana. His current research is on vodou healing practices among Haitian immigrants in south Florida. He has conducted archival research and field work among African worshiping communities in Ghana, Togo, Benin, and Canada, and among Hindu worshipers in Guyana and South Africa, with publications in the *Journal of Religion in Africa*, the *Journal of Contemporary African Studies*, and chapter contributions in edited volumes.

CONTRIBUTORS

Alice Frazer Evans is director of writing and research at Plowshares Institute, Simsbury, Connecticut; senior trainer for the Center for Empowering Reconciliation and Peace, Jakarta, Indonesia; and an adjunct faculty member at Hartford Seminary, Hartford, Connecticut. She is co-author of numerous books, including *Casebook for Christian Living*, *Pastoral Theology from a Global Context*, *Peace Skills for Community Mediators*, and *Transforming Urban Ministry*.

Robert L. Stivers is emeritus professor of Christian ethics, Pacific Lutheran University, Tacoma, Washington. He has authored, co-authored, edited, and co-edited numerous books, including *The Sustainable Society*; *Hunger, Technology, and Limits to Growth*; *The Public Vocation of Christian Ethics*, co-edited with Beverly W. Harrison and Ronald H. Stone; *Reformed Faith and Economics*; *Christian Environmental Ethics: A Case Method Approach*, co-authored with James B. Martin-Schramm; and *Resistance and Theological Ethics*, co-edited with Ronald H. Stone. He has worked extensively in the Presbyterian Church (USA) on social issues.